Object-Oriented Development Process and Metrics

Object-Oriented Development Process and Metrics

Dennis de Champeaux

Onto00, San Jose, California

An Alan R. Apt Book

Prentice Hall, Upper Saddle River, NJ 07458

Library of Congress Cataloging-in-Publication Data

de Champeaux, Dennis.
  Object-oriented development process and metrics / Dennis de Champeaux.
    p.   cm.
  Includes bibliographical references and index.
  ISBN 0-13-099755-2
    1. Object-Oriented programming (Computer Science) 2. Computer
software--Development. I. Title.
QA76.64.D42 1997   96-27587
  005.1--dc20   CIP

Acquisitions Editor: Alan Apt
Developmental Editor: Sondra Chavez
Production Editor: Joseph Scordato
Director Prod. & Mfg.: David Riccardi
Production Manager: Bayani Mendoza DeLeon
Cover Designer: Joe Sengotta
Cover Art: Courtesy of The MathWorks, Inc.
Copy Editor: Barbara Zeiders
Buyer: Donna Sullivan
Editorial Assistant : Shirley McGuire

About the Cover
Cover graphic: Riemann surface for the cube
root. Every complex number has three roots.
This plot shows the cube roots of the complex
unit disk with height equal to the real part and
hue equal to the imaginary part of the root.
Provided courtesy of The MathWorks, Inc.,
Natick, MA. (http://www.mathworks.com)

©1997 by Prentice-Hall, Inc.
Simon & Schuster/A Viacom Company
Upper Saddle River, NJ 07458

The author and publisher of this book have used their best efforts in preparing this book. These efforts
include the development, research, and testing of the theories and programs to determine their effectiveness.
The author and publisher make no warranty of any kind, expressed or implied, with regard to these programs
or the documentation contained in this book. The author and publisher shall not be liable in any event for
incidental or consequential damages in connection with, or arising out of, the furnishing, performance, or use
of these programs.

Printed in the United States of America

10 9 8 7 6 5 4 3 2 1

ISBN 0-13-099755-2

Prentice-Hall International (UK) Limited, London
Prentice-Hall of Australia Pty. Limited, Sydney
Prentice-Hall Canada Inc., Toronto
Prentice-Hall Hispanoamericana, S.A., Mexico
Prentice-Hall of India Private Limited, New Delhi
Prentice-Hall of Japan, Inc., Tokyo
Simon & Schuster Asia Pte. Ltd., Singapore
Editora Prentice-Hall do Brasil, Ltda., Rio de Janeiro

Foreword

This book gives a refreshingly interesting and different perspective on object technology for the practitioner. It has twin foci of process and metrics. This book is unique in combining these two elements, both of which are vital for the successful management of a software development. A process defines an orderliness in development, while metrics offers a tool with which to evaluate success. Software development can never attain quality without process and metrics: the topics of this book.

The type of software process used in an organization is indicative of the company's maturity. A well-defined process is needed if successes are to be understood sufficiently that they can be repeated. Increasing organizational maturity supports a process that can be managed in the sense of continual improvement — lessons learned are incorporated into future modifications to the software development process so that eventually the process itself is fully optimized. Metrics have a key role to play in quantifying both the process as it matures and also the products that are produced. Better processes produce higher quality products.

In many ways, this book encompasses the interests of both practitioners and researchers: an interesting and most important area in which to work. Object technology is itself still a relatively new and maturing discipline in commercial applications: today's research is tomorrow's practice. Managers of object technology need to monitor and understand the results of the researchers, and in turn, the researchers need to focus their attention on areas of immediate relevance to the software industry. Here is no "silver bullet" gained by merely combining process and metrics: Caveats are clearly stated and exciting opportunities publicized. For success in object technology, it is in fact critical that managers be fully aware of both pros and cons. This book focuses on those knowns and unknowns such that success can be maximized. All in all, this is a thoughtful and thought-provoking book.

B. Henderson-Sellers
Director, Centre for Object Technology Applications and Research (Victoria)

Preface

A software development organization switching to the object-oriented (OO) paradigm faces quite a challenge. All phases of the life cycle are affected: analysis, design, implementation, testing, and maintenance. An organization that has made the switch still has a long way to go to become a mature development organization - mature in the sense of CMU's SEI maturity criteria.

It is not enough to use an OO programming language and any of the OO analysis and design methods currently available. A level 3 organization as defined by the Software Engineering Institute (SEI) must routinely use a defined development process. In this book we describe a generic OO analysis and design process. The ability to monitor progress is also required. Planning, not only of the coding phases, needs estimators. Metrics for progress monitoring and the estimation of effort are developed in this book.

Object-oriented quality metrics is a novel topic. Dreaming up metrics is the easy part. Associating with numeric ranges the qualifications *good* and *bad* (and intermediate judgments) is the hard part. Going beyond measuring many artifacts in a system and identifying exceptional cases with respect to a certain metric is unrealistic at this point. Hence our presentation of quality metrics should be seen as a framework for organizations that want to collect historical data systematically. Alternatively, it is hopefully a source of inspiration for CASE tool companies that may want to automate the gathering of metrics.

This book is aimed primarily at practitioners. In particular, we want to illustrate with an example how to go from requirements through analysis and design to implementation. On the way, we show how micro processes are followed, how effort prediction can be carried out, and how quality metrics can be applied.

Execution of this agenda requires choosing an example that is not too trivial, yet not too hard, and that is easily understood by a broad range of readers. We have chosen a fancy home heating system that has been used by both Kerth [45] and by Booch [12]. We present an analysis of this system that is unusual in that all entities such as rooms, temperature sensors, and water valves, are made into autonomous objects. This gives us ample opportunity to illustrate how to deal with the removal of paralellism during design since our target implementation is a C++ simulation program that has only a single thread of control.

Using C++ is not a happy choice. We are quite embarrassed by this language. In fact, we take the position that software development should stop after a high-level design is completed. Commercial tools are already available that can execute high-level designs, often with satisfactory performance.

The structure of this book is as follows. An introductory chapter is followed by three parts that cover analysis, design, and implementation. Each part has four chapters that cover concepts, micro process, metrics, and the running example in which these notions are applied to the home heating system.[1]

Is this book aimed at software developers or at project managers? It is aimed at both. We want developers to become more aware of development processes and metrics, which are traditionally more in the realm of management. Software engineers are often weary when their activities are planned. Unrealistic schedules in the past are typically responsible for this situation. We claim that more detailed micro processes outlined in this book will be helpful for all parties. Sometimes it is claimed that an articulated process impinges on the creativity of a developer. Divide and conquer is the most important technique in problem solving. Capturing software development experience and expressing it in the form of a micro process should be recognized by all as a contribution to the state of the art. This presumes that a micro process is used as a guideline from which one can deviate instead of as dictums that are carved in granite.

We downplay the features of our graphical notation. Everything we express can be done in any of the existing popular notations. A neutral notation was needed to avoid the impression that the key topic of this book - process and metrics - applies only to a specific method. The graphical notation has been used before in de Champeaux et al. [24]. In contrast with what was done in [24], we use the same graphical notation, with extensions, for design activities.

---

[1]Of course, we do *not* suggest that software development always follows a waterfall macro process. At the same time, we do not rule out situations where a waterfall process can be applied. We discuss multiple macro processes and outline which one to use when.

Acknowledgments

A generous grant from Alan Apt, our editor, allowed us to obtain the equipment on which this book was produced in camera-ready form. His patience and trust were crucial for having this book ultimately produced.

Students at the Santa Clara University were the perfect "guinea pigs" for the analysis micro process and they provided effort metric data reported in Chapter 5.

Robert Martin wrote a report that peeked our interest. He granted us permission to use it; see Appendix A.

Numerous reviewers have given extensive feedback and have helped to beat the English into shape. Special thanks go to Brian Henderson-Sellers, Doug Lea, Simon Moser, and Darrell Parlee. We are happy to maintain full credit for all remaining errors. Feedback is welcome at our e-mail address: ddc@netcom.com.

DdC

Contents

IV   Last Words   401

14 One Step Beyond   403

A Category Quality Metric   409

Object-Oriented Development
Process and Metrics

Chapter 1

Introduction

A software (SW) development organization switching to the object-oriented (OO) paradigm faces quite a challenge. All phases of the life cycle are affected: analysis, design, implementation, test, and maintenance. An organization that has made the switch still has a long way to go to become a mature development organization. We use "mature" here in the sense of Carnegie-Mellon's SEI[1] maturity criteria. What is involved?

The great majority of SW organizations are in the "initial" phase. They depend on "magicians". The job gets done but one cannot claim that the result was produced by an orderly process. Most of this chaos has nothing to do with OO. When a product definition is vague, ambiguous, incomplete, or changes during development, we have an excellent source for chaos. At the same time, one would like discipline in the development process that dampens or contains and at best controls the perturbations induced by evolving product definitions.

Not devoting enough attention to analysis and design is another reason for a chaotic development process. This is unfortunate but understandable. Discontinuities between structured analysis, structured design, and structured implementations has given analysis and design unfavorable reputations. Too often, a design must start anew and, too often, analysis and design are seen as bureaucratic hassles that stand in the way of doing the real thing: programming the target system. The OO (programming) paradigm even promised that analysis and design would be obsolete. Early successes with OO programming reinforced these hopes. However, when a system becomes large - large in the sense that it can no longer be handled by a single brilliant OO programmer - we have to take analysis and design seriously again.

---

[1]SEI, Software Engineering Institute.

The nonintegration of analysis, design, and implementation tools is another excuse for not doing enough analysis and design. A recent study by Grady [29] shows that this practice comes with a hefty price tag. This study shows that 27% of the total life cycle cost (including maintenance) is devoted to program understanding (i.e., programmers staring at code to figure out how the system works, which does *not* include making modifications). With proper CASE tool support, one could do maintenance differently: One would first modify a design and/or the specifications and propagate these modifications forward into the code. Traceability links would facilitate quick identification of relevant fragments.

The data in the Grady study illustrate that the ratio of effort spent during the first round of analysis, design, and implementation is 1:1:2. We conjecture that this ratio is the key to high maintenance costs, which are 60% of the total life-cycle. Coding is started before the task is sufficiently understood and before the design has been sufficiently thought through. The inability to maintain consistency among analysis, design, and implementation system descriptions also plays a role; this is due to weak tool support.

Grady's account is based largely on data collected on non-OO projects. There is reasonable hope that the OO paradigm will alleviate some of the problems described above. First, there is greater conceptual continuity in going from OO analysis, via design into an implementation. The project described in de Champeaux et al. [22] observed that most classes identified during the analysis phase ultimately showed up in the implementation, and we observe the same for the example used in this book. Second, this conceptual continuity can be exploited for providing better integrated tools. Third, reuse of (domain-specific) artifacts in all phases of the life cycle is more plausible, as supported by a follow-up of the project reported in [22].

The next maturity level beyond initial, in terms of the SEI criteria, is repeatable. This entails a minimal awareness of what a SW organization is doing. Some measurements should be taken. This opens up the expectations that similar tasks should require similar efforts. An organization at this level has laid the foundation for detailed planning. Keeping track of how much effort is spent on what is certainly do-able for an organization that has switched to the OO paradigm.

The subsequent level is called defined. This directs that an organization follow an articulated and publicized development process. The entire life cycle should be covered: analysis, design, implementation, test, and defect removal. Systematizing the product definition phase is desirable as well. This level is already challenging for an organization adopting OO. Adhering to an iterative macro process until the job is done does not give enough guidance to a development team. Instead, one needs a more detailed plan that outlines many more intermediate checkpoints. The construction of such project-specific plans would benefit from the availability of a generic OO development process. This book covers such generic processes for the OO analysis, design phases, and implementation phases.[2]

The fourth level is labeled managed. An organization at this level measures more and keeps track of more details. Since the organization has elaborate macro and micro processes, there is more opportunity for measurements. Exception handling processes are defined and the need to rely on them is observed and measured as well. As a result, an organization has at this stage a higher awareness level of what is going on, can react faster to deadends, and can deal more effectively with changes such as product definition modifications.

Planning becomes less of a dart-throwing exercise. In this book we exploit the OO analysis and design processes described and formulate metrics regarding the artifacts that are produced during development. These product metrics will be the basis for the definition of effort predictors.

The last level in the SEI maturity ranking is called optimizing. An optimizing organization exploits the wealth of data that are generated continuously to improve the underlying processes. For example, plan execution may yield systematic deviations that require replanning. Such a phenomenon may be attributed to a flaw in an underlying generic process. As another example, procedures can be customized to exploit features of certain development tasks. Obviously, an organization that is engaged in these subtleties needs well-defined processes and detailed metrics. Hence for sizable development tasks it is not enough to use an OO programming language and any of the OO analysis and design methods that are now available. In the remainder of this chapter we detail ramifications of this observation and preview the content of subsequent material.

1.1 Components of a Software Method

Booch [12] makes a distinction between method and methodology as follows:

> A *method* is a disciplined process for generating a set of models that describe various aspects of a software system under development, using

---

[2]Lacking are processes for testing and maintenance. The Oopsla 95 conference had a panel discussion on testing. This is a clear indication that only anecdotes are as yet available in this area. A systematic approach to maintenance relies on a bug-tracking system that includes the incorporation of user feedback. Such a system helps to close the development cycle by providing feedback into the requirements for the next version. Processes for testing and maintenance are not discussed in this book beyond some scattered remarks.

some well-defined notation. A *methodology* is a collection of methods applied across the development life cycle and unified by some general, philosophical approach.

Methodology has traditionally held a different meaning: The study of methods. It belongs to the territory of philosophers. Since a collection of related methods can also be seen as a method, we are quite happy to leave methodology in the hands of philosophers.

We agree with the characterizations "well-defined notation" and "disciplined process". However, an ingredient is missing: One needs a way to decide whether progress is being made when a method is applied, and one needs a criterion that determines the appropriateness of an action: a termination condition. Hence we extend (and rewrite) the characterization as follows:

A *software development method* has as components:

- Well-defined core concepts for which there exist agreed-upon notations, which can be used to describe domain artifacts and models of the intended system from different perspectives.

- A process that outlines the steps for utilizing the core concepts, which defines intermediate deliverables and characterizes dependencies between these deliverables.

- A criterion for measuring progress that can indicate when a development (subordinate) activity has been completed.

This definition covers the description of a method that covers the full life cycle as well as a method that addresses only a single phase in the life cycle.

Let's look at some examples. A programming language is not a method. It has core concepts with well-defined notations that can be used for describing domain artifacts. We may even argue that certain programming languages support different perspectives; they allow characterization of complex data structures for representing domain concepts and they allow for detailed behavioral descriptions.

However, the second and third ingredients, the generic process component and the criterion for measuring progress, are lacking. This deficiency is exactly the reason why we have analysis and design activities. Hence a programming language can be seen as a *component* of a development method for the implementation phase when it is complemented with a process. For instance, a (weak) process could be a bottom-up transformation of a low-level design. A criterion for progress could be the fraction of the design that has been realized in code.

According to our definition, structured analysis is a method. There are core concepts and notations: processes, data flow diagrams, data dictionaries, and so on. The development process is: One must expand process "bubbles" into subprocesses and one must describe data on the arcs in terms of representable constituents. As a criterion for measuring progress, we could use the number of bubbles that do not need further decomposition because their meaning is obvious.[3]

None of the OO methods in the literature (e.g. Shlaer and Mellor [72, 73], Booch [12, 13], Rumbaugh et al. [70], Wirfs-Brock et al. [87], Jacobson el al. [41]) satisfy our definition. All of them give ample attention to the characterization of the core concepts, but their process dimension is quite weak. Of the ones listed, Rumbaugh et al. give the most attention, to the process dimension. However, the third component is not addressed because OO metrics have not been given adequate attention.

We proceed by distinguishing various kinds of development processes.

1.2 Development Processes

The notion of a development process is usually associated with the issue of whether analysis, design, and implementation can be done (or alternatively, is to be done):

- Sequentially, the waterfall model (Royce [68])

- Iteratively, the spiral model (Boehm [11])

- Opportunistically, the fountain model (Henderson-Sellers and Edwards [35])

- Frivolously/desperately, the whirlpool model

Control obviously becomes more event and situation driven as we go down this list.

Sometimes one has no choice which global process to follow. A contract can prescribe a waterfall life cycle; an organization may have "hardwired" a life cycle. We advocate that if one has a choice, one should look at features of a project to make an informed decision. Complete, unambiguous requirements that will be stable during development allow following a sequential waterfall approach. (Observe that we do not stipulate that one *must* follow a waterfall approach in these circumstances. In addition, see another consideration below which can prescribe an iterative process for another reason.)

---

[3]In analogy with one person's floor is another person's ceiling: What is obvious for one can be a challenge for someone else.

When the requirements are tentative and/or incomplete, it pays to follow an iterative or opportunistic approach. As an extreme case when the requirements are very unclear and one has merely a hunch as to the system to be developed, the development is not aimed initially at producing a system, but instead, is aimed at producing new insights that will narrow the requirements. Hence the whirlpool model should be chosen when we are guided only by systematized intuitions.

Planning development has intrinsic error margins. Thus even when one can follow a waterfall approach, one may be concerned about missing a narrow market window. A "clean-room" approach may be advised in such situations. This applies when the functionality of an intended system can be decomposed into nested subsets: $f1$, $f2$, $f3$, ... [i.e., the functionality of a system satisfying $f(n + 1)$ has all the functionality of a system that corresponds with $f(n)$ and satisfies another requirement in addition]. For example, although one may aim to deliver a system with a functionality of $f27$, marketable products are $f15$, $f16$, and up. If so, one may consider a waterfall approach to produce $f15$ and iterate - with short cycles - to produce $f16$, $f17$, and up. After producing $f15$ there is always a product ready to be shipped, although it may have restricted functionality.

These procedures can be called *macro processes* because they characterize the development process at the top level. *Micro processes*, in contrast, are especially relevant for OO development activities due to the great diversity of representational apparatus. It is to be observed that these micro processes are still, at the time of this writing, underdefined. Project leaders/managers still feel uncomfortable about how to schedule OO projects. We consider this state of affairs a major inhibitor for the widespread acceptance of the OO paradigm by the commercial world. Hence our attention in this book to micro processes for OO analysis and design.

The combination of a macro process with micro processes for analysis, design, and implementation provides a generic default process for OO software development. The articulation of such generic processes helps the formulation of a development plan. Taking into account the details of a project, corporate culture, and resources available, the plan can be refined into a schedule. Such a schedule is enacted and executed by a team and/or by tools.

Monitoring plan execution and enactment allow observation of deviations from the schedule. Replanning will update the development plan. A mature software development organization[4] will monitor replanning activities. Certain regularities observed in the replanning activities may be ascribed to inherit deficiencies in the generic development process which, will have to be modified accordingly (see Figure 1.1).

---

[4]A level 5 organization in the Software Engineering Institute (SEI) classification.

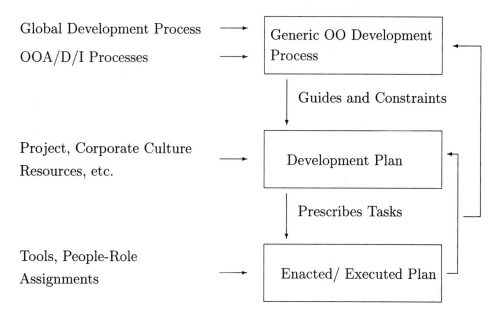

Figure 1.1: Dependencies between the generic process, the top box, which is a combination of a macro process and micro processes; the development plan, the middle box, which has the details of a schedule; and the plan enacted or executed, the bottom box. The upward arrows correspond with replanning induced by deviations from the schedule and a process improvement process to rectify intrinsic deficiencies in the generic process.

1.3 Dealing with the Unexpected

As alluded to above, obtaining new insights into the requirements during development is a major side effect. This phenomenon induces a discontinuity in the development process that requires a twist in overall effort estimation. As a consequence of a new insight, one may have to abandon developed artifacts, start a salvaging operation, and replan. Hence, as the base case we will assume that we have stable requirements, or alternatively, we will assume that we are dealing with a single cycle of a spiral process. In the latter case, there is the dual purpose of generating another round of incremental functionality to a system and verifying conjectures generated by risk assessments (see Boehm [11]). When it is clear that iterations are required, because the requirements are incomplete or because a phased approach is chosen, we can do effort estimation roughly via a multiplier, accounting for the number of iterations, or more precisely (it is to be hoped) via a summation of the estimates for the different iterations. In this book we concentrate on the base case where we have stable requirements or where there is a single cycle of an iterative macro process.

1.4   Metrics in General

Multiple aspects of software (SW) metrics are distinguished in this section. This will facilitate positioning the kind of metrics that we are mainly interested in. Here are some definitions that are common. In Mills [54] we find: "SW metrics deals with the measurements of the SW product and the process by which it is developed." Mills elaborates this definition as follows: "... the SW product should be viewed as an abstract object that evolves from an initial statement of need to a finished SW system, including source and object code and the various forms of documentation produced during development." In other words: "The product measured should be interpreted in a wide sense; i.e., metrics can be applied to any artifact constructed during development, including not only code but also analysis and design models as well as their components. Spin-off results like contributions to analysis, design and/or code libraries may be taken into account also."

A teleological definition by Mills is: "The goal of SW metrics is the identification and measurement of the essential parameters that affect SW development." More specifically, we can list as goals, among others:

- Measurement of actual development costs for a particular time period, possibly qualified per type of development activity

- Measurement of development fragments in order to predict or estimate future subsequent development costs

- Measurement of quality aspects in order to predict or estimate subsequent development costs to achieve acceptable product quality

- Measurement of development aspects to enhance a general awareness of "where we are and where we are going"

We will focus on the construction of metrics that allow the estimated prediction of future development efforts. Desirable characteristics of a metric are:

1. A metric is either elementary, in that it measures only a single well-defined aspect, or alternatively, it is an aggregation of more elementary metrics within a definition of the aggregation function.

2. It is objective in that it does not depend on the judgment of a human user and can be preferably expressed in a machine-executable algorithm.

3. It can be applied at reasonable cost.

4. It is intuitive.

5. It is compositional; a metric applied to a composite artifact should be some kind of sum of the metric applied to the components of the artifact.

6. Its value domain is numerical and allows meaningful arithmetic operations.

Obviously, we can have metrics that violate these desirable features. For example, a complexity metric may violate compositionality: The complexity of an aggregate is in general not the sum of the complexities of the constituents. We may have to admit unintuitive metrics when they turn out to be effective.

Metrics can be classified along multiple dimensions. We follow in part a classification given in [54]:

- Effort metrics measure the human, machine, and so on, resources spend during a particular time period on a specific set of development tasks.

- Static product metrics measure the volume and complexity of artifacts produced in the life cycle.

- Dynamic product metrics measure the volume of fixed and transient objects of an executing target system and the complexity of the communication graph of the objects.

Since a system configuration can vary over time, the values produced by these metrics can also vary over time. Thus we may consider derived metrics such as averages, minima and maxima, pseudoderivatives, and so on. The last entry in this classification, dynamic product metrics, is potentially significant for estimating maintenance efforts but is not discussed elaborated in this book.

1.5 Creating Development Effort Estimators

In this section we look at effort estimation, where we assume that at least some analysis activities have been completed. In Part 4 we make some remarks about earlier cost estimation in the requirements phase. Observe as well that the perspective is coarsegrained with respect to the applicability range of metrics. We will look at metrics that apply to fine-grained applicability ranges in subsequent chapters.

A premise for this book is that a SW development organization follows a disciplined process. In addition to iterations, we can observe producer-consumer relationships in the development process and hence a sequential dependency between the activities:

- Requirements: demarcation of what a system is supposed to do.

- Analysis: elaboration of the requirements in terms of a precise (graphical) formalism.

- Design: construction of a blueprint solution.

- Implementation: realization of this blueprint.

- Maintenance: removing imperfections from this solution.

Our key assumptions with respect to these activities (and their subsidiary activities) are:

1. *Phase-Effort* For each development (sub)phase we can formulate a product metric and an effort metric that correlate. These correlations are expressed by the vertical bidirectional arrows in Figure 1.2.

2. *Phase(N)-Phase(N+1)* Product metrics of adjacent phases correlate due to the conceptual continuity of the OO paradigm. These correlations are expressed by the horizontal bidirectional arrows in Figure 1.2.

Product $\underset{\text{---}}{A}$ ↔ $\underset{\text{---}}{D}$ ↔ $\underset{\text{---}}{I}$ ↔ $\underset{\text{---}}{T}$ ↔ $\underset{\text{---}}{M}$

Effort $\underset{\text{---}}{\updownarrow}$ $\underset{\text{---}}{\updownarrow}$ $\underset{\text{---}}{\updownarrow}$ $\underset{\text{---}}{\updownarrow}$ $\underset{\text{---}}{\updownarrow}$

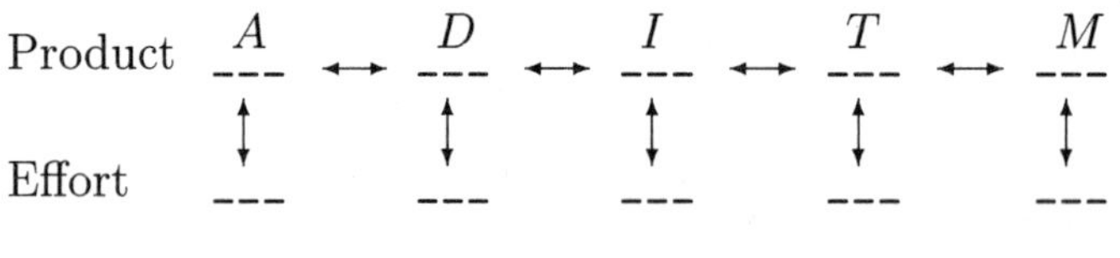

Figure 1.2: Activity correlations. Explanation of the symbols: *A*, analysis; *D*, design; *I*, implementation; *T*, test; *M*, maintenance; ---, the application of a product or effort metric to an artifact that carries over by transformations across the life cycle, such as a class or representation of an intended system.

Transitivity of the correlations in Figure 1.2 yields the derived correlations in Figure 1.3. Hence, given our assumptions, we can use the result of upstream product and/or effort metrics as estimators for product and/or effort metrics downstream.

Effort $\quad \underset{\text{---}}{A} \quad \longleftrightarrow \quad \underset{\text{---}}{D} \quad \longleftrightarrow \quad \underset{\text{---}}{I} \quad \longleftrightarrow \quad \underset{\text{---}}{T} \quad \longleftrightarrow \quad \underset{\text{---}}{M}$

Figure 1.3: Result of activity correlations. See the legend in the previous Figure for a description of the symbols.

We should stress that at this point we do not have a covering set of empirical evidence for our assumptions. Still, conceptual continuity across the phases of the life cycle is a hallmark of the OO paradigm. Hence we feel that our assumptions are more than a working hypothesis. In Part 4, we revisit Figures 1.2 and 1.3 and discuss the empirical data reported in this book, which are in support of our assumptions.

1.6 Impact of Reuse

Reuse is not a new concept in the realm of software development. Libraries have been around for a long time with such components as matrix operations, statistical packages, operating system primitives, and basic data structures and their operations. In addition, we have user-interface frameworks, persistency services, frameworks for distributed processing, and so on. Still it is felt that the OO paradigm will allow for another kind of reuse. An object bundling local state and behavior captures a domain-specific knowledge capsule. A follow-on project at Hewlett-Packard of the one reported in de Champeaux et al. [22] confirms the feasibility of incremental analysis, incremental design, and incremental implementation, by exploiting artifacts developed earlier and, as a result, reduced development efforts.

Hence development processes must allow for accessing external resources. Effort metrics must be parametrized to account for development *with* reuse. At the same time, we should acknowledge that domain-specific reuse is a nontrivial affair. We cannot simply assume that reusable artifacts can be picked up for free. The cost of constructing a reusable artifact must somehow be accounted for. Finding the right artifact may also not be obvious. In addition, having to adjust an artifact "a little bit" may become a costly nightmare. Thus, to account for reuse, one must introduce reuse effort adjustment coefficients in effort estimation formulas.

1.7   Impact of CASE Tools

We are in the midst of a not-so-small revolution in the way that software is developed. The paradigm switch to object orientation is just one aspect. In addition, we are witnessing a rapid development of CASE tools. As yet, they have only scratched the surface from the perspective of the OO paradigm. The ultimate CASE tool will support and integrate:

- *Control management.* A change made in a tool associated with a particular phase of the life cycle will trigger tasks for other tools responsible for other phases. These other tasks may be taken care of automatically, or they will be registered on agendas and notifications will be generated.

- *Data management.* Instead of each tool maintaining its own files, the CASE tool environment supports an integrated repository that maintains all artifacts and traceability links. Thus all entries are connected backward and forward, which helps explain elaboration connections.

- *Common look and feel.* All tools support a consistent user-interface protocol.

- *Team integration.* The environment allows developers to cooperate and supervises all required lock management.

- *Task management.* The environment has intimate knowledge of the generic OO development process for all phases of the life cycle and, as a result, can maintain agendas of subsidiary activities and can recommend which agenda items require urgent attention. These services are sensitive to the sophistication level of a developer.

- *Version management.* Version control is built in.

- *Knowledge management.* Domain-specific knowledge can be expressed and exploited (semi)automatically, as can design cliches and frameworks, domain-specific design and implementation constructs, and generic design and implementation constructs. Also, the development process can be customized to exploit special features of a domain.

Realizing these capabilities in a CASE tool will have an impact on the productivity of all participants in a development activity. At the same time, these advances will not be free. It has been estimated that the CASE tool environment sketched above is more complex than the most complex operating system (Humphrey [39]).

In addition, knowledge management may require extra human support: developers for the construction of reusable artifacts, component librarians, and component managers, to list just a few of them. Despite these hard-to-estimate costs, it is prudent to make metrics sensitive to the impact of (partial) mechanization of the development process.

There are currently a few integrated systems available or under development. Menga et al. [53] has an experimental development environment called G++ that integrates design, C++ implementation, and part of the analysis. This development environment is specialized for the construction of manufacturing control systems. Cubicon, another prototype environment, produced by Klausner [46], integrates analysis and high-level design and facilitates the generation of early prototypes. In both cases we see partial automatization of the construction of artifacts downstream, exploiting the conceptual continuity of the OO paradigm. The ObjecTime system is an industrial-strength development environment that yields executable models (see Selic et al. [71]). It is aimed at real-time applications.

Maintenance of a system is an ambiguous concept because it refers to two distinct activities: defect repair and functionality enhancement. Integrated tool support should greatly facilitate both activities. Observe that functionality enhancement can be seen as a special case of reuse, especially when version control management is provided by a tool.

1.8 Early Development Cost Estimation

Described above is our programme to relate product and process metrics for the analysis and design phases. This aims at the construction of effort estimators for subsequent activities. In practice, cost estimators, after having completed a requirements document, are more critical. In this section we provide an overview of earlier approaches.

1.8.1 Wolverton 1974

Wolverton [88] exploits the availability of historical data from similar projects for estimation of the cost of a new project; in short, this is estimation by analogy. In more detail, Mills writes [54]:

> The method assumes that a waterfall-style life cycle model is used. A 25 * 7 structural forecast matrix is used to allocate resources to various phases of the life cycle. In order to determine actual software costs, each

software module is first classified as belonging to one of six basic types –
control, I/O, etc. Then a level of difficulty is assigned by categorizing the
module as new or old and as easy, medium or hard. This gives a total of
six levels of module difficulty. Finally, the size of the module is estimated,
and the system cost is determined from historical cost data for software
with similar size, type and difficulty ratings.

1.8.2   Boehm (COCOMO) 1981 and Jalote 1991

Boehm [10] exploits another kind of historical data, which is an empirical relationship
between project size (in terms of lines of code) and effort (in terms of person-months):

$$InitialEffort = a * Size^b$$

where a and b are constants determined by historical data. An initial effort calculated by this formula is adjusted by multiplication factors, which are determined
by attributes of the project (called *cost drivers*). These attributes are grouped into
categories shown below with typical examples:

- *Product attributes*
  – Product complexity $(0.70/0.85/1.0/1.15/1.30/1.65)$

- *Computer attributes*
  – Execution-time constraint $(1.0/1.11/1.3/1.66)$

- *Personnel attributes*
  – Applications experience $(1.29/1.13/1.0/0.91/0.82)$

- *Project attributes*
  – Use of software tools $(1.24/1.1/1.0/0.91/0.82)$

The numbers in parentheses indicate the multiplier for a particular cost driver with
respect to the assessment categories: very low, low, nominal, high, very high, extra
high. For example: a low product complexity, a nominal execution-time constraint,
a very high applications experience and a very low use of software tools would give
the multipliers 0.85, 1.0, 0.82, and 1.24.

A key question remains how the initial *Size* parameter is to be obtained. Jalote
[42] observes:

There is no known method for estimating the size very accurately. ... [after half a page of avoiding the issue head on] ... With more detail about the system, and the subsystems and modules that will be required, the estimation should begin with estimating the sizes of the modules and subsystems, and then add up these estimates to obtain the overall estimates.

Given the difficulty of coming up with an initial *Size* estimate, one may question why the costdriver multipliers were given in three-digit accuracy (see also the result of a comparative study below). At the same time we should acknowledge that productivity in terms of produced lines of code is one of the few items of hard data available. Thus, attempts to relate to these data is a feasible strategy. On the other hand, this approach does not address, for example, the impact of (code) reuse.

1.8.3 Albrecht 1983 and Kemerer 1993

Albrecht [3] addressed the key problem of Boehm's approach by exploiting data that are available early in the life cycle. The idea is to assess the functionality of a target system and measure *function points*. Albrecht claims a high correlation between measured function points and the eventual number of source lines of code as well as between measured function points and the work effort required to develop the code. This method has been developed over time and has many adherents.[5]

Kemerer [44] gives the following characterization of the technique:

Calculation of Function Points (FP) begins with counting five components of the proposed or implemented system, namely, the number of external inputs (e.g., transaction types), external output (e.g., report types), logical internal files (files as the user may conceive of them, not physical files), external interface files (files accessed by the application but not maintained, i.e. updated by it), and external inquiries (types of on-line inquiries supported). Their complexity is classified as being relatively low, average, or high, according to a set of standards that define complexity in terms of objective guidelines. Table 1.1 is an example of such a guideline, in this case the table is used to assess the relative complexity of External Outputs, such as reports.

To use this table for counting the number of FPs in an application, a report would first be classified as an External Output. By determining

---

[5]Kemerer [44] reports that the International Function Point User Group (IFPUG) has over 300 members.

Table 1.1: Complexity Assignment for External Outputs

	1-5 Data Element Types	6-19 Data Element Types	20+ Data Element Types
0-1 File Types Referenced	Low	Low	Average
2-3 File Types Referenced	Low	Average	High
4+ File Types Referenced	Average	High	High

the number of unique files used to generate the report ("File Type Referenced"), and the number of fields on the report ("Data Element Types"),
it can be classified as a relatively low-, average-, or high-complexity External Output. After making such determinations for each of the five
component types, the number of each component type present is placed
into its assigned cell next to its weight in the matrix shown in Table 1.2.
Then, the total number of function counts (FCs) is computed by the equation

$$FC = \sum_{i=1}^{5} \sum_{j=1}^{3} W_{ij} * X_{ij}$$

where W_{ij} = weight for row i, column j, and X_{ij} = value in cell i, j.

Table 1.2: Function Count Weighting Factors

	Low	Average	High
External Input	*3	*4	*6
External Output	*4	*5	*7
Logical Internal File	*7	*10	*15
External Interface File	*5	*7	*10
External Inquiry	*3	*4	*6

The second step involves assessing the impact of 14 general system
characteristics that are rated on a scale from 0 to 5 in terms of their likely
effect for the system being counted. These characteristics are: (1) data
communications, (2) distributed functions, (3) performance, (4) heavily
used configuration, (5) transaction rate, (6) on-line data entry, (7) end

user efficiency, (8) on-line update, (9) complex processing, (10) reusability, (11) installation ease, (12) operational ease, (13) multiple sites, and (14) facilitates change. These values are summed and then modified to compute the Value Adjustment Factor, or VAF

$$VAF = 0.65 + 0.01 * \sum_{i=1}^{14} C_i$$

where C_i = value of general system characteristic i, with $0 \le C_i \le 5$.

Finally, the two values are multiplied to create the number of Function Points: $FP = FC * VAF$.

For a complete description of this technique, see the IFPUG Standard, Release 3.0 [76].

Given the subjective aspects of this technique, one can investigate the interrater stability. Kemerer [44] reports the result of an extensive field study that addressed this issue: "... the median difference in FP counts from pairs of raters using the standard method was approximately 12% ..." Hence he concludes that the interrater stability is high enough to use the FP count as the basis for size and effort estimation.

Interestingly enough, he describes in [44] an alternative technique and provides analogous empirical results. The techniques are compared as well. The second technique is based on entity-relationship modeling and apparently also uses top-level data-flow diagrams. The latter are used to identify the three types of transactions that are counted in the Function Point Analysis. Interrater stability of this variant is not as favorable as for the first one but is still satisfactory. In addition, the two techniques correlate as high as 0.95 for the data in this study.

We can conclude that these techniques are coherent and measure "something" that is plausibly correlated with the target system size. However, it is to be observed that the applicability range for this technique is probably restricted. A table in [44] that describes the types of systems used in the empirical study lists seven entries and indicates that 85% of the systems were either batch MIS applications (15%) or interactive MIS applications (70%). The entries Scientific or Mathematical application, Communications or Telecommunications application, and Embedded or real-time applications each had a 0% representation.

The impact of reuse and the utilization of CASE tools on a development effort appears not to be addressed. That is not necessarily a disadvantage, because one can argue that the function point approach aims at estimating only target system *size*, not the *effort* required to develop the system.

1.8.4   Thebaut (COPMO) 1984

The metric developed by Thebaut [79] is a generalization of Boehm's approach in that it also takes into account whether a team effort is required for effort estimation. The effort formula becomes

$$E = a + b * S + c * P^d$$

with a, b, c, and d constants to be determined from empirical data, S the program size in terms of lines of code, and P the average personnel level over the life of the project.

We agree with Mill's concern: "Unfortunately, this model requires not one but two input parameters whose actual values are not known until the project has been completed."

1.8.5   Kemerer 1987

Kemerer reports [43] the results of an empirical comparative study of several software cost estimation techniques. The following approaches were compared: Putnam's SLIM [65], Boehm's COCOMO [10], Albrecht's FP [3], and Rubin's ESTIMACS [69]. The results of this study imply that "... the resulting errors in predicted person-months are large (COCOMO 600%, SLIM 771%, FP 102%, ESTIMACS 85%)." In addition, it was observed that "the models not developed in business data-processing environments showed significant needs for calibration."

1.8.6   Summary

We can draw the following conclusions from the historic overview presented above:

- Effort estimation can be formulated in a general fashion, but application probably requires domain-specific calibration.

- An unstructured requirements document does not provide enough foundation for system effort estimation; instead, some preliminary analysis activity is to be performed.

- Experience (i.e., access to historical data) allows estimation by analogy.

- Breaking a system down into subsystems may help estimation activities.

- The impact of CASE tools and reuse is as yet not well incorporated in effort estimation metrics.

Obviously, the earlier in the life cycle one can produce (reliable) effort estimation, the better. Albrecht's technique and its modification described by Kemerer suggest that one may exploit artifacts constructed early in the life cycle. We will follow the same strategy for artifacts developed early in the OO analysis process.

1.9 Structure of This Book

The remainder of this book has been split up in parts devoted to analysis, design, and implementation, respectively. These parts have as substructure the four chapters dealing with concepts, process, metrics, and examples.

In the concepts chapters we review notions and notations that are available for representing artifacts in a particular development phase. We summarize the material developed in de Champeaux et al. [24], which by itself is a condensation of key notions presented by Shlaer and Mellor [72, 73], Booch [12], Wirfs-Brock et al. [87], Rumbaugh et al. [70], Jacobson et al. [41], among others.

The process chapters outline default procedures for a particular development phase. These procedures cannot be applied blindly for a particular development task; they need to be refined to fit the specific circumstances of a specific task.

The metrics chapters define product metrics for the artifacts that are developed in a particular subphase of the development process. Process metrics are defined as well.

In the example chapters we apply the theory developed in preceding chapters on an example that is used throughout the book, for which the requirements are described in the next section.

Appendices cover additional details of the example in C++ code.

1.10 Example Requirements

The example below has a history. It is taken from Booch [12], who reports that it was originally proposed by White [85] and extended by Kerth [45]. The example has excellent ambiguities; it reflects the reality of analysts.

Home Heating System Requirements

The Figure 1.4 provides a block diagram of the home heating system. The basic function of the system is to regulate the flow of heat to individual rooms of a home in an attempt to maintain a working temperature tw, established for each room. The working temperature for each room is calculated by the system as a function of a single desired temperature td, (set by the user through a manual input device) and whether or not the room is occupied. If the room is occupied, the working temperature is set to the desired temperature. If the room is vacant, the working temperature is set to $(td - 5)$ degrees Fahrenheit. Additionally, the system maintains a weekly living pattern and attempts to raise room temperatures thirty minutes before occupancy is anticipated for a given room. The weekly living pattern is updated when variations to the established pattern occur two weeks in a row.

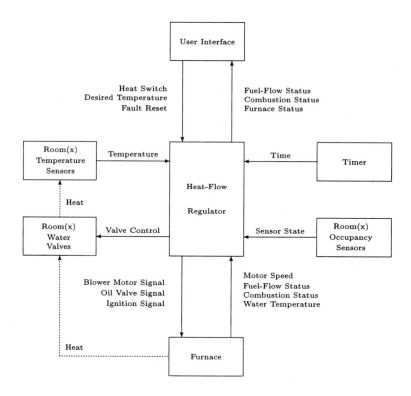

Figure 1.4: Home Heating System Block Diagram.

Each room of the home is equipped with a sensor that continuously measures temperature. Each room of the home is also equipped with an infrared sensor that continuously determines whether or not the room is occupied.

The user interface permits the user to control and monitor the furnace. The following input devices exist:

- **Heat switch** The heat switch controls the functioning of the furnace; it can be turned on and off by the user.

- **Desired temperature input device** The desired temperature input device (one per room) continuously provides the value of the desired temperature set by the user.

- **Fault reset switch/indicator** This is a combined switch and indicator; the user can reset a fault by setting the fault reset switch/ indicator to on.

The following display devices are provided:

- **Furnace status indicator** The furnace status indicator displays the running/not running state of the furnace.

- **Fault reset switch/indicator** This is a combined switch and indicator; the fault reset switch/indicator is automatically turned off by the heat-flow regulator upon the detection of either a fuel-flow or combustion-state fault.

The timer provides a continuously incrementing count, one increment for every second of elapsed time.

Heat is provided to each room of the home by circulating hot water, which is heated by the furnace. Each room is equipped with a water valve that controls the flow of hot water into the room. The valve can be commanded to be either fully open or fully closed.

The furnace consists of a boiler, an oil valve, an ignitor, a blower, and a water-temperature sensor. The furnace heats water in the boiler, and the water can then be circulated to one or more rooms of the home. The furnace is alternately activated and deactivated by the heat-flow regulator as needed to maintain the required temperature for each room. The furnace activation procedure is as follows:

- The system activates the blower motor.

- The system monitors the blower motor speed; when it reaches a predetermined RPM value the system opens the oil valve and ignites the oil.

- When the water temperature reaches a predetermined value, the system opens the appropriate room water valves.

- The furnace status indicator is turned on.

The furnace deactivation procedure is as follows:

- The system closes the oil valve and then, after five seconds, stops the blower motor.

- The system turns the furnace indicator off.

- The system closes all the room water valves.

A fuel-flow status sensor and an optical combustion sensor signal the system if abnormalities occur, in which case the system deactivates the furnace, turns the fault reset switch/indicator off, and closes all the room water valves.

The heat-flow regulator interacts with other components of the home heating system to determine the heating needs for each room and to control the flow of heat necessary to satisfy those requirements. The heat-flow regulator maintains a working temperature, tw, and a weekly living pattern for each room without regard to the running/not running state of the furnace. The heat-flow regulator determines that a given room needs heat whenever the room temperature is equal to or less than $(tw - 2)$ degrees Fahrenheit and determines that a given room does not need heat whenever the room temperature is equal to or greater than $(tw + 2)$ degrees Fahrenheit. If the furnace is not running, the heat switch and the fault reset switch/indicator are both on, and at least one room needs heat, the heat-flow regulator activates the furnace and then routes heat to the appropriate rooms. If the furnace is running, the heat-flow regulator deactivates the furnace whenever either the heat switch or the fault reset switch/indicator is off and no rooms need heat. The minimum time for furnace restart after prior operation is five minutes.

1.11 Summary

We described three key components of a software development method: (1) well-defined core concepts, (2) a process for utilizing these core concepts, and (3) a criterion for measuring progress. The distinction between macro and micro processes was elaborated and we explained that we would concentrate on micro processes for analysis, design, and implementation. We described metrics in general and distinguished between the major categories of effort and product metrics. We outlined our strategy for developing effort metrics via product metrics.

We summarized previous work in this area and drew the following major conclusions:

- Effort estimation can be formulated in a general fashion, but applications probably require domain-specific calibration.

- An unstructured requirements document does not provide enough foundation for a system effort estimation; instead, a preliminary analysis activity is required.

- Experience - preferably with access to historical data - allows estimation by analogy.

- Breaking down a system into subsystems may help estimation activities.

- The impact of CASE tools and reuse is not well incorporated into effort estimation metrics.

1.12 Further Reading

We are not aware of alternative book on object-oriented development processes beyond our own earlier text, de Champeaux et al. [24]. Regarding object-oriented metrics, we have found an alternative: Henderson-Sellers and Edwards [36], and a newer text devoted exclusively to OO metrics: Henderson-Sellers [37]. Workshops at ECOOP and OOPSLA are at the time of this writing still the best source for the emerging field of OO metrics. At the metrics workshop at OOPSLA 1994 the conclusion was reached that effort estimation metrics are to be distinguished from quality metrics. The OOPSLA 1995 workshop concentrated on development processes and effort metrics.

1.13   Exercises

1. Can the function point effort estimation technique be applied to object-oriented software development? Give arguments pro and con.

2. The maintenance costs of software outweigh the costs of initial development (over 60% versus less than 40%). Do we need OO specific metrics for the maintenance phase? Give arguments pro and con.

Part I

Analysis

Chapter 2

Analysis Concepts

This chapter gives a fast-paced introduction to OO analysis notions. A treatment with more details and at a slower pace can be found in de Champeaux et al. [24].

2.1 Purpose of Analysis

The purpose of analysis, simply put, is to reformulate a requirements document into a semiformalized notation. This exercise will help reveal ambiguities, incompleteness, and contradictions in the initial requirements. Exposing these imperfections early in the process will save costly reworkings later. A study in the 1970s demonstrated that fixing requirements errors in the maintenance phase is 100 to 1000 times more costly than fixing these same problems in the analysis phase.

The analysis will address only a subset of the total requirements. Analysis concentrates on the functional dimension and can also deal with performance demands. Other aspects, such as resource constraints, contextual constraints, specifications of programming languages, databases, UIs, and implementation frameworks are ignored. In other words, analysis is transparent to these additional requirements; they are passed on to the design phase.

A common definition of analysis is that it yields a description of *what* a system is supposed to do. In contrast, design describes *how* a system will work. The boundary between analysis and design is clear in theory but opaque in practice. Analysis should concentrate on a clarification of the task at hand without attempting to construct a partial blueprint solution; this is the responsibility of the design phase. In practice it is hard to formulate *what* a task is without digressing into solution sketches.

A prospective homeowner may formulate abstract requirements such as number

of rooms, total amount of floor space, and number of bathrooms, but will probably
rely on sketches to express a style preference or to formulate a floor plan. The same
thing happens with analysis.

The analysis core concepts that we introduce will be used to construct models of
the target system. Although one may argue that these models are abstract, they are
quite likely to capture structural elements that will carry over into the design. For
instance, when the intended system is large, one will try to decompose the system
into subsystems. A requirements document will probably contain some kind of block
diagram with some ad hoc interpretation of the blocks and their connections.[1] It is
quite unlikely that an analysis will ignore such a decomposition. As a consequence,
a logical architecture will be carried over and will be forced onto the design.

At the same time, we insist that one should remain aware of the difference between
analysis and design during analysis and design. While doing analysis, one should be
alert not to digress into details that will not help elucidate *what* the development task
is all about. Similarly, a designer should not make requirements decisions when it
turns out that the analysis output is still ambiguous.[2]

Key notion

OO analysis is obviously rooted in the notion of an object. We refer to the literature for many alternative definitions of objects. Here we reuse the object definition
formulated in de Champeaux et al. [24]. An object is a conceptual entity that:

- Is identifiable

- Has features that span a local state space

- Has operators that can change the status of the system locally while possibly
  inducing invocations of operations in peer objects

- Refers to something that is identifiable by the users of the target system: either
  a tangible thing or a mental construct

The first three items in this list apply to objects in general. The last item in the
list is specific for analysis objects. It can be used as a check to avoid wandering off
into design country.

---

[1] We encountered such a diagram in the requirements for the home heating system in Chapter 1.

[2] We do *not* suggest that analysis and design are to be done by different people. We only insist
that the person in the role of designer not make requirements decisions - and vice versa, as we have
insisted before.

Objects are not the only key concept - relations can also be used. In fact, we can import entity-relationship thinking into analysis after abstracting objects into entities. It is to be observed, however, that relationships are not supported directly in OO programming languages. Hence relationships must later be "designed away". Whether to use relationships as in relational database schema design is a matter of taste.[3]

Object role versus generic object properties

Most systems in the past were custom made. Hence most of their components were constructed to play a specific role and nothing else. The situation is different for the components at the lowest level. Strings, numbers, sets, and so on, have generic features that are independent of the use of these components. Thus we can distinguish between these generic features and specializations that allow an entity to play a specific role. For example, a generic hash table, which can be described abstractly, may be used in the role of, say, repository of city names. Wide-spectrum reuse of a component relies on being able to *instantiate* the generic features of the component into multiple roles.

These observations can apply to objects as well. In fact, the promise of reuse is one of the driving forces of the popularity of OO. But we should realize immediately that reusability has its price. One cannot develop objects on the basis of the requirements of a particular system and assume that an object will be reusable. Target system-specific features may have been "welded" in. Consequently, we face as a trade-off: the quick and dirty development of objects that will fit the role to be played in an intended system versus the development of more costly but potentially reusable objects that may need some specialization to fit into a target system.

The computational model in analysis

Although we do not emphasize computation in analysis, since we should avoid a digression into design, we still need agreement on the basics of object behavior and object interaction. Otherwise, our behavioral models would not be grounded. Another reason for addressing this issue is that we have to deal with a major difference between the computational model in analysis and in implementation. Programming language objects are passive. They are activated from the outside, perform their role

---

[3]The availability of relationships in OO analysis methods creates at least a pleasant illusion for database experts. Their use in practice is debatable.

and return control. There is only a single thread of control. The parallel connotation evoked by interobject message passing is just an illusion. Message passing is a procedure or function call from a control perspective.

This programming-level computational model is not attractive for the analysis phase. Entities encountered in a domain of interest probably have a degree of autonomy or can be modeled that way. A manufacturing environment can have multiple employees, dealing with many pieces of equipment, connected by numerous transportation mechanisms, producing many products in parallel, and so on. Similarly, an airline company has many different things that operate in parallel and semiautonomously. Hence, for analysis we adopt active objects where each object has its own thread of control. Although some methods allow an object to have more than one thread of control, we refrain from this liberty; see de Champeaux et al. [24] for arguments.

We support a multitude of interaction styles. Along one dimension we can distinguish one-way from bidirectional interaction. *Producer-consumer* is a good metaphor for one-way interaction; *client-server* corresponds with bidirectional interaction. Interactions can be extended with a time-out option when an initiator depends on a recipient for a reply or an acknowledgment of reception.

Along another dimension we can distinguish between buffered and unbuffered interaction. We take buffering as the default. How buffering is achieved is uncommitted. It may be done by "magic" in recipients or by the "ether" between objects. Unbuffered interaction is supported to represent faithfully connections between entities where buffering obviously does not occur. For example, the construction of a buffer will, at a certain low level, rely on unbuffered communication, such as atomic test-and-set instructions.

2.2   Overview of the Representational Apparatus

The notations employed in analysis can be classified by several characteristics:

1. The level of formalization

2. Whether the target system is described from the outside or the inside

3. Whether a static or a dynamic aspect is addressed

4. Whether a system-specific aspect is formulated, or whether generic aspects are described

We discuss these distinctions some before delving into the representational apparatus.

2.2.1 Level of formalization

The level of formalization varies and depends on whether a notation serves an artifact close to the unformalized requirements or whether it takes its input from intermediate representations. Hence we provide for a gradual increase in formality from the initial requirements to the analysis model. Consequently, analysis is an inherently fuzzy business. Formal verification of the analysis output against the requirements is impossible because the requirements themselves are informal. Validation of the analysis output consists of walk-throughs by analysts and by the client or customer (and by intimidating the customer sufficiently until a sign-off is obtained).

2.2.2 Inside-outside distinction

The inside-outside distinction is somewhat vague. We give attention to the inside structure of the target system by modeling its architecture. However, we do not descend deeply. These descriptions cover aspects that are "visible" from the outside, such as subsystems, obvious components, states that make sense from the perspective of a user of the system (as well as states that can be postulated to interconnect observable states), and so on. Characterizations from the outside, for example, are input-output response descriptions. Performance constraints are another example.

2.2.3 Static versus dynamic

The static versus dynamic distinction pertains to whether we describe aspects that remain constant for the target system or whether we describe behavioral aspects. Dynamic aspects can refer to components or to the system as a whole.

2.2.4 System-specific versus generic

The requirements are a driving force for the analysis process. Hence all artifacts developed are aimed primarily aimed playing a role in the target system. Thus they are system specific. At the same time, one may improve the quality of the system, and therefore its maintainability, by "ruggedizing" components such that they become potentially reusable. Even when reuse of a component will not take place, the additional effort to make it reusable will probably have improved its quality: for instance, by decoupling unrelated behaviors, closing off access paths, or enhancing exception handling.

2.3   Basic Concepts for Analysis

In this section we deal with the core representations of the target system. A middle-out approach is followed: starting with core concepts that are at the center of the analysis micro process, proceeding with representations that feed into the core representations, and finishing with representations that take the core representations as input. The core concepts for representing systems can be classified along two orthogonal dimensions (as in de Champeaux et al. [24]): (1) whether the focus is on a single object versus whether multiple objects are involved; and (2) whether a static aspect is covered or a dynamic aspect is addressed. See Table 2.1 for the matrix form. We elaborate on these core concepts below.

Table 2.1: Classification of the core OO analysis models

	Single object	Between objects
Static	Attribute	Relationship
	Constraint	Acquaintanceship
Dynamic	Transition	Service interaction or
	network	event

2.3.1   Recognizing objects

A general recipe for identifying objects cannot be provided at this time - if ever. Tangible entities are a candidate for objecthood. For example, a car can be seen as an object for car manufacturers, for auto insurance, for car rental agencies, for car repair centers, and so on. It is to be observed right away that a formalized characterization of *Car* is likely to be different in each application domain. Still it is plausible that cars will show up as objects in each of these domains. Nontangibles can become objects as well: a transfer between accounts, an ATM session, a phone call, and so on.

We can make a pragmatic distinction between enduring and transient objects. This distinction is pragmatic because trying to define their difference is an elusive enterprise. As an approximation: Enduring objects are involved with an unbounded number of interactions; transient objects are engaged in a limited number of interactions.

Other methods distinguish between active and passive objects: Active objects are said to have a certain "autonomy", passive objects are only acted upon. We don't adopt this distinction. In our perspective, all objects (in analysis) are autonomous (i.e., they have their own thread of control).

2.3.2 Instances

The carriers for the core notions are simply objects. An individual object is described predominantly via its membership in a class,[4] but in addition, some unique distinguishing characteristic must be provided. A particular class is defined through a prototypical instance such that all features ascribed to the prototypical instance apply to all instances of the class. Instances can be distinguished initially through a unique label. For example, a particular airplane of the *Fly Fast* company can be identified through its name: *Antelope*. A particular employee of a company can be identified by, for instance, the social security number of that employee. A graphical notation for an instance is simply a filled circle, as in Figure 2.1.

• *Eiffel Tower*   • *John Johnson*

Figure 2.1: Notation for the instances *Eiffel Tower* and *John Johnson*.

Sometimes we need to represent instances that are still generic. For instance, when we make a model of a car, we may want to zoom in on the carburetor. Hence we are interested in describing a carburetor - not a particular one for a particular car but a generic carburetor for a generic brand of car. We may do so by describing a certain class of carburetors. That is a good and recommended way. Still, we may want to refer to a generic instance - say, for a simulation purpose. To serve this need, we introduce the notion of a *parametric* instance. Its notation is an open circle, as in Figure 2.2. Below we will reencounter the parametric notion in the context of relations.

○ *aCarburetor*   ○ *aB747*   ○ *theCFOofTheCompany*

Figure 2.2: Notation for parametric instances.

We could proceed with detailing the static and dynamic dimensions of individual (parametric) objects, and similarly for the other dimension: individual objects versus

---

[4]See below for a formal definition of class.

object interaction. However, traditionally these extensions are covered with respect
to classes, our next topic.

2.3.3   Classes

A *class* prescribes a minimal set of properties - structural and behavioral - that are
shared by intended items in a collection, the object instances of that class. Alternatively, a class can be seen as a *template* for the generation of its instances. To
elaborate on what is perhaps obvious: A class does *not* represent a particular set of
objects at a particular time. Instead, a class defines what all (potential) objects have
in common.

Each class has, in fact, two templates: one for the static features and one for the
dynamic properties. We address both of them in the following subsections.

Object statics

The static template of a class consists, to a first approximation, of a set of object
attributes. An attribute is a function on the set of instances of a class to a value
domain. The value domain can be a set of instances of a class or a set of non-class
elements. For example, if every person (in a certain population) has health insurance
we can give the class *Person* the attribute *healthInsurance* with *HealthInsuranceCo* as
value domain. Thus in this case we find the health insurance company for a person
by looking up the *healthInsurance* attribute value.

We can choose the domain *HealthInsuranceCo* to be represented as a class or as a
plain data domain. (We do *not* insist that every entity represented be an object, but
we do, of course, alalow any reader or analyst to insist on this.)

As another example, consider the class *Dwelling*. One is likely to want to give
Dwelling the attribute *address*. The value domain could be a class *Address*, or if we
don't want to deal with these values as objects, we can choose a composite data value,
a structure, or the like for them.

Graphical notations for these concepts are:

- A class is denoted by a rectangle.

- An attribute is attached to its class and points toward its value domain, while
  the attribute name, sometimes called the *role name*, is a label on the arc.

These examples are represented in Figures 2.3, 2.4, and 2.5.

As another example we consider the class *PhoneCall* with the following attributes:

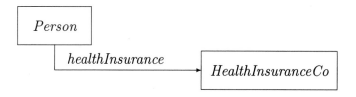

Figure 2.3: The class *Person*, with the attribute *healthInsurance* having the value domain *HealthInsuranceCo*.

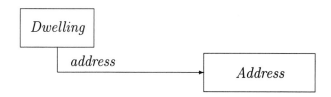

Figure 2.4: Value domain of the attribute *address* as the class *Address*.

- *caller* with value domain *Subscriber#*

- *callee* with value domain *Subscriber#*

- *initializationTime* with value domain *DateTime*

- *duration* with value domain *Duration*

Figure 2.5: Value domain of the attribute *address* represented not as a class but as a plain value.

See Figure 2.6.

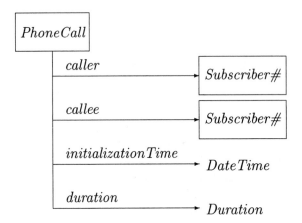

Figure 2.6: Graphical representation of the class *PhoneCall*.

Figure 2.6 has two occurrences of the class *Subscriber#*, for the caller and the callee respectively. In an alternative representation we can avoid repeating the *Subscriber#* box (without implying that the caller and callee are the same entity!), as in Figure 2.7.

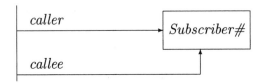

Figure 2.7: Alternative representation for the attributes *caller* and *callee* in the class *PhoneCall*. The two attributes share the same value domain.

Note that we represented the value domains of *duration* as well as of *initialization-Time* as data domains instead of as classes. Time and time intervals are usually not fruitfully represented as classes. Similarly, location is usually adequately represented by a data domain.

Attribute features   We can attach features to attributes to capture more detailed insight. For example, we may want to initialize an attribute value for a new instance with a default value. *Pink* would be a reasonable default value for the color of a pig (see Figure 2.8).

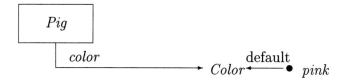

Figure 2.8: A pig has the color pink as the default value.

Color stands here for a nonclass value domain and could be an enumeration, as in:

$$Color = \{red, blue, green, yellow, brown, pink, white, black\}$$

Sometimes we can have multiple values associated with an attribute. Consider a class *DreamVilla*, where an instance always has at least 5 and at most 7 rooms, 1 kitchen, and 4 bathrooms. We add these attribute multiplicity features as in Figure 2.9.

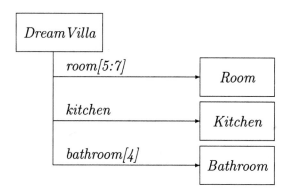

Figure 2.9: Attributes of the class *DreamVilla*. The attributes *room* and *bathroom* are multivalued and have a multiplicity feature.

The general form is $[N : M]$, with $0 <= N <= M$; N is the lower bound and M is the upper bound. $[N : N]$ can be abbreviated to $[N]$; $[1]$ is usually omitted; $[5 : M]$ stands for at least five attribute copies.

As an other example, consider the attribute *wheel* for the class *Cycle* with the repetition feature $[1 : 3]$ to represent monocycles, bicycles, and tricycles.

This notation does not handle all conceivable cases. For example, a car in a particular family of *Cars* may have either 3, 4, 6 or 10 wheels. Our notation does not handle this case. Analysts are invited to extend the notation for those situations as they see fit. For example, the notation [3, 4, 6, 10] would be an acceptable choice for the *wheel* attribute.

Attributes are generally used to express properties that apply to all instances of a class. Our [N : M] notation allows a sneaky way to have instances that lack an attribute. For example, if we have *fingers* as an attribute of *Hand*, we should have a multiplicity indicator of *fingers* that allows 0, since a hand may have lost all fingers. If *spouse* is an attribute of *Person*, we should allow for nonoccurrence of this attribute to account for unmarried people.

We may have more knowledge about an attribute that may be useful for a design and/or for an implementation. We may have knowledge as to the probabilities of occurrences of attribute values. For example, when we have an attribute for a *Person* that expresses the most recently used car rental company, if any, we may have access to marketing data that express the likelihood of a value to be Hertz, National, or oyher company.

We may have similar useful knowledge about attribute multiplicities. For example, *Car*s have predominantly four *wheel*s and *Hand*s usually have five *finger*s. In both cases, the analyst is invited to invent ad hoc notation to represent this type of knowledge.

If desired, we can impose more structure on a multivalued attribute. We give examples of domains with SET, BAG, SEQUENCE, and ARRAY structures, respectively. An analyst can add similar containers with other properties when necessary.

The class *Cheese* may have the attribute *hole* with a set of *Holes* as value domain (see Figure 2.10). A conceptually equivalent notation would use *Hole* as the value domain and [0 : M] as the multiplicity feature. The 0 allows for a piece of cheese not to have a hole, as is allowed with the SET notation by using an empty set of *Hole* instances.

A *Warehouse* can have the attribute *inventory* with *Merchandise* as value domain. In case we do not distinguish items that have the same characteristics, except being physically distinct, we can represent the domain using the BAG construct (a bag differs from a set in that a bag can have multiple appearances of the same element; see Figure 2.11).

To illustrate using SEQUENCE, we give a *ToDo* class the attribute *action*, with *Task*s as values. The SEQUENCE construct can imply some kind of ordering (priorities) of the *Task*s (see Figure 2.12).

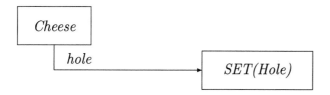

Figure 2.10: Multivalued attribute using the SET container.

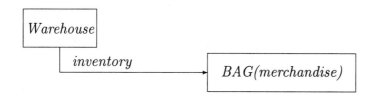

Figure 2.11: Multivalued attribute using the BAG container.

Finally, we illustrate the ARRAY construct by giving a *Window* class the attribute display with as values *Point*s (see Figure 2.13). The ARRAY example in Figure 2.13 shows that arguments of a container can be a nonclass, (i.e., a plain data value). 800 and 900 are not objects. The container itself, however, is a class. As a prototypical example we can describe a class *String* with characters as data values (see Figure 2.14).

An analyst should feel free to introduce other container constructs as the need arises. Notice that we have not provided details on how to operate on the container constructs. That is okay since we do not deal here with the dynamic aspects. However, we will ignore them when we discuss the dynamic aspects. Obviously, we need *get* and *set* operations, index operations, and so on. We leave those details to the imagination of the reader and/or as an exercise.

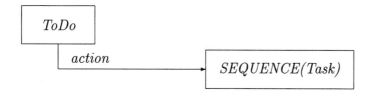

Figure 2.12: Multivalued attribute using the BAG container.

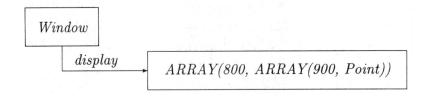

Figure 2.13: Multivalued attribute using the ARRAY container.

Figure 2.14: SEQUENCE container producing a class.

Constraints   A set of attributes of a class can be called minimal when no attribute can be formulated in terms of the others. A *2D Point* class with Cartesian coordinate attributes and polar coordinates obviously does *not* have a minimal set of attributes. Although we may simplify a nonminimal set into a minimal set, it is another matter whether we should always do that. Limited computational resources or performance reasons may prescribe caching redundant attribute values.

Another reason can be that there are multiple minimal attribute subsets and that they are all equally desirable. For example, we may describe a triangle with its three vertices, or alternatively, with its three arcs. On the other hand, having them all as attributes may be preferable.

When we describe a class with a nonminimal set of attributes, it pays to formulate the interdependencies between attribute values and/or with respect to other attribute features. Constraint expressions can be employed for those formulations. Certain restricted constraint expressions can be transformed readily, via a design, into code that will maintain a constraint by modifying dependent attributes when a primary attribute changes. We do not provide a special notation for this and point out only that one can use any mathematical notation or, if that is not expressive enough, one can fall back to logical notations, provided, of course, that one needs their precision in the first place.

To boost intuition we list some situations where constraints can be helpful:

- When a class has attributes that represent a temperature in the Kelvin, Celsius, Fahrenheit, and Réaumur scales, we can expresses their dependencies with linear equations.

- When a class has an attribute A with a nonfixed multiplicity indicator, we can have an additional attribute $A\#$ with a numeric value so that an instance has the knowledge of how many values are attached to its A attribute. The constraint that represents their connection is of the form

$$value(A\#) = |value(A)|$$

- When an *Account* class maintains an attribute that represents a log of balances and another attribute that represents a log of transactions, we have invariants of the form
$$balance(i + 1) = balance(i) + transaction(i)$$

Fixed attribute values   An attribute value may be determined once and for all instances when a class is defined. Hence all instances of that class will have that nonmutable attribute value. For example, the class *Albino* has the attribute *color* with the immutable value *white*. The class *BMW* has its *brandName* attribute fixed into *"BMW"*.

We can also freeze other aspects of an attribute like a multiplicity indicator; the class *Bicycle* will have its *wheel* attribute multiplicity feature frozen into two. We will revisit these "tricks" when we discuss inheritance.

An alternative for class-wide fixing is freezing attribute aspects per instance, say when an instance is initialized. As an example, we may have the policy that bank accounts are never recycled. Hence an *owner* attribute of *Account* and its identification number would be fixed at the initialization time of an account. An annotation in the graphical representation can express these properties as in Figure 2.15.

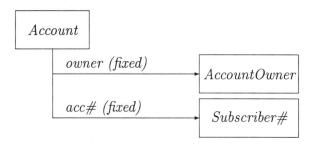

Figure 2.15: Immutable attribute values through the annotation *fixed*.

Object dynamics

This subsection is devoted to the behavior of objects. We restrict ourselves here to the behavior of individual, single, isolated objects. That is unrealistic because an OO system cannot consist in practice of a single object. Hence the ability of an object to interact is an intrinsic feature of objects.

Still, we want to distinguish between the generic dynamic behavior of an object [i.e., behavior independent of the *role(s)* that the object plays in a target system] and the behavior, the role, that the object displays to fulfill particular expectations and obligations in a specific context of a system.

This distinction is not always clear. Sometimes classes are defined for which their instances are handcrafted for one and only one role. For example, a mediator object that shields an object representing a heartbeat from a user interface displaying heartbeats may be too specialized to be perceived as a generic capability, unless it turns out that there are different types of heartbeats, each requiring somewhat different types of mediators. As a result, one may have to introduce a generic intermediary for which the instances will play different roles. But then again, the argument of highly specialized objects would arise for subclasses of the generic intermediary.

Despite these arguments pro and con regarding the universal applicability of the distinction between generic and specific behavior, we recommend describing any class as if it is generic. This enhances not only chances for its reusability, but much more significant, it will probably increase the quality of the class. For instance, scrutinizing a class for genericness may lead to the decoupling of functionality that is only incidental to a particular application and that makes a class more "voluminous" than required.

As an example, consider again our heartbeat mediator. In addition to being a mediator, it may have built-in smarts such as performing some caching operation. Although one can argue that from a performance perspective it is necessary to have the caching ability hardwired inside the mediator, one may argue otherwise - that the additional functionality is not intrinsic to the mediator capability and thus is best factored out from a conceptual perspective, which is our focus in OO analysis. By bundling the two capabilities, an analyst may in fact have transgressed prematurely into design! As a corollary of our recommendation, we advocate formulating interaction capabilities of objects in a fashion that avoids hardwiring the interaction partnerships.

More general considerations regarding behavior descriptions   Analysts have their hands tied behind their back when it comes to describing system behavior. For example, differential equations are in general not applicable. All the formalisms offered by programming languages are off limit because they aim at facilitating the description of *solutions* instead of producing *problem* descriptions.

An option is describing behavior only through state descriptions (i.e., by using pairs of states). The first one in the pair refers to the state of the "world" before an operation occurs, and the second one describes the world after the operation has terminated. Examples:

- *Cleaning* transforms something dirty into something clean.

- *Eating* transforms something hungry into something satisfied.

- A *bank transaction* transforms an initial pair of balances into a new pair of balances.

In a somewhat more formal vein, an operation has the form
```
operation: initial state --> final state
```
As an example, we have

```
Transfer C from account1 to account2:
   initial state:
      account1.balance = A
      account2.balance = B
-->
   final state:
      account1.balance' = A - C
      account2.balance' = B + C
```

Note that we have adorned attribute values in the final state with a quote (') to avoid clashes between the naming of values in the initial and in the final state.

As a special case we have service operations where the initial and final state are the same:
```
operation: state --> state
```
A generic example is

```
getInput Process & GenerateOutput
   initial state:
      Ready
```

```
-->
    final state:
      Ready
```

This example shows that such a service operation is not explained at all by knowing that it returns to the originating state. We will rely upon, among others, *guards* to elucidate service operations (see below).

The state-operation line of thinking for representing behavior leads to the utilization of transition networks for describing the overall dynamics of an object. A transition network is a notation for expressing the behavior of objects consisting of states and guarded transitions between these states. A transition is said to "fire" when control resides in the start state of the transition and:

– a transition-specific event arrives and a guard condition of the transition, if any, evaluates to true; or

– the transition does not depend on an event and its guard condition evaluates to true.

A transition network can be represented as a connected directed graph with the vertices representing states and the arcs representing transitions, while operations (also called *actions*) are part of the transitions. Below we discuss an extension where operations are also associated with states. This extension does not increase the expressive power of transition networks, but adds convenience since it permits suppressing details where warranted.

Every state of a transition network should be reachable from an initial state. An object can appear to have more than one transition network, but we can always take the Cartesian product of disjoint networks to produce a single transition network. Due to combinatorial explosions, it is not advisable to actually construct these Cartesian products.

We limit ourselves to objects having only a single thread of control. Consequently, when an object has multiple disjoint transition networks, only one transition can occur at a time.

Entities with apparent internal parallelism are modeled as ensembles, where an ensemble represents a family of constituent objects and/or subensembles (see below). Consequently, we can have our cake and eat it, too: Each object is sequential, but an ensemble appears from the outside to harbor parallelism.

Operations are associated with the arcs in transition networks. This raises the question of whether their description needs more details beyond the context of the transition network. Other methodologists [70, 72, 73] have advocated the use of data flow diagrams. We are not yet convinced that an expansion of action descriptions into data flow diagrams is required for an analysis.

Methodologists have different opinions of what a state can be. Often, a distinction is made between passive and active states. Nothing happens when an object is in a passive state, except the passage of time. An object is in an active state when it executes an interruptible process. Since the advocates of active states do not detail whether entering an active state entails starting a new process or resuming a suspended process, and similarly whether leaving an active state leads to process suspension or a process kill, we stay away from active states. Interruptibility is also too powerful a concept without precise delineation of its semantics. This does not entail rejecting active states completely. Below we provide for an emulation of active states using a passive state and a looping transition.

Having summarized our philosophy regarding generic object behavior, we progress to the details.

States One cannot say much about single-state transition networks. All associated transitions leave that state and return to it. We will call that state Ready (i.e., the object is always ready for one of these transitions). There is no formal description of Ready beyond saying that its characterization is simply *True*.

A transition network with multiple states needs discriminating state descriptors. Such descriptive names as

- *Open, Ajar,* and *Closed* for a *door*

- *Empty, Full,* and *Available* for a *buffer*

- *Off, Suspended, Accelerating,* and *Cruising* for a

- *car cruise control system*

- *Off, Cooling, Heating,* and *Standby* for a *climate control system*

are good first characterizations for these states.

A next step is to describe states in terms of the attributes of the corresponding object. Such an exercise provides a check on the attributes. We can express the states of the *door* in terms of an attribute that describes the position of the door with respect to the frame, say:
– *frameAngle* is 0 degrees for *Closed*,
– *frameAngle* is between 0 and 10 degrees for *Ajar*,
– otherwise, the door is *Open*.

The states of a buffer are defined by:
- $min = index$ if and only if the buffer is *Empty*,
- $max = index$ if and only if the buffer is *Full*,
- otherwise, the buffer is *Available*.

These definitions rely, respectively, on the attributes *frameAngle* and *index*.

Finding such an attribute is sometimes impossible (i.e., one has to retrofit an attribute that accounts for different states). The *car cruise control* example can be given an attribute *State* with the obvious values {*Off, Suspended, Accelerating, Cruising*}. The actual states in a transition network obviously correspond very closely with the value of this attribute.

The states of the climate control system are tricky in another way. At first sight we have the four states *Off, Cooling, Heating* and *Standby*. However, these states can be factored as *Off* and *On*, where the transitions between these two states are under the control of an outside "daemon", while the *On* state decomposes into *Cooling, Heating*, and *Standby*. The latter can be described in terms of the attribute *desiredTemperature* as, for instance:

- Cooling: $desiredTemperature < currentTemperature - 1$

- Heating: $desiredTemperature > currentTemperature + 1$

- Standby: $currentTemperature - 1 \leq desiredTemperature$ and $desiredTemperature \leq currentTemperature + 1$

Note that states must be defined in such a way that they exclude each other. This captures the intuition that an object can be only in one state at a time. This principle gives us a check on the definition of states. The reader is invited to *prove* that the definitions of *Cooling, Heating*, and *Standby* indeed satisfy mutual exclusion.

Question: How do we obtain mutual exclusion with the *Off* state?

Transitions   A transition represents an object leaving a state, performing (optionally) an action or multiple actions, optionally creating events targeted for other objects and entering a successor state, which can be the same state as the originating state. A key feature of a transaction is its *atomicity* (i.e., an object is uninterruptible while engaged in its transaction). This assumption simplifies the computational model substantially for objects in the analysis phase.

Multiple outgoing transitions can be associated with a single state. Guards associated with these transitions determine which transition, if any, can "fire". Hence we have the following components of a transition:

1. Initial state

2. Guard

3. Action(s)

4. Event(s)

5. Successor state

6. Transition name

In pictorial form, we have Figure 2.16.

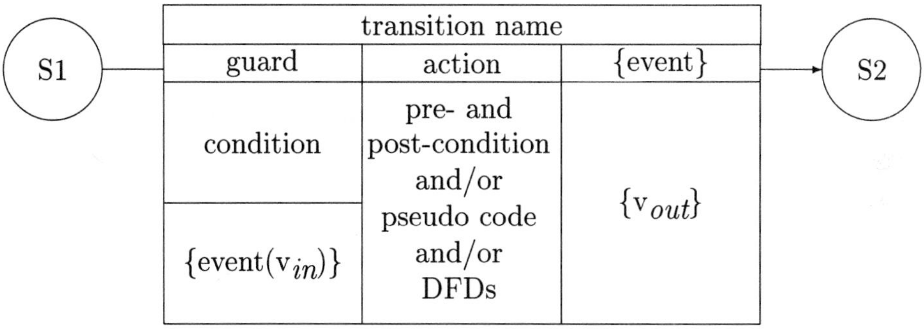

	transition name		
guard	action	{event}	
condition	pre- and post-condition and/or		{v_{out}}
{event(v_{in})}	pseudo code and/or DFDs		

S1 → [table] → S2

Figure 2.16: Graphical representation of a transition. DFD is an acronym for "data-flow diagram". Usually, DFDs can be avoided. An action component can be a service request involving another object.

Guards A guard on a transition consists of a condition to be satisfied and/or an event that has to occur (or that has occurred when events can be queued). The guard must be satisfied for the transition to fire. When multiple transitions emanate from a state, these guards must satisfy a mutual exclusion constraint to guarantee that at most one guard can be true at the time.

A guard consists of up to two parts: a Boolean expression that refers to internal attributes and or to attributes of other objects, and/or an external event. The second part, external events, are discussed in Section 2.3.4. References to attributes of other objects, although allowed, may require special care. Due to its autonomy, another object may change its attributes between the time that its attribute is consulted and the time that an action is performed by the investigating object. Either this is semantically acceptable or the external object must cooperate (according to some locking protocol) in not changing its contributing attribute until being released. Service providing transitions, including event-driven transitions, are special cases that are discussed below.

Examples of guards:

- In an ATM machine, we may encounter a transition *PINok*. Its guard checks whether information in the magnetic strip corresponds with the value obtained by applying the function *foo* onto the user-provided *PIN*. This can be expressed in the guard, for example, as $magneticCode = foo(PIN)$.

- An account may have a transition *ReportToIRS* when a balance on the account gets above \$1M. The guard would have the condition $balance \geq \$1M$.

- An example that illustrates mutual exclusion of guards associated with transitions emanating from the same state is shown in Figure 2.17.

Actions   An action is an operation that causes a local change of state or that invokes a service request in an external object. Actions are performed after a guard has "turned on" the transition and before events, if any, are produced. Not being able to produce events in the action part restricts expressive power somewhat. But this setup allows for easier recovery from an exception raised during Action execution than when events can be produced throughout action execution.

Actions must be terminating operations. An Action part can consist of a "noop" operation. Since a transition cannot be interrupted, its action part cannot be interrupted. However, we do allow for a transition to time-out.

An action can affect the values of the local attributes. Service interactions with external objects are possible as well. The latter are discussed in Section 2.3.4.

Actions are already partly described in a precondition-postcondition fashion by virtue of the starting state and guard description for the precondition and with the

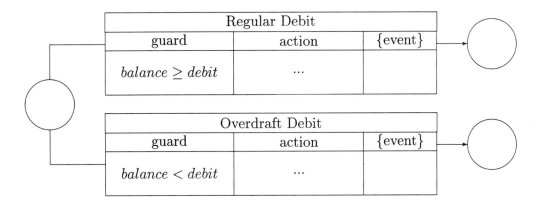

Figure 2.17: Example of two guards that are mutually exclusive. Hence there is a guarantee that at most one (and at least one) can be satisfied.

goal state for the postcondition. If this characterization is insufficient, further elaboration is required. An analyst is free to be as formal or informal as the situation demands.

A formal characterization of the Regular Debit transition yields an Action description like

```
balance' = balance - transaction
```

The expression in the action box is an equation and is *not* to be interpreted as an assignment statement. We could have written equivalently:

```
balance - transaction = balance'
```

There are other ways to expand on the semantics actions. Plain English may do the job. Data-flow diagrams may be useful for those that have been "brain damaged" by the structured paradigm.

Sometimes the name of a transition is sufficient. Consider a transition *Sort* with the action specification:

```
sort(sequence) = sequence'
```

Apparently, some kind of sorting is to be performed. It is usually *unlikely* that the understanding of this situation is improved with the elaboration:

- There is an isomorphism between **sequence** and **sequence'** (to guarantee that no elements of **sequence** are lost or added).

- There is a binary transitive predicate R, the sorting criterion, and adjacent elements in **sequence'** satisfy R (to express the sorted property).

On the other hand, when provably correct software is to be produced, we must push formalization of the analysis output to its limits. This will facilitate proving a design correct against the analysis specifications, which will in turn be the basis for showing an implementation to satisfy the design.

At the same time, formalizing the analysis output carries the risk that something is specified that does not correspond with the intention of the customer, because he or she may not have the ability to recognize a deviation between an intention and cryptic precise formulations. It is the responsibility of the analyst to provide faithful intermediate descriptions.

Events   An event is a one-way communication between the issuing object and the audience of the event. Events are discussed further in Section 2.3.4.

Timing notations   There are different aspects of timing that one may want to express. A performance constraint expresses that a transition, a sequence of transitions, or a set of transition sequences (that start in a common state and end up in a common state) has to be traversed within a certain time period.

For a single transition we can use the notation in Figure 2.18. Alternatively, we can annotate the arcs and add a constraint as in Figure 2.19. If we have one or more paths between states *S1* and *S2* and all paths starting in *S1* will reach *S2*, we can express for all these paths a single time constraint as in Figure 2.20.

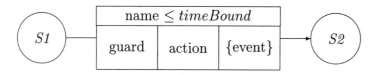

Figure 2.18: Transition that must complete within *timeBound* time.

We have expressed with these annotations that a certain *minimum* speed is to be obtained. The converse situation where we want to express that certain state may

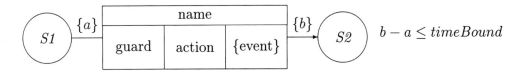

Figure 2.19: Alternative notation for a single transition that must complete within *timeBound* time.

Figure 2.20: All paths between *S1* and *S2* must complete within *timeBound* time.

not be reached too *early* can be expressed as in Figure 2.21. In a similar way, we can express a minimum time *and* a maximum time (i.e., a time window).

Figure 2.21: All paths between *S1* and *S2* must complete not *faster* than *timeBound*.

A different kind of time constraint refers to how long an object can stay in a particular state of one of its transition network(s). We call these alertness conditions. To express such a constraint, we add to a state "bubble" with name *S1* a time constraint, as in Figure 2.22. For example, an ATM machine may have the state *wait-for-first-digit* with 30 seconds as an upper bound for the waiting time.

This illustrates our term *alertness condition*: The ATM must be alert to recognize that an external object (a human being probably) is not responding in time. This allows us to formulate a remedial action when an alertness condition is violated.

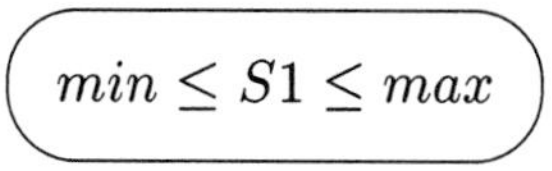

$$min \leq S1 \leq max$$

Figure 2.22: The object should stay at least *min* time in *S1* and at most *max* time.

Notations for dealing with exceptions to these timing constraints are elaborated below.

Notice that two objects interacting under time constraints have two independent ways to deal with violations. Assume that object $C(lient)$ expects an event within a certain time limit from an object $S(erver)$. C waits in an alert mode and will take action when no event shows up. Similarly, S can take a remedial action when it cannot honor the service to C fast enough. Hence speed constraints and alertness constraints are in a sense dual.

Exception transitions   An analyst may strengthen a transition network by adding exception transitions. There are multiple sources of exceptions. A rough categorization is as follows:

- A guard part obtains input arguments that do not satisfy preconditions.

- The evaluation of an action part goes astray, either internally or a communication with an external object goes wrong.

- An object resides in a state for too long.

Hence we have "regular" exceptions, transition time-outs, and alertness actions. A transition time-out is to a remedial action performed by the system when an object is not "happy" with the performance of other service peer objects. An alertness condition is raised when the context of the system or a producer object is not acting in time.

The distinction between a time-out and an alertness exception is relative. When a system and its context are seen as a single system, an alertness exception becomes a regular time-out. Similarly, an alertness exception in a subsystem with respect to another subsystem is a time-out exception from a bird's-eye system perspective.

For an exception occurring during a transition we have the notations in Figure 2.23. This form can be used for a regular exception and/or for a service time-out.

We must also deal with the situation that an object may violate a timing constraint regarding residing in a state. Figure 2.24 gives the unsurprising notation. Since more than one transition can emanate from state $S1$, the exception transition occurs when none of the "normal" transitions are activated.

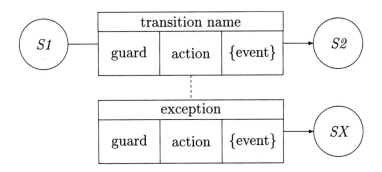

Figure 2.23: Exception handler for when the transition "transition name" gets into trouble.

Active-state emulation We recall that an active state represents an object engaged in an interruptible process. We can emulate this state of affairs by a looping transition that performs "small" increments of a certain process. Interruptibility is obtained by visiting the "active state" each time and allowing for an alternative transition that breaks the looping (see Figure 2.25).[5]

2.3.4   Object connections

In this section, we discuss static and dynamic interconnections between objects. We have advocated developing objects and their classes so that the results transcend a particular application in order to make them more robust and more reusable by decoupling incidental combinations that are appropriate only for a particular system. The constructs in this section are geared much more towards the idiosyncrasies of a particular system. Nevertheless, we urge always staying alert for opportunities for ways to generalize artifacts beyond the peculiarities of a particular setting.

---

[5]It is very well possible that the active-state notation of Rumbaugh et al. [70] and Embley et al. [25] is essentially "syntactic sugar" for this looping construct.

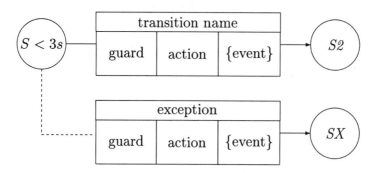

Figure 2.24: Exception handler for when an object violates a timing constraint associated with a state. The constraint here is that the object should stay less than 3 seconds in state S.

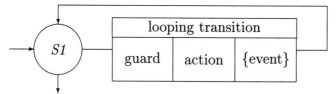

Here a transition that can break the looping transition
when the guard turns false

Figure 2.25: Transition network setup that emulates an active state through an interruptible activity.

Static object connections

OO analysis borrows relationship thinking from the relational database world. A relationship represent more-or-less static connections between objects and/or elements of data domains. "More-or-less static" here is admittedly vague. We simply discourage using relationships for representing rapidly changing object and data interconnections.

The *arity* of a relationship is fixed. The *signature*, the description of its ranges (classes and/or data domains) from which the constituents of relationship instances are recruited, is fixed as well.

Relationships are used for representing "factual" data. Hence we exclude relationships that correspond with tuples that one can calculate. For example, it does not make much sense to have a ternary relationship of integers $< a, b, c >$ defined by $a + b = c$. However, calculability of a relationship may depend on the context.

For example, *Grandparenthood* can be calculated in the presence of a *Parenthood* relationship, but in its absence could represent factual data. A caching strategy may override our dictum that a relationship should not be used to represent computable tuples.

The common diamond notation is used to represent relationships graphically as in Figure 2.26. Arcs in such a relationship diagram can be annotated to express multiple occurrences of participants of a relationship. If an employee must work for at least one and at most one department, and a department has minimally 15 and maximally 20 employees, we obtain the extended diagram in Figure 2.27.[6]

Figure 2.26: Example of a binary *WorksFor* relationship between *Employee* and *Department*. *WF* abbreviates *WorksFor*.

Figure 2.27: An employee works for precisely one department and a department has minimally 15 and maximally 25 members. As before, *WF* stands for *WorksFor*.

The graphical notation may lead to ambiguities with respect to the roles of the participating members, as in the reflexive Parent relationship (see Figure 2.28). Which box represent the parent and which the child? To clarify we add role names as in Figure 2.29.

Relationships support navigation from one object to another. For example, via an *employ* relationship we can move from an *employee* object to a corresponding *employer* object, or the other way around.

Binary relationships are a special case and can support a use other than navigation. An object that communicates with another need two things: the identity of the

---

[6]Notations of some other methods exchange the positions of *[1:1]* and *[15:25]*. Their convention reads more easily but does not scale to ternary relationships.

Figure 2.28: Example of an ambiguity regarding the role of the members of the binary *Parent* relationship.

Figure 2.29: The members of the relationship *Parent* have been clarified by the addition of the role names *parent* and *child*.

partner object and either the name of the service provided by the partner or the name of the event that can be picked up by the consumer. Identity knowledge is expressed by acquaintance relationships. Alternatively, this knowledge can be absorbed in a class by an attribute that has as its value domain the class from which the communication partner is recruited. The attribute representation format is seen by some as a design decision (see Embley et al. [25]).

Dynamic object connections

Objects can interact in different manners. Two extremes are:

- Asynchronous, one-way, send-and-forget triggering

- Synchronous, bidirectional, send-and-wait-for-reply

Intermediate forms are, among others:

- One-way with data send along (in addition to the trigger)

- One-way but blocking for an acknowledgment of reception

- Versions complemented with time-outs when waiting is involved

A one-way interaction can be seen as connecting objects in a producer-consumer fashion; bidirectional interaction represents a client-server relationship. The interactions between objects can be seen at the local level as the perspective of engaged objects and at the global level as the perspective of classes whose instances can communicate. The former, local perspective deals more with generic interaction capabilities: the latter, global perspective deals with interactions that realize the communications to satisfy the goals of the target system.

Local One-way interactions are expressed through named events. Bidirectional interactions are expressed through named service requests. A transition can produce one or more events after it has completed the operations in its action box. An event consists of a target audience, event name, and optional data that should become available to the recipients of the event.

The guard section of a transition is split into:

- A part that gives a condition that needs to be satisfied as explained above on page 47

- A part that lists an event (or a disjunction of events) that occurs or has occurred.

Both parts of a guard need to be satisfied for a transition to fire. A part (or both parts) may be *true*. Note that we do *not* allow a guard to refer to a conjunction of events or to refer to the *absence* of an event.

The action part of a transition may contain one or more blocking synchronized interactions with other objects. Such a service interaction can be realized at the service side by a single transition in the server or by a sequence of transitions. In both cases one may envision control to be preserved by *continuation passing semantics* (i.e., the client sends over, among others, its identity; a final transition in the server uses this identify to channel back a result, if any, and the control to revive the client).

Atomicity of a transition entails that an analysis object cannot be engaged in direct or indirect recursive service invocations. In case this restriction is seen as a limitation, the reader may want to remember that we are in the business of problem elucidation and we do not attempt to describe proto solutions.

Interaction timing mismatch Since objects "live their own life", we have to address the issue of what is to be done when an object is not in the proper state to deal with an incoming event or with an incoming service request. We have three distinct protocols:

- The event or service request is lost or ignored. In the case of a service request, control is returned immediately to the client. Obviously, the client needs to be prepared for not obtaining any service.

- The event or service request is queued in a queue associated, say, with the consumer or server. Variants of this case have to do with whether the queue is bounded or not and with what queue protocol is used by the consumer or server. Producers waiting for an acknowledgment and clients waiting for a reply can express their impatience using time-outs.

- The incoming event or service request raises an exception and triggers subsequent error handling.

Global   The global view of object interaction captures the roles that objects play to realize system behavior. We capture this perspective by class interaction diagrams. The nodes in such diagrams stand for classes. The labeled arcs stand either for one-way interactions corresponding with event producers and event consumers or for bidirectional client-server interactions. The interpretation of an arc between class A and class B is read: Any instance of class A has the ability to interact with an instance of class B, while the label indicates an operation in B. The diagram does not capture which instance of B is the interaction partner for an instance of A. For these details one has to look inside the class definition of A.

The classes referred to in a class interaction diagram are clearly specific for a target system. Hence class A in such a diagram may have been obtained by subclassing from, say, class AA, where class A has a commitment about the communication partners of its instances, while class AA leaves the identity of its partners open.

Target-system-specific classes have multiple ways to capture interaction partner information, such as acquaintance relationships, attributes, and forwarding/brokering intermediaries. In analysis, we usually do not go into the details of these mechanics. During design we may elaborate on what is the best strategy while trading off flexibility, maintainability, and genericness.

Dynamic notation   The diamond notation is used for depicting static connections between objects. The main purpose of the static connections is to facilitate traversal between objects. Objects that need to know each other to interact when there is not a static connection between them have to be equipped with an acquaintance relationship.[7] The notation for these relationships is given in Figure 2.30.

---

[7]Which Booch calls a "use" relationship [13].

Figure 2.30: An asymmetric link between classes A and B which says that each instance of class A knows an instance of class B. Examples are: A_1, gaspedal; B_1 carburetor; and A_2, elevator floor button; B_1, elevator controller.

This notation does *not* capture the mode of the interaction (i.e., whether the communication is one-way or two-way, whether or not a time-out is involved or not, etc.). These refinements are usually postponed to the design phase.

2.4 Beyond the Core Concepts

The sections above deal with objects from a static perspective as well as from a dynamic perspective. In addition, we discussed relationships as connections between objects and/or data values. Target-system-specific object interactions were described as well. In this section we amplify these core concepts by discussing (multiple) inheritance. We also introduce prerequisite notions and notations that are employed before the core concepts are put to work. We end up with some comments about an OOA model, the output of the analysis.

2.4.1 Inheritance

While relationships discussed earlier connect objects, the inheritance relationship connects classes. Inheritance is a binary, asymmetric connection between pairs of classes. A representation of the inheritance relationship as arcs in a graph yields an acyclic graph. Hence, as a special case, we do not let a class inherit from itself. The class from which the inheritance is done is called a *superclass*; the class that inherits is called a *subclass*.

Before defining of inheritance, we strengthen the intuition. A concept close to that of an inheritance graph is a classification hierarchy. Such a hierarchy has two key benefits:

1. Economy of representation of existing concepts. A descendant node shares all descriptions associated with nodes "higher up".

2. The introduction of a new concept is facilitated. For a new node one needs to locate the lowest node in the hierarchy that captures all properties shared with

the new descendant. Subsequently, one has to attach with the new node only the part that has not yet been captured by this parent node. We ignore here the tricky questions of how to find such a parent node, whether there is always a unique parent, and so on.

Both of these key benefits are important for class inheritance. A formal definition of inheritance is:
The class Q inherits from the class P if and only if:

- Every attribute A of P is an attribute of Q

- Every constraint C of P is a constraint of Q

- Every state S of P is a state of Q

- Every transition T of P is a transition of Q, while it is allowed in Q to weaken a guard in a transition and/or the strengthen an effect

- When P appears in a relationship, Q can appear in the same role as well

- Q formulates an additional restriction.

We have already seen a form of an additional restriction: strengthened post conditions of an operation in a transition. Other ways to strengthen a class are:

- Adding an attribute

- Narrowing a multiplicity description of an attribute

- Adding a constraint

- Adding a transition

- Adding a state in combination with adding transitions

- Using a subclass as a value domain of an attribute

- Narrowing an attribute value into a fixed value in the case of attributes that have nonobject values or into a fixed object in the case of object-valued attributes

The next-to-last example in the list shows that subclassness has a recursive component. The last example - narrowing into a single value or object - may be seen as a special case of the preceding case: narrowing a value domain into a subclass.

As formulated here, inheritance is rooted in the static dimension: sharing of declarative properties such as attributes and constraints. In our treatment, inheritance of behavior, which is the emphasis in OO programming languages, is a secondary effect that "rolls out" from the reduction of behavior to transition networks, which themselves are defined in terms of changes of attribute values.

To be frank, we have given an idealized picture of property and behavior inheritance. First, it is not always easy to define the states in a transition network purely in terms of attribute value combinations. Second, describing actions rigorously through pre- and postconditions again in terms of states and/or attribute value combinations is often a tourdeforce. Finally, we cannot insist that an analyst formulate the static dimension exhaustively before addressing the dynamic dimension.

Multiple inheritance

We have presented inheritance essentially as adding (compatible) properties to the characterization of a superclass. A powerful way to add properties to a superclass is to add all descriptions of another class: hence having two superclasses. It is easier to give examples of multiple inheritance when the superclasses do not yet have an associated transition network. For example, an *amphibiousVehicle* class inherits the static attributes from *landVehicle* and from *waterVehicle*. It cannot inherit their behavior descriptions because this would mean that an amphibious vehicle can move on land and on water at the same time. Another outstanding example is the class *SwissArmyKnife*. It inherits from *Knife*, *CanOpener*, *Scissors*, *Screwdriver*, etc. But again, it inherits only their static features because such a contraption can be used in the mode of only one of its superclasses at the time.

Somewhat bizarre devices that inherit not only attributes but behavior as well:

- Flashlight with weather report radio

- Gas stove with oven and clock (three superclasses)

- Toilet-paper holder with built-in radio

- Sound system with clock

- Instrument panel that displays multiple aspects of a device.

This is a good opportunity to point out that a class should denote a concept that can have at least one instance. This prohibits the introduction of questionable classes via multiple inheritance such as *SquareCircles*, *FemaleSteers*, and *MachoCoward*.

To go into more detail: All attributes from the superclasses are carried over in the subclass and similarly for constraints. Transition networks are carried over as well. The effective transition network in the subclass is the Cartesian product of the component transition networks. However, to avoid a combinatorial explosion we keep them notationally apart using a convention introduced by Harel [33, 34]. In Figure 2.31 we show a stove that inherits behavior from *clock*, *oven*, and from four different *burner*s.

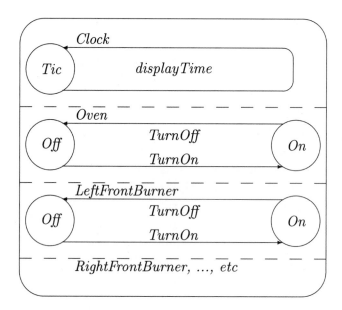

Figure 2.31: Stove that has a clock, an oven, and four burners (of which we show only the left front). This representation technique prevents construction of a single transition network where we would take all combination of states of the component transition networks.

In case a subclass inherits the same attribute via more than one superclass, we have a problem. We can distinguish two different cases (we discuss here only the situation where *two* attributes with the same attribute name show up in a subclass):

- Although the attribute names are the same, they differ in some other aspect: for instance, a cardinality is different and/or a value domain is different. We can often *prohibit* this situation right away. An example illustrates the situation. When *Raven* has the attribute *color* with the hardwired value *black*, and *Albino* has the *color* attribute with the value *white*, we cannot introduce *AlbinoRaven*, inheriting from *Raven* and from *Albino*, because its *color* attribute has contradictory values. However, here is another situation. Let the class *Animal* have the attribute *sexOrgan* with value domain *SexOrgan*. Assume that we have the subclasses *MaleSexOrgan* and *FemaleSexOrgan*. Hence we can introduce the subclasses *MaleAnimal* and *FemaleAnimal* that have as attribute value domains *MaleSexOrgan* and *FemaleSexOrgan*, respectively. Now consider the subclass *HermaphroditeAnimal* that inherits from *MaleAnimal* and *FemaleAnimal*. It obtains two different *SexOrgan* attributes. This time we must accept the situation and come up with an ad hoc solution for naming these attributes.

- The attributes are identical (i.e., they agree not only in their names but also in all their other features). An attractive solution is to merge the two attributes in one. In case the two attributes emerge from a single, common base (here the super-superclass), this strategy seems quite defensible. As an example, consider the base *Person* with attribute *ss#*. Let *Employee* and *Client* be subclasses of *Person*. The class *EmployeeClient* as a subclass of *Employee* and of *Client* inherits twice the attribute *ss#*. Merging them is obviously okay here.

Unfortunately, there are exceptions to the merging strategy. A counterexample has *Channel* as a base class with the attribute *channelId*. Two subclasses are *AudioChannel* and *ImageChannel* respectively. The class *Video* inherits from both *AudioChannel* and *ImageChannel*. This time we certainly do *not* want to merge the two attributes *channelId*. See Figure 2.32 for the pictorial representations of these two cases of multiple inheritance. Notice that two parallel lines have been added to the top diagram as a reminder that attributes get merged. Again we have to come up with an ad hoc solution to distinguish between the two channels.

Substitutability

We have set up inheritance such that substitutability is guaranteed (i.e., whatever can be done to an instance of a superclass can also be done to an instance of a subclass). Substitutability exerts a powerful influence on inheritance. We give two examples where the substitutability requirement effectively prohibits inheritance.

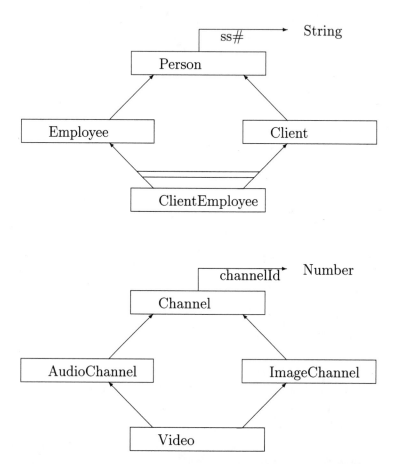

Figure 2.32: Different cases of merges of identical attributes. Attribute pairs coming from *Person* into *ClientEmployee* must be merged. In contrast, the attribute pairs coming from *Channel* into *Video* must *not* be merged. The two horizontal lines in the top diagram are a reminder that attributes will be merged.

Suppose we have a *Furniture* class that has an attribute *color* with as value domain the enumerated values {*red, blue, green, purple, white*}. It is reasonable to have a subclass *WhiteFurniture* that has its color attribute obviously frozen into *white*. This is indeed okay given this context. However, if we assume that *Furniture* has a transition network with a transition *Paint* that allows changing the value of the *color* attribute, it is now *not* possible to introduce *WhiteFurniture* as a subclass of *Furniture* because a resulting state of *Paint* cannot guarantee that the resulting state is *white*.

Another example is the class *Account* with the attribute *balance*, which is any number greater than or equal to zero. A *SavingsAccount* is a subclass with the additional constraint that its *balance* should not be less than $100. Again this subclass gets in trouble when *Account* has a transition that changes the *balance* while checking only that the *balance* does not become negative. Such a check is not sufficient for *SavingsAccount*. We would have to strengthen the precondition of the debit operation (whereas a subclass can strengthen a *post*condition of an operation, it can only *weaken* a *pre*condition).

The moral of these examples is that we have to be careful with subclassing when we want to adhere to the substitutability principle. Should we abandon substitutability? We don't believe so. Substitutability corresponds with theory inheritance. Everything we know about a superclass will carry over into a subclass. Every test program that runs successfully on instances of the superclass will yield the same result on instances of a subclass. Hence substitutability is a cornerstone for black-box reuse of classes.

Polymorphism

Substitutability yields polymorphism[8] as an unexpected bonus. A subclass should minimally adhere to what the superclass prescribes, but it is allowed to do more. More precisely, it may strengthen a postcondition of a transition in a superclass. In other words, different peer subclasses can define an operation differently as long as they conform minimally to what a subclass prescribes. Hence, when a manipulator object has a reference to an entity that conforms to a superclass, the manipulator can invoke an operation that is promised by the superclass, while the operation executed is determined by the object that is actually being referred to. The standard example has, as manipulator object, a manager of window graphical entities such as lines, circles, texts, and so on, where these graphical entities are subclasses of a superclass that supports a display operation. Regarding the display operation, the superclass

---

[8]An operation is polymorphic when its semantics depend on the context of invocation.

only commits to displaying an instance. The subclasses line, circle, text, and so on, live up to this promise and do the actual work. Thus the system's display capability is distributed over the classes that have firsthand knowledge of their particular features.

Polymorphism is usually taken for granted. Phones use pulse or tone dialing; the user sees only one operation. The + operation adds things up: integers, floats, combinations of these, vectors, matrices, strings, etc. The operating expenses of a department are calculated from the employees, temporary workers, contractors, consultants, and so on. All of these can support an operation "expense", which is different for each category. Each object that must contribute to the monthly total must know about the details of the category to which it belongs, while there is a class "contributor" that supports a generic "expense" operation that shields a client object from all the different versions. Adding and deleting types (i.e., subclasses) can be done without disturbing clients of contributor.

The home heating example can exploit polymorphism. There is a clock that broadcasts ticks to interested parties. Candidates are of multiple types: room, furnace, and furnace monitor. Consequently, to obtain a generic clock that can broadcast to any kind of entity, it pays to introduce a superclass that supports a transition *tic* and let room, furnace, and furnace monitor be subclasses.

Polymorphism can be used to simplify designs. The book *Design Patterns* [28] devotes close to 400 pages to 23 design patterns, and most if not all of them rely on polymorphism. As argued here, an analysis that cares about the types of attribute values and the types of the entities on which operations apply must take polymorphism into account.

2.4.2   Use case

As discussed, inheritance amplifies the core concepts described earlier. In this and the subsequent two sections on subsystems and vocabulary, we switch to notions that play a role *before* notations grounded in the core concepts are invoked.

Use cases are the brainchild of Ivar Jacobson [40, 41]. He describes them as follows:

> The actors represent what interacts with the system. They represent everything that needs to exchange information with the system. ... An instance of an actor does a number of different operations to the system. When a user uses the system, she or he will perform a behaviorally related sequence of transactions in a dialogue with the system. We call such a special sequence a *use case*.

A user or actor need not be a human being, as, for example when the target system is in fact an embedded component of a larger system. Hence we can characterize a use case as a prototypical interaction sequence between a system and its context, whatever the context is.

A prototypical interaction sequence should give a maximal explanation of the intention of the interaction at minimal cost of descriptive complexity. A variant of an interaction sequence, if feasible, would describe, instead, all possible kind of variants, either in the form of a tree structure, or when branches would have common tails, a lattice structure could be provided. To give complete coverage, these variants should have branches representing corner cases as well as exceptions.

In either case, a sequence can be described formally as

state, (user action, state, system action, state)*

where the * indicates one or more repetitions of this sequence. As an example, consider an interactive Unix session:

> Prompt displayed
> User types *ls*
> System determines the current directory and displays result
> Prompt displayed

As another example, consider starting your car:

> Car idle
> Insert key
> Key inserted
> Key turned
> Circuits powered
> Contact light on
> Circuits powered and contact light on
> Key turned further
> Start engine activated
> Engine starts
> Engine runs/contact light off
> Key returned to previous contact position
> Engine still runs
> Etc.

As we have demonstrated in these examples, the "formalism" used for use cases is just restricted, templated natural language.

A requirements document is the primary source for the construction of use cases. Filling in gaps in the requirements document is encouraged, but these creative interpretations must be checked for accuracy with the customer and may lead to extensions and/or modifications of the requirements document.

2.4.3   Scenario

A use case is just an initial description of a user-system interaction sequence. Often we know more about the intended system and we can expand the use case into a *scenario*. A scenario is an extension of a use case by filling in "obvious" actions that decompose "large" operations, where the intermediate actions involve intermediate objects and/or subsystems. This description of scenarios is deliberately vague. Opportunities to elaborate a use case depend on the charter of the analysis. An example may be helpful. Consider a use case that describes how to change floors using an elevator. Suppose that the use case describes a user standing on a floor and "selecting a desired direction". This may be okay for this use case, but an analyst may question how this selection is actually done. By speaking? Hence the scenario may elaborate the use case by committing to "selecting a desired direction by pushing the up button". Thus a scenario can fill in the "obvious" details omitted in a use case.

A requirements document may already have outlined a (logical) architecture, which is an element of a high-level design. The task of the analysis is then to elucidate *what* the components of this architecture have to do. If so, a scenario can exploit this insight and split up a system response into action/activities of the subsystem components.

Scenario diagram

A scenario can be extended further into a *scenario diagram*.[9] Such a diagram consists of (prototypical) instances of classes, and numbered interaction links between them. The numbering corresponds with the sequential ordering of the interactions in the originating scenario. An interaction link label describes either a one-way event, a bidirectional service request, or a reply to a service request. *Interaction diagrams* are an alternative, slightly condensed representation to scenario diagrams (see Jacobson [41]). For an example of a scenario diagram and an interaction diagram, see Figure 2.33. Additional examples of scenario diagrams are given in Section 5.13, page 203.

---

[9]Scenario diagrams resemble object diagrams as described in Booch [13].

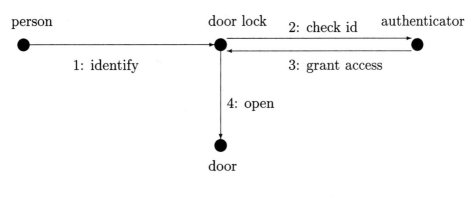

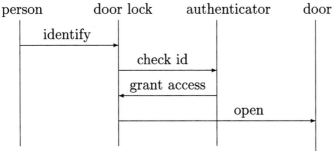

Figure 2.33: A scenario diagram appears at the top and the equivalent interaction diagram at the bottom. The scenario depicted regards a person identifying himself or herself at a door lock, the door lock contacting a authorization agent, the authorization agent granting access, and the door lock opening the door.

The collection of use cases and scenarios help develop the vocabulary regarding classes, relationships, and instances of the intended system. Use cases, scenarios, and scenario diagrams play a role in the validation of a constructed OO analysis model. As a third role, test programs for the implementation of the target system can be derived from them.

2.4.4 Subsystem

Even small systems are composed of subsystems. At the very least we can distinguish a subsystem that is responsible for interacting with the "outside world" and a subsystem that does the thing that embodies the core functionality of the overall system. A system that needs a "lot of memory" will have a repository subsystem. A system may be a "player" in a large setting of peer "players". If so, there is quite likely to be a peer-interaction subsystem. The core functionality of the system may be quite complex, and hence it helps to describe the overall functionality in terms of the functionality of subsystems.

For example:

- A washing machine has subsystems for loading and unloading, a program selection component, an execution controller, a waterhandler, a wash-motion device, and others.

- A car has traction , steering, braking, electrical, starting, and additional subsystems.

- A retail shop has an inventory, an acquisition component, a sales department, and a restocking unit, among others.

Some of these decompositions of a system into subsystems may seem to be forays into design country. The defense is that we must, at all costs, split up a system to fight complexity.

A description of a subsystem should be small. To give arbitrary definitions of smallness: it should fit on a page and/or on a computer screen, a transparency, or the back of an envelope. The overall description should be small as well.

We already have powerful decomposition facilities: objects, classes, and relationships. A slight modification of objects into *ensembles* will give us a formal apparatus to represent subsystems. Ensembles are elaborated on in Section 2.4.5. What remains is to have a disciplined way to describe subsystems informally early in the process.

As for use cases, we will use a templated form of natural language, which the analyst can extend as necessary. The template can have minimally:

- The name of the subsystem

- A brief description of its functionality

- Its parent subsystem, if any

- Children subsystems, if any

- Peer subsystems that are interacted with

Filling in these templates and the ones we describe below can be done gradually. Newer insights obtained downstream will help to fill in and/or modify templates started earlier.

The construction of one or more subsystem diagrams is obviously recommended. A rooted tree with "the system" as root and subsystem instances as nodes is the notation of choice for such a diagram.

2.4.5   Vocabulary

Analysis can be seen as a rewriting activity: rewriting an unstructured, unformalized requirements document into precise notations that culminate in a (descriptive) model of the intended system. It pays to smooth the formalization by making this transition gradually. Use case and scenario descriptions and subsystem identifications are the first step in this transition. A next step is the development of a vocabulary, which prepares for the formal description of object classes, ensemble classes, relationships, and their instances. The language for describing the vocabulary is again templated natural language. We describe each one in turn.

Class

The class template is:

1. Name of the class

2. Parent class(es), if any

3. Generic functionality

4. Producers or clients of the class, if any

5. Consumers or servers of the class, if any

6. Other interaction classes, if any

7. Salient features shared by all instances

8. Salient states shared by all instances

9. Salient transitions shared by all instances

10. Miscellaneous features, like constraints

11. Participation in relationships

Ensemble class

An ensemble class is a special kind of class. It has typically only a single instance in an application. Such an instance will represent a subsystem. Its description in the vocabulary corresponds with the one for classes. See below for a detailed treatment of ensembles.

Relationship

The template for a relationship is:

1. Name of the relationship

2. Arity of the relationship

3. Parent relationship, if any

4. Participant classes

5. Participant value domains, if any

6. Multiplicity of the occurrences of participant instances, if any

7. Miscellaneous properties, such as symmetry and transitivity

Class instance

The template for a class instance:

1. Class to which the instance belongs

2. Identifying characteristics for the instance in terms of the attributes of the class to which the object belongs

3. An auxiliary name that abbreviates the instance for diagramming purposes

Ensemble

An ensemble is an object that represents a subsystem. Since a system probably has only dissimilar subsystems, we describe ensembles here at the instance level, although it is certainly advisable to introduce ensemble classes for modeling. An ensemble is defined as follows in de Champeaux et al. [24]:

- An ensemble is an object with other objects and/or subensembles as its functional components.

- A constituent is a part of at least one and at most one ensemble (thus the constituent-ensemble relationship is *not* transitive).

- An ensemble mediates all interaction between constituents and entities outside the ensemble.

- Constituents may interact with each other.

- An ensemble is responsible for the construction and deletion of constituents.

On the basis of this definition, ensembles form a tree structure provided that we see the overall system as an ensemble as well. Hence, in addition to the global class interaction diagram, we have a global subsystem tree. The subset of the class interaction diagram restricted to ensembles (which we can produce because there is a one-to-one correspondence between ensembles and ensemble classes) gives us the big picture of the dynamics of the intended system; or conversely, provides a starting point for a detailed description of the dynamics at the class level and subsequently at the object level.

A template for an ensemble includes:

1. Its name

2. Its parent ensemble, if any

3. Constituent objects and/or subensembles

4. Other attribute values, if any

5. Occurrences in relationship instances, if any

6. Miscellaneous other information to characterize the ensemble

Relationship instance

The template for a relationship instance has the set of participant objects, ensembles, and/or values that play a role in a relationship instance.

2.4.6   Miscellaneous constructs

In this section we describe advanced constructs that can be ignored in a first pass.

Parametrized classes

The classes
StackOfRecords
StackOfTokens
StackOfAccounts
StackOfProcesses
StackOfXYZ
have "stackness" in common. Given our persistent desire to eliminate redundancies, we allow to be a variable the type of "things" to be stacked. Thus, after defining a *parametrized* class *StackOf(T)* within its body references to the stack elements of type *T*, we get "for free" the classes *StackOf(Record)*, *StackOf(Token)*, *StackOf(Account)*, *StackOf(Process)*, and *StackOf(XYZ)*, provided, of course, that we have the classes *Record, Token, Account, Process,* and *XYZ*. Connoisseurs of C++ recognize here the equivalent template construct.

Multiple class parameters are possible as well. Container classes are obvious customers of this parametrization construct. Consider *Set(T)*, *List(T)*, *Array(T)*, *Bag(T)*, and so on.

Parametric relationship instances

We have already introduced parametric instances. A parametric instance represents a prototypical object in a model that has been generalized with respect to irrelevant details. For instance, we may want to simulate the operations of a typical branch of a bank, instead of a particular branch that is located at a particular address, that has a particular branch manager, etc.

Our model may have several parametric instances. A parametric instance of *Branch* will have a branch manager who is a parametric instance of *Employee*, or the like. Hence we may need parametric instances of relationships, for instance to express that the branch manager *Heads* the branch; see Figure 2.34 for the chosen representation of a parametric instance of a relationship.

These parametric class instances correspond with *existential* logical expressions: "There is an instance x of the class X such that ..." without being specific about an actual corresponding entity in a target domain. Parametric instances of relationships connect these postulated entities.

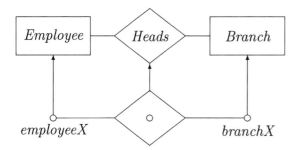

Figure 2.34: *EmployeeX* and *branchX* are parametric instances of the classes *Employee* and *Branch* respectively, while these parametric instances are related through the relationship *Heads*.

Inside a class we may encounter a parametric instance of a relationship in a somewhat different role. It may express a constraint with respect to attribute values. For example, if we have a class *Family* with the multivalued attributes *parent* and *child* each with attribute domain *Person*, we may express more semantics of the *Family* class with the constraint that a parent is the custodian of a child. A parametric instance of the relationship *Custody* can connect the attribute values of both *parent* and *child*. Note that the parametric instances in this case are wrapped inside a *universal* logical expression: "For each instance of *Family*, if p is a *parent* and c is a *child*, then p is in the *Custody* relationship with c."

2.4.7 Target model

The output of an analysis activity is a model of the intended system. This model will have the following ingredients:

1. Ensemble classes that describe the subsystem components of the system

2. Specialized classes (i.e., classes that have hardwired communication obligations for their instances)

3. Relationships

4. Ensembles that represent subsystems

5. (Parametric) instances (of the specialized classes) that represent unique entities in the system

6. (Parametric) relationship instances.

We should be able to translate all scenarios (and thus the originating use cases) into scenario diagrams (or interaction diagrams). This corresponds with "executing" all use cases and their corresponding scenarios against this model. We have put "execute" in quotes because the transitions in our transition networks are not executable: their operations are at best described with pre- and postconditions, which are in general not executable.

Our model description is spartan. It helps to adjoin summary views. For instance, we can add class interaction diagrams and subsystem hierarchies. The former is a graph with classes as nodes and with arcs between them that express that service or one-way interactions between instances are defined. A subsystem hierarchy simply expresses how a subsystem is composed of other subsystems. Other summary views or close-up views can be introduced as the need arises.

2.5   Summary

In this chapter we have presented OO analysis at a fast pace to set the scene for process and metrics in the next chapters. Most attention is given to concepts rather than to how they are represented graphically. Analysis is essentially a translation and elaboration activity with, as input, a requirements document and, as output, the total analysis model. The notions presented allow for a gradual transition in formality in this transformation process. Analysis aims at clarifying the requirements; finding ambiguities; incompleteness due to the omission of "obvious" assumptions; resolving contradictions caused, for example, by different expectations by different stakeholders of the target system; and so on.

Use cases are examples of user-system interaction sequences that are expanded into scenarios. Subsystems can be identified to break down the complexity of the overall system. A vocabulary captures in templated English all significant entities. Classes can be characterized intrinsically by capturing their inherent static features, and the generic behavior of instances and classes can be described regarding the roles that the instances will play in the system. Target-system-specific descriptions are done with class interaction diagrams and with class relationship diagrams. Validation of the analysis model can be done by rewriting scenarios into scenario diagrams or interaction diagrams. Inheritance diagrams help demonstrate how the application domain concepts are classified to avoid redundancies.

2.6 Further Reading

There are many books that cover the material in this section at a leisurely pace. The classics are Shlaer and Mellor [72, 73], Booch [12, 13], and Rumbaugh et al. [70]. Newer books are: Jacobson et al. [41], de Champeaux et al. [24], Berard [7], Firesmith [26], Lorenz [50], Henderson-Sellers and Edwards [36], Selic et al. [71], and Reenskaug et al. [66]. The commonalities of all these texts outweigh their differences, in our opinion. There is a great diversity of graphical notations, but the underlying concepts are similar if not identical. All authors have adopted use cases from Jacobson et al., and many authors have "borrowed" other features from other methods as well.

Some differences are:

- Shlaer and Mellor use state machines where the actions are associated with the state "bubbles", while everyone else associates actions with the transitions.

- de Champeaux et al. present a textual, separate design language, while everyone else uses either the analysis notations or a programming language for design (in this book we do *not* use this textual design language).

- Henderson-Sellers and Edwards start presenting OO metrics.

- Selic et al. give a method specialized for real-time applications that is supported by a development environment that covers the total development cycle.

Here is an example of a minor difference between these books. Our notion of subsystem defines the "logical" architecture of the target system (i.e., the decomposition of the system in components that make sense from the perspective of the client). Booch [12, 13] has a radically different meaning for subsystem. A subsystem in his world stands for a collection of modules that realizes the system. Hence if a module corresponds with a file, a subsystem corresponds with a directory. His subsystems constitute the physical architecture, which represents the dependencies between subsystems that are captured (although he doesn't say this explicitly) by a makefile. In contrast, we reserve the notion of physical architecture for the components and their connections in a distributed system.

This is clearly more a difference of terminology than of substance. The good news is that efforts are under way to merge all notations. This will facilitate the development of tools that support a standard notation with a standard method.

2.7   Exercises

1. Does OO analysis apply only to software systems?

2. Suppose that a software system implemented originally in Fortran has to be reimplemented in C++. Is an OO analysis required? Is it recommended? Is it to be avoided? Can it be done?

3. States have to exclude each other. How do we ascertain that the states *Off, Cooling, Heating* and *Standby* of the Home Heating System, described on page 46, are mutually exclusive? Give proofs.

4. Can we model a faucet that supplies cold and hot water via multiple inheritance?

5. Model the concept *EggHead* through multiple inheritance with as much detail as possible. Consider also the dynamic dimension.

6. Construct a solution to the *sexOrgan* multiple inheritance problem described on page 63.

Chapter 3

Analysis Process

We recollect that a software development method has three major components:

1. Key notions supported by (graphical) notations, the topic of Chapter 2

2. A process that outlines steps to produce (intermediate) artifacts, the topic of this chapter

3. Criteria for measuring progress and to estimate the remaining effort required, the topic of Chapter 4.

We approach the OO analysis process from different directions. Minimal requirements are formulated which any OO analysis process should satisfy. We give a working definition of the analysis process. Subsequently, we formulate some additional auxiliary features. This sets the stage for a detailed description of an OO analysis process tailored to our notations. Yet another perspective is given by describing alternative processes and by providing some comparisons.

3.1 Requirements for an OO Analysis Process

In this section we formulate some requirements that any OO analysis process should satisfy.

3.1.1 Compatibility with the global process

The analysis process is a fragment of the overall process. Variants of the global, macro, process are: waterfall, spiral, fountain, whirlpool. These variants differ with

respect to the scheduling of analysis, design and implementation. The waterfall, at
one extreme, prescribes a linear temporal order for these activities. At the other
extreme, the whirlpool model allows "random" traversals of the analysis, design, and
implementation activity space. A choice in this spectrum depends on the stability
and completeness of the requirements. Stable and complete requirements allow a
waterfall macro process. Fluid and incomplete requirements prescribe a whirlpool
process.

Maintaining consistency is obviously more challenging and will profit more from
CASE tool support in a whirlpool setting than in a waterfall process. Whatever
choice is made for the macro process at the top level, the OO analysis process should
be compatible. This entails that an analysis activity can be primed with mandates
such as the following:

- Don't finish before a complete model is constructed

- Produce a partial analysis, concentrating on subsystem XYZ (this presumes an
  initial insight about the global architecture that in fact precedes the analysis
  process).

An analysis process is interruptible for diverse reasons:

1. An infeasibility is encountered.

2. An external requirement changes.

3. A contradiction is encountered.

4. An incompleteness in the requirements is encountered.

5. A new insight forces a major reorganization.

These discontinuities happen, of course, nearly continuously. Still, we will dis-
regard them at our abstraction level. Suffice it to say that one should strive to set
up a concrete process where these interrupts can get through only in "clean states":
Bombarding developers continuously with "stop the show" information does not contribute to a high concentration level.

3.1.2   Control inside the OOA process

The "algorithm" of OOA has conflicting demands. Sometimes, we want the process
to be "smart" (i.e., give us guidance). Sometimes we know better and we don't want

the process to get in the way. Sometimes it pays to be systematic in one way - just working layer by layer to get through a massive amount of detail; at other times we want to probe deeply the ramifications of a particular choice. Consequently, the process must have nondeterminism to accommodate these differences. Still we want the process to be specific with respect to preconditions that must be satisfied for a step to be applicable. This usually translates into artifacts being available for further elaboration.

3.1.3   Analysis team size

An analysis process should apply equally well whether a single analyst is doing all the work or when a team is sharing the work. Of course, we agree that the latter case involves coordination, communication, and special attention to global consistency. However, we see these issues, although important, as orthogonal to the underlying analysis process.

3.1.4   Precision of the analysis process

The formulation of the analysis process can have as one extreme the precision of an algorithm, and as another extreme it can just consist of a list of issues to pay attention to. The first extreme is attractive but unrealistic, since we transform unformalized input into formalized output. Major breakthroughs in artificial intelligence are required to obtain a machine transformation of the requirements into an analysis model. Such a program would probably not be algorithmic either since it would depend on human interventions to help resolve ambiguities. The latter extreme is too loose to be effectively helpful. Within this spectrum we need a description to be precise enough to serve, potentially, as the requirements for a process support tool. Such a tool would assist and cooperate with a CASE acquisition component used for constructing OOA artifacts.

At the same time, we do not insist that an analysis process must be realized into a CASE tool component. We only want to have enough precision that analysts need not have to puzzle over which step is applicable, what its prerequisites are, and what is to be produced.

3.1.5   Users of the methods

Without doubts, practice breeds excellence. Still, we want as a requirement for an analysis process that one, as the saying goes, "doesn't have to be a rocket scientist" to use it. As an associated requirement, the analysis process should be teachable (i.e., it does not require to be under the tutelage of a guru). We feel that this is not a strong delimiting requirement. Modeling is quite likely already more demanding than is executing a default analysis recipe.

3.1.6   Reuse

Analysis as an activity boils down to the construction of many different kinds of artifacts. When the construction of an artifact is more costly than buying, "borrowing", or "stealing" it from an external source, it is obviously attractive when the analysis process accommodates a reuse strategy. At the same time, we are not too optimistic about the applicability of reuse at this juncture. Only when software development practices are routinely guided by well-articulated processes do we feel that reuse can take off. Management of artifact libraries, accounting for the reimbursement of producers and charging consumers of artifacts, minimizing search time in artifacts libraries, assessing the applicability of an artifact without having to look "inside", and similar activities are all daunting obstacles.

An auxiliary optional feature of an analysis process consists of contributing to a repository of domain concepts. [We used the domain restriction deliberately: Reuse across application domains at this point is much too difficult; that is, impossible beyond low-level CS concepts, which are out of reach during analysis.]

3.1.7   Information flows

Although we will present the OO analysis process in an OO fashion, i.e. we will anchor the description in the artifacts to be produced, it doesn't hurt to exploit an information flow principle from the data-flow realm. The (OO) analysis process is composed of subprocesses. These subprocesses are connected with information flows. We have the following constraints:

1. A subprocess accounts for all its inputs; i.e., all inputs are produced by other subprocesses or are extracted explicitly from a requirements document or another external source; hence we cannot have a "magic" input.

2. A subprocess produces no spurious output; i.e., all outputs are consumed by other processes or contribute to the OO analysis model; hence we cannot have a "black hole".

3.1.8 Granularity of subprocesses

The (elaboration) subprocesses in the analysis process are not too small, yielding only microscopic progress, and are not too big, begging the question of how output artifacts are produced from their inputs. An analyst should not have to ponder how to jump the Grand Canyon.

As a first approximation we want to have subprocesses that have similar complexity. In case a subprocess is significantly larger, it is to be elaborated on in subactivities.

3.1.9 Specificity of the process to OO

An analysis process should be specific for OO. In fact, we have a stronger requirement: The process must exploit the key concepts of the method; i.e., it should cover the production and consumption of all the different kinds of artifacts advocated by a method. Specificity does not entail uniqueness. It is conceivable to have two methods that agree completely as to key concept and notations while still advocating different procedures on how to develop intermediate artifacts. The order in which attention is given to the static and dynamic dimensions of classes is an example of where processes can differ.

3.1.10 Independence of target system size

The genericity of the analysis process precludes considerations of system size. At the same time we acknowledge, of course, that system size affects the "details" of the process. While a small system need not depend on tool support, enforcement of a process for a large system "by hand" may become unwieldy. For example, keeping track manually of artifacts that have to be elaborated may be virtually impossible for a large system. As a corollary, we demand that the process scale perfectly with the size of the target system. This means simply that we abstract the process up to the "30,000 ft level" and we delegate to the "instantiation" of the process the management issues induced by large system size.

3.1.11 OOA for OOA?

Yes, the heading of this section is worrisome. We simply mean that if we imagine the OOA process to be executed by a system with the analysts and the artifacts as "objects", we can wonder whether this system can be described using OOA. We think that the OOA notation should be able to do this, provided that the OOA process has been explained in enough detail. Hence we see this as a sanity check of the OOA method. An (OO) methodologist should first be able to swallow his or her own medicine - preferably in public.

3.2 Summary of Requirements for the OO Analysis Process

An OO analysis process (OOAP) prescribes how to construct, from an unformalized system requirements document as input, a formalized OO model of the target system as output. An OOAP should be generic in being:

1. Independent of intended system size

2. Independent of the size of the analysis team

3. Compatible with any global SW development process

4. Independent of application domains

5. Compatible with any corporate constraints

6. Capable of accommodating reuse

7. Capable of accommodating product and process metrics

8. Articulated with sufficient precision so that a tool can be built that "enforces" the process in the sense that at least assistance can be provided to novices and an active agenda can be maintained for pending tasks

3.3 Our Analysis Process

As we will see in the next section, processes are often described as numbered steps, where each step outlines a particular activity. The magnitude of a step can vary from the monumental, as in "find and document the objects" to the more minute, as in "define attributes ... position the attributes".

Most methodologists downplay the ordering of the steps. A prescription to iterate over the steps, globally and locally, is a popular cop-out. These process descriptions resemble the set of rules in an expert system: If a rule applies, execute the body and go to the next rule. If you reach the end of the list, cycle back provided that at least one rule "fired" in the last iteration.

Our OOA process description is slightly different in that our formulation is "OO-ish." We give more attention to the description of the intermediate artifacts that are produced in the process, and we outline what the dependencies are between the different types of artifacts. A dependency corresponds with a step to be executed by an analyst which can be circumscribed as an elaboration activity. The intermediate artifacts can be seen as stepping-stones in the analysis space.

Analysis has a unique feature in the overall development process: It provides the bridge between an unformalized requirement input and the formalized output that is transformed into executable code during design and implementation. Our analysis process provides a gradual transition from the nonformal input into the formalized output model. We proceed by giving a bird's-eye view of the process, and in the subsequent section we provide details.

3.4 Main Stepping Stones

For each stepping stone/ artifact type we describe its local features and what the input artifacts are that feed into its construction.

3.4.1 Requirements document

This document is usually at the other side of the analysis boundary. If such a document is not available, it has to be produced first. It has to cover a great diversity of topics. Its format depends on what role the software plays, which ranges from independent product, substantial component of a product, to embedded component of a larger system. The latter in this sequence may have much more rigid contextual constraints than the former in the sequence.

Another aspect of the requirements document regards whether there is an early commitment to an architecture that may have come from an earlier domain analysis or is simply dictated for political reasons that are beyond discussion. If so, the charter of an analysis is to clarify the components of the architecture and their connections.

We assume here that one of these documents has been produced and that a best effort has been made to describe the software in sufficient detail. In case certain aspects cannot be described due to lack of insight, it is essential that these "white areas on the map" be explicitly acknowledged so that further investigations can invade these areas through iterative prototyping.

Minimal sections in the requirements document should address functionality; prototypical interaction sequences between the software system and the context must be detailed whatever the context is; performance is to be described; resource consumption is to be formulated; user interfaces are to be sketched; and so on. A pictorial "data-flow" representation of the input stream to the requirements document is shown in Figure 3.1.

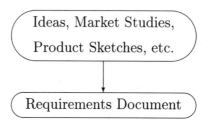

Figure 3.1: Source for the requirements document. Obviously, we do not investigate here how the ideas, market studies, etc. are produced.

3.4.2   Use case

For an earlier description of use cases, we refer to Section 2.4.2. Use cases embody a simple idea: describe the behavior of a system through examples. In addition to "common" examples, it helps to give "corner" cases. The primary sources for the construction of use cases are the requirements document and common sense.

The notion of a use case can be generalized from a prototypical interaction sequence to a tree-like format that covers all possible branches on the basis of choices by the user/context and/or by the intended system logic.

The language for the description of sequential use cases can be as formal as required. As indicated before, the general format is

use-case-sequential = state, (user action, state, system action, state)*

with the * indicating one or more repetitions of the bracketed four-tuple.

In case we want to go beyond sequential prototypical interaction descriptions, we need more powerful notations. For instance, we may want to represent all choices that can be made by the user or context in a particular state. The system may have different response types as well. Alternatives are separated by "|". The alternative choices for the system response are either nondeterministic or, alternatively, one may expand *systemAction* into a guard-action pair, where, obviously, the guards should be provably exclusive. As in the sequential case, we may want to describe repeating patterns. See below for the label-constructs:

use-case-tree = state, ([label:]) userSystem [| userSystem]*)*

userSystem = (userAction, state, (sysResponse [| sysResponse]*) [label])

sysResponse = systemAction, state

The *label:* expression permits us to name a position in the expansion. A recursive "invocation" is possible inside a *userSystem* four-tuple. We used square brackets in *[label]* to suggest a guarded recursion expression.

Hence we can model a user-system interaction where a user provides a list of input data in two ways: through the *-iteration construct or via the recursion-label construct.

The vanilla sequential notation or an even less formal version will do in most circumstances and is in fact preferred since it is most easily understood by customers. Detailed protocols for embedded systems may exploit the more sophisticated notation, which may have to be customized further to fit a situation.

A pictorial representation of the input stream to the use case artifacts is shown in Figure 3.2.

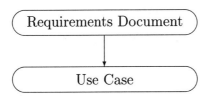

Figure 3.2: Source for the use cases.

3.4.3 Scenario

Specification of a use case may yield insights in gaps. Gaps emerge when it is not obvious how the results of an action lead to a subsequent action or state. Such gaps are in general unavoidable: We are doing analysis and we should avoid worrying about realization aspects. However, when an architecture has been prescribed or when a domain of interest prescribes participating constituents, we can fill in these gaps by showing how these architectural components or participating constituents cooperate to achieve a use case. These elaborations constitute scenarios. Hence scenarios are produced with use cases, architectures, and/or descriptions of major "players" in the target system as input. A pictorial representation of the input stream to the scenario artifacts is shown in Figure 3.3.

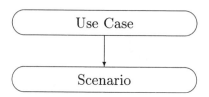

Figure 3.3: Source for the scenarios.

3.4.4   Subsystem

Understanding the requirements of a system is not likely to happen if we cannot decompose the system into subcomponents early in the process. In fact, it is very plausible that a requirements document already contains a block diagram with semimysterious arcs that provides an initial split up into peer subsystems. If not, an analyst has to rely upon commonsense knowledge to construct a high-level decomposition. Early feedback from the customer for such decompositions is essential.

As we have outlined in the previous chapter, each subsystem is to be described in more detail with:

1. The name of the subsystem

2. A short narrative of the functionality

3. An indication of the parent system, if any

4. A list of children subsystems, if any

5. A list of peer subsystems, if any

Each arc in the block diagram mentioned above that depicts a subsystem interaction can be detailed as well:

- Is it a control interaction or an information interaction?

- Is it a producer-consumer interaction or a client-server interaction?

- What kind of information is exchanged, if any?

- Which use case(s) will rely on this interaction?

A subsystem should become so well understood that one can decompose it further. However, such a decomposition is to be done only when it helps to further an understanding of the system as a whole. Otherwise, it is likely that a premature design effort is under way.

A pictorial representation of the input stream to the subsystem artifacts is shown in Figure 3.4.

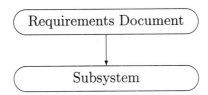

Figure 3.4: Source for the subsystems.

3.4.5 Vocabulary

Use cases, scenarios, and descriptions of subsystems feed into the vocabulary. The vocabulary is simply a set of templated narratives of all classes, relationships, ensemble classes, and their instances that are expected to play a role in the formal model to be constructed. The identification of the entries for the vocabulary is a matter of good taste, experience, gut-level intuition, unjustified braveness, etc.

Nouns and noun phrases employed in the use cases and scenarios are to be investigated to see whether objects lurk underneath them. Verbs should be looked at to see whether they can be interpreted as relationships or as object operations that are to be mapped later onto transitions in transition networks.

Subsystems are the natural candidates to be represented as ensembles and are a start for the enumeration of unique (parametric) (enduring) objects. Identification of other unique instances of classes and/or relationships is highly dependent on the intended system. Certain systems consist only or mainly of unique objects. The ubiquitous car-cruise-control system is an example. Our home heating system also has many unique objects: the boiler, the furnace, the heat-switch, etc. However, as mentioned before, we should always model all instances through their classes, even when we know that we will never create more than one instance of a class.

It is very likely that the information expressed in the vocabulary through templated natural language overlaps with the information expressed by class diagrams, scenario diagrams, inheritance diagrams, transition network diagrams, etc. Maintaining consistency is the price to pay for this redundancy. The transformation from a templated textual representation to a structured graphical representation likely yield new insights, expose gaps, and generate another round of questions. The gains from these new insights outweigh the costs of maintaining consistency, in our experience.

A pictorial representation of the input stream to the vocabulary artifacts is shown in Figure 3.5.

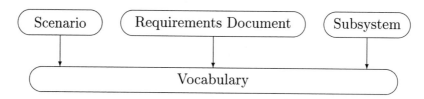

Figure 3.5: Source for the vocabulary.

3.4.6   Top-level diagrams

Subsystem diagrams depict major classes as nodes and relationships as links between them. As mentioned before, the relationships represent an opportunity for navigation and/or communication linkages. At the highest level, such a diagram depicts a logical architecture. Most, if not all, classes will have in the intended system a single instance that corresponds with a subsystem, and such an instance will represent an enduring or persistent entity. Subsystems can be expanded similarly. Class-relationship diagrams extend subsystem diagrams by the incorporation of all classes and all relationships.

Initial inheritance diagrams are useful to fight redundancies early in the process. The representation of inheritance is a "joker" from a process perspective. At all times during the construction of classes, we have to consider whether a class under construction is a (close) special case of an existing class, or whether there is another class already around that shares sufficient structure to justify an abstraction.

All these diagrams take their input from the vocabulary. A pictorial representation of the input streams to these artifacts is shown in Figure 3.6.

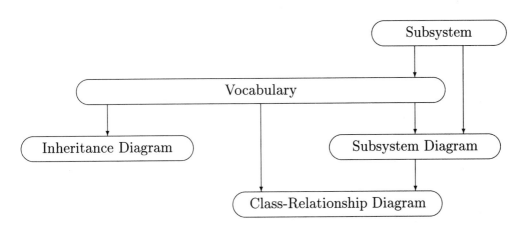

Figure 3.6: Sources for the inheritance diagram, the subsystem diagram, and the class-relationship diagram.

3.4.7 Class

Class descriptions take their input from "everywhere": the vocabulary, the inheritance diagram, and the class-relationship diagrams.

We have two main variants of the micro process regarding the generation of classes:

1. We concentrate on the production of classes that are customized for the task at hand and we leave to a postprocessing phase their generalizations that fit in a domain repository; or alternatively,

2. We concentrate on the intrinsics of classes and subsequently specialize them for the task at hand.

The former is advisable when there is a low chance for reuse and/or when the project is already behind schedule. The latter is to be done when we can afford to invest in the future right from the start. We assume the former in the sequel.

Classes are elaborated via two different roads: (1) static descriptions: attribute structures and constraints, and (2) dynamic descriptions: transition networks. These are strongly mutually dependent. Attributes must be justified by the existence of actions on transitions that access them, states are defined in terms of attribute values, and transition guards and actions are grounded in attributes. Consequently, the mutual dependencies between these diagrams precludes, formulating a rigid order in which these diagrams are to be developed.

Personal preference can play a role. Some people need to develop a foundation of static structures before they can address the dynamic dimension. Other people must address the behavioral aspects before they feel confident to formulate the static structures that carry the dynamics.

As a result of the inherent duality between static and dynamic modeling, we are uncommitted about what is to be done first. We demand only that the respective descriptions be mutually consistent:

- Each component of the static structures is used at least once in the dynamic descriptions.

- Dynamic descriptions are grounded in the static structures and respect invariants.

In summary, we have the situation represented pictorially in Figure 3.7.

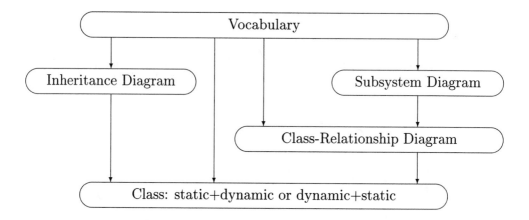

Figure 3.7: Inputs for detailed class descriptions. As discussed in the text, we are uncommitted as to whether class statics or class dynamics are to be addressed first.

One can also wonder whether at an even more detailed level, states are to be defined before transitions in transition networks, or the other way around. Given that we are uncommitted about the static-dynamic ordering, we avoid formulating an ordering here as well.

3.4.8 Relationship

Relationships are usually covered sufficiently well by class-relationship diagrams. In case cardinality annotations have been ignored initially, they can be added at this stage. It is wise to check whether binary relationships can be reduced faithfully to attributes in the participating classes or whether we have a genuine "loose" connection between the classes. It is wise as well to have a closer look at attributes in classes and to check whether they are in fact relationships that have prematurely been made into attributes.

Consequently, we can depict the position of this step as in Figure 3.8.

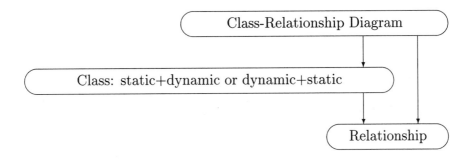

Figure 3.8: Inputs for elaborations of relationships in class-relationship diagrams.

3.4.9 Instance

The identification of unique instances, if any, will probably have been done earlier, and if so, the vocabulary covers them informally. Their description can be firmed up once classes and relationships are nailed down. This will lead to a characterization via attribute values, relationship instances, and/or descriptions of communication partners.

Hence the dependencies of instances with respect to the other artifacts can be depicted as in Figure 3.9.

3.4.10 Scenario diagram

We recall that a scenario diagram is a graphical depiction of a scenario. The nodes of the diagram are (prototypical) instances of classes. An interaction link between two

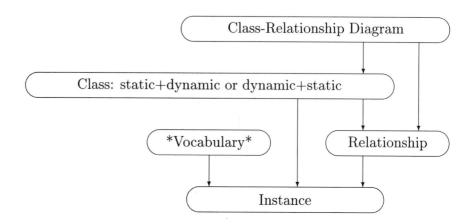

Figure 3.9: Inputs for instances. We put the "Vocabulary" inside asterisks to remind ourselves that the Vocabulary box is a copy from higher up in the diagram.

objects is labeled with a sequence number and with a description of a communication event between the objects (see Section 2.4.3).

Obviously, these diagrams take their input from scenarios and from instances. The communication labels on the interaction links prescribe that class transition networks are input as well.

This gives us the dependencies shown in pictorial form in Figure 3.10.

3.4.11   Interaction diagram

Interaction diagrams are an alternative notion for scenario diagrams and serve the same purpose: testing the adequacy of the formal model against the scenarios. Hence we omit them explicitly from our process.

3.4.12   OOA model

The final output of an OO analysis is just the sum of all the artifacts produced thus far. Hence we get for the grand total the pictorial form shown in Figure 3.11.

We should point out that slight transformations may have affected classes when they contribute to the OOA output. A class may have been developed earlier with reuse in mind. If so, generality may be instantiated away to service the needs of a

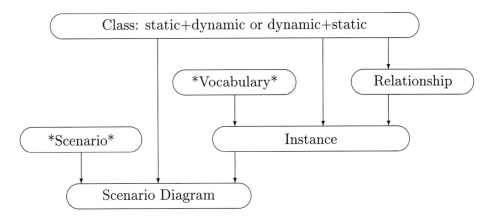

Figure 3.10: Inputs for scenario diagrams. Again, *Scenario* refers to a box higher up.

particular application. Communication dependencies, which are well known in the application, are an obvious candidate for specialization.

Our diagram represents the analysis process in an object-object fashion in the sense that it emphasizes the artifacts to be produced. Control of the development process is insufficiently expressed, to say the least. In fact, our diagram still allows for a great amount of nondeterminism. The diagram can be traversed in a top-down fashion, in a depth-first left-to-right fashion, or in other conceivable fashions. Vertical slicing on the basis of choosing a subsystem is an obvious candidate.

More generally, this OOA micro process can take as input a mandate from a chosen macro process that prescribes development of a prototype for a particular aspect of the target system. Hence the micro process description constrains development activities primarily by demanding that the required input for the construction of an artifact is available, while it is flexible enough to accommodate additional demands from a macro process or from any other source.

3.5 Process of Other Methods

Most other OOA methods give only a little attention, if any, to their micro process. An exception is the OMT method (Rumbaugh et al. [70]). We describe and compare

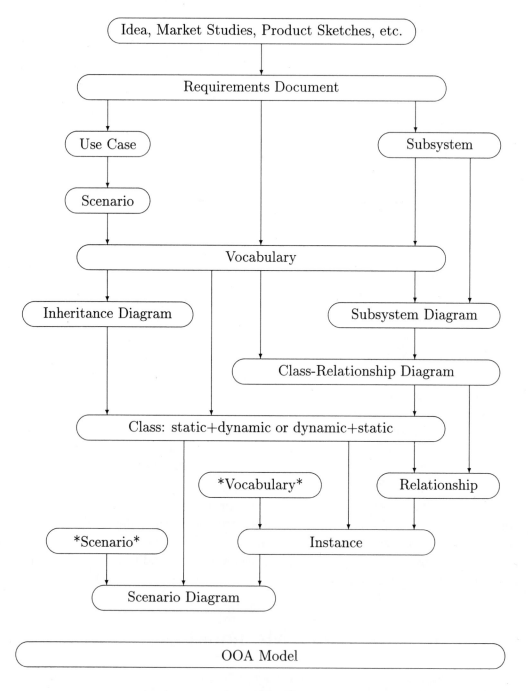

Figure 3.11: All the artifacts that contribute to the OOA model. The items within asterisks are copies of an item from higher up.

their process. The OMT OOA process is as follows:[1]

1. Write or obtain an initial description of the problem (Problem Statement).

2. Build an Object Model:

   - Identify object classes.
   - Begin a data dictionary containing descriptions of classes, attributes and associations.
   - Add associations between classes.
   - Add attributes for objects and links.
   - Organize and simplify object classes using inheritance.
   - Test access paths using scenarios and iterate the above steps as necessary.
   - Group classes into modules, based on close coupling and related function.
     ⇒ **Object Model** = object model diagram + data dictionary.

3. Develop a Dynamic Model:

   - Prepare scenarios of typical interaction sequences.
   - Identify events between objects and prepare an event trace for each scenario.
   - Prepare an event flow diagram for the system.
   - Develop a state diagram for each class that has important dynamic behavior.
   - Check for consistency and completeness of events shared among the state diagrams.
     ⇒ **Dynamic Model** = state diagrams + global event flow diagram.

4. Construct a Functional Model:

   - Identify input and output values.
   - Use data flow diagrams as needed to show functional dependencies.
   - Describe what each function does.
   - Identify constraints.
   - Specify optimization criteria.
     ⇒ **Functional Model** = data flow diagrams + constraints.

---

[1]The reader is warned that some of the terminology used for the OMT process can have a somewhat different interpretation.

5. Verify, iterate, and refine the three models:

- Add key operations that were discovered during preparation of the functional model to the object model. Do not show all operations during analysis as this would clutter the object model; just show the most important operations.

- Verify that the classes, associations, attributes, and operations are consistent and complete at the chosen level of abstraction. Compare the three models with the problem statement and relevant domain knowledge, and test the models using scenarios.

- Develop more detailed scenarios (including error conditions) as variants on the basic scenarios. Use these "what-if" scenarios to further verify the three models.

- Iterate the above steps as needed to complete the analysis.
  $\Rightarrow$ **Analysis Document** = Problem Statement + Object Model + Dynamic Model + Functional Model

It is certainly reassuring that there is sizable overlap in the artifacts developed in our and OMT's micro process (although Rumbaugh et al. do not call their description a micro process). Both start with a requirement document. Both produce a set of (graphical) formal artifacts. Obviously, objects, classes, attributes, inheritance, transition networks (which they call state diagrams), and scenarios are shared as well.

A major difference is their *functional model*. Rumbaugh et al. feel that the combination of transition networks, use case, scenarios, and scenario diagrams is insufficient to describe the dynamic dimension. Consequently they advocate the use of data-flow diagrams to expand operations in transition networks. Our experience does not support their position.[2] [3]

There is substantial overlap as well in the development activities of our and the OMT method: identification of objects and classes, construction of a vocabulary/ data dictionary, identification of attributes, construction of an inheritance diagram, construction of transition networks, and other details.

The only difference of significance, as we see it, concerns the "algorithms" in both micro processes. Our "algorithm" is determined by producer-consumer connections between the artifacts to be developed. Since our process still allows for an abundance

---

[2]Incorporation of data-flow diagrams *does* have an advantage: Analysts trained in structured analysis obtain a backdoor migration path.

[3]The Shlaer-Mellor method [72, 73] also relies on data-flow diagrams to describe behavioral details. This method, however, does not, as far as we know, exploit use cases, scenarios and scenario diagrams.

of nondeterminism (depth first, breadth first, mini-waterfall, mini-spiral, etc.), we can't really claim it to be an algorithm. The OMT process, in contrast, resembles a set of rules from an expert system. If a rule applies, execute the body; otherwise, go farther down the list. At the end of the list, start all over again when at least one rule fired (or go back to the beginning of the list each time when a rule was applied successfully).

CASE tools will ultimately provide nonintrusive support for the development process. They will have "insight" into the ramifications for a chosen macro and micro process. They will maintain agendas for pending tasks and they will "know" about the dependencies of tasks on artifacts. We hope that our micro process will help the development of such process managers.

3.6 Summary

In this chapter we have described a micro process for analysis. This description is OO-ish by virtue of the fact that the description concentrates on the intermediate deliverables. The process dimension enters by the introduction of elaboration dependencies between the different analysis artifacts. We are uncommitted about the details for developing classes. In particular, we leave it to the analyst as to whether to concentrate first on the static dimension or attack first the dynamic dimension. This description is loose in the sense that it allows for nondeterminism. At each point, one can choose to work on an artifact that has not been elaborated in a downstream artifact. Breadth-first, depth-first, and any mixture of the two can be chosen as a strategy. We compared this process with the process description of the OMT method.

3.7 Further Reading

Rumbaugh's OMT method [70] is obvious recommended reading. This method and process are also described in Henderson-Sellers and Edwards, [36]; many other methods are described there as well. This text, which can act as a reference book for all these methods, is a methodologist's delight - a must for researchers in this field. There are process descriptions, but all of them merge macro process and micro process. The best example is the process from Booch [12]:

1. Identify the classes and objects at a given level of abstraction.

2. Identify the semantics of these classes and objects.

3. Identify the relationships among these classes and objects (perhaps using CRC cards).

4. Implement these classes and objects.

CRC (for "Class, Responsibility and Collaboration") cards are small index cards on which one can write a class name, some phrases that describe the responsibility, and some phrases that describe other classes for interaction. These cards can be used in a group setting to identify classes and their main features. Subsequently, one can "play-act" the target system using the cards. Someone has called this "method" the west-coast, laid-back way of doing OO analysis. The technique was pioneered by Beck [6] and adopted and extended by Wirfs-Brock [87], leading to "responsibility driven design".

CRC cards appear to be an informal variant of our vocabulary. However, there is a key difference, as revealed by the term "responsibility". A CRC card describes how the instances of a class play a role in the target system, in combination with instances of other classes. In contrast, we advocate that an entry in the vocabulary has gone through an abstraction process that reveals its intrinsic features that are independent of the target system. As a result, our classes should have a wider applicability range as well. Scenario diagrams subsequently illustrate that their "pure" instances are capable of assuming their intended responsibility and play their intended roles.

Role modeling is a cornerstone aspect of Reenskaug et al. [66]. It appears that a role model is mapped directly on an implementation without the role abstraction that is part of our process. For an application of our process, see Chapter 5.

3.8   Exercises

1. In Section 3.1 we listed requirements for an OO analysis process. Check whether our process meets these requirements.

2. Check whether the process of the OMT method meets these requirements.

3. Figure 3.11 can be reinterpreted, with some squinting, as a class interaction diagram where the ovals represent classes and the lines interactions. Develop attributes for some classes and try to develop transition networks.

Chapter 4

Analysis Metrics

Analysis aims to clarify *what* a system is supposed to do. All the notations described in Chapter 2 help to capture and represent required functionality and performance. An analysis activity can convince a customer that a system to be constructed will satisfy their intentions. However, the customer may also want to know the development costs for a system's design, implementation, and testing before it can be deployed. In fact, this question may have come up already before any analysis is done.

Development cost estimation based on only a (partial) requirements document is obviously a perilous enterprise. It need not be totally hopeless, though. We may be in the fortunate situation that a similar project was completed earlier. If so, we have an estimate of the development time and effort which can include the effort required for a detailed analysis.

In the absence of such luck, we have to rely on other sources. The size and apparent complexity of a requirements document gives us a first inkling as to the required development effort. However, basing an effort estimate metric only on requirement documents as the input source is an unlikely strategy. These documents are as formal as a spynovel. They can belabor the obvious or omit "obvious" "details" that will require major work during design and implementation.

We are not the first to have made these observations. In Section 1.8.3 we described earlier work on function points that addressed this issue. It pays to revisit the approach followed to calculate function points. (Recollect that the function point metric correlates with target system size and thus with development effort - provided that reuse does not play a major role.) First, five components are to be identified for the proposed system: the number of external inputs, external outputs, logical internal files, external interface files, and external queries. Second, these components are classified according to their complexity. Third, 14 general system characteristics are rated for the intended system. We omit further details and look at the general picture. Clearly, a requirements document is, in general, insufficient to produce the data that feed into the function point computation. To produce these data, one has to do a "mini" analysis to ferret out the data required.

The applicability of a function points analysis (FPA) for development effort estimation of OO systems is a priori not infeasible. In fact, Paul C. George argues:

> One can thus estimate the size of an OO project just like a "conventional" one, the packaging and granularity is merely different. Indeed it may be easier on an OO project as the "architectural elements" are more modular with better defined interfaces.[1]

Calibration of a computed function point output against the size of the system in an OO language and against a development effort remains unsurprisingly a nasty issue (which we will have to face as well).

However, function point analysis also has drawbacks. First, it appears that it is geared toward MIS applications instead of being a generic estimation technique. The terminology "logical internal files, external files, and external queries" leads to this conjecture. The publication by Kemerer [44] underwrites this conjecture by the observation that 85% of the systems in that study were MIS applications.

Second, it has a magic component: the matrices with numbers that somehow capture experience from previous projects. One wonders whether these projects will be similar enough to a new project. In the same contribution, Paul George observes:

> ... it appears that 60-80% of the variance in actual versus estimated project effort is not attributable to factors covered by FPA. They involve such things as personnel, technical complexity or unknowns, constraints, etc.

Third, FPA is not compatible with the OO philosophy. It is an ad hoc procedure that does not contribute to OO activities, and more important, the FPA outcome is not refined incrementally by subsequent OO development activities. As noted by Kathy Reinold [67]:

> ... estimation must be almost a by-product of development – not an extra step; and of course, it must be easy to track progress and therefore measure the reliability of our estimates.

---

[1]Contribution to the Newsgroup comp.object on October 28, 1993.

Consequently, we advocate using OO metrics right from the start to estimate development efforts. In addition, we aim at an estimation procedure that is tightly interwoven with the development process. Although initial estimates may rely on historical data, subsequent, "continuously" evolving estimates are to be based on measurements of the ongoing project. In that way, one captures, or at least one hopes to capture, such things as personnel, technical complexity or unknowns, and constraints.

A coarse-grained illustration of this strategy was already outlined on page 10 and illustrated in Figure 1.2. There we argued that the conceptual continuity of the OO paradigm will facilitate the effort estimation of downstream activities based on upstream activities. We go into detail here and concentrate on the OOA micro process depicted in Figure 3.11.

4.1 Analysis Effort Estimation

In contrast with the deliberations above, we take a global, outside perspective and from there we proceed into the details of effort estimation. Our assumptions here are that we perform analysis as part of either a waterfall global process or a single cycle of an iterative global process. We use the following terms:

t_0 = the time when the analysis starts
t_e = the time when the analysis terminates
T = a particular time of interest with $t_0 < T < t_e$ and with the default interpretation "now"
$C(T) = A(T) + B(T)$, the effort cost function, with the functions A and B defined as
$A(T)$ = the actual development costs in the period (t_0, T)
$B(T)$ = the estimated development costs in the period (T, t_e)

Obviously, $A(t_0) = B(t_e) = 0$ and $A(t_e) = C(t_e)$ is the true cost of doing analysis. A $C(T)$ value below $C(t_e)$ is an optimistic underestimate of the ultimate costs, while a $C(T)$ value over $C(t_e)$ is a pessimistic overestimate. In the case when the function $C(T)$ fluctuates above and below $C(t_e)$, we could say that the effort estimation procedure is "manic-depressive". See Figure 4.1 for the description of estimation points.

As suggested in this example, the estimates get progressively closer to the true value $C(t_e)$. There are two reasons:

1. The ratio of $A(T)/C(T)$ will automatically get closer to 1 when T approaches

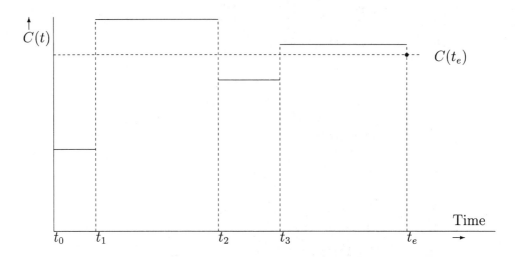

Figure 4.1: Example of a cost estimation function. The development starts at time t_0 and terminates at time t_e. In this example there are four estimates performed at times t_0, t_1, t_2, and t_3, respectively. The estimate at time t_0 is based only on an intuition fueled by experience and a thorough understanding of a requirements document. The estimates in the other time points exploit the artifacts already developed and the effort required for their construction. The estimates at times t_0 and t_2 are underestimates of the ultimate effort $C(t_e)$; the estimates at t_1 and t_3 are overestimates.

t_e.

2. The estimation of the development of remaining artifacts, $B(T)$, gets easier over time because more artifacts have been developed already and their development effort is available - provided, of course, that systematic measurement and record keeping are done.

Certainly, the crucial question remains of how the function $B(T)$ is constructed.

4.1.1   The $B(T)$ function

The estimation function $B(T)$ is constructed in several steps. As a simplification we assume first that at time T we have the following situation for all artifact types (an artifact type in analysis corresponds with an oval in Figure 3.11 on page 96): Either *all* artifacts of a particular type have been constructed or *none* of them have. Hence we can split the artifact types into two sets:

1. P, the completed types

2. Q, the types for which all artifacts are still to be constructed.

As a working example:

1. $P = \{$Use Case, Scenario, Subsystem, Vocabulary, Inheritance Diagram, Subsystem Diagram, Class-Relationship Diagram$\}$

2. $Q = \{$Class, Relationship, Instance, Scenario Diagram$\}$

For a completed type τ in P, we should have minimally available:

1. The number of artifacts in the type

2. The total amount of effort spent to construct all these artifacts, which we denote by $\Omega(\tau)$

In addition, we may have also available:

1. The effort spend on constructing each artifact

2. A measure of each artifact, where such a measure can be a composite of a size metric and a complexity metric

We proceed by dealing first with the situation where we have available only the aggregate information per artifact type. The value of $B(T)$ is constructed in a sequence of iterations:

1. If there is still an artifact type in Q that has not yet been assigned an effort estimate:

2.
   - Select such an artifact type q in Q for which the artifact types on which it depends, $\{r_j\}_j$, have either a known effort or for which an effort estimation has been done already.
   - The function ω represents the effort for a type and is defined on all these r_i's as follows:
   $\omega(r_i) = \Omega(r_i)$ when r_i is an artifact type in P,
   $\omega(r_i) = B_T(r_i)$ when r_i is an artifact type in Q and an effort estimation has already been done in a previous iteration.

- With these definitions we can denote the effort estimate for q in terms of $\{\omega(r_i)\}$ and denoted by $B_T(q)$ as:
  $B_T(q) = f_q(\omega(r_1), \omega(r_2), ...),$
  where f_q is a simple (preferably linear) composite function of its arguments, and where q still represents an artifact type in Q.

3. After all artifact types in Q have been estimated, we obtain:
   $B(T) = \sum_{q \epsilon Q} B_T(q)$

Certainly, we still have to provide more details about the f_q functions. Each such function, say $f_q(e_1, e_2, e_3)$, is defined as:

$$f_q(e_1, e_2, e_3) = fq_0 + fq_1 * e_1 + fq_2 * e_2 + fq_3 * e_3$$

for certain constants $\{fq_k\}_k$.[2]

How do we define these constants? The best answer is: We don't. We calculate them on the basis of previous experience. The second best answer is that we "guesstimate" them first and adjust their values later, while monitoring the changes to assess the validity of the estimation procedure.

An example is warranted at this point. We will elaborate on the example given above where we had:

1. $P = \{$Use Case, Scenario, Subsystem, Vocabulary, Inheritance Diagram, Subsystem Diagram, Class-Relationship Diagram$\}$

2. $Q = \{$Class, Relationship, Instance, Scenario Diagram$\}$

We will calculate the total cost $C(T)$.

Assume that we have for the artifact types in P at time T:
$\Omega(UseCase) = 100$ [3]
$\Omega(Scenario) = 130$
$\Omega(Subsystem) = 45$
$\Omega(Vocabulary) = 375$
$\Omega(InheritanceDiagram) = 80$
$\Omega(SubsystemDiagram) = 35$
$\Omega(ClassRelationshipDiagram) = 20$

---

[2]Obviously, we have chosen simple linear polynomial functions. Any other type of function could be chosen as well, but given the inherent fuzziness of the estimation process, more complex functions are likely to be overkill.

[3]The unit in which we measure effort is, say, person * hours.

The known costs for the analysis effort $A(T)$ at time T is:

$$
\begin{aligned}
A(T) \; = \;\; & \Omega(UseCase) + \Omega(Scenario) + \Omega(Subsystem) + \\
& \Omega(Vocabulary) + \Omega(InheritanceDiagram) + \\
& \Omega(SubsystemDiagram) + \Omega(ClassRelationshipDiagram) \\
= \;\; & 100 + 130 + 45 + 375 + 80 + 35 + 20 = 785
\end{aligned}
$$

We proceed with the calculation of an estimate of the remaining analysis effort $B(T)$. Assume that we have the following estimation function for f_{Class}:

$$
\begin{aligned}
& f_{Class}(e_{InheritanceDiagram}, e_{Vocabulary}, e_{ClassRelationshipDiagram}) \\
& = 10 + 0.5 * e_{InheritanceDiagram} + 3 * e_{Vocabulary} + 0.2 * e_{ClassRelationshipDiagram}
\end{aligned}
$$

All argument values of f_{Class} have known Ω values. Thus we obtain:

$$
\begin{aligned}
& B_T(Class) \\
& = \;\; 10 + 0.5 * \Omega(InheritanceDiagram) + 3 * \Omega(Vocabulary) + \\
& \quad\;\; 0.2 * \Omega(ClassRelationshipDiagram) \\
& = \;\; 10 + 0.5 * 80 + 3 * 375 + 0.2 * 20 = 1185
\end{aligned}
$$

Similarly, assume that we have for $f_{Relationship}$

$$
\begin{aligned}
& f_{Relationship}(e_{ClassRelationshipDiagram}, e_{Class}) \\
& = 10 + 1 * e_{ClassRelationshipDiagram} + 0.02 * e_{Class}
\end{aligned}
$$

In this case we know the actual value of $e_{ClassRelationshipDiagram}$, while we have an estimate for e_{Class}. Hence we obtain[4]

$$
\begin{aligned}
& B_T(Relationship) \\
& = 10 + 1 * \Omega(ClassRelationshipDiagram) + 0.02 * B_T(Class) \\
& = 10 + 1 * 20 + 0.02 * 1185 = 53
\end{aligned}
$$

Again, assume that we have for $f_{Instance}$

$$
\begin{aligned}
& f_{Instance}(e_{Vocabulary}, e_{Class}, e_{Relationship}) \\
& = 10 + 0.05 * e_{Vocabulary} + 0.01 * e_{Class} + 0.01 * e_{Relationship}
\end{aligned}
$$

---

[4]The calculations are rounded to integer values.

We have a mixed case again. We know the value for $e_{Vocabulary}$ and we have estimates for e_{Class} and $e_{Relationship}$. Consequently, we get

$$
\begin{aligned}
&B_T(Instance) \\
&= \quad 10 + 0.05 * \Omega(Vocabulary) + 0.01 * B_T(Class) + 0.01 * B_T(Relationship) \\
&= \quad 10 + 0.05 * 375 + 0.01 * 1185 + 0.01 * 53 = 41
\end{aligned}
$$

Finally, assume that we have for $f_{ScenarioDiagram}$

$$
\begin{aligned}
&f_{ScenarioDiagram}(e_{Scenario}, e_{Class}, e_{Instance}) \\
&\quad = 10 + 0.9 * e_{Scenario} + 0.001 * e_{Class} + 2 * e_{Instance}
\end{aligned}
$$

The value of $e_{Scenario}$ is known, while the two other arguments have been estimated. This gives us

$$
\begin{aligned}
&B_T(ScenarioDiagram) \\
&\quad = 10 + 0.9 * \Omega(Scenario) + 0.001 * B_T(Class) + 2 * B_T(Instance) \\
&\quad = 10 + 0.9 * 130 + 0.1 * 1185 + 2 * 41 = 328
\end{aligned}
$$

Since we have defined the estimate of the remaining analysis effort, $B(T)$, as

$$
B(T) = \sum_{q \in Q} B_T(q)
$$

we obtain in our example:

$$
\begin{aligned}
&B(T) \\
&\quad = B_T(Class) + B_T(Relationship) + B_T(Instance) + B_T(ScenarioDiagram) \\
&\quad = 1185 + 53 + 41 + 328 = 1607
\end{aligned}
$$

The total cost of analysis $C(T)$, which is at time T a mixture of known actual development effort $A(T)$ and an estimate of remaining development effort $B(T)$, is now easily obtained:

$$
C(T) = A(T) + B(T) = 785 + 1607 = 2392
$$

Thus at time T we estimate that the total costs for the analysis is 2392 person-hours.

4.1.2 Incomplete artifact types

In the previous section, we dealt with the "clean" situation where the development reached the utopian situation where all artifacts of a particular type had already been developed or none of them had been developed. This situation is unlikely to occur in practice. Hence we have not only the set P, for which all artifacts are completed, and the set Q for which no artifact is completed, but also a set R of artifact types which are partially completed.

We can reduce the calculation of $C(T)$ in this case to the preceding case, provided that we estimate for each artifact type r in R the completion fraction, notated as, say, ρ_r, with, obviously, $0 < \rho_r < 1$. The contribution of the type r to $C(T)$ becomes

$$\Omega'(r) + (1 - \rho_r) * B_T(r)$$

where $\Omega'(r)$ is the effort already expended on the artifacts of type r and $(1-\rho_r)*B_T(r)$ represents the estimate for the remaining effort to construct the artifacts of type r.

The next refinement to the development cost estimation business requires that we have more detailed knowledge about artifacts already developed.

4.1.3 Disaggregation of an artifact type

To facilitate the discussion, we return to the situation where we have at time T only the two sets P and Q of artifact types for which, respectively, all and none of the artifacts have been developed. Instead of estimating the aggregate development costs of all artifacts in a type q in Q, we take a closer look at the cost of constructing each individual artifact of type q. This works only if we know which artifacts will show up of type q (allowing, of course, for midstream deviations). Examples where we have a good feel for the artifacts to be constructed: scenarios when we know the use cases, a scenario diagram when we know the scenarios, classes and relationships from knowing class-relationship diagrams. All these examples have in common that we already know (roughly) the number of artifacts for a type q still to be developed.

Disaggregation of an input type p in the set P for the development cost estimation of a target type q would not make sense when all artifacts in the input type p are similar - similar in terms of their size and complexity according to as yet unspecified metrics. In such a situation we could use an arbitrary artifact of type p, estimate with an estimation function as defined in an earlier section the development cost of a target artifact of type q, and multiply the result by the number of input artifacts (which is equal to the number of output artifacts).

It is unlikely that this situation occurs in practice. Usually, we have many small artifacts and a few large ones. It is to be observed as well that the development effort of a new artifact is, statistically, *not* a simple linear function of its size. More likely we have a quadratic, if not an exponential function.

To sharpen up this description, we need a few more definitions. Assume that p and q are artifact types and are, respectively, elements in P and Q. In addition, each artifact in p will induce an artifact in q. Let p_i be an artifact of type p and let q_i represent the hypothetical artifact that will be constructed of type q using p_i as its primary input. We assume further that we have available for each artifact of type p the effort to construct it, which we denote as $e(p_i)$ for p_i, and a certain product metric μ, which we denote as $\mu(p_i)$ for p_i. Finally, we denote the development effort estimate for q_i as

$$\mathcal{F}(e(p_i), \mu(p_i))$$

where $\mathcal{F}(e, m)$ is an appropriate quadratic or exponential function. Hence we can define the effort estimate for the artifacts of type q, $B'_T(q)$, as

$$B'_T(q) = \sum_{p_i \in p} \mathcal{F}(e(p_i), \mu(p_i))$$

We do not need to stop here, but we can continue with the "phantom" elements q_i in q. If we can construct an estimation function for a metric $\mu'(q_i)$ based on the values $\mathcal{F}(e(p_i), \mu(p_i))$ and $\mu(p_i)$ (assuming again that q_i is the artifact constructed from p_i), we have all the ingredients in place to estimate the effort of constructing a phantom artifact q'_i that is based on the phantom q_i. Thus we can estimate $B'_T(q')$ where all artifacts q'_i's are of the type q'.

Consequently, we have obtained an alternative route to estimate $B(T)$. We may argue that the first version, using only aggregate values for the artifact types, is only weakly OO-ish. OO comes to play only through the micro development process and the continuity postulate, which allows to come up with the hypothesis of simple estimation functions connecting the different artifact types. The second version using the estimates $B'_T(q)$ is much more OO-ish because the $\mathcal{F}$ function takes as an argument value the result of an OO artifact metric.

The second version is also more sophisticated because it uses two different sources of estimation. This is reflected in the two arguments in $\mathcal{F}(e(p_i), \mu(p_i))$. This function can be written – approximately – as a composite function dependent on a parameter β as

$$\mathcal{F}(e(p_i), \mu(p_i)) = \beta * \mathcal{F}_1(e(p_i)) + (1 - \beta) * \mathcal{F}_2(\mu(p_i))$$

where we have $0 \leq \beta \leq 1$. The function $\mathcal{F}_1(e)$ takes into account only the effort expended to construct p_i in order to estimate the construction of q_i. Hence this function resembles the f_q functions used for the calculation of $B_T(q)$. The other function $\mathcal{F}_2(m)$ relies solely upon a measurement of the volume and complexity of p_i to estimate the development cost of q_i. As long as we don't have a reliable estimation function that uses $\mu(p_i)$, we set β close to 1. When we obtain better insights into the correlations between effort metrics and product metrics, we can decrease the β value.

Keeping track of the expended effort to construct artifacts is quite error prone unless developers use a (hypothetical) sophisticated CASE tool that keeps a record of the time spent to construct an artifact. Automatic tracking by a CASE tool of artifact metrics is a more plausible prospect.

This section should have prepared the reader for a treatment of analysis product metrics, the topic of the next section.

4.2   Analysis Artifact Metrics

In this section we concentrate on product metrics. We start off by reviewing the results of a seminal paper, Chidamber and Kemerer [16]. That paper defines six metrics. These metrics are evaluated analytically against a set of measurement principles proposed by Weyuker [84], and they are evaluated empirically against two libraries of C++ and Smalltalk code. We look first at some theoretical principles for metrics.

4.2.1   Theory of metrics

A metric, in our context, is a function from a domain of artifacts to a range of assessment values. We are already quite familiar with artifact domains. Examples include use cases, vocabulary, inheritance graphs, and classes. An artifact domain can also be taken from other phases of the life cycle.

Ranges of assessment values come in different versions. A very simple one is a range with two elements labeled, say, *bad* and *good*. Another range can have the three elements *small*, *medium* and *large*. Instead, we use assessment values represented by positive numbers. Thus a metric μ is a function[5]

$$\mu: \{\text{artifact domain}\} \rightarrow R^+$$

We discuss characteristics of metrics that are desirable although not necessary for an acceptable metric. Most of our concrete metrics will, in fact, not satisfy one or more of these desired features. The characteristics below come from Chidamber and Kemerer [16], who obtained them from Weyuker [84].

---

[5]R^+ stands for the nonnegative numbers.

Order property

At the very least, we want to have a correspondence between an intuitive, preformalized ordering in the artifact domain with an ordering induced by a metric. For each two artifacts a_1 and a_2, if our premeasurement intuition suggests that a_1 is less than a_2 with respect to some common aspect of a_1 and a_2, we expect that $\mu(a_1) < \mu(a_2)$. Using an example in [16]: If we eyeball two schoolchildren and estimate that one is taller than the other, we expect the taller-ordering to correspond with the ordering induced by measuring their heights.

Relative metric

The numeric values produced by a metric do not have an absolute interpretation. More specifically, the two metrics μ and $m * \mu$ for a positive value of m are equivalent metrics. The advantage of this feature is that we can scale a metric when we want to combine various metrics.

Artifact separation

Thus far we are not protected against a bizarre metric that maps all artifacts in a domain to a single value, say, 93. Thus we assume that a metric separates artifacts sufficiently. This necessitates that a metric operating on a domain allowing arbitrary "large" artifacts should yield arbitrary large values as well. Weyuker addresses this feature as reported in [16]. She calls this issue *granularity* and demands that only finitely many artifacts in a domain have the same metric value. Chidamber and Kemerer [16], call this property *non-coarseness* and formulate it as: For each class p one can always find a class q such that $\mu(p) \neq \mu(q)$.[6]

Incidental collusion

Despite the previous feature, it is acceptable that two different artifacts score the same on a metric.

Artifact composition

An artifact domain can have a composition operation. For example:

---

[6]Their noncoarseness check is quite insufficient. It does not preclude a metric that maps all artifacts to only two values. It is somewhat funny that they reject Weyuker's granularity test as being irrelevant while they clearly have the same idea in mind.

- One may be able to combine two use cases, notated as $u = u_1 + u_2$, where u_1 is the first part of u and sets the stage for the second use case u_2.

- A class c may be obtained through multiple inheritance from the classes c_1 and c_2: $c = c_1 + c_2$.

The meaning of + obviously changes in these two examples.

In case we have such a composition operation for an artifact domain and we have two artifacts a_1 and a_2 that can be composed, we usually assume that

$$\mu(a_1) + \mu(a_2) \leq \mu(a_1 + a_2)$$

Its slogan justification: The sum is greater than its parts. This sounds right for metrics that capture some form of complexity. However, we have to watch for merging effects. An example that does *not* satisfy the composition principle is the following: Choose sets as artifacts, and as a metric take the cardinality of a set. For this choice, we have a "reverse" inequality. Consider: s_1 and s_2 are sets, + in $s_1 + s_2$ stands for the set union operation:

$$\mu(s_1 + s_2) \leq \mu(s_1) + \mu(s_2)$$

If still in doubt, consider the special case $\emptyset \neq s_1 = s_2$. Thus our metric inequality may apply only to those situations where these merging effects do not take place.

Artifact structure

Weyuker has formulated another requirement that takes into account the internal structure of an artifact. Apparently, this requirement applies to code written with block structures. She requires that the metric of an artifact change when program statements are permuted. We assume that she refers to nesting depths being affected by these permutations. We follow Chidamber and Kemerer [16] in casting doubt that this requirement is relevant for our OOA metrics.[7] OOA artifacts do not have internal structure that lends itself to permutations.

Artifact renaming

Weyuker insists that renaming an artifact should not affect its metric. We agree.

---

[7]However, Weyuker's permutation requirement may still apply to metrics that measure C++ member functions.

Form versus meaning

A metric does not measure meaning. For example, two different classes that have the same functionality do not necessarily have the same metric. This feature is a blessing in disguise. A metric being invariant to functionality is hard to construe, if possible at all. Thus our metrics depend on syntactic aspects of the artifacts.

Monotonicity

Adding something to an artifact does not decrease its value by any applicable metric. Chidamber and Kemerer [16] describe a special case: For all classes p and q if they can be combined as a class denoted by $p+q$, we have $\mu(p) \leq \mu(p+q)$ and $\mu(q) \leq \mu(p+q)$. A stronger principle prescribes the $<$-inequality in these equations instead of the $\leq$-relationship.

Composition instability

Composition of p with r and q with r need not maintain the measured difference between p and q. In terms of an equation, the formula $\mu(p) - \mu(q) = \mu(p+r) - \mu(q+r)$ may fail to hold. Obviously, this is a quite weak feature. Insisting on the converse would be more informative, but artifact composition is here too weakly defined to insist on such an invariant. The composition instability feature is too weak to be of any help.[8]

This completes our theoretical discussion of metrics. We proceed by describing metrics for the artifacts encountered in OO analysis.

4.2.2   Analysis metrics

Analysis artifacts can be classified into multivalued and single-valued types, which are respectively:

- Those for which arbitrarily many entities can be introduced: for example, use cases, scenarios, vocabulary entries, relationships, classes, subsystems, ensembles, (parametric) class and relationship instances, relationships, and classes

---

[8]We have generalized the composition instability property somewhat. The original formulation in Chidamber and Kemerer [16] required only: $\mu(p) = \mu(q)$ does not imply that $\mu(p+r) = \mu(q+r)$. Our generalization is too weak to make a fuss about it.

- Those for which at most one entity can be introduced: for example, an inheritance lattice and a subsystem diagram

A special case of a single-valued metric takes as argument a complete OOA model. As an example of a such a metric we could take the total development effort of an OOA model.

For each type τ for which there are multiple entities $\{t_i\}$, we denote their contribution to the complete model by summing up the metrics of all entities of that type. Hence if μ_τ is a metric that applies to artifacts of type τ, we define the contribution of type τ, D_τ, as

$$D_\tau = \sum_i \mu_\tau(t_i)$$

The contribution of all these types, D, can be obtained by weighting the contributions with weights w_τ as in

$$D = \sum_\tau w_\tau * D_\tau$$

Adding to D the contribution of the remaining types can easily be achieved with certain weights. This gives us an alternative way to assign an "effort" value to the complete analysis model. This value can also be used to estimate downstream development effort. Again we can use the aggregated approach as well the disaggregated approach as outlined above for effort estimation based on upstream effort measurements.

What remains is the "detail" of the metrics μ_τ for the different types τ. We consider each analysis artifact in turn. The description below outlines many more product metrics than we actually used for the home heating system. Values tracked in Chapter 5 are sizes of vocabulary entries, number of attributes, number of states, number of transitions, number of events in transitions, number of service requests in transitions, and number of events targeted at other objects in transitions. This subset of product metrics allows us to study internal correlations of the home heating system's analysis.

Use case

A formal format for use cases, as suggested in Section 2.4.2 on page 66, helps to formulate a metric for them. We repeat that format:

state, (user action, state, system action, state)*

where the $*$ indicates one or more repetitions of this sequence.

A straightforward metric, $\mu_{useCase}$, simply counts the number of user actions, or equivalently the number of system actions, which again is equivalent to the number of bracketed 4-tuples. In practice, when this format is not adhered to strictly, we can count the number of sentences that describes the use case. Hence we get for a use case u:

$$\mu_{useCase}(u) = \text{the number of sentences in } u$$

Scenario

Scenarios are an elaboration of use cases in that hidden objects are added to bridge obvious gaps in a scenario. These additions stop when there are no more gaps or when further additions cannot be interpreted by an outsider of the system and instead, are design notions. These scenarios are structurally the same as use cases and thus the same metric applies to them.

Subsystem

Subsystems are described through a template as detailed in Section 3.4.4. There are two approaches here for defining a metric. A simple approach is to count the number of identified subsystems and hence each subsystem has 1 as a metric value. This gives for a subsystem ss

$$\mu_{subsystem}(ss) = 1$$

Alternatively, we can look at fields in the template that can be quantified. For example, the field "a list of children subsystem, if any" can be quantified by taking the length of this list, and similarly for the field "a list of peer subsystems, if any". Other fields can be quantified as well. The different quantifications can be combined using a linear polynomial with proper weighting coefficients.

Vocabulary

Vocabulary entries describe relationships, object classes, ensemble classes, (parametric) relationship instances, (parametric) objects, and ensembles (which correspond to subsystems). All of these have templates. As for subsystems, a simple approach is to give all vocabulary entries the metric value 1, and consequently, the contribution to the model is their number. Alternatively, as for subsystems, we can exploit fields that can be quantified. A class description template can list attributes and operations, a

relationship can describe its arity, an ensemble can describe the list of subensembles, and so on.

Inheritance diagram

Only a single artifact is constructed of the inheritance diagram type: a semilattice with classes as nodes and the inheritance relationship as arcs. This graph can be measured by counting the number of nonroot nodes. A more sophisticated metric weights each class in the lattice with respect to its number of parent classes. Since multiple inheritance is a complex feature, which remains under debate, a class can be weighted, say, by an exponential function:

$$\mu_{inheritanceDiagram} = \sum_{i \neq root} class_i$$

where we have

$$class_i = c^{\#parent(i)-1}$$

in which $\#parent(i)$ represents the number of parent classes of $class_i$ and c is an appropriate parameter larger than 1.

Subsystem diagram

The subsystem diagram is an artifact type for which only a single artifact is produced: a graph with as nodes the labeled subsystems and as arcs some kind of high-level interaction connection between them. At this level of abstraction, one does not have to be too concerned about the exact semantics of these links, although it doesn't hurt, of course, if they are labeled with whatever seems pertinent.

A simple metric for such subsystem diagram is a weighted sum of the number of nodes and the number of arcs:

$$\mu_{subsystems}(graph) = w_{node} * \#\_nodes(graph) + w_{arc} * \#\_arcs(graph)$$

Just counting the number of nodes can be done with $w_{node} = 1$ and $w_{arc} = 0$.

A more sophisticated metric takes the complexity of the subsystems into account. The complexity of a subsystem can be measured by its number of links with other subsystems. Thus if we denote with $subs_i$ the number of links that the subsystem i has with its peers, we obtain as an alternative metric,

$$\mu'_{subsystems}(graph) = \sum_{i \epsilon graph} subs_i$$

The metric $\mu'_{subsystems}$ is more sensitive than $\mu_{subsystems}$ to the complexity of the graph. Another metric that counts cycles in the graph can be even more sensitive to the complexity of the subsystems graph. At this point we don't have empirical data to formulate a preference for one over another.

Class-relationship diagram

The class-relationship diagram is another artifact type of which we have only one instance. The complexity of this graph is a function of the number of relationship nodes and the number of class nodes. The arity of a relationship is at least 2, which corresponds with the number of arcs in the graph attached to a relationship node. A class node has at least one arc attached to it. We can measure this diagram by counting the number of class nodes and adding for each relationship its arity:

$$\mu_{classRelationships} = \#classNodes + \sum_{r \, relationship} arity(r)$$

A more sophisticated metric would use weights for the contributions of the class nodes and the relationship nodes. We can also have a closer look at cardinalities associated with the arcs as we will do later in the section Relationship.

Class

This artifact type is the *pièce de résistance*. We discuss several metrics that apply to classes. Several of them have been described in the seminal paper by Chidamber and Kemerer [16]. Below we denote by C a class on which we apply a metric μ.

Attribute A straightforward way to measure a class is to count its attributes:

$\mu_{classAttribute}(C)$ = the number of attributes of C.

This metric can be refined by taking into account distinctions as:

1. The value of the attribute is a single entity or is multivalued.

2. The value of the attribute is an object, a simple elementary data element (e.g., a number, a string, etc.), or a structure.

3. The attribute is recursive.

Thus we can sum up entries for each attribute and weight every entry multiplicatively dependent on these features. A multivalued attribute with, say, five values would get the weight 5. An attribute with as value an elementary data type would get the weight 1; with as value an object O it would get some measure of that object, or if this complicates matters too much, we can agree on a certain constant value, $c_{classAttributeObject}$; and similarly for an attribute that has a structure as a value.

Our silent assumption here has been that we measure all attributes that are visible to a class (i.e., the local attributes and all the attributes that are inherited from any ancestor class).

Constraints Attribute value combinations can be ruled out by constraints. Hence we can count the number of constraints formulated for a class:

$$\mu_{classConstraint}(C) = \text{the number of constraints of } C.$$

Constraints translate during design into operations that propagate changes in an attribute to affected attributes. A more realistic measure weights each constraint based on the impact it will have on the operations that modify attribute values.

Transition network Several metrics can be defined on transition networks:

$$\mu_{classTNs}(C) = \text{the number of disjoint transition networks of } C.$$

Recall that an object has only a single thread of control but that we allow an object to inherit multiple transition networks. Multiple networks can be merged conceptually through a Cartesian product into a single transition network. To avoid an exponential explosion of states and transitions it is better to keep them separate. Hence these metrics:

$$\mu_{classState}(C) = \text{the number of states in } C\text{'s transition network(s)}$$
$$\mu_{classTransition}(C) = \text{the number of transitions in } C\text{'s transition network(s)}$$

The latter metric can be refined by weighting the transitions. Relevant features of a transition to play a role in a weighing scheme are: whether a transition depends on an event in addition to a condition, whether at least one event gets generated, and whether the action part of the transition contains a service request. Further refinements would entail a complexity assessment of the action part of the transition. A step beyond would count the number of distinct cycles in a transition network.

Event and service requests A measure of the "socialness" of the instances of a class is the number of different events that it can respond to

$$\mu_{classEvent}(C) = \text{the number of different events in } C\text{'s transitions}$$

It is to be observed that an event *ev* can be referred to on multiple transitions in *C*'s transition networks. This allows different responses to *ev* dependent on the state of the object in which *ev* is accepted. An event occurring on multiple transitions will be counted only once.

Another measure of socialness is the number of different service requests formulated in *C*'s transition networks. Again identical service requests are counted only once.[9]

$$\mu_{classServiceRequest}(C) = \text{the number of different service requests in } C\text{'s transitions}$$

Yet another metric in this realm regards events produced by *C*'s transition networks:

$$\mu_{classEventProduced}(C) = \text{the number of different events targeted at other objects in } C\text{'s transitions}$$

Depth of Inheritance Tree (DIT) This metric was defined in Chidamber and Kemerer [16] as the class *C*'s depth in the inheritance tree:

$$\mu_{DIT}(C) = \text{the distance of } C \text{ to the root; in case there are multiple paths, due to multiple inheritance, the longest path is taken for the distance}$$

This metric indicates how many levels of inheritance one has to investigate for obtaining the total picture for *C*.

Number of Ancestors (NOA) This metric, $\mu_{NOA}(C)$, measures the number of ancestor classes of *C*. The metric coincides with the DIT metric in the absence of multiple inheritance. Thus we have in general: $\mu_{DIT}(C) \leq \mu_{NOA}(C)$. The μ_{NOA} metric is more accurate than the μ_{DIT} metric in measuring the dependency of *C* on its ancestor classes.

Number of Children (NOC) This metric was also defined in Chidamber and Kemerer [16]:

$$\mu_{NOC}(C) = \text{the number of immediate subclasses of } C$$

This metric can be used to prioritize quality assurance efforts. The more children a class has, the more vulnerable the analysis is to its correctness (and similarly for

---

[9]We ignore different arguments as we do for the counting of events.

the design and the implementation).

Number of all Children (NOAC) This metric is a variation on the preceding one:

$$\mu_{NOAC}(C) = \text{the number of immediate and indirect sub-classes of } C$$

It gives us a more accurate figure on the impact of C on the analysis (and on the design and the implementation).

Coupling Between Object Classes (CBO) This metric was defined in Chidamber and Kemerer [16] for classes in C++ and Smalltalk. We adjust their definition here for the analysis phase as

$\mu_{CBO}(C) = $ the number of couples that C has with other classes. A couple between C and C' is defined as a directed couple between C and C' or a directed couple between C' and C. A directed couple between C and C' is defined as one of the following:

- The occurrence of a service request in a transition inside C to an instance of C'

- The sending of an event to an instance of C'

- The transmission of an instance of C' in a C transition through a service request or an event

- The reception of an instance of C' in an event or service request

We can't have zero coupling, because this would entail that instances cannot communicate, but we want to have low coupling to maximize modularity, or alternatively, to minimize the dependence on other parties.

Response For a Class (RFC) This metric was also defined in Chidamber and Kemerer [16] and needs adjustment as well:

$\mu_{RFC}(C) = $ the size of the response set of C. An element in the response set for C is defined as an event or service request that can activate a transition inside C, or an event or service request that can be generated by a transition inside C.
Both metrics μ_{CBO} and μ_{RFC} measure aspects of object interaction, but while μ_{CBO} measures communication partners, μ_{RFC} measures service requests and events.

Lack Of Cohesion (LCOM) This metric is introduced in Chidamber and Kemerer [16]. LCOM stands for "Lack of Cohesion in Methods".[10] It measures how

---

[10] "Method" is the pompous term in Smalltalk for what is known as a member function in C++.

"splitable" a C++ or Smalltalk class is by checking whether the set of instances variables used by a method intersect with similar sets of other methods in C. We don't have methods in analysis, and thus one should adjust the notion of cohesion to the realm of analysis. Since the definition in the following footnote does not cover our intuition about cohesion, we recommend this topic for research; see also page 354.[11]

Other metrics Certainly it is possible to conceive of more metrics on classes: constancy of attributes, the number of references to attributes in transition networks, the number of changes to attributes in transition networks (which can be described by postconditions of operations), the complexity structure of transition networks with respect to cycles along the directed edges, the complexity of transitions, etc.

Relationship

Measuring a relationship R can be straightforward:

$$\mu_{Relationship}(R) = \text{the } arity(R)$$

Hence we obtain

$$\mu_{Relationships} = \sum_{r \epsilon relationship} \mu_{Relationship}(r)$$

A more sophisticated metric can be obtained by having a closer look at the arcs that are attached to a relationship node. A cardinality description unequal to 1 entails more work in the design phase. Hence, instead of simply counting the arcs, as done by $arity(R)$, we can attach a weight to each arc dependent on the specified cardinality according to the schema:

- If the cardinality $= 1$, then w_1

- If the cardinality is fixed, then w_2

---

[11]A somewhat analogous metric could be applied to classes that have more than one transition network.

Let P be defined as the pairs of transition networks of C where the attributes referred to in one transition network of a pair have an empty intersection with the attributes referred to in the other transition network of the pair. In contrast, Q is defined as those pairs where the similar intersections are not empty. Let p be the size of P and q be the size of P. Finally, we define $\mu_{LCOM}(C) = $ if $p > q$, then $p - q$, else 0.

An excellent example of a class with lack of cohesion is obtained through multiple inheritance when the transition networks obtained from the parents are not extended with cross references. Since the classes in our running example do not have multiple transition networks, we ignore μ_{LCOM}.

- If the cardinality is a small fixed range, then w_3[12]

- If the cardinality is a small variable range, then w_4[13]

- Otherwise, w_5[14]

With this approach we get:

$\mu_{Relationship}(R) =$ the sum of the weights on the arcs attached to R.

Instance

Instances can be distinguished pragmatically into two categories: enduring versus transient objects. The former are unique, stable objects that form the "backbone" of a system. The latter are created and deleted on the fly. Every OO system has enduring objects, while transient objects are optional. We define two metrics:

$\mu_{EndInstances} =$ the number of enduring instances
$\mu_{TranInstances} =$ the number of classes whose instances are transient

Scenario diagram

A scenario diagram is a detailed description of a scenario using class instances and their transition networks. Such a diagram consists of a graph (sometimes multiple graphs), where a node represents a (prototypical) object and the directed and numbered arcs correspond with object interactions, i.e., they represent service requests, replies, or one-way communications.

A measure for a scenario diagram SD for suitable weights $w1_{SD}$ and $w2_{SD}$:

$$\mu_{ScenarioDiagram}(SD) = w1_{SD} * \#ObjectsIn(SD) + w2_{SD} * \#ArcsIn(SD)$$

One-way communications require more design efforts since the current OO programming languages do not support concurrency (except through ad hoc extensions via libraries). Hence, given this situation, it pays to refine the scenario diagram metric

---

[12] "Small" is quite subjective here; it can be interpreted as bounded by such numbers as 8, 16, 32, 64, 128, and 256. A plausible design would be an array construct.

[13] "Small" can be different here. A plausible design could be a linked list.

[14] General purpose containers are required for this case.

by counting separately the arcs that correspond with one-way communications and the arcs that are service requests or replies:

$$\mu_{ScenarioDiagram}(SD) = w1_{SD} * \#ObjectsIn(SD) + w2_{SD} * \#OneWayArcsIn(SD)$$
$$+ w3_{SD} * \#ServiceRequestsIn(SD) + w4_{SD} * \#RepliesIn(SD)$$

Summing up all the different scenario diagrams gives us

$$\mu_{ScenarioDiagrams} = \sum_{sd \epsilon ScenarioDiagram} \mu_{ScenarioDiagram}(sd)$$

OOA model

The metric of the total OOA model can be just the weighted sum of all the components described in previous sections. But, as we did before, we can have second thoughts. As we mentioned in the previous Chapter, if one has done a domain analysis, classes are obtained that are more general than needed in a target system. If so, we have a second round of class definitions devoted to their specializations.

4.2.3   Application of the theory on metrics

In summary, most of the metrics defined satisfy most of the desirable properties outlined in Section 4.2.1. The metrics seem to satisfy intuition; thus the order property is okay. The relative property is satisfied as well. The metrics are sensitive to volume aspects of the artifacts measured. This yields the artifact separation property. Incidental collusion is not prevented. Artifact composition can be violated when the artifacts are classes and "+" stands for multiple inheritance. Merging effects are the cause. Renaming of artifacts has no ramification for the metrics discussed. The metrics also do not depend on any semantics: they just look at syntactic features. Adding something to an artifact doesn't cause a metric to decrease; hence monotonicity is satisfied.

4.3   Summary

According to Grady [30] there are four major categories where metrics impact development:

1. Project estimation and process monitoring

2. Evaluation of work products

3. Process improvement through defect analysis (refers to the practice of measuring defects and ascribing systematic errors to flaws in the development process)

4. Experimental validation of best practices (refers to not accepting excellent ideas for improving software development unless empirical data has proven the value of the measure in practice)

We have concentrated in this chapter on the first two items in this list.

Jalote observes that "software metrics is an emerging area" [42]. OO metrics are also obviously still under development. Many questions are still open: Are these metrics independent? Are they defined precisely enough so that they can be incorporated in CASE tools? Do these metrics cover all topics of interest? Are they significant? Are they effective? Is the world stable enough to pay for the cost of collecting them? Clearly, we need much more work in this area and more experience to settle these questions.

The next chapter is devoted to an example where we adhere to the process described in the previous chapter and where we apply the metrics developed in this chapter. We will observe promising correlations between effort metrics collected for different artifact types. Product metrics also yield good correlations that can be the basis for an alternative route for effort prediction.

4.4 Further Reading

The book by Jalote [42], is a good general introduction to software engineering. For example, it introduces the distinction between product and process metrics. The COCOMO effort estimation technique is described but object specific metrics are not mentioned.

Bob Grady's book [30], also has virtually nothing to say about object-oriented metrics. Instead, it is full of "nuggets" about metrics in general. For example, he reports that effort ratios between requirements/specifications, design, implementation, and test vary depending on whether a software project belongs to the following categories: firmware, systems, or applications. Table 4.1 shows the various ratios. Hence one cannot expect to come up with an effort prediction technique that ignores these, and possibly other, categories. In addition Grady reminds us that:

> Managers use metrics data far too little for progress monitoring, even though intuition and evidence suggest that such use is highly practical.

	Firmware	Systems	Applications
Requirements/specifications	15	14	22
Design	21	19	16
Implementation	39	30	34
Test	25	37	28

Table 4.1: Effort ratios (%) between different phases in the development phase dependent on the target category. Averages were calculated over the following number of projects: firmware, 31 projects; systems, 48 projects; applications, 53 projects.

> One reason that metrics aren't used is that project managers often don't have time. Another reason is that we seem to be held back by our fears of people's reactions to measurement.

These fears have to be alleviated but are not the full story. Metrics should be positioned as worthwhile tools for the developers themselves. What is a carpenter without a measuring band? What would your author be without a spell checker?[15]

A seminal paper on object-oriented metrics is Chidamber and Kemerer, [15]. All of our quotations are from their subsequent report [16]. It is to be observed that their metrics have been developed by investigating implementations in Smalltalk and C++. The generalization to the analysis realm is ours.

4.5   Exercises

1. Work out the numerics of an example where we have incomplete artifact types (see Section 4.1.2) as we did in Section 4.1.1 for completed artifact types.

2. As the previous exercise but give a brief example of where the artifact types are disaggregated (see Section 4.1.3).

3. Prove that our version of the composition instability property (see page 114) implies the one formulated by Chidamber, see the footnote.

---

[15]Quite miserable.

Chapter 5

Example: Home Heating System

This chapter is devoted to an illustration of the material developed in earlier chapters. We explore a home heating system by applying the notations introduced in Chapter 2, we follow the process described in Chapter 3 and we apply the metrics outlined in Chapter 4. The presentation is not representative for a real-life example for several reasons:

1. The example is quite small, although it is not trivial. In fact, despite its size, it has surprising complexity.

2. The representation is streamlined in the sense that no backtracking occurs. In practice an analysis has many "random" traversals when new insights force re-arrangements of earlier conceptions and hence of previously developed artifacts.

3. The effects of teamwork are not covered. However, at the end of the chapter we present some data developed by student teams that worked on the home heating system as part of an OO analysis course.

4. We present a complete home heating system instead of going through a fragment as part of an iterative and incremental macro process.

Most of the balance of the chapter consists of sections devoted to artifact types in which we describe artifacts and the values of metrics applied to them. While working on this problem we maintained a log to monitor progress and to record events. Some of the observations are reported.

5.1   Requirements

The very first step in the analysis consists of simply reading the requirements document and resolving questions as they arise from this preliminary understanding.[1]

Our readings – we recommend strongly that the reader go over section 1.10 at least three times – yielded the following issues and their resolutions:

- The initialization of the living pattern is not specified. We assume that upon installation time a default pattern gets established.

- It is not clear whether the room occupancy status is still recorded and living patterns are maintained when the system is turned off. We assume that it is maintained.

- Similarly, it is not clear what happens when the power is turned off. Is there a battery backup for the clock, for the sensors, and for the maintenance of the living pattern and the occupancy history? We assume that there is.

- The timer is incremented every second. We assume that this timer has sufficient capacity so that no one has to worry about overflow problems, or alternatively, that the timer takes care of these problems.

- The system "learns" continuously the living pattern of the occupants and hence one does not have to worry about the timer drifting off in the long run. Still we have to assume that the timer is accurate enough so that occupancy patterns collected a week earlier can be compared.

- We prefer to make each room "responsible" for maintaining the room occupancy history and the weekly living pattern (instead of giving the heat-flow regulator this responsibility).

- In the sentence before last in the specification "... and no rooms need heat", we assume that the intended meaning is "... or no room needs heat."

- The specification can be extended by the addition of a "vacation mode" to be activated and deactivated by an occupant. The vacation mode avoids a living pattern being wiped out due to an extended absence. In addition a vacation mode can maintain the room temperatures at a minimum level.[2] Our

---

[1]If there is no requirements document, ... well then it has to be *written* first. We emphasize *written* because one will get an abundance of insights by having to formulate precisely a customer's ideas – no matter how sketchy these are.

[2]Doug Lea suggested the vacation-mode feature.

description will, however, not incorporate the vacation-mode feature.

It is also recommended that the algorithmic fragments of the requirements be rewritten in a more formal language to determine whether they are coherent, consistent, and complete. The room temperature and the living pattern both benefit from some formal rewriting.

Room Temperature

ta = the actual temperature of a room

td = the desired temperature for a room that is set by an occupant using the input device for that room

tw = the working temperature of a room, calculated as:

tw = if the room is occupied or the room is expected to be occupied within 30 minutes, then td, else $td - 5$;

NeedsHeat describes whether or not a room needs heat and is defined in the requirements as "... a given room needs heat whenever the room temperature is equal to or less than $(tw - 2)$ degrees Fahrenheit and determines that a given room does not need heat whenever the room temperature is equal to or greater than $(tw + 2)$ ...". This begs the question of whether a room needs heat when its temperature is between $(tw - 2)$ and $(tw + 2)$. The way out is to say that in those circumstances the value of *NeedsHeat* does not change. The following behavior is obtained: If the current temperature is equal to or less than $(tw - 2)$, the room needs heat until the temperature equals $(tw + 2)$. Similarly, when it is decided that the room does not need heat, this situation persists until the room temperature is $(tw - 2)$. Hence, when a room receives an event from the clock:

$NeedsHeat =$
if $ta \leq tw - 2$ then *True* else
if $ta \geq tw + 2$ then *False* else
use the current *NeedsHeat* value.

Room Living Pattern

Tn = the current time

$OHOR(t)$ = the Occupancy History Of a Room as a function of time; the history of only the last 7 days needs to be maintained

$OHOR(Tn)$ = the value of the occupancy sensor

$LPOR(t)$ = the Living Pattern Of a Room as a function of time; again only a 7 day period has to be recorded

The expression "$LPOR(t \sim 7days)$" stands for the value of $LPOR$ at time t modulo 7 days. When a clock event arrives, a new value of $LPOR(Tn)$ is calculated as

$LPOR(Tn \sim 7days) =$
if $OHOR(Tn) \neq OHOR(Tn - 7days)$
then the current value of $LPOR(Tn \sim 7days)$
else $OHOR(Tn)$.

Hence we do *not* change the living pattern when the current occupancy differs from the occupancy a week earlier. Otherwise, we set the pattern to the current occupancy status. Observe that the latter case need not have changed the stored value of $LPOR(Tn \sim 7days)$.

Note that we have not done any design here. Instead, we have clarified and made explicit the paragraph that ended with "The weekly living pattern is updated when variations to the established pattern occur two weeks in a row."

In a real-life situation, one must check these formalizations with the customer to make sure that the correct intentions have been obtained.

5.1.1 Metrics

Scrutinizing the requirements and formulating clarifications took about 120 minutes.

5.1.2 Notes

Puzzling were the weekly occupancy patterns:

> Read the $2\frac{1}{4}$ page requirements several times. ... Did some brewing in the background. For instance, I worried about the requirement to maintain a weekly room occupancy pattern. And the complication that the pattern must be updated when changes are persistent over two weeks.
>
> I guess that I did not understand this at first. I "solved this" by constructing a representation of the weekly pattern – which felt initially like jumping prematurely into design.

My first attempt was to maintain a circular list of time points: total time points 2 weeks[3] and with a 1 second granularity. This would represent the occupancy history. A similar list would represent the occupancy pattern. Each second one would advance through both lists and do the following ...

But in the meantime I worried already about the representation of this data – which is a design/implementation concern but can also be seen as an attempt to clarify my understandings of the requirements. I dreamed up the following representation ...

These quotations testify that staying focused purely on the requirements did not occur. There was some need to see whether the conceptualizations could be "grounded" in an, albeit naive, implementation.[4] We have observed that the need to do this type of grounding happens to some extent in each analysis. Whether it is as explicit as reported in the quotation will depend on the complexity of the situation, the familiarity with the subject matter, the personality of the analyst, the willingness to admit these discursions, etc.

5.2 Use Case

The home heating system allows for many use cases. Here are three:

- The user turns on the heat switch while the current temperature in room A is 5 degrees below its working temperature.

  Since room A needs heat, the furnace is started.

- A user enters a room, which causes activation of the furnace.

  An ignition error occurs and the fault/reset indicator is turned off.

- The temperature of a room that is being heated rises above its working temperature + 2 and consequently does no longer needs heat.

  Since it was the only room being heated, the furnace shuts down.

  Another room needs heat but must wait until the 5 minute delay period has expired before the furnace is restarted.

---

[3]Note that only 1 week + 1 second of historical data is required.

[4]The representation chosen were long arrays of bits representing a week of time points with the granularity of a second. This representation is sufficient to represent an occupancy history and an occupancy pattern.

Many other use cases can be formulated: changing the living pattern of a room, adding a room that needs heat while the furnace is running, removing a room that needs heat while another room continues to be heated, a user changing the desired temperature causing a room to be heated, or alternatively, causing a room not to be heated, etc. In a real-life situation one should describe these cases and more. When to stop is difficult to answer in general and depends on many factors. Unfamiliarity with the domain, vague and incomplete requirements, and the fail-safeness of the intended system are all good reasons to explore the intended system deeply with typical and corner use cases. When additional use cases do not lead to new insights, one may have reached coverage.

5.2.1   Metrics

Constructing and formulating the use cases took about 120 minutes. The use cases are unformalized. Hence to obtain their metric we can simply count the number of sentences used. Instead of counting sentences naively, we can split up compound sentences when more than one entity appears to be involved. For example, the second sentence in the second use case, "An ignition error occurs and the fault reset indicator is turned off" appears to involve more than one entity: an "observer" of the ignition error and the fault/reset indicator. Thus we obtain

$\mu_{useCase}(UC1) = 3$

$\mu_{useCase}(UC2) = 4$

$\mu_{useCase}(UC3) = 5$

Measuring the use cases is admittedly a subjective affair.

5.2.2   Notes

Working on use cases forces a deeper understanding of the intended system. For example, what happens when the power is switched off? Will the clock continue, for instance, because there is a battery backup? If so, will the occupancy sensors continue? If not, how do we deal with a gap in the occupancy history? What happens with the living pattern? Should we extend the system by having it make periodic backups of the patterns and the histories so that we can reconstruct a consistent state when the power is restored? These and similar questions will help an analyst to interact better with the customer. It will further increase the customer's trust that the system developed will be robust and reliable and will correspond with the customer's intentions.

5.3 Scenario

A scenario expands a use case by filling in gaps that were omitted because they were obvious and/or because they were forgotten. Additions can be descriptions of assumed states of affairs or of intermediate actions and/or states. The analyst has to walk a fine line to ascertain that premature design is avoided during scenario construction. We expand each use case in turn.

Use Case 1

> The user turns on the heat switch while the current temperature in room A is 5 degrees below its working temperature.
>
> Since room A needs heat, the furnace is started.

Scenario 1 is developed by observing that the use case needs to be extended since the room does not control the furnace directly. Since we know that the furnace is started, we know as well that the system is enabled; i.e., that the fault/reset switch is already in the *on* position. The use case is partitioned to indicate the involvements of objects. A partition boundary is denoted by "//". This partitioning is certainly based only on educated intuitions. More insights developed later may lead, as for all other artifacts, to revisions and refinements.

Scenario 1

> The user turns on the heat switch (while the current temperature in room A is 5 degrees below its working temperature).//
> The heat switch informs a heat flow regulator that it is switched on.//
> The heat flow regulator informs a furnace controller that the furnace is enabled (since the fault/reset switch is on).//
> The furnace controller informs the furnace to startup since it knows already that there is at least one room that needs heat.//

This scenario has introduced the new entities "heat flow regulator" and "furnace controller" as mediators between the heat switch and the furnace.

Use Case 2

> A user enters a room, which causes activation of the furnace.
>
> An ignition error occurs and the fault reset indicator is turned off.

This use case will be expanded in a similar fashion.

Scenario 2

A user enters a room ...

The room occupancy sensor informs the room that it is occupied.//

The room registers the occupancy and changes the weekly living pattern if necessary.//

The room verifies the actual temperature, ta, against the working temperature, tw; since $ta \leq tw - 2$, it informs the room controller that it needs heat.//

The room controller adds the room to the set of rooms that needs heat and informs the furnace controller that a room needs heat.//

... which causes activation of the furnace.

The furnace controller informs the furnace to start up.//

The furnace starts the blower motor.//

The blower motor informs the furnace that it has reached the sufficient RPM level.//

The furnace informs the oil valve to open.//

The furnace activates the igniter.//

The furnace activates the furnace monitor.//

The furnace monitor finds an ignition error.//

The furnace monitor informs the furnace to shut down.//

The furnace monitor informs the furnace controller to disable the system.//

The furnace monitor sets the fault reset indicator to off.//

The following new entities have been introduced: "room controller" and "furnace monitor." As was the case for the entities introduced in scenario 1, we can ask questions like: How do we ascertain that they are necessary? By what mechanism have they been selected? Their necessity is hard to prove. Quite likely it is possible to describe the system without them. Their introduction is an attempt to simplify the description by splitting up bundled functionality into smaller self-contained pieces. The mechanism for their introduction? We are not aware of any guidelines or heuristics that help the introduction of intermediate entities. A certain playfulness and fearlessness seem to be prerequisites - and a willingness to abandon good ideas, see the Notes section below.

Use Case 3

The temperature of a room that is being heated rises above its working temperature + 2 and consequently it does not need heat any longer.

Since it was the only room being heated, the furnace shuts down.

Another room needs heat but must wait until the 5 minute delay period has expired before the furnace is restarted.

We leave the construction of scenario 3 as an exercise for the reader.

5.3.1 Metrics

The construction of the two scenarios took about 40 and 90 minutes, respectively.
    Their metrics by counting sentences is:

$\mu_{scenario}(SC1) = 4$

$\mu_{scenario}(SC2) = 14$

    Scenarios are derived from use cases. Thus it is of interest to see whether there is a relationship between the metrics of use cases and scenarios, see Table 5.1.

Use Cases & Scenarios	1		2	
	Effort	Metric	Effort	Metric
Use case	40	3	40	4
Scenario	60	4	90	14

Table 5.1: Summary of the development effort (minutes) for the two use cases and scenarios and their scores on the metric that counts sentences.

Before discussing these data we should observe that we can't draw statistically significant conclusions from two data points. Thus we can admit right away that these data do not fit too well our conjectures for effort prediction. The use case/scenario ratios regarding effort for 1 and 2 are, respectively, 1.5 and 2.25. This is too wide a range for predicting the effort of scenario development based on the effort to develop a use case. Similarly, the use case/scenario ratios regarding the metrics for 1 and 2 have a wide range and are, respectively, 1.3 and 3.5.

Clearly, we need more empirical data to validate effort and metric ratios. For now, we can use as a rough heuristic that scenarios double the size of use cases and take twice more effort.

5.3.2 Notes

As we will see later, the introduction in scenario 1 of the "heat flow regulator" and "furnace controller" is only part of the story. Another entity will be introduced, a "system controller", to simplify the different ways thar the furnace controller is impacted. The heat switch will interact in this extended setup with the system controller instead of interacting with the heat flow regulator. This is an excellent example showing how a system's architectural description is obtained in an incremental fashion.

As we will see below, the introduction of the room controller turned out not to be necessary. A room acts as a controller of its sensors and its other components. The addition of the furnace monitor turned out to be useful.

5.4　Subsystem

We will describe systems only through a characteristic name and through an enumeration of their components, which are possibly subsystems also.

Home Heating System The Home Heating System is the top-level system. It has, at this early stage, the following components:
- the user interface
- the system controller
- the heat flow regulator
- the furnace controller
- the furnace
- the furnace monitor

User Interface This subsystem is just a collection of independent components:
- the heat switch
- the fault reset switch/indicator
- the furnace status indicator

Heat Flow Regulator This subsystem seems to be odd because it has only one kind of component, although there are multiple instances:
- the rooms

Room Each room can be seen as a subsystem:
- the occupancy sensor
- the room temperature sensor
- the device for registering the desired temperature
- the water valve

The reader may wonder why the device used by an occupant to set a room's desired temperature is not a part of the user-interface subsystem. In fact, Figure 1.4 on page 20 depicts the desired temperature devices as part of the user interface. However, we prefer our setup because each room has such a device and the data produced by such a device are exclusively consumed by a room. Hence there is no reason to "hide" this input device in another system.

Furnace The furnace has, among others, the following components:
- the blower motor
- the oil valve
- the igniter
- the water temperature sensor

A realistic furnace has other components as well: a boiler, the water in the boiler (and in the pipes and radiators), possibly a hot water pump, a pressure release valve, a valve to add water to the system, etc. Since we do not need these objects for the description of our system, we exclude them.

Now that we are at it: The water in the system is a problematic entity. It is hard to justify being an object. For example, it does not have an obvious identify, which is one of the requirements for objecthood. Water is an example of *mass terms*, which are all poor objects.[5]

Furnace Monitor This subsystem has as components:
- the fuel flow sensor
- the optical combustion sensor

5.4.1 Metrics

The development of these subsystems took a total of 20 minutes.

As discussed in the previous chapter, there are several ways to measure the artifacts. The simplest way is to give a subsystem the metric value of 1. Hence for each subsystem ss: $\mu_{subsystem}(ss) = 1$. Another extreme uses a detailed template for a description of subsystems which can be used to assign weights to quantifiable fields in the template. For example, a distinction can be made between components of a subsystem that are subsystems by themselves and components that aren't. We follow as middle ground a metric that counts the number of components. (In fact, we count component types; the heat flow regulator has multiple rooms as components but only one component type.) Hence we obtain

$\mu_{subsystem}(HomeHeatingSystem) = 5$
$\mu_{subsystem}(UserInterface) = 3$
$\mu_{subsystem}(HeatFlowRegulator) = 1$
$\mu_{subsystem}(Room) = 4$
$\mu_{subsystem}(Furnace) = 4$

---

[5]Mass terms are notoriously hard to handle in a formal manner. Philosophers are still struggling with them, see, e.g. Bunt [14].

$$\mu_{subsystem}(FurnaceMonitor) = 2$$

5.4.2   Notes

The room appears to be incomplete. The occupancy history and the living pattern are obvious candidates to be added to a room as components. The clock does not show up in this list of subsystems. We left these omissions to illustrate that it is virtually impossible to get things correct the first time around.

5.5   List of Candidate Classes

Although making a list of candidate classes is not a part of the analysis micro process, it is a good preparation for constructing the vocabulary. The following list is just a "flattening" of the entities encountered while constructing subsystems:

HomeHeatingSystem
UserInterface
HeatSwitch
FaultResetSwitch/Indicator
FurnaceStatusIndicator
SystemController
HeatFlowRegulator
Room
OccupancySensor
RoomTemperatureSensor
DesiredTemperatureInputDevice
WaterValve
FurnaceController
Furnace
BlowerMotor
OilValve
Igniter
WaterTemperatureSensor
FurnaceMonitor
FuelFlowSensor
OpticalCombustionSensor

Again this is incomplete. Subsequent development led to the following additions:
OccupancyHistory

LivingPattern
Clock
ValveController
Timer
ClockClient

The last one in this list is a class with a design flavor that had to be introduced to allow the clock to handle a heterogeneous set of recipients for clock ticks.

5.5.1 Metrics

Constructing this list took 10 minutes. Artifact metrics do not apply. The reader is invited to count the length of this list, but as mentioned above, we will add classes.

5.5.2 Notes

Scrutinizing the list of classes yields the suggestion that we can factor out commonalities from the class RoomTemperatureSensor and the class WaterTemperatureSensor. Similarly, one can wonder whether the XYZsensor classes can be abstracted further, yielding a class Sensor.

These abstractions make sense when the subclasses share structure. We don't know yet at this point whether that will be the case. This abstraction conjecture can be passed on to the downstream activity that deals with inheritance.

5.6 Vocabulary

The vocabulary deals with subsystems (formulated not as instances but as classes), classes of "normal" objects, relationships, and unique instances. In our running example, we deal only with classes. The vocabulary will be described with the template:
- Purpose
- Attributes/components
- States
- Operations

HeatSwitch
  - Purpose: This is an input device with which the furnace can be turned on or off. This switch does not affect the clock, the occupancy sensors, the maintenance of the living patterns and the occupancy histories.

– Attributes/components: onOffStatus
– States: on, off
– Operations: turnOn(), turnOff()

FaultResetSwitch/Indicator

– Purpose: A furnace error turns the indicator and the switch into off; the user can reset the switch and the indicator.
– Attributes/components: onOffStatus
– States: on, off
– Operations: turnOn(), turnOff()

FurnaceStatusIndicator

– Purpose: This indicator displays whether or not the furnace is running.
– Attributes/components: onOffStatus
– States: on, off
– Operations: turnOn(), turnOff()

Comment: The entities above share a remarkable amount of structure, which suggests that there is an opportunity for abstraction.

HeatFlowRegulator

– Purpose: This is a mediator between the rooms and the furnace controller.
– Attributes/components: roomsThatNeedHeat
– States: noRoomNeedsHeat, aRoomNeedsHeat
– Operations: register(room), unregister(room)

Comment: As can be inferred from the names of the states in HeatFlowRegulator, this object will keep track of whether or not the furnace has to be on or not based on the "opinions" of the rooms. Whether or not the furnace will in fact be on or not depends on other factors as well. The furnace controller integrates all these factors and makes the final decision.

SystemController

– Purpose: This entity integrates the settings of the heat switch and fault/reset indicator and contributes their conjunction to the furnace controller.
– Attributes/components: *None*
– States: hsOff&frOff, hsOff&frOn, hsOn&frOff, hsOn&frOn
– Operations: hsOff(), hsOn(), frOn(), frOff()

Comment: This description needs some explication, due to the cryptic names. The state hsOff&frOn, for example, describes that the heat switch is in the off state and that the fault/reset indicator is in the on state. Hence the furnace can be running provided only that the system controller is in the state: hsOn&frOn!

The operation hsOff() is to be used by the heat switch to report to the system controller that it changed in the off state. Similarly, the operation frOn is used by the fault/reset indicator when it changes into the on state.

Clock
– Purpose: This entity activates registered parties every second. It is also able to reply to requests for the time.
– Attributes/components: currentTime, clients
– States: ready
– Operations: ticToc(), getTime()

Comment: The operation ticToc() is activated every second by an actual clock that is outside the system boundary. The transition triggered by the ticToc event is the main engine of the system. All rooms get activated, which allows them to review their state of affairs and act accordingly.

Room
– Purpose: A room maintains its weekly living pattern and the weekly occupancy history. It checks the actual temperature, determines the working temperature, and determines whether it needs heat. The heat flow regulator is informed when a change with respect to heating requirements is determined.
– Attributes/components: theOccupancySensor, theRoomTemperatureSensor, theDesiredTemperatureInputDevice, theWaterValve, theOccupancyHistory, the-LivingPattern, needsHeat? (= NH?)[6], registeredHeatRequest? (= RHR?), occupiedOrToBeOccupied? (= OOTBO?)
– States: waitForClockTic, decideToChangeHeatingRequest
– Operations: openValve(), closeValve(), tic(dateTime)

Comment: The tic operation will update the occupancy history, and the living pattern if necessary. In addition, it will determine whether or not the room needs heat and will set the attribute NH? accordingly.

The name of the state decideToChangeHeatingRequest is slightly inaccurate. In fact, the decision is prepared *whether* to change requesting heat.

The attributes that have the prefix "the" have as value an object of the type

---

[6]The expression between brackets are abbreviations that are used below in state transition diagrams.

suggested by the second part of the attribute name. For example, the attribute theWaterValve has as value an instance of the class WaterValve.

OccupancySensor
– Purpose: This sensor keeps track of the occupancy of a room.
– Attributes/components: occupied?
– States: ready
– Operations: setOccupied?() (beyond the system boundary), getOccupied?()

Comment: Most objects modeled in the home heating system "push" their data around. The sensors are an exception: They reply to requests for their sensed data; their data are "pulled" from them. An object that "pushes" is engaged in a one-way, producer-consumer interaction; a "pulling" object is part of a client-server, two-way interaction.

RoomTemperatureSensor
– Purpose: Obviously, this entity measures the current room temperature.
– Attributes/components: currentTemperature
– States: ready
– Operations: setCurrentTemperature() (beyond the system boundary), getCurrentTemperature()

Comment: When an object has only one state, this state is usually given the name "ready", as we have done previously.

DesiredTemperatureInputDevice
– Purpose: This device is used by an occupant to register the desired room temperature when the room is occupied.
– Attributes/components: desiredTemperature
– States: ready
– Operations: setDesiredTemperature(), getDesiredTemperature()

WaterValve
– Purpose: This valve controls the flow of hot water in a room's radiator.
– Attributes/components: *None*
– States: opened, closed
– Operations: turnOpen(), turnClose()

FurnaceController
– Purpose: This entity is an intermediary between, on the one hand, the heat flow regulator and the system controller, and on the other hand, the furnace.

The furnace controller works similarly to the system controller in that it acts
like an and-gate.
– Attributes/components: *None*
– States: disabled&noHeatNeeded, enabled&noHeatNeeded, disabled&needs-
Heat, enabled&needsHeat
– Operations: enable(), disable(), startup(), shutdown()

Furnace
– Purpose: This entity manages all the components of the furnace.
– Attributes/components: theBlowerMotor, theOilValve, theIgniter, theWa-
terTemperatureSensor, lastShutDownTime
– States: furnaceOff, waitToFireUp, waitForBlowerMotor, oilValveOpened, wait-
ForHotWater, furnaceOn, oilValveClosed
– Operations: startup(), shutdown()

Comment: Again, all the attributes prefixed with "the" have components as
attribute values.

BlowerMotor
– Purpose: This entity controls the blower motor, which blows air in the (phys-
ical) furnace.
– Attributes/components: theRPM
– States: on, off
– Operations: turnOn(), turnOff(), getRPM()

OilValve
– Purpose: This entity controls the flow of oil in the furnace.
– Attributes/components: *None*
– States: opened, closed
– Operations: turnOpen(), turnClose()

Igniter
– Purpose: This entity ignites the oil in the furnace.
– Attributes/components: *None*
– States: ready
– Operations: ignite()

WaterTemperatureSensor
– Purpose: This entity measures the temperature in the boiler.
– Attributes/components: currentTemperature

– States: ready

– Operations: setCurrentTemperature() (beyond the system boundary), setCurrentTemperature()

Comment: One has to agree that the previous objects are "boring" from the perspective of the home heating system. At the same time, they provide the requirements for these components at *their* abstraction level.

FurnaceMonitor

– Purpose: This entity checks the furnace after it has been ignited.

– Attributes/components: theFuelFlowSensor, theOpticalCombustionSensor, oilFlow?, combustion?

– States: off, on, check

– Operations: enable(), disable(), tic(dateTime)

FuelFlowSensor

– Purpose: This sensor checks whether oil flows in the furnace.

– Attributes/components: fuelFlow?

– States: ready

– Operations: setFuelFlow?() (beyond the system boundary), getFuelFlow?()

OpticalCombustionSensor

– Purpose: This sensor checks whether the oil is burning.

– Attributes/components: combustion?

– States: ready

– Operations: setCombustion?() (beyond the system boundary), getCombustion?()

OccupancyHistory

– Purpose: This entity keeps track of the occupancy history of a room during the preceding week. Hence it is possible to ask for the occupancy status a week earlier and check whether a current occupancy corresponds with the one a week before.

– Attributes/components: history

– States: ready

– Operations: setOccupancyRecord(dateTime, occupancy), getOccupancyRecord(dateTime)

LivingPattern

– Purpose: This object records the living pattern of a room. A current occu-

pancy that is equal to the occupancy a week earlier will set the living pattern, which may or may not entail a change of the living pattern.
– Attributes/components: pattern
– States: ready
– Operations: setPattern(dateTime, occupancy), occupationExpected?(dateTime, period)

Comment: The occupationExpected? operation can be used to check whether occupation is expected within 30 minutes of the current time (which is to be determined when the room is not currently occupied).

5.6.1 Metrics

Developing this vocabulary took about 7 hours (420 minutes). Unfortunately, the amount of time per vocabulary entry was not tracked.

As an artifact metric for a vocabulary entry VE we will use

$$\mu_{vocabulary}(VE) = \text{\# attributes in } VE + \text{\# states in } VE + \text{\# operations in } VE.$$

According to this definition, we obtain:
$\mu_{vocabulary}(HeatSwitch) = 5$
$\mu_{vocabulary}(FaultResetSwitch/Indicator) = 5$
$\mu_{vocabulary}(FurnaceStatusIndicator) = 5$
$\mu_{vocabulary}(HeatFlowRegulator) = 5$
$\mu_{vocabulary}(SystemController) = 8$
$\mu_{vocabulary}(Clock) = 5$
$\mu_{vocabulary}(Room) = 14$
$\mu_{vocabulary}(OccupancySensor) = 4$
$\mu_{vocabulary}(RoomTemperatureSensor) = 4$
$\mu_{vocabulary}(DesiredTemperatureInputDevice) = 4$
$\mu_{vocabulary}(WaterValve) = 4$
$\mu_{vocabulary}(FurnaceController) = 8$
$\mu_{vocabulary}(Furnace) = 14$
$\mu_{vocabulary}(BlowerMotor) = 6$
$\mu_{vocabulary}(OilValve) = 4$
$\mu_{vocabulary}(Igniter) = 2$
$\mu_{vocabulary}(WaterTemperatureSensor) = 4$
$\mu_{vocabulary}(FurnaceMonitor) = 10$

$\mu_{vocabulary}(FuelFlowSensor) = 4$
$\mu_{vocabulary}(OpticalCombustionSensor) = 4$
$\mu_{vocabulary}(OccupancyHistory) = 4$
$\mu_{vocabulary}(LivingPattern) = 4$

It is interesting to see how the metrics are distributed:

- Total number of artifacts in the vocabulary (thus far): 22

- The minimum metric value: 2

- The maximum metric value: 14

- The median value of the metric: 4.5

- The average value of the metric: 5.8

A histogram that shows the distribution is shown in Figure 5.1.

The skewedness of the distribution is typical. There are many items that are small, 16, a few in the middle, 3, and a few that are large, 3. Although these data are certainly preliminary, we obtain already a good feeling for where to focus most of the attention: the artifacts that score highest on the metric: the room and the furnace, both with metric value 14, and the furnace monitor, with score 10. In case this project would be tackled by a team, we already have an inclination of what to assign to the most capable members of the team.

5.6.2   Notes

The vocabulary as described above has more entries than given in the list of entities developed earlier. As mentioned earlier, the clock was simply forgotten. The two other entries, the occupancy history and the living pattern, were added due to "promotion": They showed up as significant components in the room's vocabulary entry. Hence these two entities were initially not given enough attention.

Noteworthy is that all entries in the vocabulary represent entities; i.e., no relationships have been identified beyond certain entities being components of other subsystem entities. Acquaintanceships - called use relationships by Booch [13] - will show up when we construct class-relationship diagrams.

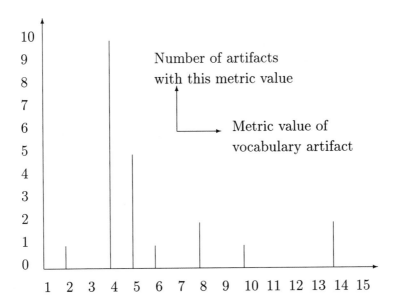

Figure 5.1: This histogram shows the number of vocabulary artifacts as a function of the vocabulary metric. This metric is defined as the sum of the number of attributes/components, the number of states, and the number of operations. The median value of the metric is 4.5, while the average value is 5.8.

5.7 Inheritance Diagram

There is virtually no benefit of exploiting inheritance in this example. Although we could introduce a class *Valve* that abstracts *WaterValve* and *OilValve*, there is no real gain: We don't have a significant discriminator between an oil valve and a water valve. Hence one tactic would be to eliminate the distinction between water valve and oil valve and simply equip the model with valves. An argument in favor of this tactic is that we do not model fluid flows, heat flows, etc. On the other hand, when our model needs to be extended and we want to describe the details of its "mechanics", it is recommended that the different valves be already in place.

The same line of reasoning applies to the various sensors in the system. We could introduce a class *Sensor* but we don't have discriminators to separate: *OccupancySensor*, *RoomTemperatureSensor*, *WaterTemperatureSensor*, *FuelFlowSensor*, and *OpticalCombustionSensor*.

The situation changes when we build a (partial) simulator for the Home Heating System. Then its helps to introduce in the design an abstract class *Sensor* and have subclasses that adjust certain parameters; see the Example chapter in the Design part.

5.8   Subsystem Diagram

A subsystem diagram can be obtained from the description of subsystems in Section 5.4, see Figure 5.2. The emphasis in this diagram is on static, component-of relationships.

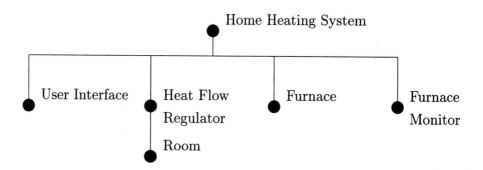

Figure 5.2: High level view of the home heating system and its subsystems. The links can be read as component-of relationships. Notice that the vocabulary does *not* have an entry for the Home Heating System. Such an entry is useful when we model this system as part of a larger system. The vocabulary also does not contain an entry for the User Interface. This node represents the heat switch, the fault reset switch/indicator, and the furnace status indicator. The User Interface is a just a grouping of these three classes; there is no need to introduce this class explicitly.

5.8.1   Metrics

The construction of this diagram took about 15 minutes.

As an artifact metric we use the node counting version of the metric formulated in Section 4.2.2:

$$\mu_{subsystems}(graph) = \#\_nodes(graph).$$

This yields: $\mu_{subsystems}(graph) = 6.$

5.8.2   Notes

The subsystem diagram is a graphical representation of textual descriptions of subsystems given in Section 5.4. This depiction can raise questions that did not arise from the textual representation.[7] Have we captured all subsystems? Are the subsystems depicted at the correct abstraction level? Is this an effective and orthogonal decomposition? Is this an intuitive decomposition?

It pays to think hard at this stage. Rearrangements after many lines of codes have been constructed can no longer be afforded.

5.9   Class-Relationship Diagram

Although we have thus far not identified relationships, we do have an inkling which objects need to communicate. A top-level diagram is given in Figure 5.3. This

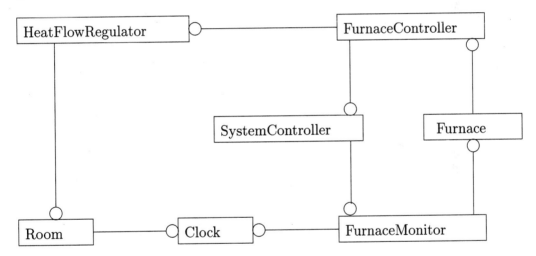

Figure 5.3: Acquaintance relationships between the major classes of the home heating systems. Notice that this diagram contains the "need to know" cycle: *FurnaceController, Furnace, FurnaceMonitor, SystemController, FurnaceController.* Such a cycle, of in our case actual instances, has ramifications for an implementation in C++. The linearity of the code and the prohibition in C++ on forward references dictate that at least one instance in this cycle cannot be initialized completely when it is introduced. Hence this diagram has "deep" ramifications for an automatic C++ code generator.

---

[7]The reverse can happen also. One starts with a pictorial sketch. Its detailed elaboration in textual form will raise issues that were "hiding" in the pictorial format.

diagram depicts the main "players" in the system. The top level nature of this diagram shows that all except one of its classes have only unique instances. Most of these objects have already been identified as subsystems.

The clock object has a remarkable feature. No other object – at this top-level – initiates a communication with it. A class that no other class needs to talk to is suspicious, unless its instances are the drivers of the system. In this preliminary stage, we cannot jump to that conclusion, but it is a good conjecture, to be carried forward into the design phase, that the clock is the key "engine" of the system.

We proceed with lower-level diagrams. Figure 5.4 depicts how user interface elements are connected with the system controller. This diagram shows how a user affects the home heating system through the system controller. This diagram is possibly incomplete. One would expect an arc coming into the fault reset switch/indicator that would explain how the indicator is impacted. It turns out – as we will see below – that the furnace monitor will provide this missing link.

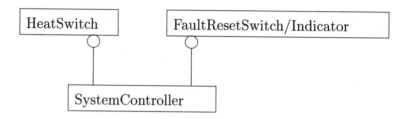

Figure 5.4: How an occupant affects the home heating system through the system controller. See the text for a discussion of how the indicator is impacted.

The relationships of the room subsystem are depicted in Figure 5.5. As we mentioned before, the room "pulls" data from its sensors. This explains the directionality of the links between the sensors and the room. A similar setup applies to the device used by an occupant to set the desired temperature. Although the customer can set this device at any time, it is at the discretion of the room to pull out the desired value. The directionality of the other links is uncontroversial.

The relationships of the furnace subsystem aredepicted in Figure 5.6. The communication with the water temperature sensor is again of the "pulling" type. The furnace interacts with the blower motor in two ways: It turns the motor on and off, and it checks after turning the motor on whether it has reached a predefined RPM value.[8] Hence the acquaintance link to the blower motor facilitates two different com-

---

[8]The requirements do *not* specify a time-out operation when the RPM level is not reached within a predefined period.

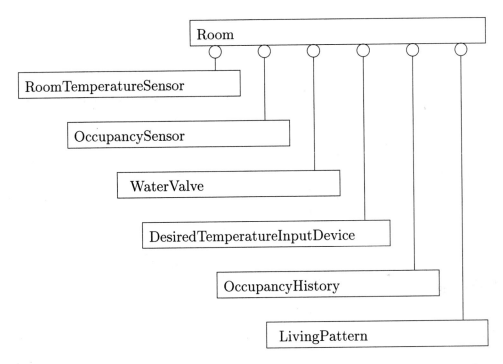

Figure 5.5: How the room communicates with its components. As discussed in the text, the initiative for communication is with the room for all of them.

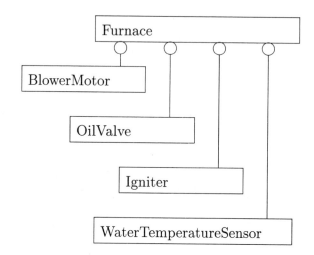

Figure 5.6: Communication relationships of the furnace subsystem.

munications. In an alternative setup, we have a link from the blower motor to the furnace. This link would support a communication initiated by the blower motor to report that it has reached the required RPM value. During the analysis phase it is not clear which way of formulating the interaction will be closer to the design and subsequent realization. Thus for now we stick with the setup depicted.

The relationships of the furnace monitor subsystem are depicted in Figure 5.7. We observed above that the fault reset switch/indicator impacts something - the system controller - but that it is not influenced by any other object, which is not as expected. As we will see below, the furnace monitor is the object that impacts the fault reset switch. Hence we expect it to occur in Figure 5.7. However, when this Figure was first constructed, this connection had not yet been identified.

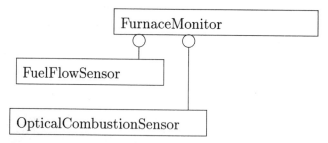

Figure 5.7: As discussed, this diagram must be extended with a communication supporting link to the class FaultResetSwitch/Indicator.

5.9.1 Metrics

Although we gave multiple figures above, they show fragments of a single class-relationship diagram. Construction of the top-level diagram and the other fragments took about 2 hours. The metric for this diagram was defined in Chapter 4 as:

$$\mu_{classRelationships} = \#classNodes + \sum_{r \epsilon relationship} arity(r)$$

All our relationships are binary. Hence our metric formula simplifies to

$$\mu_{classRelationships} = \#classNodes + 2 * \#relationships$$

Since we have 21 class nodes and 22 acquaintance relationships, we obtain:

$$\mu_{classRelationships} = 21 + 2 * 22 = 65.$$

5.9.2 Notes

Is it strange that we don't have regular relationships? It is certainly conceivable to use a part-of relationship instead of our "use" relationships. For example, one may feel that the oil valve is part-of the furnace, and similarly for the other classes in Figure 5.6. The same sentiment can be applied to the links in Figure 5.5, with the room containing the water valve, the sensors, etc. Either way is okay in this situation.[9]

5.10 Class

We now have all the prerequisites in place for expanding the description of classes. For each class, we provide a summary view consisting of the name of class attributes and the name of class operations. An example of a summary view is shown on the left-hand side of Figure 5.8. A box represents a class, with the class name at top. Below the class name there is an enumeration of the attributes, omitting their value

---

[9]Booch [13] has as notation for the aggregation relationship a variant of our acquaintance link: The circle is filled in as follows:

domains, and an enumeration of operations, where an operation corresponds with one or more transitions. Subsequently, we elaborate attribute descriptions by providing attribute value domains and multiplicity descriptions where applicable. The dynamic dimension is elaborated with (a) transition network(s).

5.10.1   UI classes

It turns out that the *HeatSwitch, the FaultResetSwitch/Indicator*, and the *FurnaceStatusIndicator* have similar structure and behavior. Hence we can introduce, for now, an abstract class, called, say, *Switch/Indicator*, that captures the common structure and behavior. The summary view is given in Figure 5.8.

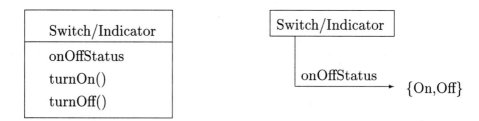

Figure 5.8: Left: the summary view of the abstract class *Switch/Indicator*; right: description of the static structure of the class. The attribute *onOffStatus* gives the instances of *Switch/Indicator* a little "self awareness" – provided, of course, that its value is properly maintained. Hence we could add, if necessary, a report operation called *onOffStatus?()* that accesses the attribute *onOffStatus*.

Switch/Indicator static

The description of the static structure of *Switch/Indicator* is given also in Figure 5.8. The value domain of the attribute *onOffStatus* is represented as a nonclass, the set containing two enumerated values *on* and *off*.

It turns out that the dynamics differ for the classes *HeatSwitch, FaultResetSwitch/Indicator*, and *FurnaceStatusIndicator*. Hence we can profitably use inheritance from the class *Switch/Indicator* to factor out the static common structure and describe the unique dynamics for each subclass.

HeatSwitch dynamic

The transition network for the *HeatSwitch* is shown in Figure 5.9. We have depicted a global view of the network showing the states *off* and *on* together with the turn-on and turn-off transitions. The details of these transitions are shown as well. The transition coming from "nowhere" that leads into the *off* states indicates that a heat switch object enters the *off* state when it is created. Initialization activities can be associated with the initialization arc. For example, the attribute *onOffStatus* must be initialized with the value *off*.

The *turnOn* transition describes that the heat switch can accept a *turnOn* event when it is in the *on* state. The transition has as action the assignment of a new value to the attribute *onOffStatus* (note the " ' " in the action box). In addition, this transition will generate the event *hsOn()* targeted at a *systemController*.[10]

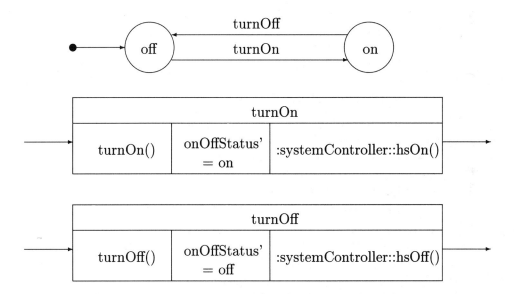

Figure 5.9: Single transition diagram of the heat switch. The top is the summary view with the states *off* and *on* and the two turn on/off transitions. See the text for the transition that enters the *off* state from the left. The details of the two transitions are depicted as well.

---

[10]Recall that a heat switch "knows about" a system controller as a result of an acquaintance link between the two corresponding classes, see page 150.

FaultResetSwitch/Indicator dynamic

The transition network of the *FaultResetSwitch/Indicator* is only slightly different from the transition network of the *HeatSwitch*, see Figure 5.10. The difference resides in the different events that are generated and targeted at the system controller.

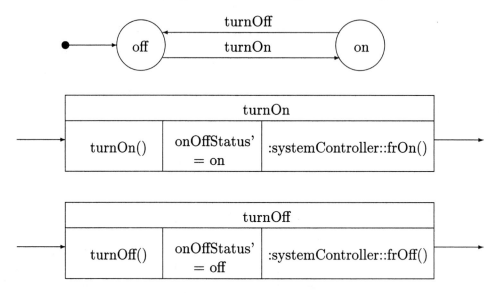

Figure 5.10: Transition network for the *FaultResetSwitch/Indicator*, which is nearly identical to the transition network for the *HeatSwitch*. Only the generated events are different.

FurnaceStatusIndicator dynamic

The summary transition network of the *FurnaceStatusIndicator* is very simple. It consists of the *off* and *on* states and the *turnOn* and *turnOff* transitions as in Figure 5.10. The expansion of the transitions is, of course, different, but is of no interest here. The controlled indicator light is outside the system boundary.

5.10.2   Heat-Flow Regulator

The summary view of the *HeatFlowRegulator* is shown in Figure 5.11. The name of the attribute *roomsThatNeedHeat* indicates that this attribute is multivalued. The summary view does not express how multiple values are handled. The two operations will clearly be used to manipulate the *roomsThatNeedHeat* attribute.

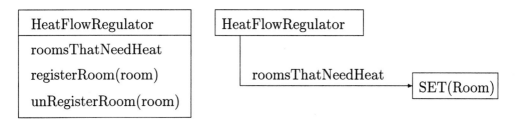

Figure 5.11: Left: summary view of the Heat-Flow Regulator class; right: expands the static dimension. The attribute *roomsThatNeedHeat* is multivalued. A set is employed as a container.

Heat-Flow Regulator static

The static structure of the *HeatFlowRegulator* is also shown in Figure 5.11. The multivalued attribute *roomsThatNeedHeat* is elaborated by using a set as a container for room instances.

Heat-Flow Regulator dynamic

The dynamic structure of the *HeatFlowRegulator* is depicted in Figure 5.12. The figure contains the following abbreviations:

nRNH = noRoomNeedsHeat
aRNH = aRoomNeedsHeat
rR = registerRoom
uRR = unRegisterRoom
rTNH = roomsThatNeedHeat
vC = valveControl
aR = addRoom
dR = deleteRoom
fC = furnaceController

Registering a room is possible in both states. The effect of a registration is, however, drastically different. When the *HeatFlowRegulator* is in the state that no other room had registered a request for heat, it leads to a request to start up the furnace targeted at the *furnaceController*. Whether the furnace is to be started up indeed depends on whether the furnace is enabled and will be decided by the *furnaceController*.

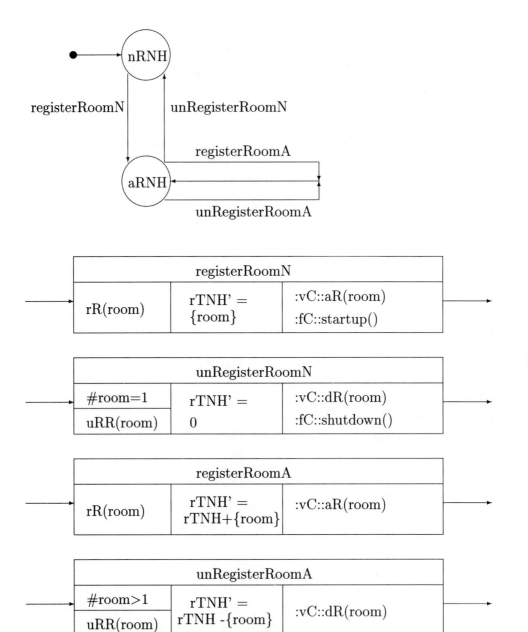

Figure 5.12: Dynamics of the heat-flow regulator. See the text for an explanation of the abbreviations used.

A room registering a request for heat need not imply that its water valve can be opened right away. There are two reason why the valve need not be opened:

1. The furnace is not on yet and it will take awhile before the water in the boiler has reached the proper temperature.

2. The furnace will not go on at all because it is not enabled, which can have diverse reasons.

As a result, the management of the room water valves has been delegated to a new entity: *valveControl*. Hence one needs to backtrack and add an entry to the vocabulary. We will assume here that this addition has been completed.

Deregistering a room leads to two different cases:

1. There is still another room that needs heat.

2. It was the only room that was registered.

As a result, the *unRegisterRoom* operation in the state *aRoomNeedsHeat* must be qualified to distinguish the two cases. The corresponding transitions have been extended with a test that checks whether or not the number of rooms registered is greater than 1. Obviously, a design can realize this test by counting the members in the set referred to by the attribute *roomsThatNeedHeat*.

5.10.3 System Controller

The summary view of the *SystemController* is shown in Figure 5.13. It is of interest that this class does not have an attribute but only operations. We can add an attribute that keeps track of the state of a system controller, but since no other object depends on this state information, we refrain from introducing it. However, one should recognize that such an attribute can be beneficial for testing.

System Controller static

As mentioned above, the System Controller class has no attributes.

System Controller dynamic

The transition network of the *SystemController* is shown in Figure 5.14. The *SystemController* behaves like an *and*-gate that integrates two inputs: the status of the

SystemController
hsOff()
hsOn()
frOn()
frOff()

Figure 5.13: Summary view of the *SystemController*. The absence of attributes is noteworthy.

heat switch and the status of the fault reset switch/indicator. The four states of the system controller correspond with the combination of states of these two inputs. For example, the state *hf&ff* represents the state of affairs where the heat switch and the fault reset switch/indicator are both *off*. Similarly, the state *hn&fn* corresponds with both of these user-interface devices being in the *on* state. The two other states represent the two remaining combinations.

We have expanded in Figure 5.14 only the transitions that reach or leave the state *hn&fn*. These transitions cause the generation of events targeted at the furnace controller, which ultimately makes the decision to activate or to deactivate the furnace.

The transitions that have not been expanded consist only of the consumption of their triggering event and cause the appropriate transition. For example, when the system controller is in the state *hf&ff*, the event *frOn()* - which is produced when an occupant flips the fault reset switch into the on state - will cause a transition of the system controller into the state *hf&fn*.

5.10.4   Clock

The summary view of the *Clock* is shown in Figure 5.15. This conception of a clock is inspired more by generic features of a clock than driven by the home heating system application. And, of course, a clock is an item that has widespread applicability.

The clock sits on the system boundary. It provides services to entities inside the system, but at the same time it is driven by a "real" clock outside the system boundary. The operation *ticToc()* straddles the system boundary. It is invoked by the "real" clock, but we can attach effects that impact the entities inside the system.

Entities affected by the clock can be of any type. Hence we have given the operations *addClient* and *deleteClient* the signature *Thing* which stands for any entity

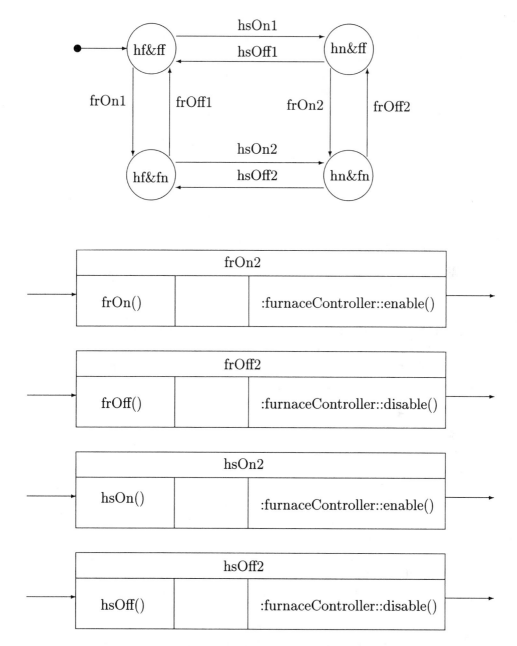

Figure 5.14: Dynamics of the *SystemController*. The transitions *hsOn1*, *hsOff1*, *frOn1*, and *frOff1* have not been expanded. See the text for their description.

whatsoever.[11]

A timer for a particular purpose can be defined easily using this clock. The timer registers itself with a clock, and as a result it will be notified of each *tic*. It is up to a timer to decide what to do with a *tic*. A count-down mechanism is an obvious choice. Expiration of a timer can induce any desired action.

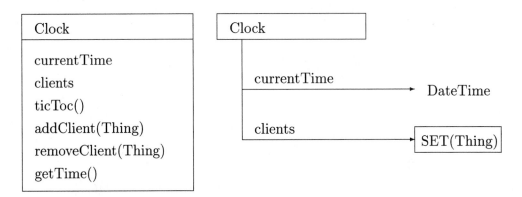

Figure 5.15: Left: summary view of a *Clock*. The clock straddles the system boundary. The operation *ticToc()* is activated periodically by a "real" clock outside the system boundary. All clients of a clock are notified of a tic. A clock can also respond to a *getTime()* request. Right: static view.

Clock static

The static structure of a *Clock* is also shown in Figure 5.15. The time is kept internally in the attribute *currentTime*, whose value is represented as a nonobject of type *DateTime*. The clients of the clock, if any, are maintained in a set container. The elements of the container are of the type *Thing*. The class *Thing* should support a transition that support *tic* events. As a result, we have a generic clock that is decoupled from its actual clients in this application: rooms, furnace, and furnace monitor.

---

[11]Giving a clock the ability to communicate with any *Thing* does not quite work. Clients of a clock should agree minimally what events they expect from a clock. As shown in the dynamic diagram, they should support a transition that handles *tic* events. The design takes care of this detail. Note that the class *Thing* is renamed in the implementation into *ClockClient*.

Clock dynamic

The transition network of a *Clock* is shown in Figure 5.16. The *ticToc* transition is triggered by a *ticToc* event generated by an external clock. The action part describes that the *currentTime* attribute is incremented. As a side effect, events are created for all clients of a *Clock* as described by *BR(tic(dateTime), clients)*: That is, a broadcast is produced of a *tic* event targeted at all objects referred to by the attribute *clients*.

The *getTime* transition is an example of server transition that is activated as part of a client-server interaction. The *addClient* and *removeClient* transition entail only a local action. In case we want an instigator of these actions to block until these actions are completed, we can add a *Reply()* response.

5.10.5 Room

The overview picture of the *Room* is shown in Figure 5.17.

The value of the attribute *needsHeat?* is to be determined at every *tic* event of the clock. It summarizes the decision procedure, which takes into account the current temperature, the desired temperature, the working temperature, the (expected) occupancy, and due to hysteresis, the previously determined *needsHeat?* value; see below for the details of this procedure.

The attribute *registeredHeatRequest?* gives a room self-knowledge as to whether or not it has registered itself with the *HeatFlowRegulator*.

The remaining attributes represent the objects that are components of the room subsystem.

A careful reader may have observed already that there is a mismatch between the producer *Clock* and the client *Room*. A clock expects its clients to be of type *Thing*, while a room is just of type *Room*. There are several ways to resolve this mismatch. An easy way is to change the description of the clock: Make the clients of the clock be of type *Room*. This fix will not work because the clock also has clients of another type. Another solution is to make the class *Room* into a subclass of *Thing*. As a variant we can argue that the class *Thing* is too general and that it is better to replace it with a "mix-in" class named "ClockClient". As a result the class *Room* would be made a subclass of *ClockClient*. Another approach is to change the class *Clock* into a parametrized class *Clock(ClockClients)* and provide a specific class: *Clock(HHS-ClockClients)*, where the class *HHS-ClockClients* is a mixin class for the class *Room* and for other clients of the clock.

To avoid disrupting the flow of the presentation, we postpone the repair of this error. In a real-life project, we would backtrack.

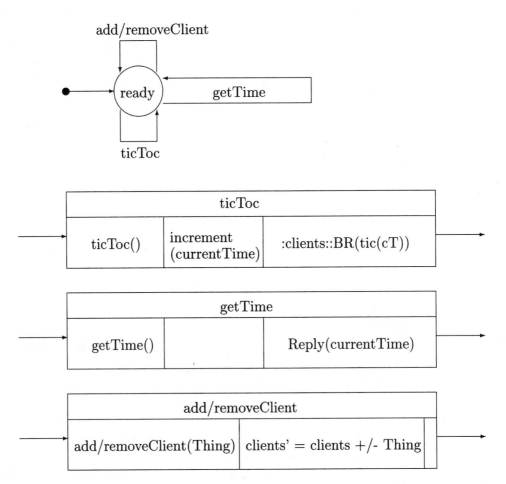

Figure 5.16: The clock has a single state, *ready*. The transition *ticToc* is triggered as a result of an event generated by a "real" clock and causes a broadcast to its clients through *:clients::BR(tic(currentTime))*. Notice the abbreviation *cT* in the figure, which stands for *currentTime*. The *getTime* transition responds to a service request and produces a reply response. The two transitions *addClient* and *removeClient* have been combined in the figure since they have a lot in common: only their action parts differ.

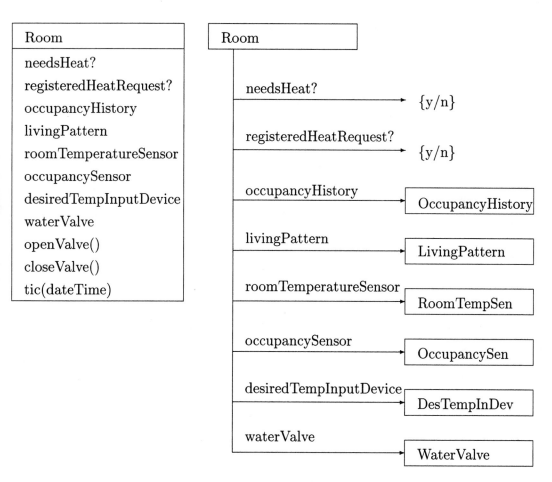

Figure 5.17: Left: static description. Most of the attributes refer to components of the room subsystem. Right: the details of the value domains.

Room static

The right-hand side of Figure 5.17 shows the static structure of instances of the class *Room*. The top two attributes have Boolean values. The other attributes represent components of the room subsystem.

Room dynamic

Figure 5.18 is a summary view of a room's transition network. The rounded boxes are states (earlier represented as circles). The diagram has three (!) states:

1. *Wait for clock tic*

2. *Decide whether to change heat request*

3. An unnamed global state that contains the two other states

With this setup, we can express succinctly that the transitions *OpenValve* and *CloseValve* apply to the state *wait for clock tic* as well as to the state *decide whether to change heat request*.

The transitions given in Figure 5.18 are elaborated on in Figure 5.19, which uses the following abbreviations:

NH? = *needsHeat?*
RHR? = *registeredHeatRequest?*

The guards of the three transitions that emanate from the state *Decide Whether To Change Heat Request* all depend only on a condition (in contrast to the other transitions that depend on events). These three transitions illustrate the guard exclusion property and the guard covering property. We can prove that at most one guard can be satisfied and we can prove that at least one guard is satisfied.

Self-knowledge about registration is maintained correctly in the *register* and *unregister* transitions.

The transitions *openValve* and *closeValve* are good examples of transducers. Their purpose is to shield the sender of *openValve()* and *closeValve()* events from the components of the room subsystem. Such a transducer can, in general, do some filtering, checking for appropriateness, and/or do exception interpretation.

The *tic* transition has a fairly complex action section for which we provide more details here:

```
currentOccupancy' = :occupancySensor::getOccupied?();
```

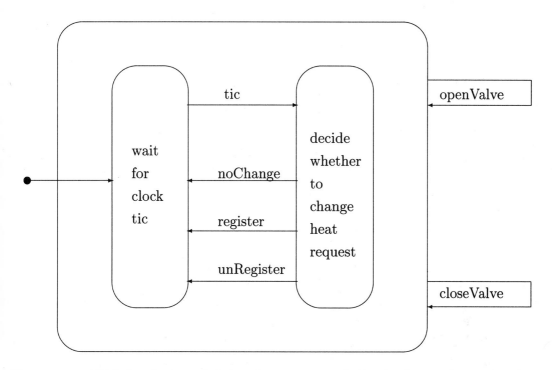

Figure 5.18: High-level view of the transition network for the *Room* class. The three rounded boxes represent states (previously represented as circles). The large box represents the "sum" of the two enclosed states. This allows to express that the transition *OpenValve* and *CloseValve* applies to both of the enclosed states.

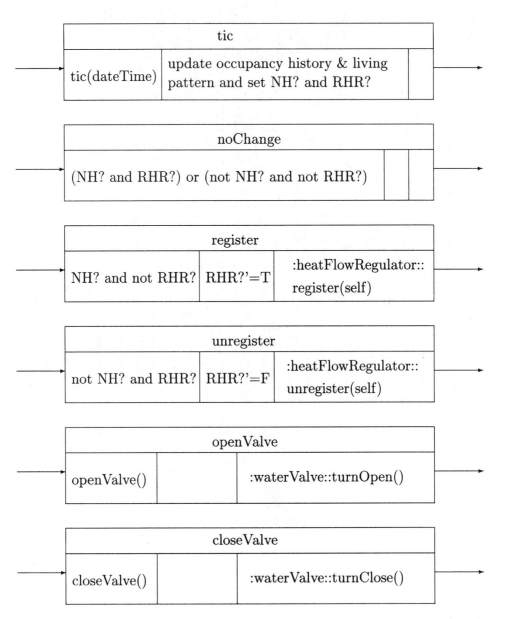

Figure 5.19: Elaborated transitions for a room. See the text for an explanation of the abbreviations used.

```
:occupancyHistory::setOccupancy(dateTime, currentOccupancy);
previousOccupancy' = :occupancyHistory::getOccupancy(dateTime -
                                                        1 week);

if (currentOccupancy == previousOccupancy)
then :livingPattern::setPattern(dateTime, currentOccupancy);
-- occupied? indicates whether the room is currently occupied or is
-- expected to be occupied within 30 minutes
occupied?' = currentOccupancy OR
             :livingPattern::getPattern(dateTime, 30 minutes);
td' = :desiredTempInputDevice::getDesiredTemperature();
if (occupied?) then tw' = td else tw' = td - 5;
temp' = :roomTemperatureSensor::getCurrentTemperature();
if temp <= tw - 2 then needsHeat' = y else
if temp >= tw + 2 then needsHeat' = n else
needsHeat' = needsHeat;
```

Notes:

1. The operation *:livingPattern::getPattern(dateTime, 30 minutes)* checks whether the room is currently occupied or whether it is expected that the room will be occupied within 30 minutes.

2. Determining whether the room needs heat is surprisingly subtle. Hysteresis is employed, through the temperature bands, to prevent the furnace from going on and off too rapidly.

The reader may argue that the elaboration provided for the *tic* transition action description has a design flavor. We disagree: We have only detailed and rewritten what was formulated less formally in the requirements. A pseudo code formalism is required due to the nature of the subject matter: determining whether a room needs heat or not as a function of the sensors, the user input device, and the occupancy history.

5.10.6 Occupancy Sensor

Figure 5.20 gives an overview diagram of the *OccupancySensor*. The operation *setOccupied?(value)* straddles the system boundary. The "real" occupancy sensor invokes this operation continuously to set the value of the *occupied?* attribute.

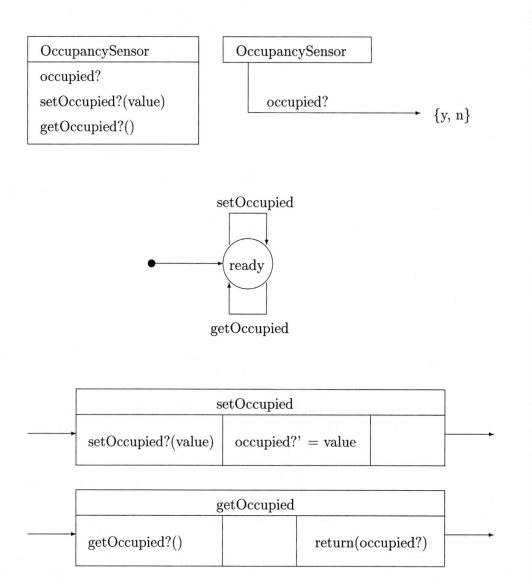

Figure 5.20: Top left: the summary view of the occupancy sensor; top right: static view; middle: summary view of the behavior; and the bottom: elaborated transitions. The *setOccupied* transition is invoked by a send-and-forget event. The *getOccupied* transition is invoked by a service request.

Occupancy Sensor static

See Figure 5.20 for the unsurprising static description of the *OccupancySensor*.

Occupancy Sensor dynamic

Figure 5.20 also shows the dynamics of the *OccupancySensor*. The transition *setOccupied* is event driven; the transition *getOccupied* is a service transition, activated by its room client.

RoomTemperatureSensor
currentTemperature
setCurrentTemperature(value)
getCurrentTemperature()

DesiredTempInputDevice
desiredTemperature
setDesiredTemperature(value)
getDesiredTemperature()

Figure 5.21: Summary diagrams for the room temperature sensor and the desired temperature input device. Their structure is similar to the structure of the occupancy sensor, and hence we do not expand them into static and dynamic diagrams.

5.10.7 Two other classes of the room subsystem

Figure 5.21 shows overview diagrams of the room temperature sensor and the desired temperature input device. Their structures are similar to the structure of the occupancy sensor. Consequently, we do not bother to provide more details of their static and dynamic descriptions. The only noteworthy difference is that while the occupancy sensor deals with boolean values, the objects we describe here deal with numeric values.

5.10.8 Water Valve

All diagrams for the *WaterValve* are shown in Figure 5.22. There is no need to give a water valve knowledge of its status, and thus it has no attributes. Hence we omitted a static diagram. The water valve also straddles the system boundary. The action parts of the transition refer to activations of the physical valve. Both transitions are triggered by send-and-forget events.

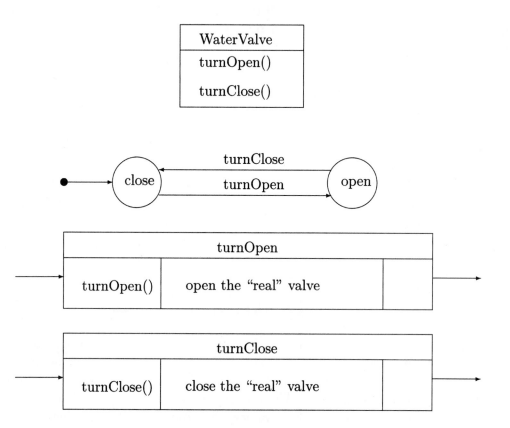

Figure 5.22: Summary diagram and dynamic diagrams for the water valve. There is no static diagram since there are no attributes.

5.10.9 Furnace Controller

The summary diagram for the *FurnaceController* is shown in Figure 5.23. The furnace controller has the same structure as the system controller. Neither has "normal" attributes and they also do not need an attribute representing self-knowledge about the internal state.

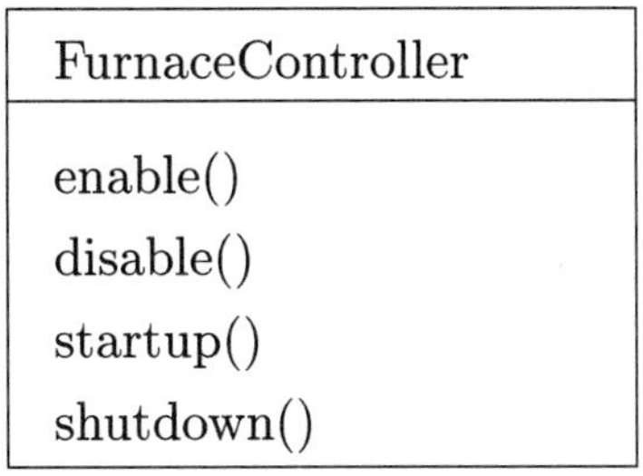

FurnaceController
enable()
disable()
startup()
shutdown()

Figure 5.23: Summary diagram of the furnace controller. Note that there are no attributes, as is the case for the system controller.

Furnace Controller dynamic

Figure 5.24 shows the furnace controller's transition network and elaborations of the transitions. The names of the states have been abbreviated in the figure. They expand as follows:

$d\&nN$ = disabled and no heat needed
$d\&N$ = disabled and needs heat
$e\&nN$ = enabled but no heat needed
$e\&N$ = enabled and needs heat

The similarity with the dynamics of the system controller should be obvious. While the transition network of the system controller is the *and*-gate for the user interface switches, the furnace controller network is the *and*-gate for the system controller and the heat flow regulator.

Only half of the transitions have been expanded in Figure 5.24, as we did for the system controller. The others can be derived easily. For example, the transition *startup1* is obtained from the transition *startup2* by elimination of the event *:furnace::startup()*.

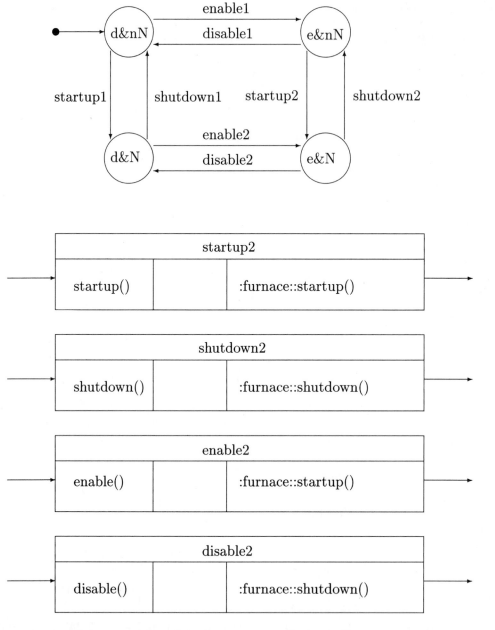

Figure 5.24: Transition network of the furnace controller. Only half of the transitions are expanded. See the text for a description of the expansions of the other transitions and for an explanation of the abbreviated state names.

5.10.10 Furnace

A summary view of the furnace is shown in Figure 5.25. Most attributes refer to other objects that the furnace has to communicate with in order to get its job done. We have here a good example of an ensemble. A furnace object acts as a coordinator for its constituents.

It may come as a surprise that the furnace shown has attributes such as *valveControl* and *furnaceMonitor*. One can argue that these attributes do not belong to a generic furnace but that these features are specific for the furnace as part of the home heating system. Hence one can advocate the introduction of a generic furnace that has a minimal set of features, say *blowerMotor, oilValve, igniter*, and that our furnace is obtained through inheritance from such a generic furnace. This tactic is warranted indeed when one foresees more usage of such a generic, stripped-down version.

Furnace static

The attribute *lastShutDownTime* is used to keep track of the last time there was a shut down to avoid a restart within 5 minutes.

A newcomer in the list of attributes is the class *ValveControl*. An instance of this class mediates between the furnace and the rooms regarding opening and closing of valves. The heat regulator keeps the valve controller up-to-date regarding the rooms that need heat. The furnace informs the valve controller whether it is able to deliver hot water. Hence the valve controller has all the information required to decide when the room water valves are to be opened and closed, and it will instruct the rooms accordingly (which will pass on these instructions to their water valves).

The clock attribute has been added because it seems prudent to have a clock around given that the furnace behavior has temporal components as indicated by:
- "the minimum time for furnace restart after prior operation is five minutes";
- "... when it reaches a predetermined RPM value ...";
- "... after five seconds, stops the blower motor".

Whether access to a clock is sufficient to handle these requirements is not clear at this point. We will reconsider the situation after describing the dynamic model of the furnace.

Furnace dynamic

The summary diagram of the furnace's transition diagram is shown in Figure 5.26. We make use of a macro state to express that the transition *shutdown* applies to all the states that are enclosed in the macro state. For example, at any time while the

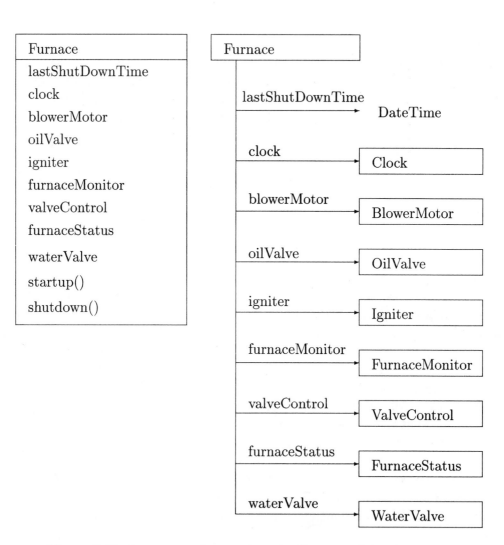

Figure 5.25: Summary view and static diagram of the furnace.

furnace is in the macro state, the user can turn off the system and thereby force a shutdown. Another possibility is that a user turns down the desired temperature of the only room that needs heat and thereby causes a shutdown.

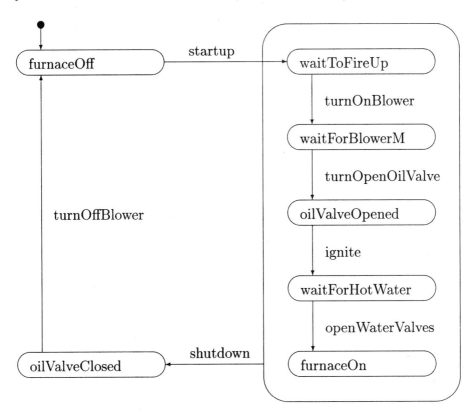

Figure 5.26: Summary diagram of the furnace's transition network. The *shutdown* transition applies to all the states enclosed in the unnamed macro state.

The expansions of the transitions are depicted in Figure 5.27. The attribute *lastShutDownTime* has been abbreviated in this figure as *lSDT*. The entity *waitPeriod* has been introduced as an attribute that has only local significance. It is used to delay, if necessary, firing up the furnace.

Some of the guards are high level in the sense that they do not refer to actual attributes and/or events produced by other objects. The first one is the guard "Wait Period Expired". We have taken for granted that when we know the delay period, it is easy to construct a wait mechanism that allows us to replace the "Wait Period Expired" description. For example, we can register the furnace as a client of the clock

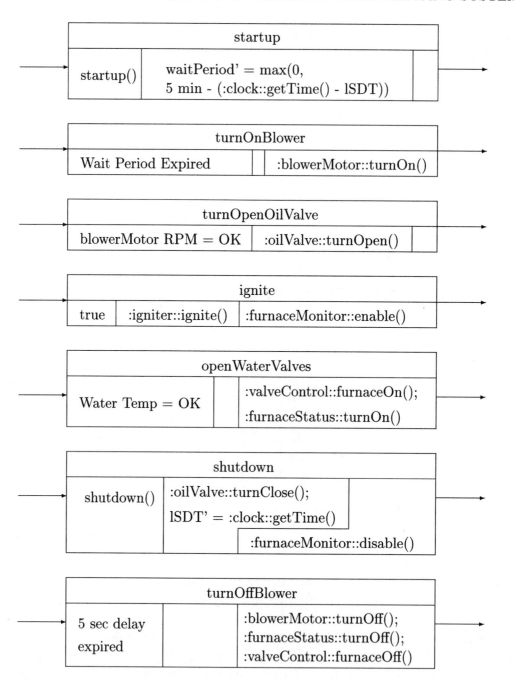

Figure 5.27: Expansions of the transitions of the furnace. See the text for a discussion of guards and for *lSDT*.

in the startup transition and add a looping *tic* transition to the *waitToFireUp* state which decreases the *waitPeriod*. The guard of the *turnOnBlower* transition would then become a test of whether *waitToFireUp* is nonpositive.

The guard "blowerMotor RPM = OK" needs attention as well. A condition of the form *:blowerMotor::getRPM() = RPM-OK* assumes implicitly that the furnace is polling the blower motor until the blower motor has reached the *RPM-OK* speed. An explicit description would also attach to the *waitForBlowerMotor* state a *tic* transition. The action part of this transition would have a *:blowerMotor::getRPM() = RPM-OK* action setting a local attribute named, say, *blowerMotorOK*. This attribute *blowerMotorOK* would be referred to in a replacement of "blowerMotor RPM = OK".

The same story applies, obviously, to the guard "Water Temp = OK" in the transition *openWaterValve* and to the guard "5 sec delay expired" in the transition *turnOffBlower*.

These four guards are good examples regarding the question of whether their replacement is appropriate during the analysis phase or whether this is an example of design activities. It depends on whether or not one feels that the requirements are faithfully represented as depicted in Figure 5.27. Alternatively phrased, we need to evaluate whether or not the description is unambiguous for a designer or from another perspective whether or not the elaborated versions have left the design space intact. We don't take a position here. The answer depends, among others, on the familiarity that the developers have with the application domain.

The *ignite* transition is worth attention. Its guard is simply *true*, indicating that this transition fires immediately after entering the *oilValveOpened* state. Why do we believe that the oil valve is open? Because the transition *turnOpenOilValve* has described the interaction with the *oilValve* as a service request, which will guarantee that the valve will be open when the *turnOpenOilValve* transition reaches its *oilValveOpened* state. This setup raises the question of what is to be done when the oil valve malfunctions. Who is responsible for detecting the malfunction? What is the recovery procedure? These and similar questions must be brought to the attention of the customer for resolution.

The igniter is activated as a service request as well. This will guarantee that it has done its action (successfully or not) before the furnace monitor is activated. If a delay is required to assure that the optical combustion sensor can report faithfully whether ignition has occurred, we should split up the ignite transition.

It is noteworthy that we have minimized service request communications. For example, in the transition *openWaterValve*, the valve controller and the furnace status objects are activated through events. The semantics of event delivery and event processing by the recipients leaves it uncommitted as to which one of the two recipient objects will have processed the events first. In fact, it doesn't matter. Another example is the three one-way communications in the *turnOffBlower* transition.

Somewhat surprising, perhaps, is the fact that we have many more transitions in the transition network diagram than the two operations *startup()* and *shutdown* listed in the summary figure on page 176. The other transitions are internal transitions that coordinate the activation and deactivation of the components of the furnace subsystem.

It pays to have a closer at Figure 5.26. Processing a shutdown operation causes the furnace to enter the state *oilValveClosed*. The furnace will stay in this state for 5 seconds before the blower motor is turned on and the furnace enters the state *furnaceOff*. What would happen if a startup event arrives while the furnace is still in the state *oilValveClosed*? Before answering this question, we should ascertain whether such an event can arrive at all. The furnace controller is the only source of startup events targeted at the furnace. A furnace shutdown transition may have been caused because there was only one room being heated and that room decided that it no longer needed heat. As a consequence of the shutdown transition, the furnace controller changed state as well. Its new state has a transition that may generate a startup event for the furnace when a room finds that it needs heat. Thus it is possible that the furnace receives a startup event while it still in the state *oilValveClosed*.

Hence we encounter an example of the general situation where an event arrives while an object is not in a state that can accept the event. There are three different policies for dealing with such situations:
– The event is ignored and discarded.
– The event is queued and will be processed when the object enters a state where this event can be processed.
– This situation is recognized as an error and exception handling is invoked.
An analyst can deal with this situation by "closing off" a transition diagram; i.e. by introducing additional transitions so that the nonapplicable event situation is avoided. Such a treatment often leads in practice to unwieldy, cluttered diagrams; see Allen and de Champeaux [4] for how to deal with this problem. In this particular case we leave the diagram as it is and delegate this issue to the design to queue startup events when the furnace is in the state *oilValveClosed*.

5.10.11   Blower motor

An overview of the *BlowerMotor* is shown in Figure 5.28.

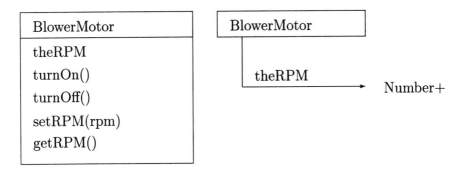

Figure 5.28: Overview of the blower motor and its static diagram.

Blower Motor static

The static diagram of the blower motor is also shown in Figure 5.28. The value domain of the attribute *theRPM* is (a finite subset of) the positive numbers. Concerns about basic data types can often be conveniently ignored. An executable design should address this "detail".

Blower Motor dynamic

The diagrams for the dynamics of the blower motor are depicted in Figure 5.29. The transition *getRPM* is the only "normal" transition. The others straddle the system boundary by interacting with the physical blower motor.

5.10.12 Oil Valve

Figure 5.30 shows all diagrams for the *OilValve*. The static diagram is omitted since there are no attributes, and we refrain from giving an oil valve self-knowledge about its opened-closed status.

An oil valve operates as a server. Hence clients will block while an oil valve changes state. Thus a client will have the guarantee that a valve has changed state when it resumes.

5.10.13 Igniter

Figure 5.31 shows all we care to know about the igniter. The *ignite* transition shows that the igniter object also straddles the system boundary. Observe that the client doesn't get any feedback from the igniter whether or not ignition was successful when

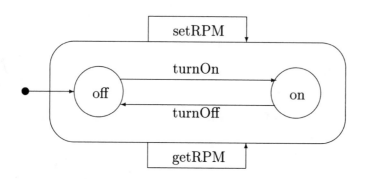

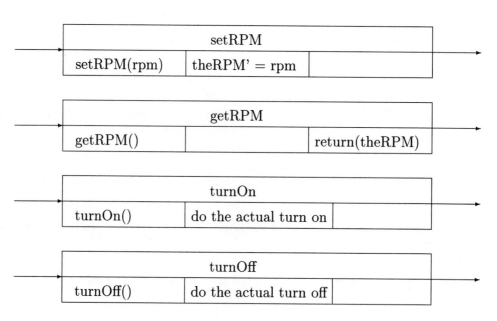

Figure 5.29: Transition network of a blower motor interface object.

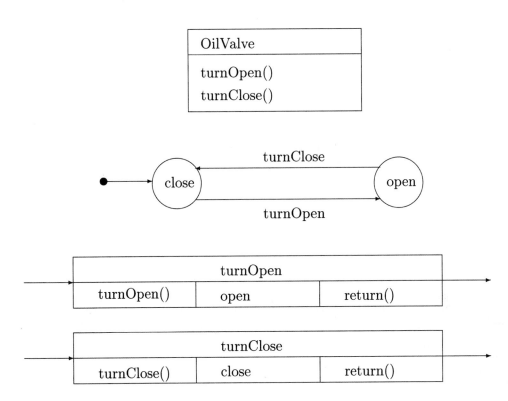

Figure 5.30: All diagrams for the oil valve.

the client is reactivated through the igniter's *return()*. The furnace relies on the furnace monitor to check whether ignition was successful (and that the oil continues burning).

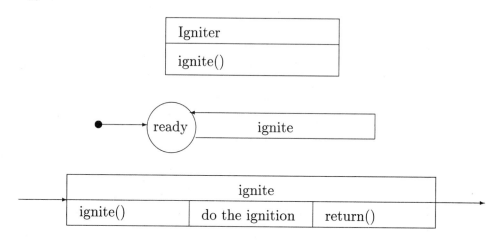

Figure 5.31: All the diagrams of the igniter. The static diagram has been omitted since the igniter has no attributes.

5.10.14   Sensors

The three sensors *WaterTemperatureSensor, FuelFlowSensor,* and *OpticalCombustionSensor* have a common structure. Hence we combine them in this section. Their diagrams all look like the diagrams in Figure 5.32. The similarity of these sensors with the occupancy sensor should be obvious.

The *WaterTemperatureSensor* can be derived from the schema in Figure 5.32 by the following replacements:

XyzSensor → *WaterTemperatureSensor*
XYZ → *Number+* (or *TemperatureRange*)
xyzAttribute → *currentTemperature*
setXyzAttribute → *setCurrentTemperature*
getXyzAttribute → *getCurrentTemperature*

Similarly for the *FuelFlowSensor*:

XyzSensor → *FuelFlowSensor*

$XYZ \rightarrow \{y,n\}$
$xyzAttribute \rightarrow fuelFlow?$
$setXyzAttribute \rightarrow setFuelFlow?$
$getXyzAttribute \rightarrow getFuelFlow?$

And again for the *OpticalCombustionSensor*:

$XyzSensor \rightarrow OpticalCombustionSensor$
$XYZ \rightarrow \{y,n\}$
$xyzAttribute \rightarrow combustion?$
$setXyzAttribute \rightarrow setCombustion?$
$getXyzAttribute \rightarrow getCombustion?$

As discussed earlier, inheritance doesn't pay to factor out commonalities. Having dedicated attribute names and dedicated names for the operations is quite convenient in this situation.

5.10.15 Furnace Monitor

Figure 5.33 shows the overview diagram of the *FurnaceMonitor*. Comparison of this figure with Figure 5.7 on page 152 shows that we have repaired the omission of the *FaultResetSwitch/Indicator*. Note as well that we have added an attribute *clock*. As a result, the *FurnaceMonitor* can communicate with the *Clock* and register and deregister itself.

Furnace Monitor static

The abbreviations in the static diagrams expand, unsurprisingly, to:

fFS = *FuelFlowSensor*
oCS = *OpticalCombustionSensor*
fRS = *FaultResetSwitch/Indicator*.

Furnace Monitor dynamic

Figure 5.34 depicts the dynamic diagrams for the *FurnaceMonitor*.

These diagrams can be used elegantly for a proof that the clock will not send a *tic* event to the *FurnaceMonitor* when it is in the *off* state (provided only that the

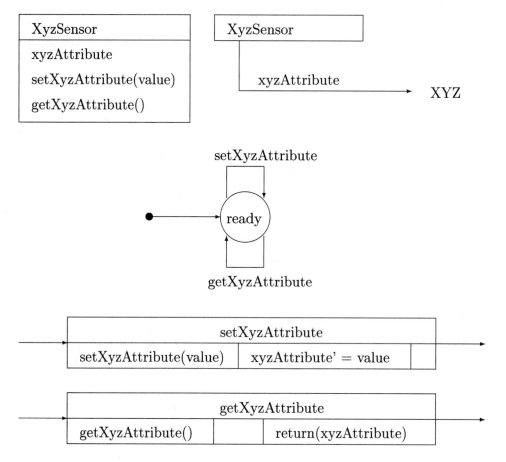

Figure 5.32: Structure and dynamics of a generic sensor.

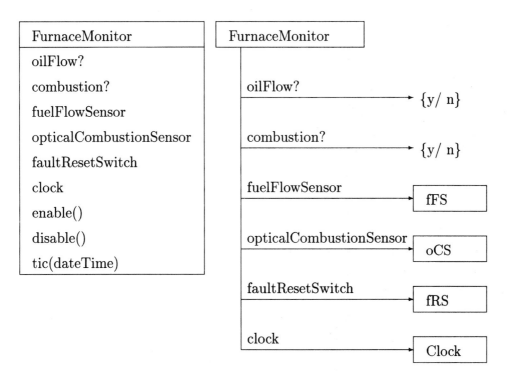

Figure 5.33: Summary view and static diagram for the furnace monitor. See the text for the abbreviations used in the static diagram.

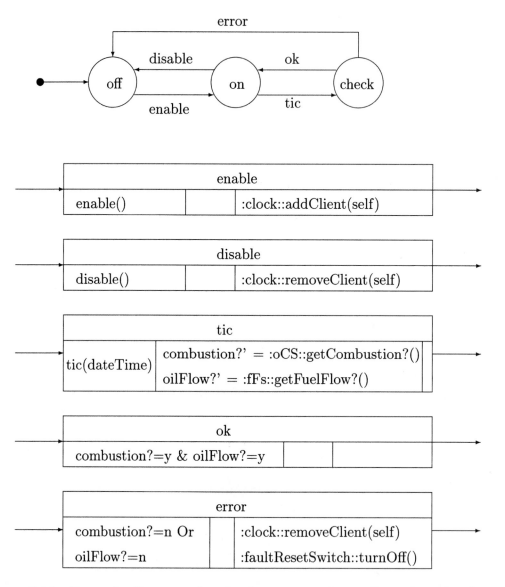

Figure 5.34: Dynamic diagrams for the furnace monitor. Note that the furnace monitor takes care of its registration and deregistration with the clock.

FurnaceMonitor registers itself with the clock). Assuming that the *FurnaceMonitor* is not registered with the clock when it is initialized, we know that the clock cannot send *tic* events in the *off* state because the two other paths into the *off* state contain a deregistration. Similarly, we know that when the *FurnaceMonitor* is in the *on* state, the *FurnaceMonitor* is registered and thus will receive *tic* events (as the result of an "obligations" description that characterize the interactive behavior of the clock[12]).

The transitions *ok* and *error* are good examples of transitions whose guards are provably mutually exclusive.

5.10.16 Occupancy History

The summary diagram of the *OccupancyHistory* class is shown in Figure 5.35. The operation names have been abbreviated in the diagram. For instance, "setOcc" stands for "setOccupancy".

Occupancy History static

Figure 5.35 shows the static diagram. Noteworthy is the value domain *occupancy-Struct* of the attribute *occupancyRecord*. This value domain should be able to represent 7 days of occupancy data with a time granularity of 1 second. Obviously, this value domain will be used by the two operations *setOccupancy* and *getOccupancy*. This value domain is a good example of an item that need not be explored further by the analyst. Its semantics are clear, while there are many different design realizations.

Occupancy History dynamic

Figure 5.35 depicts also the dynamic diagrams. The term *oR*, unsurprisingly, stands for *occupancyRecord*.

The two transitions in Figure 5.35 are good examples of supporting, respectively, producer-consumer interaction, *setOccupancy*, and client-server interaction *getOccupancy*. The *update* and *get* operations will work on the *occupancyStruct* value domain. The figure suggests that the value domain of *occupancyStruct* is *not* a class. The design may change this position.

---

[12]See [21] for a formalism based upon obligations and expectations that is used for showing the correctness of interacting processes.

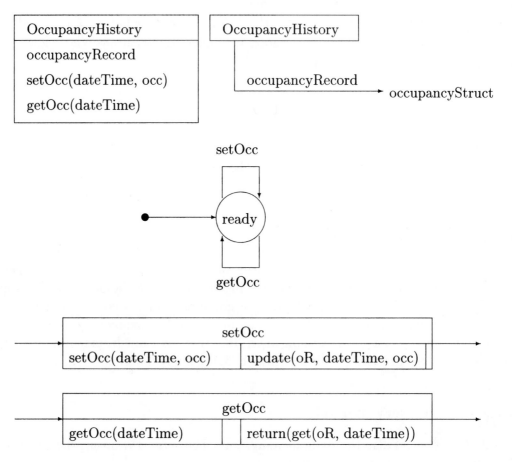

Figure 5.35: All the diagrams of the occupancy history class. The abbreviations *setOcc* and *getOcc* expand into, respectively, *setOccupancy* and *getOccupancy*; *oR* stands for *occupancyRecord.*

5.10.17 Living Pattern

The diagrams for the *LivingPattern* are all shown in Figure 5.36. The similarity of these diagrams with those for the *OccupancyHistory* class is obvious. The attribute *livingPattern* must also be capable of recording 7 days of occupancy data with a time granularity of 1 second. The only real difference is the operations *getOccRec(dateTime)* and *occExp?(dateTime, length)*. The former retrieves from the repository the occupancy of a single moment; the latter replies whether occupancy can be expected in the period *[dateTime, dateTime+length]*. The design can certainly exploit the commonalities, for instance, by making the two value domains into a class that supports the three operations.

The abbreviations used in the diagrams are

dT = *dateTime*
lP = *livingPattern*.

5.10.18 Valve Control

The class *ValveControl* has been introduced to concentrate in one place the responsibility for the opening and closing of valves and for keeping track of the rooms that need heat. The *HeatFlowRegulator* informs *ValveControl* when a room needs heat and when it no longer needs heat. The *FurnaceController* informs *ValveControl* when hot water is available and when the furnace shuts down.

Figure 5.37 shows the summary diagram. The attribute *furnaceOn?* is used to decide whether a room's water valve can be opened up right away (when the room communicates with the valve controller) or whether the room's valve cannot be opened because hot water is not yet available. The latter can have several causes:
– The furnace is on but the water is not yet hot enough.
– The user has turned off the system.
– A fault has occurred and as a result the system has turned off.
This setup, where a room's (de)registration does *not* coincide with opening (closing) its valve, minimizes unnecessary valve operations.

Valve Control static

Figure 5.37 includes a static diagram. Noticeable is the value domain of the attribute *roomsThatNeedHeat*. The domain of this multivalued attribute is represented through a set container class. We encountered the set container construct previously in the

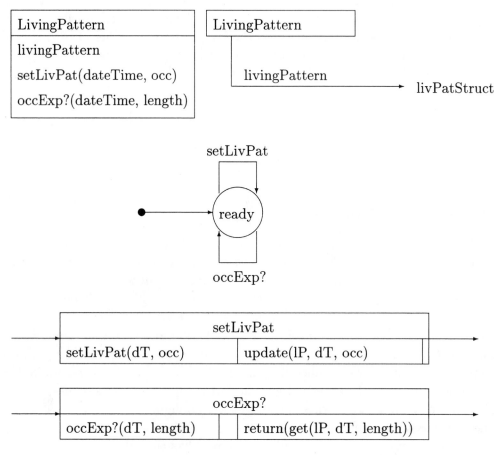

Figure 5.36: All the diagrams of the living pattern class. The similarity with the occupancy history class is striking.

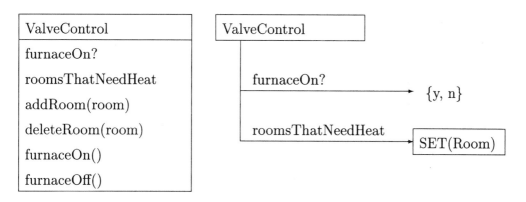

Figure 5.37: Overview diagram and the static diagram of the valve control class.

clock class, where it was used to register all the clients of the clock.

Valve Control dynamic

Half of the transitions for the *ValveControl* are shown in Figure 5.38.

The *BR* operation of the parametrized class *SET(Room)* is special, as alluded to above. Its argument within parenthesis is in fact a quoted expression and is to be broadcast to all members of the set. In this particular example, the *furnaceOn* transition prescribes that all registered rooms need to receive the event *openValve()*, and similarly, for the *furnaceOff* transition the rooms need to receive the *closeValve()* events. Note that the *ValveControl* remembers the on/off status of the furnace through its attribute *furnaceOn?*.

Figure 5.39 shows the (de)registration of a room. Both of these operation entail a two-step procedure. The first step is the addition to or the deletion from the set container. Subsequently, depending on whether or not the attribute *furnaceOn?* is true, the room's valve will be affected. Note the *add* and *del* states share the transition *noOP*. This transition leads back to the *ready* state from either *add* or *del* when *furnaceOn?* is false.

We have chosen to represent the behavior of *ValveControl* as two disjoint transition networks. They can be combined into one transition network easily by taking their Cartesian product. This doesn't increase their readability. Figure 5.40 shows an alternative merge of the two networks. It depicts clearly that the transitions *furnaceOn* and *furnaceOff* apply to the three substates and that the resulting state is the originating substate.

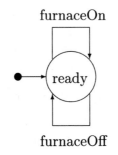

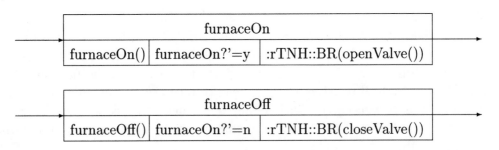

Figure 5.38: Half of the transitions of the valve control class. The abbreviation *rTNH* expands into *roomsThatNeedHeat*. The BR expression represents a broadcast operation that sends events to all the registered rooms in the set *roomsThatNeedHeat*.

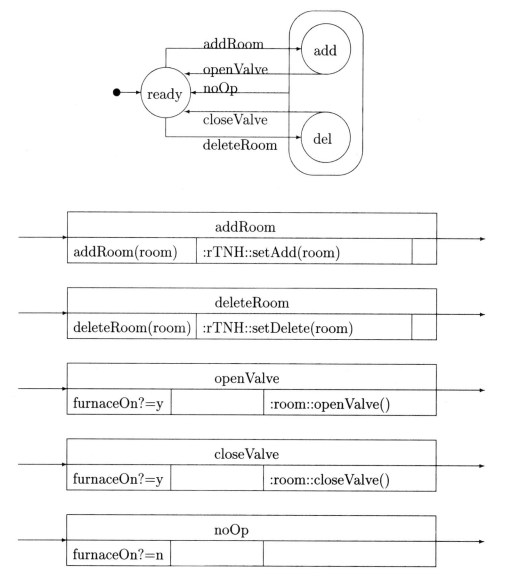

Figure 5.39: Addition and deletion of registered rooms. The *noOp* transition is shared by the *add* and *del* states. Observe that the expression *:room* refers to the argument *room* in either *addRoom* or *deleteRoom*.

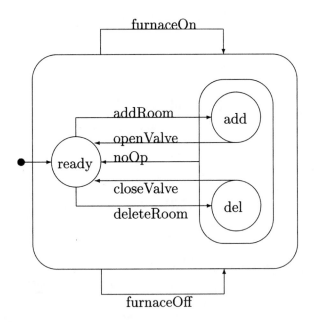

Figure 5.40: Both transition networks for the valve control class are merged in this single diagram. The transitions *furnaceOn* and *furnaceOff* can originate in any of the three substates *ready*, *add*, and *del* and will return to the originating state.

5.10.19 Metrics

As mentioned before, the construction of these class descriptions is the lion's share of the analysis effort. Unfortunately, we did not track the development effort per class – nor for that matter the finer granularity of the summary diagram, static diagram, and dynamic diagram. Our notes indicate that the summary diagrams together took 3 hours. We don't have recorded figures for the other diagrams. A best estimate is that the static diagrams took 2 hours and the dynamic diagrams took an additional 8 hours.

We have defined multiple metrics for classes in chapter 4, see page 118. In Table 5.2 we depict the results of applying the metrics $\mu_{attribute}$, $\mu_{classState}$, $\mu_{classTransition}$, $\mu_{classEvent}$, $\mu_{classServiceRequest}$, and $\mu_{classEventProduced}$ to the defined classes.

We have added, as the second column, the measurement from $\mu_{vocabulary}$ applied to the corresponding vocabulary entries previously developed. The last column, headed Ψ_A, contains a "synthetic" metric: $\mu_{attribute} + \mu_{classState} + \mu_{classTransition} + \mu_{classEvent} + \mu_{classServiceRequest} + \mu_{classEventProduced}$. This Ψ_A metric is a special case with all weight coefficients set to 1 in the metric: $w_a * \mu_{attribute} + w_s * \mu_{classState} + w_t * \mu_{classTransition} + w_e * \mu_{classEvent} + w_r * \mu_{classServiceRequest} + w_p * \mu_{classEventProduced}$. This generalized metric can exploit insights in the relative average amount of effort needed to define an attribute versus a state versus a transition versus an event versus a service request versus a produced event. Lacking this detailed insight led to the definition of Ψ_A as given above.

Of interest is whether the vocabulary metric restricted to class entries correlates with the metrics $\mu_{attribute}$, $\mu_{classState}$, $\mu_{classTransition}$, $\mu_{classEvent}$, $\mu_{classServiceRequest}$, $\mu_{classEventProduced}$, and with Ψ_A. We have investigated whether the data for classes in table 5.2 can be approximated by a linear dependence on the vocabulary data:

$$\mu_C = \beta_0 + \beta_1 * \mu_{vocabulary}$$

for certain parameters β_0 and β_1 and where C stands for, respectively, $\mu_{attribute}$, $\mu_{classState}$, $\mu_{classTransition}$, $\mu_{classEvent}$, $\mu_{classServiceRequest}$, $\mu_{classEventProduced}$, and Ψ_A.

In Table 5.3 we see the results as well as the correlation coefficients. The correlations are quite encouraging, especially the one for the synthetic Ψ_A metric. Since it is quite plausible that the product metrics $\mu_{vocabulary}$ and Ψ_A correlate with the corresponding effort metrics, we obtain an encouraging support for the conjecture that prediction of effort for OOA classes can be based on the effort spend on their vocabulary counterparts. However, we want to be the first to warn that these results must be duplicated on other and larger samples.

Class	μ_{vocab}	μ_{attr}	$\mu_{clState}$	$\mu_{clTrans}$	$\mu_{clEvent}$	μ_{clSrvR}	μ_{clEvPr}	Ψ_A
HS	5	1	2	3	2	0	2	10
FRS/I	5	1	2	3	2	0	2	10
FSI	5	1	2	3	2	0	2	10
HFR	5	1	2	5	2	0	4	14
SC	8	0	4	9	4	0	2	19
Clock	5	2	1	5	4	0	2	14
Room	14	8	3	7	3	7	4	32
OS	4	1	1	3	2	0	1	8
RTS	4	1	1	3	2	0	1	8
DTID	4	1	1	3	2	0	1	8
WV	4	0	2	3	2	2	0	9
FC	8	0	4	9	4	0	2	19
Furnace	14	8	8	8	6	5	9	44
BM	6	1	3	5	4	2	1	16
OilValve	4	0	2	3	2	2	2	11
Igniter	2	0	1	2	1	1	1	6
WTS	4	1	1	3	2	0	1	8
FM	10	6	3	6	3	2	3	23
FFS	4	1	1	3	2	0	1	8
OCS	4	1	1	3	2	0	1	8
OH	4	1	1	3	2	1	1	9
LP	4	1	1	3	2	1	1	9
VC	NA	2	4	8	4	2	4	24

Table 5.2: Values obtained from metrics defined Chapter 4 for the developed classes. Abbreviations used: HS, HeatSwitch; FRS/I, FaultResetSwitch/Indicator; FSI, FurnaceStatusIndicator; HFR, HeatFlowRegulator; SC, SystemController; OS, OccupancySensor; RTS, RoomTemperatureSensor; DTID, DesiredTemperatureInputDevice; WV, WaterValve; FC, FurnaceController; BM, BlowerMotor; WTS, WaterTemperatureSensor; FM, FurnaceMonitor; FFS, FuelFlowSensor; OCS, OpticalCombustionSensor; OH, OccupancyHistory; LP, LivingPattern; VC, ValveControl; the synthetic metric Ψ_A is defined in the text.

Metric	β_0	β_1	Correlation
$\mu_{attribute}$	-2.08947	0.65329	0.87252
$\mu_{classState}$	-0.30723	0.42330	0.81904
$\mu_{classTransition}$	1.19588	0.54087	0.80029
$\mu_{classEvent}$	1.03905	0.26883	0.74864
$\mu_{classServiceRequest}$	-1.49474	0.44003	0.77132
$\mu_{classEventProduced}$	-0.67024	0.46256	0.79347
Ψ_A	-2.32675	2.78889	0.96491

Table 5.3: The values for β_0 and β_1 are the best fits for the available data in the equation: $\mu_{Metric} = \beta_0 + \beta_1 * \mu_{vocabulary}$. The synthetic metric Ψ_A correlates quite well with the vocabulary metric $\mu_{vocabulary}$.

5.10.20   Notes

Chapter 4 has more definitions for class metrics. Several of the other metrics do not apply to our example due to the lack of inheritance: Depth of Inheritance (μ_{DIT}), Number of Ancestors (μ_{NOA}), Number of Children (μ_{NOC}),and Number of All Children (μ_{NOAC}). The remaining metrics, Coupling Between Object Classes (μ_{CBO}) and Response For a Class (μ_{RFC}), are somewhat different in that they are intended to address primarily quality aspects rather than volume/size.

Table 5.4 shows the results of the application of these metrics to our collection of classes. We have added to this table also the values reported above for the synthetic Ψ_A metric. Eye balling these data suggests that the metrics are similar. Table 5.5 shows that, indeed they all correlate.

The correlation between Ψ_A and μ_{RFC} is not too surprising. The metric Ψ_A resembles the metric $\mu_{WMC}(C)$ defined in Chidamber and Kemerer [16] as the number of methods in the class C. They mention in a footnote that μ_{WMC} and their version of μ_{RFC} correlate at 0.9.

Somewhat disturbing is the significant correlation between Ψ_A (as well as μ_{RFC}) and μ_{CBO}. As a result, their claim that μ_{RFC} and μ_{CBO} are measuring different quality dimensions instead of providing alternative views on volume/size is unconvincing. One could say that the metric μ_{CBO}, which is supposed to measure the coupling of a class with its peers, and which should be minimal, embodies the maxim "small is beautiful".

Class	Ψ_A	μ_{CBO}	μ_{RFC}
HS	10	1	4
FRS/I	10	1	4
FSI	10	1	4
HFR	14	3	6
SC	19	1	6
Clock	14	2	5
Room	32	7	13
OS	8	0	2
RTS	8	0	2
DTID	8	0	2
WV	9	0	2
FC	19	1	6
Furnace	44	7	14
BM	16	0	4
OilValve	11	0	2
Igniter	6	0	1
WTS	8	0	2
FM	23	4	9
FFS	8	0	2
OCS	8	0	2
OH	9	0	2
LP	9	0	2
VC	24	2	10

Table 5.4: Application of the metrics μ_{CBO} and μ_{RFC} to the defined classes. We have added the values for Ψ_A. See also the next Table.

Metric 1	Metric 2	β_0	β_1	Correlation
Ψ_A	μ_{CBO}	-1.61133	0.20508	0.90102
Ψ_A	μ_{RFC}	0.83489	0.38288	0.96319
μ_{CBO}	μ_{RFC}	2.47127	1.63869	0.93827

Table 5.5: The values for β_0 and β_1 are the best fits for the available data in the equation $\mu_{Metric2} = \beta_0 + \beta_1 * \mu_{Metric1}$. The last column shows the correlation coefficients.

5.11 Relationship

No relationships have been used except the ones that support communication as outlined in Section 5.9. Observe that all these relationships have been absorbed already as attributes in classes to support the descriptions of event targets in one-way communications or of servers in two-way communications.

5.12 Instance

Most classes in the Home Heating System have only a single instance. The classes in the *Room* subsystem are the exception. Here we encounter, in a sense, an incompleteness in the requirements: it is not mentioned how many rooms there are. The same applies to the number of temperature sensors, occupancy sensors, etc., although we will have one of each for each room, see Figure 5.5 on page 151. The way out is to argue that the requirements are generic: they apply to a house with any number of rooms.

To construct the scenario diagrams, we assume that a house has, say, seven rooms and hence seven room temperature sensors, seven occupancy sensors, etc. Figure 5.41 depicts two instances. They are labeled with unique names to distinguish them.

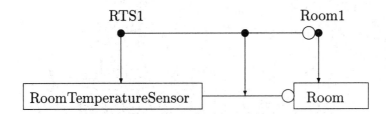

Figure 5.41: One of the seven instances of the class *Room* and one of the seven instances of the class *RoomTemperatureSensor*. We have also shown a relationship instance between the two objects that is derived from the communication acquaintance relationship between the parent classes.

Similar diagrams can be drawn for the objects in the room subsystem associated with *Room1*, for the other rooms in the room subsystem, and for all the other objects that are unique instances of their corresponding classes.

The figures in Section 5.9 can be followed closely. We have only to add an instance of the class *ValveControl* with links to *HeatFlowRegulator*, *Room*, and *Furnace*; see

Figure 5.42 for a fragment of the links attached to the instance *VC* of the class *ValveControl*.

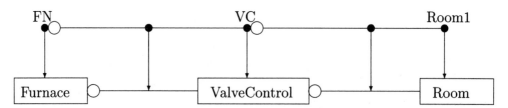

Figure 5.42: Two of the links attached to the instance *VC* of the class *ValveControl*. Not shown are links between *VC* and the other rooms and between *VC* and *HFR*, the unique instance of the *HeatFlowRegulator*.

5.12.1 Metrics

The construction of these diagrams took about 1 hour.

The product metric for instances is simply a count of them. Since all our instances are enduring (we do not create and delete objects on the fly), we obtain the following list of classes with the corresponding instances:

HeatFlowRegulator: HFR
HeatSwitch: HSW
FaultResetSwitch/Indicator: FRSI
SystemController: SC
Clock: CK
Room: RM1, ..., RM7
RoomTemperatureSensor: RTS1, ..., RTS7
OccupancySensor: OS1, ..., OS7
WaterValve: WV1, ..., WV7
DesiredTempInputDevice: DTID1, ..., DTID7
OccupancyHistory: OH1, ..., OH7
LivingPattern: LP1, ..., LP7
FurnaceController: FC
Furnace: FN
BlowerMotor: BM
OilValve: OV
Igniter: IG
FuelFlowSensor: FFS

OpticalCombustionSensor: OCS
FurnaceMonitor: FM
ValveControl: VC

Hence we have 14 classes with unique instances and 7 classes each with 7 instances. This yields $\mu_{PerInstances} = 14 + 49 = 63$. There are no transient instances: $\mu_{TranInstances} = 0$.

5.12.2   Notes

The instance diagrams do not yield much new information. The links between the objects are instances of relationships. Thus one can argue that these diagrams only increase the burden to keep everything consistent. The other side of the coin is that they provide yet another angle on the system to be developed. They force us to revisit already developed artifacts. In our case we noticed an inaccuracy in a previous version of Figure 5.3 on page 149. The previous version had a bidirectional link between *Room* and *HeatFlowRegulator*. That diagram was constructed before *ValveControl* was introduced. The original plan was that *HeatFlowRegulator* would be responsible for informing *Room* to open or close the water valves. Instead, we let *ValveControl* do this communication, as shown in Figure 5.43.

5.13   Scenario Diagram

Scenario diagrams are used to "debug" the classes, relationships, instances, etc. that have been formally developed. The set of artifacts developed should support the formally description into scenario diagrams of the initial scenarios, which themselves are expansions of the use cases. We revisit the use cases and scenarios described in section 5.3 and expand them into scenario diagrams.

Use Case 1

> The user turns on the heat switch while the current temperature in room A is 5 degrees below its working temperature.
>
> Since room A needs heat, the furnace is started.

This was expanded into:

Scenario 1

> The user turns on the heat switch (while the current temperature in room A is 5 degrees below its working temperature).//

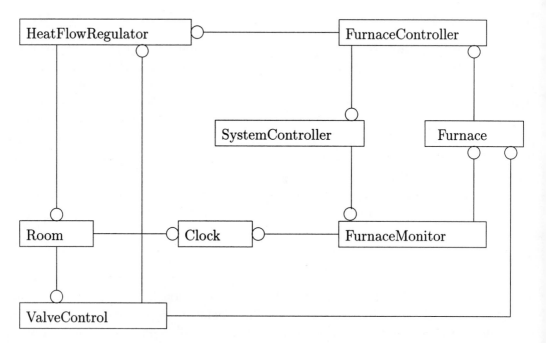

Figure 5.43: Extension of Figure 5.3. *ValveControl* receives from *HeatFlowRegulator* information as to which rooms need heat, and it is informed by *Furnace* when hot water is available or when the furnace shuts down. In turn, *ValveControl* informs the rooms to open or close their valves.

> The heat switch informs a heat-flow regulator that it is switched on.//
> The heat-flow regulator informs a furnace controller that the furnace is enabled (since the fault/reset switch is on).//
> The furnace controller informs the furnace to startup since it knows already that there is at least one room that needs heat.//

We hope that at this point the reader is at least quite concerned. The scenario indicates that "the heat switch informs a heat-flow regulator ...". However, we have seen in Figure 5.4 that the heat switch doesn't interact with the heat-flow regulator, but instead, with the system controller. Something went wrong. The explanation is that the development did not go as smooth and linearly as suggested in this chapter. An earlier version of the heat-flow regulator was quite complex. It was simplified by splitting off the system controller. Hence the scenario became, instead:

Scenario 1'

> The user turns on the heat switch (while the current temperature in room A is 5 degrees below its working temperature).//
> The heat switch informs a system controller that it is switched on.//
> The system controller informs a furnace controller that the furnace is enabled (since the fault/reset switch is on).//
> The furnace controller informs the furnace to startup since it knows already that there is at least one room that needs heat.//

See Figure 5.44 for the realization of this scenario. The nodes represent the instances in the scenario. The directed arcs represent one-way interactions. The numbers express an ordering of the events.

Arcs may be labeled with the same sequence number to indicate that they execute in parallel or that their ordering is immaterial. The ordinal numbers may be replaced by actual times to express that events have to be produced according to a prescribed timing schema. Instance description can be extended by detailing their class. For example, we could have: *HSW::HeatSwitch* instead of simply *HSW* as in the figure. Arguments in events can be provided when called for.

An arc in a scenario diagram can also represent a two-way service interaction. The client part of the arc has a single arrow, the server side a double arrow. Such an arc shows not only the calling event but also the return event. Figure 5.45 shows an example where a room calls upon its occupancy sensor to check whether it is occupied. Note that we have used the extended object notion to distinguish between the different rooms and occupancy sensors and to indicate their respective classes.

We proceed with the second use case and scenario:

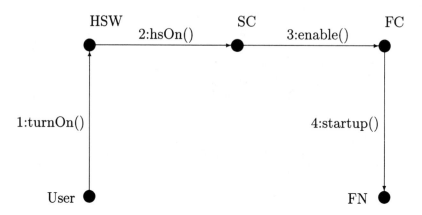

Figure 5.44: Scenario diagram for the adjusted first scenario. See the text for the modifications. The labels at the instances refer, respectively, to the *HeatSwitch*, *SystemController*, *FurnaceController*, and *Furnace*.

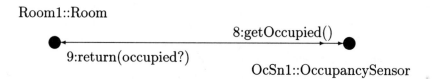

Figure 5.45: Fragment of a scenario diagram where an arc represents a two-way service interaction. The numbers 8 and 9 represent sequence numbers of the events in this fragment. The *getOccupied* transition of *OccupancySensor* produces a return value, which justifies the fact that the return event immediately follows the invocation event.

Use Case 2

A user enters a room, which causes activation of the furnace.

An ignition error occurs and the fault reset indicator is turned off.

This was expanded into:
Scenario 2

A user enters a room ...
The room occupancy sensor informs the room that it is occupied.//
The room registers the occupancy and changes the weekly living pattern
if necessary.//
The room verifies the actual temperature, ta, against the working temper-
ature, tw; since $ta \leq tw - 2$ it informs the room controller that it needs
heat.//
The room controller adds the room to the set of rooms that needs heat
and informs the furnace controller that a room needs heat.//
... which causes activation of the furnace.
The furnace controller informs the furnace to startup.//
The furnace starts the blower motor.//
The blower motor informs the furnace that it has reached a sufficient RPM
value.//
The furnace informs the oil valve to open.//
The furnace activates the igniter.//
The furnace activates the furnace monitor.//
The furnace monitor finds an ignition error.//
The furnace monitor informs the furnace to shut down.//
The furnace monitor informs the furnace controller to disable the sys-
tem.//
The furnace monitor sets the fault reset indicator to off.//

This is a relatively large scenario. We need several figures to expand this scenario
into a scenario diagram. See Figure 5.46 for the first fragment, which is centered
around room *R1*. The user who enters room *R1* and triggers this scenario is not
depicted. This figure concentrates on what happens in the room subsystem. The
last event in the figure corresponds to the room registering itself with the heat-flow
regulator.

Figure 5.47 has the second part of the scenario, which leads to activation of the
furnace. The figure continues where the previous figure left off: at the activated

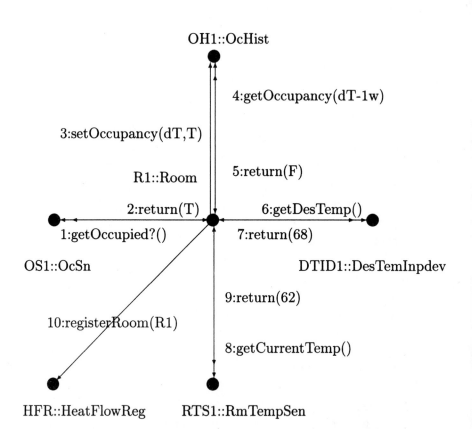

Figure 5.46: First part of the second scenario. The node in the middle is the room *R1*. This room interacts in turn with *OS1*, its occupancy sensor; *OH1*, its occupancy history; *DTID1*, its desired temperature input device; and *RTS1*, its room temperature sensor. Finally, the room registers itself with *HFR*, the heat flow regulator. Note that there are *no* interactions with the room's object which maintains the living pattern. The reasons are that the living pattern need not to be changed because the current occupancy differs from the one a week earlier; the living pattern need not to be accessed to check whether the room will be occupied within 30 minutes, because it is already known that the room is occupied.

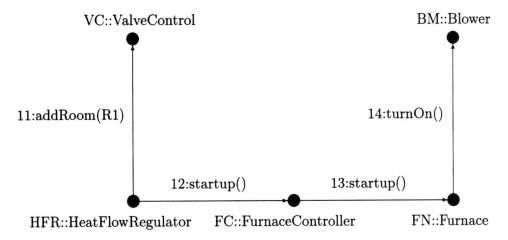

Figure 5.47: Second part of the second scenario. The heat flow regulator informs the valve controller that the room *R1* needs heat when the furnace is ready. Subsequently, the furnace controller receives the event *startup()*. This causes the furnace to receive a similar but different event *startup()*. Activation of the furnace leads to many other events, of which this figure shows only the activation of the blower motor. The subsequent events are depicted in the next figure.

heat-flow regulator. The sequence of events ends here with the furnace activating the blower motor.

One may argue that the furnace should interact first with the clock to account for the *waitToFireUp* state that prevents the furnace from being restarted within 5 minutes since the last shutdown. The omission can be justified by arguing that this interaction is "trivial" and can be delegated to the design phase. A reader uncomfortable with this omission is invited to fill this gap - see the exercises.

Figure 5.48 shows the third and last part of the second scenario. Note that the furnace object occurs twice in this figure: at the top, where it opens the oil valve, and at the bottom, where it receives the shutdown event. This scenario can be extended further. The shutdown event causes the oil valve to be closed, the clock is accessed, the furnace monitor is disabled, and so on.

As argued above, one may object to not having modeled the active state *WaitForBlowerMotor*. The reader is invited to fill in this gap.

It is noteworthy that the last three steps in the original scenario differ from those shown in Figure 5.48. We repeat the last four steps in the scenario:

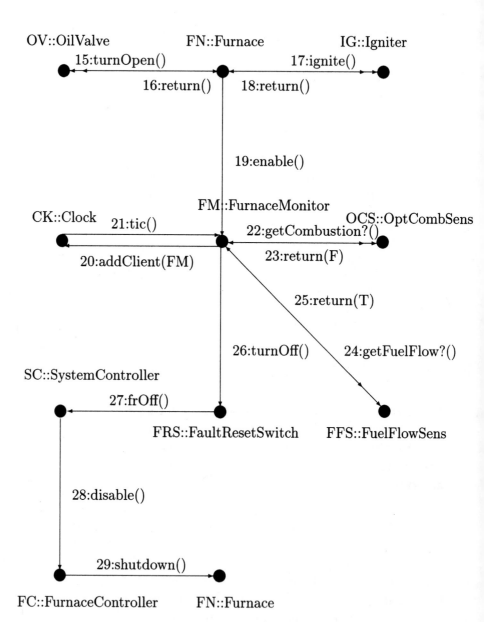

Figure 5.48: Third and last part of the second scenario. See the text for a discussion.

... The furnace monitor finds an ignition error.//
The furnace monitor informs the furnace to shut down.//
The furnace monitor informs the furnace controller to disable the system.//
The furnace monitor sets the fault reset indicator to off.//

Tripping the fault reset switch/indicator is the only thing that the furnace monitor does (in the scenario diagram) when it encounters an ignition error. Subsequently, this causes the indicator to be turned off, and ultimately, it causes the furnace to be shut down. The divergence between the scenario and the scenario diagram was caused by the emergence of the system controller, whose purpose is to integrate the settings of the heat switch and the fault reset switch. The functionality already in place that deals with shutting down the furnace permitted us to decrease the involvement of the furnace monitor.

5.13.1 Metrics

The construction of the first scenario diagram took about 1 hour. The second diagram took about 4 hours.

To calculate the metrics for the two scenario diagrams we use a special case of

$$\mu_{ScenarioDiagram}(SD) =$$
$$w1_{SD} * \#ObjectsIn(SD) + w2_{SD} * \#OneWayArcsIn(SD) +$$
$$w3_{SD} * \#ServiceRequestsIn(SD) + w4_{SD} * \#RepliesIn(SD)$$

We take for all the weights i: $wi_{SD} = 1$. Since we have only two scenario diagrams, we obtain:

$$\mu_{ScenarioDiagrams} = \mu_{ScenarioDiagram}(SD_1) + \mu_{ScenarioDiagram}(SD_2)$$

We obtain for the first scenario diagram:
$\#ObjectsIn(SD_1) = 5$
$\#OneWayArcsIn(SD_1) = 4$
$\#ServiceRequestsIn(SD_1) = 0$
$\#RepliesIn(SD_1) = 0$.
Hence $\mu_{ScenarioDiagram}(SD_1) = 9$.

We obtain for the second scenario diagram:
$\#ObjectsIn(SD_2) = 6 + 4 + 8 = 18$ (not counting duplicate instances)

Artifact	1	2	Ratio
$\mu_{useCase}$	3	4	1.3
$\mu_{scenario}$	4	14	3.5
$\mu_{ScenarioDiagram}$	9	47	5.2

Table 5.6: Metric values for use cases 1 and 2 and the derived scenarios and scenario diagrams.

$\#OneWayArcsIn(SD_2) = 2 + 4 + 7 = 13$
$\#ServiceRequestsIn(SD_2) = 4 + 0 + 4 = 8$
$\#RepliesIn(SD_2) = 4 + 0 + 4 = 8.$
Hence $\mu_{ScenarioDiagram}(SD_2) = 47$. This gives: $\mu_{ScenarioDiagrams} = 9 + 47 = 56$.

5.13.2   Notes

It should be clear that our home heating system example needs more use cases to describe in greater detail how the system behaves in different circumstances. This would permit us to check more rigorously through scenario diagrams that the model developed satisfies the corresponding scenarios.

At this point we cannot say much about the relationship between the metrics applied to use cases, scenarios, and scenario diagrams. Table 5.6 summarizes the few data we have. Scenario diagram metrics seem not to relate linearly to use case metrics. Still, according to our minimal data, their ordering is maintained:

$\mu_{useCase}(UC_1) < \mu_{useCase}(UC_2)$
$\mu_{scenario}(SC_1) < \mu_{scenario}(SC_2)$
$\mu_{ScenarioDiagram}(SD_1) < \mu_{ScenarioDiagram}(SD_2)$

5.14   Empirical Relationships

We have completed one analysis round of the home heating system. In addition to all the artifacts, we collected process (effort) and product metrics. We did not exploit reuse, nor did we tap the powers of a CASE tool. The metrics collected are summarized and superimposed on the analysis micro process in Figure 5.49.

The metric data collected can be used for postulating empirical relationships between the metrics of the OOA artifact types. Of most interest are functions that yield an effort metric value for an artifact type based on the artifact types on which

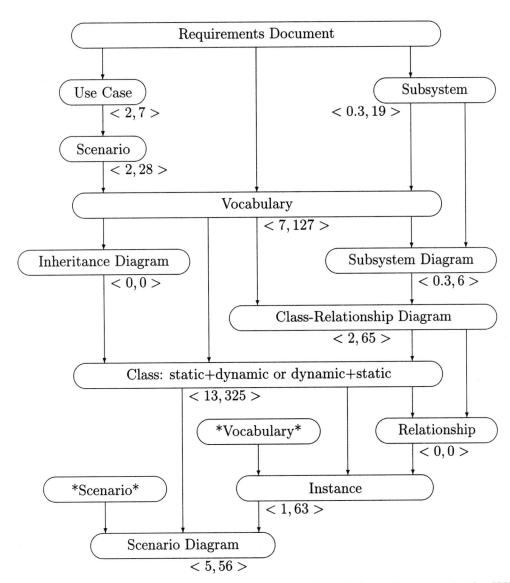

Figure 5.49: Effort and product metric are attached to each artifact type in the HHS. N in the expression $< N, M >$ stands for the number of hours used to develop all artifacts in the associated collection of artifacts. For example, it took 7 hours to develop the vocabulary. Similarly, M stands for the sum of the appropriate metric for the associated artifacts. For example, by representing the vocabulary entries by VE_i, we obtain: $\sum_i \mu_{vocabulary}(VE_i) = 127$.

it depends. For example, the effort for the vocabulary can be postulated to depend on the efforts for the scenario and the subsystem (and the requirements document, but we have no metric values available for the requirements document). The postulation of these empirical functions is a highly underconstrained affair. Many functions can map, for example, the values $< 2, 28 >$ for the scenario type and the values $< 0.3, 19 >$ for the subsystem type onto the effort metric 7 for the vocabulary type. Constraining this function to be linear still leaves many possibilities. Multiple data points would be helpful. Given the state of affairs, we supplement the lack of data with the assumptions that:

1. The linear function has a constant term with value 0.

2. The contribution of the scenario type weights 3 times that of the contribution of the subsystem type.

3. The scenario's effort metric contributes with weight equal to that of the product metric (hence the product metric value is to be divided by 14 to weight in as much as the effort metric).

4. Similarly for the subsystem type: The product metric must be weighted with the factor 0.3/19.

Now let

- $ef_{scenario}$ be the effort metrics value of the scenario type

- $pr_{scenario}$ be the product metrics value of the scenario type

- $ef_{subsystem}$ be the effort metrics value of the subsystem type

- $pr_{scenario}$ be the product metrics value of the subsystem type

- $ef'_{vocabulary}$ be an estimate for the effort metrics value of the vocabulary type

Our measured values and assumptions yield:

$$ef'_{vocabulary} =$$
$$1.31 * ef_{scenario} + 0.093 * pr_{scenario} +$$
$$2.92 * ef_{subsystem} + 0.046 * pr_{scenario}$$

Obviously, we have scaled the parameters such that $ef'_{vocabulary} = 7$ when we substitute the observed values for $ef_{scenario}$, and so on.

It should be clear that we can create similar empirical estimation functions for the other elaboration dependencies of the OOA micro process and the observed data as depicted in Figure 5.49.

It is to be noted that we refined the presentation given in Section 4.1.1. The function f_q defined there depended only on measured (or calculated) effort metric values. A function that also depends also on product metric values can be used when both values are available. Another feasible effort estimation function would depend only on earlier product metric values.

We repeat that at this point we do not have sufficient empirical data to produce a suite of effort estimation functions. We should also reemphasize that these estimation functions are probably application domain dependent. Obviously, the experience level of developers and the availability of reuse libraries and CASE tools are other factors that can easily thwart the accuracy of effort prediction functions.

5.15 Data from Student Teams

In this section we report the efforts measured by student teams working on the home heating system. These students attended an OO analysis and design class and had to apply their new insights in group projects. The quality of their results varies. Time pressures did not allow them to produce as much detail as we have shown in this chapter. Of interest is where they spend their time.

Table 5.7 shows the results for the six teams, denoted by A-F. The last column, headed by Z, shows again our values reported already in the previous section.

The row containing the totals shows that there is a substantial variation in the number of hours spend on their projects. Since the quality of the solutions fluctuates as well, we interpret these differences only as varying levels of commitment of the teams. Hence we restrict ourselves mostly to a team's relative effort in dealing with fragments of the total set of activities.

Noticeable is the small or zero amount of attention given to inheritance, subsystem diagrams, relationship,s and instances. This is ironic, given the amount of attention usually spend on these topics in the literature and in courses.

Several of the teams have split the amount of effort devoted to classes into static and dynamic parts. Table 5.8 shows the values they reported. Again noticeable is the much larger amount of attention given to the dynamic dimension than to the static parts.

	Team						
	A	B	C	D	E	F	Z
1 Use case	2.5	4.9	7.0	3.5	11.0	1.0	2.0
2 Scenario	2.5	0.0	9.0	0.0	0.0	1.5	2.0
3 Subsystem	2.5	4.0	11.0	3.5	12.0	5.7	0.3
4 Vocabulary	4.0	2.0	11.0	4.5	0.0	1.3	7.0
5 Inheritance	0.0	0.0	0.0	3.5	0.0	0.0	0.0
6 Subsystem diagram	3.0	0.0	0.0	0.0	0.0	0.0	0.3
7 Class-relationship	0.5	0.0	0.0	0.0	2.0	0.0	2.0
8 Class	39.5	22.3	35.0	30.0	38.0	41.6	13.0
9 Relationship	0.0	0.0	0.0	0.0	0.0	0.0	0.0
10 Instance	0.0	0.0	0.0	0.0	0.0	0.0	1.0
11 Scenario diagram	6.5	0.0	14.0	0.0	0.0	0.0	5.0
Total	61.0	33.2	87.0	45.0	63.0	51.1	32.6
Team size	3	4	4	3	4	3	1

Table 5.7: How for six student teams, A-F, spend their time (hours) developing artifacts for the home heating system. Column Z shows the values that we found and that we summarized in the preceding section. See the text for interpretations.

	Team					
	B	C	D	E	F	Total
Statics	10.3	13.0	9.5	14.5	13.6	60.9
Dynamics	12.0	22.0	20.5	23.5	28.0	106.0

Table 5.8: Split up of the effort spend on classes towards statics and dynamics. The last column shows the overall sum of the teams B-F. The dynamic dimension takes close to two-thirds of the total effort devoted to classes.

5.16   Heuristics for Effort Prediction

The data reported in Table 5.7 allow to formulate rough estimation functions for the total effort required to do an OOA analysis based on initial effort measurements. Table 5.9 depicts how to calculate the total effort for an analysis given measurements of initial activities. The numbers in the first column refer to artifact types as defined in Table 5.7. For example, if the use cases, scenarios, and subsystems have been completed (and their efforts have been measured), the row with 1+2+3 applies. The second column gives the correlation coefficient that yields an indication for the accuracy of the estimation.

The heuristics provided here are, obviously, very tentative since the data are based on a single task, the home heating system, and exploit only a handful of data. Accuracy improves, the more activities in the micro process are completed - as is to be expected - and conforms with Figure 4.1 on page 104. As discussed earlier, when effort metrics correlate with product metrics, we can also use product measures (in combination with effort measures) to estimate the remaining efforts.

Just in case the reader thinks that we are assuming a waterfall process, we remind you that the effort estimation discussed here applies to only one cycle of an analysis activity. Whether or not this cycle is the only analysis activity depends on what macro process is used.

We repeat our earlier disclaimers that reuse, CASE tools, the experience level of developers, and so on, have all been ignored.

5.17   Further Reading

We are aware of only one publication that discusses the home heating system: the first edition of Booch's *Object Oriented Design with Applications* [12].[13] Obviously, there are elements in common between the two different treatments. As we did, Booch prefers to give each room the responsibility of handling its living pattern, and his home diagram also shows a connection with the room and living pattern classes. We did *not* find an occupancy history class. Booch's treatment is in fact not complete. It is more like a sketch. On the other hand, he describes how to implement fragments into Smalltalk. Most significant is the fact that he intermixes analysis, design, and implementation. A general discussion of the requirements is followed by a detailed

---

[13]The second edition [13] had a changed title: *Object Oriented Analysis and Design with Applications* to stress the emerging distinction in the OO community between analysis and design. It is noteworthy is that the second edition no longer has the home heating example.

Initial phase, ip	Correlation coefficient	Total effort, te
1	0.48	$te = 41.1 + 2.66 * ip$
2	0.76	$te = 43.5 + 4.53 * ip$
3	0.76	$te = 34.9 + 3.30 * ip$
1+2	0.83	$te = 31.7 + 3.21 * ip$
1+3	0.66	$te = 36.2 + 1.69 * ip$
1+2+3	0.83	$te = 31.3 + 1.79 * ip$
1+2+3+4	0.85	$te = 27.6 + 1.55 * ip$
1+2+3+4+5	0.84	$te = 26.6 + 1.56 * ip$
1+2+3+41+5+6	0.88	$te = 24.1 + 1.67 * ip$
1+2+3+4+5+6+7	0.86	$te = 23.6 + 1.64 * ip$
1+2+3+4+5+6+7+8	0.97	$te = -3.3 + 1.14 * ip$
1+2+3+4+5+6+7+8+10	0.97	$te = -4.4 + 1.16 * ip$

Table 5.9: How to calculate an estimate of the total effort required for an OO analysis on the basis of an initial activity. For example, the row with 1+2+3+4 says that when the total effort of developing use cases, scenarios, subsystems and the vocabulary was 100 hours, the estimated total analysis effort is $27.6 + 1.55 * 100 = 182.6$. Hence the remaining effort is 82.6 hours. The correlation coefficient indicates the accuracy of the estimation.

description of how to prototype the user interface of the system. The implementation of a toggle switch is given ample attention. Subsequently, Booch returns to a high-level characterization of the major subsystems. This is followed by detailed diagrams for the room and the furnace, together with fragments of the corresponding code.

The complexity of Booch's descriptions appear larger than ours. For example, his transition diagram of a room has six states with 20 transitions. In contrast, we used only three states with six transitions. He ends his description by suggesting changes to the requirements and discusses whether these changes would lead to ripple effects (see the exercises).

5.18 Summary

In this chapter we have described an application of the OO analysis micro process to the home heating system example. Product metrics applied to the vocabulary entries and to the corresponding formal class descriptions show a high correlation (0.96). Effort metrics obtained from seven sources suggest that early analysis efforts (i.e., use cases, scenarios, subsystems, and vocabulary) correlate positively with the overall analysis effort (0.85). The analysis produced 21 classes.

5.19 Exercises

1. Construct a scenario that elaborates the third use case, see page 134.

2. Construct a scenario diagram based on the scenario developed in the preceding exercise.

3. Extend the transition network of the furnace to deal with a 5-minute waiting period following a shutdown.

4. Extend the transition network of the furnace to deal with the blower motor reaching a predefined RPM value.

5. Extend the transition network of the furnace so that activation of the monitor is delayed by 1 second after ignition occurs.

6. Extend the transition network of the furnace to deal with the water in the boiler reaching a predefined temperature.

7. Booch suggests changing the requirements so that a user can set explicitly, per room, the desired temperature when the room is unoccupied. Modify the analysis model so that this change is incorporated.

8. Change the requirements so that the user can set a vacation mode in which the rooms do not lose their living patterns while the temperature of all rooms are maintained at a user-specified uniform temperature.

Part II

Design

Chapter 6

Design Concepts

6.1 Purpose of Design

Designing is often used to refer to all the activities that precede coding and testing. It has the connotation of "smartness", in contrast to what is done in "plain" coding.[1] This meaning allows design to be done during an implementation, especially when a software development process is not adhered to, is ill defined, or is not defined at all. One can call this the wide sense of design. A good example of this usage is in the title of the first edition of the book *Object Oriented Design* by Grady Booch [12]. A much more restricted meaning of *designing* is the activity that, somehow, is interspersed between analysis and implementation activities. This is the narrow sense of design and is the topic of this chapter. Again a good example of this usage is in the second edition of Booch's book: *Object Oriented Analysis and Design.*

A precise demarcation of analysis, design, and implementation activities is not easy, due to widespread advertisements for iterative and fountain life cycles, which tend, sometimes deliberately, to blur their distinctions. In addition, one must admit that analysis as presented in Part I and as presented in Booch [12, 13], Rumbaugh et al. [70], Shlaer and Mellor [72, 73], and elsewhere has design flavors. For example, the introduction of classes during the analysis defines, partially, the solution space. In fact, the continuity induced by analysis classes showing up in the implementation is a major, if not the most important, achievement of the OO software development

---

[1] Over the years, there has been a gradual inflation in the standing of software development. When programming lost its "priest" status, programmers referred to their activity as "building systems". Coding and hacking caused more erosion and hence "designing" became *en vogue*. "Architecting" is the current rage. The terms do indicate that the key activity in software construction slowly creeps up in the life cycle.

approach.

Using a difference in notations that would separate analysis, design, and implementation is not readily available. Analysis notations are graphical; implementation notations are textual; but there is no consensus about design notations in OO. We used a textual, specially developed design language in de Champeaux et al. [24], but this language is not been widely embraced.

One may propose that the formalisms used for analysis and design differ in expressive power regarding computability. Design certainly needs a formalism that has the power of a Turing machine. The situation is less clear regarding the analysis formalism. Since analysis needs to capture only precisely *what* the requirements are, one may argue that executability is not required for the analysis formalism. In practice, one needs nearly the full power of algorithmic description to capture temporal phenomena in the requirements: One needs to provide a PIN *before* one is able to receive money from an ATM. Hence one uses happily transition networks in analysis to capture intended system behavior.

As a result, we demarcate analysis and design through the *intent* of the activities. Analysis aims at problem description and clarification, and in the process we may have to introduce concepts that define and possibly constrain the solution space. It is simply a fact of life that pure problem description languages do not exist. In contrast, design aims at the construction of the solutions to the problems formulated by analysis. Consequently, we can use a formalism that has the expressive power of a Turing machine for analysis as long as the intent of the descriptions is problem clarification and demarcation. The same formalism could then be used for design in order to express solutions in great detail and to satisfy many auxiliary requirements, such as performance, maintainability, and reusability.

The question remains how to demarcate design against implementation activities. Both aim at providing a solution. A dictionary defines design as "to devise for a specific function or end". This applies to implementation activities as well. Thus we have to look for differences elsewhere.

We can get inspiration from the deliverables in other engineering disciplines. We see obvious distinctions between, on the one hand, the construction of blueprints for a skyscraper, a bridge, a space station, or an aircraft carrier and, on the other hand, the construction of these entities themselves. One such distinction is that, making a fundamental change in any of these blueprints is fairly easy compared with establishing the corresponding changes in the real things, which may not even be possible. The distinction between a software design and the corresponding implementation is in general of a lesser magnitude: An implementation is not cast in concrete, although it may sometimes feel that way. The similarity in medium - symbolic notations - is misleading. A key difference in the case of software is the completeness of detail. Design should yield a unique solution that satisfies all functional, resource, performance, and other requirements but can leave out details that can obviously be filled in later. In contrast, the implementation activity should "plug all holes" and in addition can improve the design by exploiting features of the target implementation language.

Somewhat worrisome is still the phrase "details that can obviously be filled in later". What is obvious is a function of context. Sorting 100 Gb of data may not need an elaboration in one environment and may be a serious design issue in another environment.

At the same time, under certain circumstances, design may plug all holes as well. Still, an implementation may yield a much more detailed solution - probably with better performance - when a design formalism aims at ease of expression, say for early prototyping, over efficiency.

The design - implementation boundary delineation has been discussed thus far independent of OO-ness. The boundary between them becomes defined more sharply when we take OO into account. OO design has the responsibility to bridge a major difference between the computational "philosophy" in analysis versus the one in current OO programming languages.

While we have objects and classes all the way from analysis through design up to implementation, the nature of an object changes along the way. An analysis object is endowed with its own thread of control[2] while an implementation object normally has to share a single thread of control per process. OO design must eliminate the abundance of implicit parallelism in the analysis output model.

Satisfaction of performance requirements is another key responsibility of design. We have a little paradox here. A design is in general not executable, and in case it is executable, its performance is likely to be inferior. So how can we demand that design ensures performance requirements? A design should ensure the performance from a computational complexity perspective. This is where the notion of scalability comes in. The design should provide algorithms and data structures that will ensure that the performance requirements are met from a scalability perspective. The corollary is that when a system fails a performance requirement, one should, in general, *not* tinker with the code. The design should be changed (or the requirements loosened up).

Whether design is dependent on features of the target programming language is a matter of taste. If it is independent, one may obtain a generic design that can easily be realized in any chosen implementation language, provided, for example, that the

---

[2]Embley et al. [25] and others allow even more than one thread of control per object.

design does not use multiple inheritance when the target language supports only single inheritance. At the very least, it is helpful to distinguish between design decisions that are programming language dependent and those that are not, while postponing the ones that are based on the target language.

There are different ways to look at the *scope* of design activities. Design "in the small" concentrates on the different artifacts produced in the analysis and carries them over into a low-level design through elaboration, realization, possibly inducing the introduction of other artifacts, such as container classes, exception mechanisms, etc. A topic like sequentialization requires us to go beyond individual artifacts and obtain a global perspective. An application of design patterns may also require that we investigate multiple artifacts, see Gamma et al. [28]. Finally, one can perceive design as an activity that operates at the level of models: the transformation of an analysis model into a model that represents a complete low-level design. Choosing and instantiating a design framework is an example activity in this realm. This last global perspective will be revisited when we discuss the design process.

In summary, design is the activity that transforms the output of the analysis into the input of the implementation by constructing a scalable proto solution that satisfies the requirements. Major goals in design are: achieving (proto) executability, satisfaction of resource constraints, scalability, and sequentialization of the analysis model.

6.2 Desiderata for an OO Design Notation

Unresolved is the question of what to use for an OO design notation. This vacuum is painfully clear in a book like *Design Patterns: Elements of Reusable OO Software* [28]. There Gamma et al. resort to using some graphical analysis notations in combination with C++ and Smalltalk snippets. As mentioned before, in [24] we used a dedicated design language ODL. That language is quite adequate from an educational perspective – one can stay away from the idiosyncrasies of C++, Smalltalk, and so on. It is another matter, however, whether ODL can be used in practice, which is our orientation in this book.

Using three different formal languages during software development requires at the very least powerful support by an integrated CASE tool. Such a tool would need to generate downstream artifacts from upstream artifacts automatically, similar to the way that certain CASE tools generate C++ fragments from analysis models. Even with such a tool, we must face the reality that preserving the consistency of three distinct formal descriptions is beyond the ability of most projects. As a result, we have the choice of using for design the analysis language, a fragment of a programming language, or a middle way. Somewhat reluctantly, we will use a combination of the graphical analysis notation extended for greater precision where necessary with C++. Our discomfort is caused by the fact that this choice tends to hide the fundamental change in computational models that happens during design.

Delineating more features of a design notation requires a detour regarding OO design "styles". One can distinguish two different practices, with in between ground as well. Let's call the practitioners at one end of the spectrum the "impressionists" and the practitioners at the other end of the spectrum the "constructivists". The impressionists do not rely on precise semantics of the analysis and design notations. A key phrase in these circles is that "the design fleshes out the analysis output", and one is not welcome to ask for a definition of "fleshing out". The idea that analysis has a different computational model than the implementation is acknowledged opportunistically: The difference is welcomed when useful and is ignored when this would entail an explicit transformation. For this style of development one does not need to elaborate the design notation further. The transition to precision occurs when the implementation starts.

The constructivists have a radically different approach. They want to exploit the analysis computational model. They observe that the behavioral descriptions in analysis are "nearly" executable. Aiming for early prototyping, they put a premium on the construction of a high-level, executable design language that is as close as possible to the analysis notations. Key features of such a language are precise semantics for object communication and in particular well-defined policies for event processing. Transforming an executable prototype expressed in a high-level design notation to, say, C++ can be automated to a large extent and does not require a separate design formalism. If an executable prototype relies on garbage collection, the realization of memory management needs manual support in a transformation to C++. In case one does not want to rely on a run-time system that emulates object concurrency, one has to provide manual support for sequentialization as well.

It should not come as a surprise that most OO development work is done according to the impressionistic style. The alternative constructivist approach is, however, growing, as witnessed by the increasing number of CASE tools that allow execution of high-level designs.[3]

We will steer a middle road in this book. The mentality of the impressionist's approach is accommodated by avoiding rigorous precision of a design formalism. At

---

[3]At the time of this writing, we are aware of ObjectBench from SES, ObjectTime from ObjecTime, and OMW from Intellicorp.

the same time we will sketch design as done through adoption of the constructivist's approach.

6.3   Basic Concepts for Design

OO design is an unobvious activity. It falls under the general heading of problem solving. Naively, analysis yields the definition of the problem, design comes up with a blueprint of the solution. The situation is less grim for design than it looks. Design does not start with an empty slate. An analysis produces, in fact, an outline for a solution. Hence design is concerned with assessing that this proto solution is compatible with all auxiliary requirements beyond the functional requirements, and if so, this outline is to be elaborated. As mentioned earlier, the elaboration is done at different scopes: at the level of individual artifacts, at the level of multiple interrelated artifacts, and at the level of the system as a whole.

To ground the intuition for the assessment of the analysis proto solution, consider the following example: Analysis, as presented, forces "push" versus "pull" commitments; i.e., data are pushed out through events or data is pulled in from servers. Most communication in our home heating system is of the push type. Sensors are pulled, however. The design should challenge these choices. Actual sensors may not support pulling data from them. As another example, consider the autonomy of all objects in the home heating analysis model. The "spirit" of the model suggests that all objects have their own thread of control. But the requirements document does not endorse a distributed realization where each object has its own processor. Hence the design is incompatible with the ultimate design model.

What is to be done depends on the nature of the discrepancy (and whether design is done in an impressionistic fashion, where difference can be more tolerated than when the design is done in a constructive fashion). A buy-in means that the design will accept responsibility for an unrealistic or incomplete aspect of the analysis model. For example, if actual sensors cannot be pulled, the design may wrap them. If buy-in is not possible, or is deemed to be impossible, the design has to backtrack into the analysis when a high level of consistency between analysis and design models is called for.

Elaboration of a proto solution benefits greatly from expertise. This can take many shapes: knowing an application domain and having access to "tricks of the trade", knowing a procedure for breaking down a large problem into more tractable subproblems, knowing an array of ready-made or customizable building blocks, etc. In turn, we will look at a set of activities thar have proven effective, and subsequently consider some emerging idioms and patterns that can act as flexible building blocks.

6.3.1 Physical architecture

Logical architecture - the structure of top-level subsystem - is a major concern in the analysis. Similarly in design we are interested in how to realize the executing system as a structured collection of interacting processes which we define to be the physical architecture.[4] The base case is a system with only a single process. In fact, the majority of systems (editors, compilers, spreadsheets, etc.) are single-process systems. The growing number of networks will facilitate more distributed systems.

Systems that have more than one process, but with all of them residing on the same processor, are often assembled as pipes and filters. Unix has build-in support for this family of architectures. Pipe and filter architectures are not helpful to support multiple processes that realize an OO analysis model unless the analysis model has clear-cut boundaries while the communication across these boundaries can be squeezed through the one-way pipe and filter plumbing.

A more typical arrangement for a realization of an OO analysis model into multiple processes relies on infrastructure that allows object to communicate across process boundaries. An example of multiple processes that reside on a single processor is an integrated CASE system with among other processes:

- A user-interface process

- A process that gives support for development work flows

- Processes for point tools

- A process that acts as a forwarding agency for point tool intercommunicating messages

- A process to manage a CASE tool-wide repository of development artifacts

A multiple-process physical architecture helps to fight the inherent complexity of a large system. The integrated CASE example illustrates that a physical architecture can coincide with a logical architecture, but this is not always the case. Here

---

[4]What we call *physical architecture* is called *process architecture* by Booch [12, 13]. At the same time, by physical architecture he refers to the organization of the directories used to store the files so that the system can be compiled in an orderly fashion and so that the system can be documented and maintained easily.

are two examples where the logical architecture does not coincide with the physical architecture.

Consider a bank as a system. One of its logical subsystems is responsible for interacting with customers to take in deposits and to disburse cash. Its realization is spread out over many units, is achieved through human tellers using special terminals, and through ATMs.

Consider an advanced system for finite element analysis. Such a system is used to calculate force fields over one, two, or three dimensional artifacts that cannot be determined analytically by solving equations due to the irregularity of the artifacts. Consider, for example, an airplane. These calculations typically uses supercomputers, due to the vast amount of number crunching required. Novel approaches use distributed processing. The artifact under consideration is partitioned, the different parts are assigned to different processes, and the calculations proceed by doing local calculations while exchanging data regarding the shared boundary elements.

The latter example illustrates a system where the number of constituting subprocesses is not fixed but fluctuates during run time. Generic problem solvers are another example that may dynamically generate subprocesses that correspond to conjectured problem decompositions.

These examples illustrates that there are no general recipes for the construction of physical architectures. Generic guidelines are:
– Try to exploit boundaries defined by the logical architecture.
– Try to exploit decomposition that correspond with localized sensors, actors, and/or interactive devices.
– Try to exploit regularities in data to be manipulated so that a divide-and-conquer approach can be applied.

After a physical architecture is established, we need, at a certain point, to "spread out" the analysis model over the collection of processes that make up the physical architecture. This is discussed in Section 6.3.6 on clustering.

6.3.2   Acquaintance relationship

Impressionists and constructivists alike face designing away relationships introduced in the analysis phase. This section deals with relationships that are used to support communications. The next section deals with "normal" relationships that are used for traversals.

Acquaintance relationships express an asymmetric "know-of" connection between instances of two classes. For example, in our home heating system, each room needs to know the heat-flow regulator, the heat-flow regulator knows the valve controller and the furnace controller, etc., see Figure 5.43 on page 204. For all these examples we reduce the design of such relationships to the introduction of attributes in the objects that "need to know". See Figure 6.1 for details.

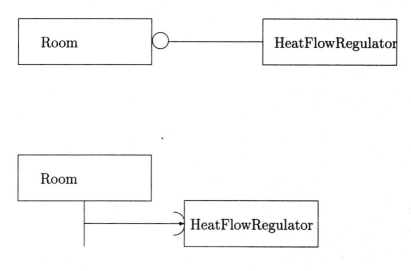

Figure 6.1: Design of acquaintance relationships. A room needs to know the heat flow regulator in order to communicate events. The design consists of the addition of an attribute to the room, with the heat-flow regulator class as the value domain. The (in this case unique) instance of *HeatFlowRegulator* is to be reached via the indirection of a reference, as indicated by the attribute link ending in a half-circle.

6.3.3 Eliminating regular relationships

Relationships that support traversals are designed away similarly to acquaintance relationships. However, multiplicities can complicate the situation. Only binary relationships are considered here. The design of ternary relationships follows corresponding patterns. For the multiplicities, we consider the following three cases:

1. *One-one relationship* for example, the *Spouse* relationship between *Husband* and *Wife*[5]

---

[5] A reviewer had to remind us that the one-one-ness of the spouse relationship does not apply uniformly to all societies.

2. *One-many relationship* for example, the *WorksFor* relationship between *Employee* and *Department*

3. *Many-many relationship* for example, the *Owns* relationship between *Account* and *Client*, assuming that an account can have multiple owners and a client can have multiple accounts

Each of these is discussed in turn. Reflexive relationships are also considered.

A symmetric solution is recommended for a one-one relationship. Hence we add attributes to both parties of the relationship with, as referenced value domains, the other class. See Figure 6.2 for the design of the *Spouse* relationship relationship. This design does *not* provide for manipulating the set of all husband and wife pairs. If this is needed, one has to extend the design by the introduction of either the class *SET(Husband)* or the class *SET(Wife)*. A symmetric solution would use a template Pair as in *SET(Pair(Husband, Wife))*.

A one-many relationship will yield an asymmetric design. For example, in the *WorksFor* relationship, an employee gets an attribute with *Department* as value domain, while a department gets an attribute that refers to a parametrized container class, see Figure 6.3. Supporting the set of pairs of (employee, department) is somewhat different than in the preceding case. A simple solution is to introduce a class *SET(Department)*. This yields effectively a set of sets of employee-department pairs.

A many-many relationship yields again a symmetric design; see Figure 6.4 for the *Owns* relationship between *Account* and *Client*. To traverse all client-account pairs, we need either a class *SET(Client)*, *SET(Account)*, or *SET(Pair(Client, Account))*.

(Set) container classes are usually equipped with iterator operations that traverse the elements and execute a specifiable operation on each traversed element in turn. Faster access to subsets in a container requires additional infrastructure. Techniques developed for relational databases can be employed as necessary.

Containment between directories in a hierarchical structure is an example of a reflexive relationship. A directory has optionally a parent directory and can contain optionally other directories. See Figure 6.5 for the design of the containment relationship.

6.3.4   Attributes

The design of an attribute depends on:
– The representation of the attribute's value domain
– The way an attribute value is incorporated: by value or through a referring pointer
We discuss each point in turn.

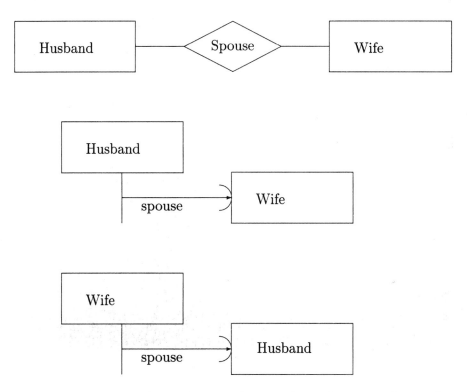

Figure 6.2: How a one-one relationship can be transformed into attributes. Note that both attribute value domains are attached through a reference, as indicated by the attribute links ending in a half-circle.

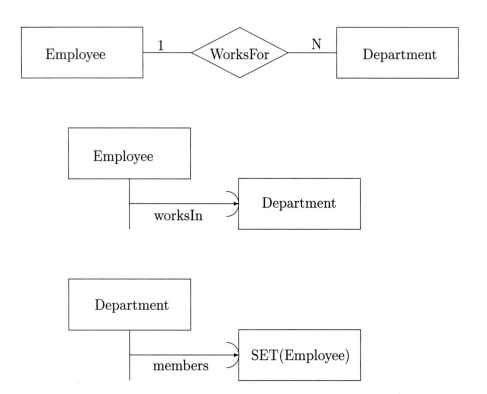

Figure 6.3: Design of a one-many relationship. The "1" at the left-hand side of the relationship indicates that an employee occurs exactly once in the *WorksFor* relationship. The "N" at the other side indicates that a department can occur many times in the *WorksFor* relationship.

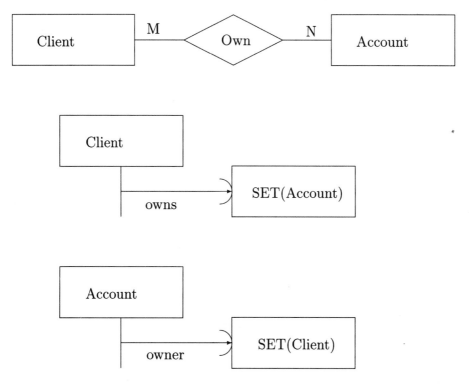

Figure 6.4: Design of a many-many relationship. A client can have M different accounts and an account can have N different owners. N and M are unconstrained here. In practice, constraints will be available. These constraints are propagated to the sets. This is relevant for the decision as to how to implement these sets.

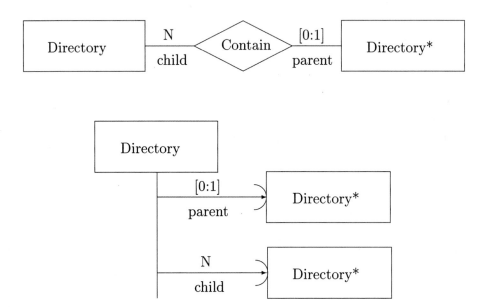

Figure 6.5: Design of a reflexive relationship. The binary *Contain* relationship is called reflexive because its two classes are the same. The asterisk is a reminder that the class has another, primary, occurrence elsewhere. Notice that the links between the diamond and the classes must be labeled to disambiguate them. The same labeling can be used for the names of the corresponding attributes in the design. Obviously, the attributes domains *must* be referenced - an object cannot incorporate an object of the same type.

An analysis can make a commitment about an attribute's value domain. For example, Figure 2.6 on page 36 depicted the *caller* and the *callee* domains as being represented as classes with the domains of *initializationTime* and *duration* being represented as nonclasses. The design may accept these choices or change nonclasses into classes after all. Having code available in the form of a class for a value domain can be a convincing argument to a switch over in the design.[6]

The analysis ignores whether the value of an attribute is physically inside an object (incorporation by value) or whether the value is to be accessed indirectly through a pointer.[7] A uniform policy can prescribe a design where all attributes are reached through an indirection. If feasible, one can make a tighter coupling between an attribute value and the corresponding object through an incorporation by value. Incorporation by value of instances of, say, the class A in instances of the class B is not possible when instances of B are already incorporated by value in the class A, see page 318.

We can extend the notation for attributes to indicate whether an attribute value is physically incorporated or whether a reference is to be used. See Figure 6.6 for details. Deciding whether to use incorporation by value or whether to use a reference is subtle. Incorporation by value yields more encapsulation and is faster. A referenced attribute value gets more "respect" for its identity. When an attribute value needs to do business with other parties, a reference is appropriate.

6.3.5 Executability

The previous sections dealt with the static dimension. Here we address the design of the dynamics. Making an analysis model executable involves only three activities (ignoring the infrastructure required for distributed systems):
- Making transition networks executable
- Creating constructors for all classes
- Creating an initializer for the system
In this section we focus on the transition networks. The two other tasks are application system specific and are ignored. However, see Gamma et al. [28] for creational patterns.

As described above, there is the constructivist approach and the impressionistic approach. The constructivists will produce an executable high-level design that is

---

[6]Note that C++ supports non-object-valued attributes. Smalltalk has only object-valued attributes.

[7]The two ways of incorporation of an attribute value map directly on corresponding C++ constructs. Smalltalk supports only attributes values that are referenced.

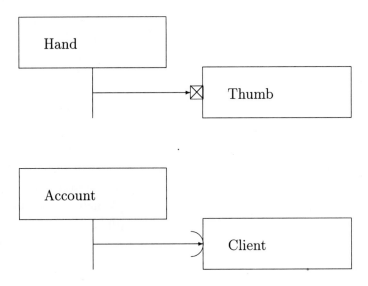

Figure 6.6: Notation for how an attribute value is attached to an object. The box connection between *Hand* and *Thumb* denotes an incorporation by value. In contrast, the half-circle connection between *Account* and *Client* denotes attachment through a pointer. Note that the incorporation by value encapsulates the attribute value much more than does attachment through a reference.

close to the analysis model. Subsequently, they may produce a low-level design if the performance is not acceptable or when the target system is distributed. The low-level design differs from the high-level design in that the abundance of parallelism has been removed. The impressionists bypass the constructivist's high-level design and start with the sequentialization. To illustrate these different approaches, we apply them to a simple artificial example.

Example Set Exchange

The following example is fairly atypical and should be appreciated only for the illustration of design phenomena. The "requirements document" is as follows:

> An entity x has possession of two nonempty sets p and q whose members are of a certain type T. The intersection of p and q is empty. Two elements of type T can be compared as if they are numbers. Elements of the sets p and q can be replaced; i.e., elements can only be inserted or deleted as part of a replacement operation; hence the sizes of p and q remain the same. The set p is less than or equal to ($\leq$) the set q if and and only if the maximum of the elements in p is less or equal than the minimum in q. The situation is to be reached where $p \leq q$.

A symmetric approach yields a description where a third party takes care of the comparison of elements of p and q. See Figure 6.7 for the static descriptions. The class *Tset* delegates "setness" to a standard templated class *SET*. The dynamic dimension is captured in Figure 6.8. The reader is invited to verify that the description in Figure 6.8 is a high-level characterization, with inherent parallelism, of a solution to the set exchange problem. Observe that p and q are both instances of the class *Tset* and that the transition networks of p and q are triggered, respectively, with *p.trigger(max)* and *q.trigger(min)*. As a result, the transition networks for p and q will search, respectively, for maximum and minimum values.

Constructivist approach

Assuming having an interpreter available for our transition diagrams, filling in gaps is what remains. The following omissions must be dealt with:

1. The unknown guard in the transition network of X. The requirements are not of much help here. A simple solution is to make the guard *true*. However, this will lead to an infinite cycle. Introducing a dependence on an external event,

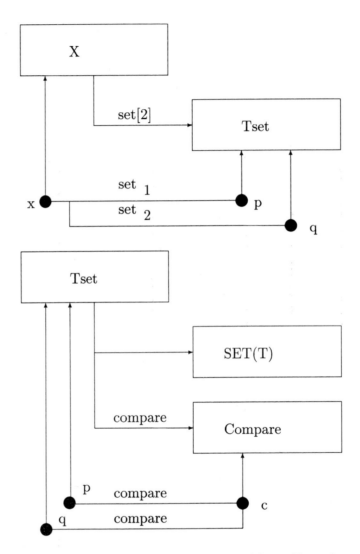

Figure 6.7: Static description for the set exchange problem. Note that p and q appear twice: as attribute values and as instances. The class X has a handle on two sets of the type *Tset*. *Tset* uses delegation to a parametrized set. This construct allows us to use a standard set and to supplement the basic features with additional ones as calls for by the situation.

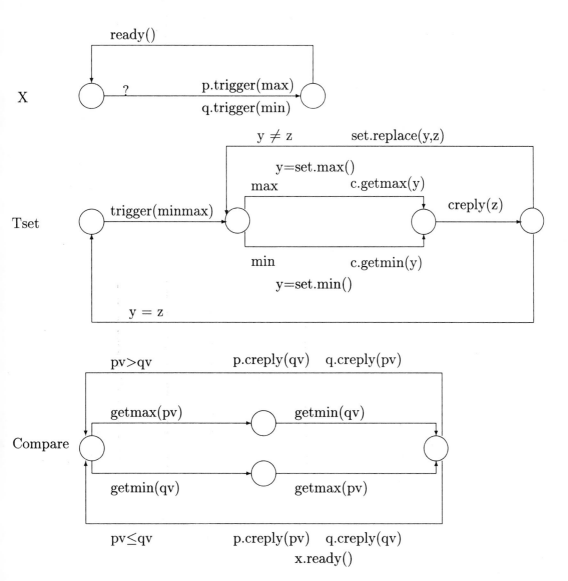

Figure 6.8: Dynamics of the classes X, $Tset$, and $Compare$. The start event in X is unknown. The start trigger in $Tset$ carries in the value min or max. Note that $Compare$ signals x an instance of X explicitly when the exchanges are completed with the event $x.ready()$. Since Compare does not know the sequence in which the $getmax(pv)$ and $getmin(qv)$ events arrive, it has two parallel routes to accepts these input events.

say *startExchange()*, is probably the best solution but begs the question as to which object will generate this event. A stopgap solution is to add a Boolean-valued attribute *exchange* to X, initialize this attribute as *true*, and reset this attribute to *false* on the return transition that is triggered by the *ready()* event.

2. The operations *max()* and *min()* in *Set*. It is not realistic to assume that a generic templated container class *Set* will support this functionality. Hence a delegation construct can be employed where *SET(T)* is replaced by *MySet(T)*. *MySet(T)* will use internally an attribute with value domain *SET(T)* and will have the machinery to find a maximum and a minimum relying on an element traversal mechanism of *SET(T)*. Alternatively, we replace *set.max()* and *set.min()* by local operations *max()* and *min()*, respectively, which rely on element traversal of *SET(T)*. It is unlikely that an analyst will object against this replacement. In fact, we have found an "error" in the analysis characterization!

3. The operation *set.replace(y.z)*. Again it is unlikely that *SET* will support this operation. Hence we have to follow the same tactic as for the realization of *max()* and *min()*.

4. The guards $pv > qv$ and $pv \leq qv$. If the type T of pv (and hence of qv) is indeed a number, it is possible to do the comparison inside *Compare*. Otherwise, comparison operations must be introduced inside the class T.

5. The guards $pv > qv$ and $pv \leq qv$ again. It is not really necessary to test the values themselves in the guards. One $\leq$-comparison can be done as soon as both pv and qv values have arrived inside *Compare*. Thus the guards can be replaced by *pvGreaterQv* and *not pvGreaterQv* respectively, when we capture in *pvGreaterQv* the boolean value of the result of this comparison.

6. The guards *max* and *min*. They must be replaced by *minmax = max* and *minmax = min* respectively. An analysis model syntax checker should have prevented the sloppy formulation of these guards.

   The states in these transition networks fall into two disjoint categories: Emanating transitions are driven by events only or emanating transitions are driven by boolean conditions only.[8] An execution engine for transition networks must be proactive

---

[8]We have not yet encountered in practice a state that had an emanating transition driven only by a boolean condition in addition to a transition driven only by an event. We have encountered a situation where an emanating transition is driven only by an event, while there is another transition that has a boolean condition *and* an event; see the heat-flow regulator on page 158.

when a state is entered that has transitions driven by boolean conditions.[9] Either the emanating transition with a true guard is executed immediately, or that transition is added to a first-in-first-out event queue.

With these replacements and elaborations, we obtain an executable prototype.[10] Clustering, sequentializing, and optimizing this prototype are discussed in the following sections.

6.3.6 Clustering

A cluster is a component in the physical architecture of the design that will be realized as a process in the implementation. Clustering plays a role when a system is to be realized as a collection of interacting processes. We have discussed above considerations that play a role in delineating a physical architecture. Mapping objects onto the processes in the architecture should exploit the rationale for splitting up the system and the resulting characterizations of the individual processes.

Since the rationale for distribution is quite diverse and ranges from fault-tolerant concerns, obtaining speedup by exploiting parallelism, catering for I/O components that are geographically distributed, and so on, there is not a single recipe to construe maps from objects to processes. Hence it will suffice here give some suggestions.

Architecture isomorphism

When the physical architecture coincides with the logical architecture, we can apply the following strategy. The top-level subsystems are realized as instances of ensemble classes. Hence these classes are assigned to their respective components of the physical architecture. Subsequently, we apply repeatedly the rule that if the class of an object reachable from an already allocated object has not been allocated, its class is to be allocated to the same component. If the class, say C, has already been allocated, we need to investigate whether or not we have the situation where this class must be present in more than one system component. Low-level utility classes are an example thar we expect to be present in more than one component.

---

[9] Normally, one of the emanating transitions should have a guard that evaluates to true. If not, a dead end is reached, unless the object has an orthogonal network that can still change a guard from a transition in the dead-end state. These are esoteric situations that we have not encountered in practice.

[10] Of course, we do not claim that obtaining an executable design from an analysis model will always be that simple.

If we decide that instances of the already allocated class C must not reside in multiple components, we must have a closer look at the situation. Is the current allocation of the class C acceptable at giving the newly established communication needs, which would entail interaction crossing component boundaries? If we accept the current allocation, we have established the need for a pair of classes that need to communicate across component boundaries. If we change the allocation of the class C, we may want to reassess the other communication obligations.

In general, we can make our life arbitrarily difficult since we deal with an NP-complete bin-packing problem - or worse. In practice, we can exploit additional insights, make decisions, and learn to live with them.

Data parallelism

Data parallelism can be caused by duplicated fault-tolerant computation or by the need to exploit multiple computing resources to obtain speedup. In both cases we have duplications of logical subsystems, and hence all objects and their classes are being made available in multiple processes. The division of labor between a supervisory process and compute "slaves" should prescribe how to allocate classes to a supervisor process.

Geographic distribution

Processes that cooperate while being distributed geographically can be special cases of either of the two cases described above. A distributed bank's branches is an example of data parallelism. A satellite tracking system is another example. A distributed manufacturing company with an integrated information system is an example where logical architecture and physical architecture may partially overlap. A combination of allocation strategies may have to be applied.

More detailed considerations that play a role in clustering can be found in de Champeaux et al. [24].

6.3.7   Sequentialization

Each cluster, or a single cluster if we have a nondistributed target system, has to be sequentialized if the target system is to be implemented in C++, Smalltalk, or a reader's favored OO language or perhaps in a non-OO programming language.[11] The set exchange example is revisited in Section 6.3.9 to illustrates the impressionistic approach. The set exchange example demonstrates that sequentialization can require nonlocal adjustments to the participating classes.

A standard approach is to wrap a cluster in an indefinite loop that starts with reading events. A branching logic at the beginning of the loop leads to execution threads which ultimately die out. Dependencies among objects should lead to the formation of these threads. Objectification of these threads can be considered, see Figure 6.11 on page 254.

Sequentialization of the transition network of a class can be a nontrivial affair. If the transition network has only a single state such that all transitions emanate from this state and return to this state, we need to work only on the events, if any, generated on transitions. These events must be transformed into blocking service interactions. Certainly, we must assure that we do not introduce calling cycles by making these modifications.

If the transition network has more than one state, we have several choices. The first choice is to take a global perspective and identify chains of events that are to be represented as chains of service requests. This will define the semantics of the operations to be translated into (C++) member functions. This approach is illustrated below with the set exchange example.

The second choice is to transform a multi state transition network into a single state network by qualifying the transitions with boolean conditions that represent the emanating states in the original transition network. Figure 6.9 shows how a transition network with two states is transformed in a transition network with one state that has qualified transitions. The corresponding class must be extended with a state attribute that is consulted in a transition's guard.

A third choice changes the value domain of the state attribute to unique members of subclasses of the class to be transformed. In the example of Figure 6.9 we would introduce the subclasses P and Q. These subclasses would have unique instances, say, p and q. The value domain of the state attribute in the main class would be $\{p, q\}$. The main class would be equipped with a single state that has the following transitions:

– *forwardA*: This transition would have a nil body and would never be invoked.
– *A*: This transition would invoke: `state->forwardA(...)`.

---

[11]Superimposing a generic lightweight thread package on, say, C++ is unlikely to yield a happy combination. Objects communicate in C++ through blocking member function calls. Analysis objects communicate preferably through the generation of targeted events in a send-and-forget mode.

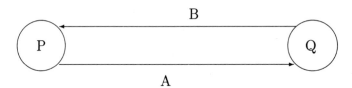

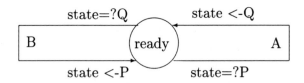

Figure 6.9: How to transform a transition network with multiple states in a network with a single state. The corresponding class is extended with an attribute named *state* that has as value domain the names of the states in the original network, in this example {*P, Q*}. The transitions are modified at two places. The guard should check whether the state attribute has the proper value. Second, the state attribute should be modified before the transition is completed to reflect the new state.

Similarly, we have the transitions *forwardB* and *B*.

The subclass *P* has a single state and the following transitions:

– *forwardA*: This transition would have as body the activities of the *A* transition in the original network and before completing would set the state attribute to *q*.

– *forwardB*: This operation would have a nil body because the state attribute has the value *p*.

Similarly, the subclass *Q* also has the transitions *forwardA* and *forwardB*, but here *forwardA* is a "no-operation", and *forwardB* has the original *B* operation extended with setting the state attribute. This third choice is illustrated in greater detail, using the heat switch, in Section 9.1.3 on page 292.

In part III we follow the second choice for the implementation of the Home Heating System.

6.3.8 Optimization

Sequentialized clusters must be optimized. There is not much generic algorithmic advice to be formulated. Features of the design constructed will drive optimization. See Table 6.1, from de Champeaux et al. [24], for some considerations.

6.3.9 Impressionistic approach

In this section we visit briefly the impressionistic approach. This approach aims at the construction of one or more sequentialized executable processes and bypassing the construction of an executable model where each object has its own private control thread. For now we assume that the target system is not distributed. Sequentializing the OOA model is the main concern in this approach. Let's revisit the set exchange problem. This example illustrates that serialization can be nontrivial. The analysis description exploits parallelism by calculating in parallel the maximum in *p* and the minimum in *q*. Another complication is the interaction between *Compare* and *X*: *Compare* informs *X* directly, "over the heads of *p* and *q*", when the exchanges are completed. The interaction between *X*, *Tset*, and *Compare* is dedicated to the set exchange problem. As a result, it is not feasible to obtain a sequentialization through local transformations.

The first observation to make is that the originating object *x* is effectively blocked while waiting for *p*, *q* and *c* to reach an agreement. Hence an operation performing a service request in *x* is a plausible first step. What would be the candidate object to receive this request? Symmetry rules out *p* and *q*. This leaves a service request to *c* (or the introduction of another mediating entity). Thus we obtain a transition in

Usually Faster	Usually Slower	Usually Faster	Usually Slower
Internal	External	Hardware	Software
Storage	Computation	Direct	Indirect
Unmediated	Mediated	Fixed	Variable
Implicit	Explicit	Special Purpose	General Purpose
Unguarded	Guarded	Immediate	Queued
Unconditional	Conditional	Computed	Symbolic
Approximate	Exact	Compile-Time	Run-Time
Optimistic	Pessimistic	Transient	Persistent
Control	Coordination	Event-Driven	Polled
Cooperation	Coordination	Point-to-Point	Routed
Dispatching	Forwarding	Local Call	Remote Call
Inline expansion	Call	Reply	Exception
Signaling	Blocking	Update	Construction
Invocation	Construction	Recycling	Construction
Chunked	One-at-a-time	Binding	Evaluation
Indexing	Searching	Lazy	Eager
Reference	Copy	Better Algorithm	Better Code

Table 6.1: Some performance trade-offs.

x that invokes, say, $c.exchange(\&p, \&q)$. This operation can be expanded, exploiting recursion, into

```
pv = pa->max();
qv = qa->min();
if (pv > qv) {
   pa->replace(pv,qv);
   qa->replace(qv,pv);
   exchange(pa,qa); };
```

This design (which is a fragment of the implementation) assumes that *Tset* forwards the *max()* and *min()* operations to the instance of its internal set attribute. X must be extended with a handle to a substantially modified compare instance. *Tset* no longer requires handle on a compare instance, and its behavior description is simplified.

This example demonstrates that one may have to mangle classes substantially when an analysis description exploits the power of parallelism in an intricate fashion. In common practice, the objects of most classes are engaged in extensive sequential threads, and hence the design of these classes does not require discontinuous modifications.

6.4   Beyond the Core Concepts

Thus far we have described generic notions. This section is devoted to some "nifty constructs". Coplien [19] calls them *idioms*. Gamma et al. [28] refer to them as *design patterns*. What is a nifty construct? It is a combination of primitive language elements that have been encountered repeatedly over time. Given that a construct has been reused, one can expect and hope that it may be applicable in more contexts. An example idiom in the realm of C, taken from Coplien [19], is

```
while (*cp1++ = *cp2++)
```

This is quite a concise construct, and it exemplifies the spirit of C: its obtuseness. It is a pure idiom because the example does not specify the type of `cp1` and `cp2`. As long as the `cp2` sequence terminates with a zero, we can use this copy construct. An idiom in the analysis realm is the *and*-gate that we encountered in the system controller, page 161 and in the furnace controller, page 174.

Absorbing the content of this section is not a trivial pursuit. Idioms/patterns/nifty constructs are explained primarily through examples. To reach the essence of the construct, the reader has to abstract away auxiliary details from a particular example.

Subsequently, a feel is to be developed for the applicability range so that the relevance of an idiom can be recognized later. Building up private idioms through experience is relatively easier than absorbing idioms through educational exposure. Hence we encourage the reader to study these idioms carefully - and repeatedly. See also Coplien, [19] and Gamma et al. [28].

6.4.1 Delegation

Delegation is a particular construct that has many different uses - in fact, an open-ended number of then.[12] To explain the construct, we start with a simple example. Suppose that we need "defensive" objects; i.e., objects whose operations test their preconditions and generate exceptions if a precondition is violated. Suppose as well that we have available a "naive" helper class that supports the proper functionality but doesn't check any preconditions. The trick here is to construct operations in a delegating class, as in:

```
if (event/service request) {
   if (preconditionOK) {
      invoke event/service request in helper object }
   else {
      raise an exception }
}
```

Operations in the delegating class have in common that they need to know an instance of the helper class. Hence we need a special attribute in the delegating class that has, as value domain, the helper class, see Figure 6.10.

This example suggests that the application of the delegation idiom is easy. It depends on where one starts. When one is familiar with the helper class and the task is to "ruggedize" it, the applicability of the idiom is straightforward. When one starts with requirements for a class and one considers exploiting, via delegation, an existing class, one must ascertain that a helper class indeed provides the necessary functionality. The costs of this investigation - a special case of reuse - must be compared against the costs of developing the functionality of the helper class from scratch.

Adaptation of a helper class to another context is another application of delegation. As an example, consider a helper class that does exception handling through

---

[12]Delegation is yet another instance of the postulate that all problem's in CS can be solved by another level of indirection.

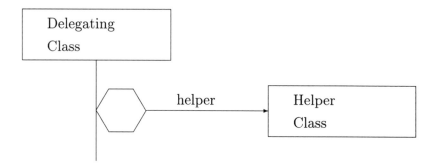

Figure 6.10: Structural dimension of delegation: The helper class is an attribute of the delegating class. Operations in the delegating class act as transducers and activate operations in the helper class.

catch-and-throw while the overall exception-handling policy is passing-the-buck. The delegating class can shield the system against the aberrant class.

Yet another example: The helper class has the wrong set of operation names and/or provides a desired functionality only partially. The delegating class can act as the intermediary and provide additional services as needed. This pattern is called the *adaptor* by Gamma et al. [28]. We can see this as a special case of wrapping because wrapping is usually referred to as providing an OO veneer to a legacy system.

These examples suggest that the delegating class and the helper class have similar purposes in this idiom. That is not required. The helper class can be arbitrarily different as long as its behavior can be overlaid to realize the behavior demanded of the delegating class. As a weird example, a stirrer for a teacup can be designed through delegation to a spoon that supports swirling, or through delegation to a screwdriver that supports swirling. One can ignore behavior that is not relevant in the helper class. For example, a stirrer class can ignore the spooning behavior of a teaspoon and the screwing capability of a screwdriver. In this example, we overlay the behavior of one entity, the teaspoon or screwdriver, with another interpretation. Pre-OO examples where the same phenomenon occurs include:
– Using a sequence of adjacent memory cells to represent an array
– Using an array to represent a vector
– Using a vector to represent a force
– Using an array in combination with link lists to represent a hash table
– Using a hash table to emulate associative memory

It should be clear by now that delegation can be very powerful but also that it can require genuine creativity to leverage an existing helper class.

6.4.2   Object existence management

Memory management is a headache in the absence of automatic garbage collection. Counting references to an object can help to keep track of the aliveness of an object. Coplien describes a scheme in [19] involving double indirections that can be applied to a class whose instances are to be managed. This scheme avoids having to do any modification of a managed helper class. It is based on overloading of the assignment operator. As such, one can argue that this is a target-language-specific design idiom.

6.4.3   Object creation and deletion management

Creation of transient objects with a high frequency may lead to performance problems. This can be ameliorated by creating objects in bulk, allocating them from a pool and recycling obsolete objects back into the pool. This can be done through overloading of the `new` and `delete` operations. For details of this idiom see, Coplien [19].

6.4.4   Client-Server

Client-server architectures enjoy a growing popularity since one can combine legacy systems on mainframes with cheap, powerful peripheral equipment with its snazzy graphics. It is the first step on the road in migrating from centralized to fully distributed computing.

Communication from a client to a server can be realized as remote procedure calls. This is not a good design if this entails that an application blocks, since it means that a user has lost control. Allowing the user to cancel a client-server interaction is a poor way to regain control. Instead, a client application should communicate in a nonblocking fashion. This will allow the user to maintain control and, if desired, to issue multiple requests concurrently to multiple servers or even to a single server – provided, of course, that a server entertains concurrent services.

A client application that allows a user to remain in control should "listen" to events coming from multiple directions: from the user and from any server that is opened which can generate expected replies or even "unexpected" events.[13] These requirements can be satisfied by a client architecture that transforms events into thread-objects. Such a thread-object receives control after its initialization, fulfills its mission, and self-destructs. There are three basic types of these thread objects:

---

[13]As an example of an unexpected event: The Z39.50, version 3, library access protocol, prescribes that a client should be prepared to handle a close event at all times.

1. Achieving a local change. *Examples:* A user may stipulate that future displays be done in a specific format; A server may generate data that are locally cached.

2. Causing output at the "same side". *Examples:* A user issues a display request for locally available data; a server issues a security challenge that can be replied to with data available in the client application.

3. Causing output at the "other side". *Examples:* a user issues a request to a server; a server returns data that can be displayed.

See Figure 6.11 for more details; see also Section 10.16, page 333.

6.5 OMT

This section is devoted to a discussion of design as described in the OMT method of Rumbaugh et al. [70]. We feel that this book is closest to what is described in this chapter. By going over some details, we contrast their approach versus ours. This gives us another way to clarify design activities.

"Traditionally", software design is split up into system design and detailed design. Rumbaugh et al. [70] replaced the detailed design of this pair and obtained the pair system design – object design. System design was not considered by them to be specific for OO, as witnessed by:

> The object-oriented paradigm introduces no special insights into system design, but we include system design for complete coverage of the software development process.

They describe system design as containing the following set of activities:

1. Organize the system into subsystems.

2. Identify concurrency inherent in the problem.

3. Allocate subsystems to processors and tasks.

4. Choose the basic strategy for implementing data stores in terms of data structures, files, and databases.

5. Identify global resources and determine mechanisms for controlling access to them.

User

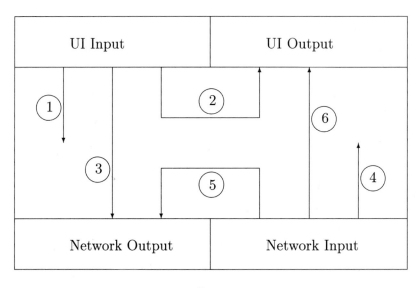

Server

Figure 6.11: Base architecture for a generic client that is part of a client-server pair. The user always remains in control, provided that threads complete quickly. Events are produced by the user or by the server. Events are transformed into transient thread-objects that are given control after they have been created. Threads 1 and 4 cause a local change in the client. Thread 2 causes a display of local data. Thread 3 represents a user initiated-request that is shipped to the server. Thread 5 is a server-initiated request that is replied to based on local data. Thread 6 is a server event that causes data to be displayed. Other threads can be construed as well. For example, a remote procedure call can be modeled by a thread that suspends itself after causing communication with the server, while the thread will be revived when the server's reply event arrives.

6. Choose an approach to implementing software control:
   - Use the location within a program to hold state, or
   - Directly implement a state machine, or
   - Use concurrent tasks.

7. Consider boundary conditions.

8. Establish trade-off priorities.

We will take a closer look at these activities. Although these activities are numbered, the significance of the ordering is not 100% clear. In fact, we rearrange things in the Chapter 7 on Design Process. The last two items on the list appear to be of a different magnitude, and their deliverables are less obvious.

We are sympathetic with the idea that system decompositions and subsystem interrelationships are to be addressed in the design phase. Indeed, system decomposition has a problem decomposition flavor and, as such, can be seen as belonging to design. However, as demonstrated in Part I, we have promoted subsystem delineation to the analysis phase, because a large system has to be decomposed early to control its complexity.

Identification of inherent *concurrency* is quite likely to be interpreted as the identification of inherent *parallelism*. Splitting up a process in multiple processes residing on the same processor cannot be an inherent feature of a target system.[14]

Finding inherent parallelism may be easy. For example, a requirements document may dictate that the system is geographically distributed or that parallelism is required to ensure a higher degree of fault tolerance. Parallelism may be required for performance reasons. This can be arbitrarily hard when a new algorithm has to be developed. However, this has little to do with OO.

The allocation of subsystems to processors and tasks is a questionable activity. It may not be possible. Assigning *objects* to processors and processes needs to be done when inherent parallelism has been found. But there is no guarantee that the process fault lines coincide with subsystem boundaries. For example, a subsystem responsible for maintaining persistent data may be distributed over multiple sites; a subsystem for data acquisition of an airline reservation system is inherently spread out over many many processors; a communication relay system through multiple satellites is inherently spread out over multiple processors. Hence we see the heuristics:

---

[14]Two processes are concurrent when the second one starts before the first one terminates, while only one executes at a time; two processes are in parallel when there is a period where they execute at the same time.

1. When feasible, assign subsystems to processors and processes. (Multiple processes on a processor are sometimes attractive: for example, when an existing process, such as a server, can be reused as is.)

2. When feasible, assign classes to processes. This entails that all instances of a class reside on a single processor. This is not always possible. The examples given above illustrate that this constraint can be too restrictive.

3. When feasible, assign objects to processes. We leave the door open for non-assignability of individual objects; this allows object migration from one process to another. At present we recommend staying away from object migration. The heuristic to assign objects to processes gives no guidance as to how to do these assignments. As a first shot, ensemble objects may be placed relatively easily. Using them as anchor points, one may get inspiration for other objects. Proximities to support communication as described in scenario and/or interaction diagrams can be used as a guideline.

The three choices listed for realizing control may need some elaboration. The first choice, "use the location within a program to hold state", is the least obvious. This entails "flattening" all transition networks into member functions, possibly equipped with conditions that depend on local state attributes, and coercing all event communications into member function invocations. A careful analysis has to be done to guarantee that the semantics realized through unbounded object parallelism is preserved in the sequentialized setting.

The second choice, "directly implement a state machine", refers to the realization of transition networks through low-level constructs such as labels and gotos, through case statements, or through similar techniques. Every service request and event communication is to be designed as a relaying member function that causes an addition to a queue attached to the recipient object. Each object having a nontrivial transition network has an attribute that keeps track of the current state of affairs. It resembles a program counter but can be more complex in the presence of parallel transition networks. An object with a nonempty queue is considered active and will reside as a member on a process-wide queue. An interpreter picks an object from the process queue, investigates the object queue, checks which transition can fire, if any, and if there is one, the interpreter executes the transition's actions. This can lead to the generation of service requests and/or of events that cause additions to the queues of the recipient objects.

The third choice, "use concurrent tasks", resembles the second choice with respect to the realization of transition networks. However, the interpreter is replaced by the machinery of the operating system or by a package supporting lightweight threads.

The item "consider boundary conditions" stands for initialization and for normal and abnormal termination procedures. It is not clear from [70] what they propose as the deliverables of this activity. The item "setting trade-off priorities" refers to design choices such as space versus time, complete and slow versus prototype and fast, portable versus dedicated, etc. A spiral life cycle with risk analysis will, in general, prescribe these priorities for a particular iteration of the cycle.

It should be clear from our elaboration that we do not underwrite the position that system design is independent of the OO paradigm. For example, all three approaches to the design of control depend intimately on how behavior is modeled in OO. We proceed by considering the Rumbaugh et al. view on object design:

1. Obtain operations for the object model from the other models:
   – Find an operation for each process in the functional model.
   – Define an operation for each event in the dynamic model, depending on the implementation of control.

2. Design algorithms to implement operations:
   – Choose algorithms that minimize the cost of implementing operations.
   – Select data structures appropriate to the algorithms.
   – Define new internal classes and operations as necessary.
   – Assign responsibility for operations that are not clearly associated with a single class.

3. Optimize access paths to data:
   – Add redundant associations to minimize access cost and maximize convenience.
   – Rearrange the computation for greater efficiency.
   – Save derived values to avoid recomputation of complicated expressions.

4. Implement software control by fleshing out the approach chosen during system design.

5. Adjust class structure to increase inheritance:
   – Rearrange and adjust classes and operations to increase inheritance.
   – Abstract common behavior out of groups of classes.
   – Use delegation to share behavior where inheritance is semantically invalid.

6. Design implementation of associations:
   – Analyze the traversal of associations.

  – Implement each association as a distinct object or by adding object-valued attributes to one or both classes in the association.

7. Determine the exact representation of object attributes.

8. Package classes and associations into modules.

We will also take a closer look at some of these object design activities. The activity "obtain operations for the object model from the other models" refers to the design of member functions. Input for this activities are the transitions, events, and the functional models, which are quite specific for the OMT method. These functional models detail the semantics of object behavior through structure charts. The phrase "define an operation ... depending on the implementation of control" parametrizes what is to be done with respect to choices: overall serialization and emulation of transition networks using an interpreter or relying upon the operating system or thread package.

The activity "assign responsibility for operations that are not clearly associated with a single class" is somewhat of an anomaly. Where would such an operation come from? All significant operations to be designed originate from the given analysis descriptions which are all attached to classes. Hence we recommend skipping this activity.

The last two subactivities under "optimize access paths to data" are generic design tricks and do not depend on OO. The addition of redundant associations has pros and cons. The rationale is to improve performance by introducing communication shortcuts. Increased coupling between classes is the price to pay. Rearranging things in the analysis model is to be considered.

"Implement software control by fleshing out the approach chosen during system design" is easier said than done. This refers to the design of the manner chosen to realize control from the list of three: sequentialize and flatten all transition networks, create an interpreter for emulated transition networks, map objects to processes and use the operating system to schedule them. We are not aware of any project that has realized the third choice. Process context switching is currently quite costly. On the other hand, certain operating systems make interprocess communication transparent with respect to the location of two communicating processes; i.e., communication between two processes residing on the same processor is treated in the same fashion as when they are on different processors. This solves elegantly the design and implementation of object communication in distributed systems. Due to the price tag of this solution, current practice is to sequentialize transition networks and to rely on CORBA services, or the like [55] for interprocess object communication.

"Adjust class structure to increase inheritance" is not a design activity to be scheduled separately; it is more a "demon"-like activity. At all times during OO development (not only in design), one should be alert to recognize abstraction possibilities. The introduction of new classes in design should retrigger the abstraction demon.

"Design implementation of associations" refers to the translation of relations in the analysis output since relationships are not supported directly in OO programming languages. Rumbaugh et al. [70] use only binary relations, although they allow features to be attached to these associations. Design of relationship can be complex by requiring auxiliary indices or hash tables to provide efficient navigations.

"Determine the exact representation of object attributes" refers to how attribute values are incorporated: by value or by reference. It can also refer to the determination of the value domains: classes or "normal" value types – unless, of course, one adheres to the "everything is an object" dogma.

6.6 Further Reading

We have referred several times to Gamma et al. [28]. This book contains 23 design patterns. A design pattern is a mini architecture for small-scale design problem that appears to recur in OO systems. See the Glossary for a more extensive description. They describe five patterns that apply to the creation of objects. Seven patterns are given to help structure a system. They can be used to add flexibility to a design, to provide another level of run-time flexibility, to connect objects that have incompatible interfaces, etc. Eleven patterns are described that apply to the behavioral realm. For example, their state pattern appears to correspond to the result of transforming a transition network with multiple states by using subclassing.

Vigorous work is under way to extend the number of generic patterns. Others attempt to develop domain-specific patterns and presumably even proprietary patterns; see Best [8].

A dedicated Object Design Language (ODL) was developed in de Champeaux et al. [24]. This language is wide spectrum in that it covers high-level design, where each object has its own thread of control as well as low-level design after sequentialization has taken place. Many design idioms and patterns are discussed. Given that over 250 pages are devoted to OO design, the pace is different than that in this chapter and many more aspects are covered in depth.

6.7   Summary

This chapter delineates the main activities in OO design. Physical architecture is contrasted against logical architecture. Transformation of relationships into attributes is followed by a description of how to expand attributes in the design. Obtaining executability is a key aspect that must be dealt with. A distinction is made between a constructive approach and an impressionistic approach. The main difference between the two is that the constructive approach makes the analysis model executable before sequentialization takes place, while the impressionistic approach bypasses this activity and produces a sequential system directly. Different techniques for sequentialization are outlined. Advanced design idioms and patterns are visited briefly. The chapter ends with an extensive comparison with design activities as advocated by the OMT method.

6.8   Exercises

1. Define a ternary relationship and describe its design.

2. Can we expect that design patterns will be lifted up into analysis patterns? Argue pro and con.

3. Transform the transition networks of the set exchange example using the qualification of the transitions through Boolean guards.

4. Transform the transition networks of the set exchange example using the introduction of subclasses to qualify transitions.

Chapter 7

Design Process

Many design activities were described in the preceding chapter. This chapter gives an ordering of activities in a fashion somewhat similar to the one we used for the analysis activities. In particular, we outline the elaboration dependencies of design artifacts. A distinction was made in Chapter 6 between two approaches: the "neat" constructivist and the "scruffy" impressionistic approaches. Both approaches follow a distinct process - insofar as the impressionists follow a process - and hence we treat each of them in turn.

7.1 Constructive Process

At a high level we can describe the constructivist approach as the transformation of target system models. The following sequence of (partial) models is encountered:

1. **Analysis model** This is the input to the design.

2. **Executable model** This artifact is an extension of the analysis model in that non-executable action specifications in transition diagrams are replaced by executable versions. Relationships are replaced as outlined in the previous chapter. Actual executability relies on the availability of an interpreter/compiler for the extended analysis language. Note that in this executable model every object has its own thread of control.

3. **Clustered model** A clustered model prepares for a distributed realization of the target system - when the executable model is decomposed in more than one cluster. Objects are assigned to clusters, where each cluster corresponds with a

different process in the implementation. Each object still has its own thread of control. Actual executability requires that there is sufficient infrastructure to support object inter-cluster communication.

4. **Sequentialized clusters** This model has all clusters sequentialized; i.e., all objects in a cluster share a single thread of control. The system still has parallelism, provided that there is more than one cluster. Executability requires an interpreter per cluster and support for object inter-cluster interaction. From a computational perspective, this model corresponds with a target system consisting of communicating "normal" processes, where each process has objects living in the same address space.

5. **Optimized clusters** This model should account for performance issues "abstractly"; i.e., chosen data structures and algorithms should ensure scalability.

Since we obtain executability early in this micro process (provided that we have an execution engine for the design language), it is possible to stop right there and avoid going into the implementation altogether. Tidwell [80], see also below, reported early successes with this approach. Even when the performance of the high-level design is unacceptable, one obtains a prototype that can be used to validate the intended functionality. This may lead to the insight that identified and agreed-upon requirements have to be adjusted. Postponing obtaining such insights can be quite costly. On the other hand, producing these executable high-level designs is not for free. Tools that embody the execution engines are still costly. Plus, the transformation of the high level design model into an implementation model requires handcrafting that relies on scarce expertise.

These models address the major design requirements; see Figure 7.1 which appeared earlier in de Champeaux et al. [23]. Other topics such as extensibility, maintainability, faulttolerance, failsafety, etc. are not covered explicitly but are supposed to be taken care of along the way. The model with optimized clusters may be complemented optionally by a model that adjusts the design to exploit target-language-specific features. Alternatively, these modifications take place directly during the implementation.

Hence the constructive high-level design process is simply a linear sequence of gradual transformations from the analysis model into a design model. Obviously, each high-level transformation relies on a multitude of lower-level activities, many of which were discussed in the previous chapter. We summarize here the lower-level activities per intermediate model.

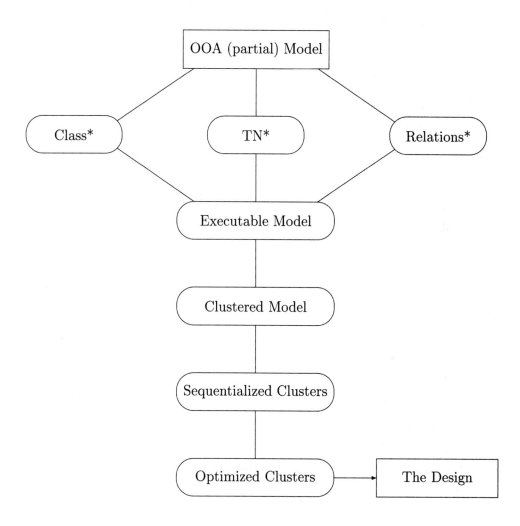

Figure 7.1: Design process from a bird's-eye perspective. The ovals with *Class**, *TN**, and *Relations** refer the modifications of these entities to obtain an executable model. For example, classes must be equipped with constructors and destructors, operations on transition diagrams must be extended into algorithms, and relationships must be designed away.

Executable model

1. Acquaintance relationships are replaced via a design attribute, see Section 6.3.2.

2. Regular relationships are eliminated using design attributes and/or containers, see Section 6.3.3.

3. Multivalued attributes must be replaced by container-valued attributes of the proper type.

4. Attribute value domains may have to be objectified.

5. Incorporation by value or by reference must be decided, see Section 6.3.4.

6. Operations on transitions must be made executable.

7. Queueing of events must be arranged where called for.

8. Object constructors and destructors must be provided.

9. A system initializer that creates all enduring instances and that starts up the system must be constructed.

Clustered model

1. The physical architecture that determines the number of clusters and their names must be committed.

2. The mechanism that creates the clusters when the system is initialized (and the mechanism for a clean teardown) must be constructed.

3. For each cluster we must determine which classes are required so that we can support the necessary map of objects to clusters.

4. Per cluster we must identify the inter-cluster communication requirements and adjust a communication infrastructure accordingly.

Sequentialized clusters

1. For each cluster, we choose an overall framework, for example a loop that takes in events followed by a switch that branches on different events.

2. Required control threads are determined based on dependencies between objects as expressed by use cases and/or scenario diagrams.

3. Threads can (optionally) be objectified.

Optimized clusters

1. Inefficient, naive algorithms introduced to obtain early executability are to be replaced.

2. Caches can be introduced where profitable.

3. Redundant relationship link attributes may be introduced to shorten access paths.

4. We can consider the introduction of specialized classes which may do less checking when an application context provably guarantees preconditions.

Activities for optimization are open ended and are driven mainly by the features of a specific design.

7.2 Impressionistic Process

Bypassing the explicit construction of an executable design in which each object still has its own thread of control makes the design quite murky. In fact, projects often jump directly to implementation activities. This happens when an analysis is done with a single thread of control per system mind-set, which is the result of *too much* experience with "normal" programming. For example, while database operations can be conceptualized as parallel operations performed on elements of sets (or as timeless set operations), most often one thinks in terms of cursors that process one record at the time. In general, business processing lends itself easily to a one thread of control per system mindset, especially when a target system consists only of a single process.[1]

In case the temptation to jump into coding is resisted, we have the following sequence of activities (for a nondistributed system):

1. As in the constructive process, we deal with the static aspects of the analysis model; i.e, we transform acquaintance relationships and regular relationships using design attributes with containers as necessary, we transform multivalued attributes, we objectify attribute value domains as necessary, and we decide how attribute values are incorporated.

---

[1]Client-server architectures come to mind as a counterexample. However, the presence of more than one thread of control in the client-server setting is massaged away at all costs through database "beachheads" at the client side. They provide the illusion that the database is at the client side as well. Blocking calls from the client into the server complete the end of any illusion of parallelism.

2. We sequentialize the OO analysis model or verify that the model is already sequentialized.

3. We fill in the details of the operational specifications. Transition diagrams must be flattened, e.g., states must be represented by an attribute and transitions must be prefixed with guards that refer to this state attribute.

4. Constructors and destructors must be introduced.

5. A system initializer that generates the enduring objects must be constructed.

6. The resulting design must be optimized depending on its features.

7.3   Comparison with Other Processes

In this section we describe some other processes. In Chapter 6 we gave a detailed description of the design process as seen by Rumbaugh et al. [70], see page 253 and 257. Their process belongs to the impressionistic category since they do not strive to develop an early executable prototype. It appears that the system design activities precede, in general, the object design activities. The steps inside these two major blocks appear to be unordered: If a step applies, do it; otherwise, check another activity. The activities regarding the removal of relationships (called associations) and the representation of attributes are listed last by Rumbaugh et al. We recommend addressing these early in design. As a matter of fact, attribute value domains are described in our analysis phase.

A completely different design process is given in Coad and Yourdon [17]:

Designing the Problem Domain Component

- Apply OOA
- Use OOA results - and improve them during OOD
- Use OOA results - and add to them during OOD
    - Reuse design and programming classes
    - Group problem-domain-specific classes together
    - Establish a protocol by adding a generalization class
    - Accommodate the supported level of inheritance
    - Improve performance

  - Support the data management component
  - Add lower-level components
  - Don't modify just to reflect team assignments
  - Review and challenge the additions to OOA results

Designing the Human Interaction Component

- Classify the humans

- Describe the humans and their task scenarios

- Design the command hierarchy

- Design the detailed interaction

- Continue to prototype

- Design the Human Interaction Component classes

- Design accounting for graphical user interfaces (when applicable)

Designing the Task Management Component

- Identify event-driven tasks

- Identify clock-driven tasks

- Identify priority tasks and critical tasks

- Identify a coordinator

- Challenge each task

- Define each task

Designing the Data Management Component

- Select data management approach (flat file/relational DB/OO DB)

- Assess data management tools

- Design the data management component[2]

Distinguishing four major components of a system is the "trick" in this process. Each system can be seen as having an optional user interface, an optional data management component, an optional process communication component, and a core logic component. For each of these, Coad and Yourdon formulate a separate process.

---

[2]The original expands this item; this is *not* a recursive definition.

None of the activities appear to be ordered. Some of them are a bit peculiar, such as "Don't modify just to reflect team assignments" and "Continue to prototype". The entry "Reuse design and programming classes" is not a particular design step but is a recommendation to look in libraries first before embarking on constructing an artifact.

The activity "Classify the humans" is a precursor to the generation of use cases, which Coad and Yourdon call task scenarios. Classifying the users is not only helpful to decompose the task of developing use cases but helps a preanalysis to check whether the different users are stakeholders of the intended system with conflicting interests. If there are conflicting interests, they must be resolved. Otherwise, one may end up with a system that may satisfy no one, while nobody realizes that analysts (implicitly) generated a compromise description of the intended system. Obviously, we believe that the "Classify the humans" and the "Describe the humans and their task scenarios" activities belongs to analysis and *not* to design as suggested by Coad and Yourdon.

Somewhat remarkable is the design process in Booch [12, 13]. He describes the OO software development process as an iteration (which corresponds with a hardwired spiral life cycle) over the following:

1. Identify the classes and objects at a given level of abstraction.

2. Identify the semantics of these classes and objects.

3. Identify the relationships among these classes and objects.

4. Implement these classes and objects.

As we see it, these listed activities belong to the analysis realm or to the implementation realm while nothing is mentioned about design![3]

7.4   Summary

In this chapter we describe two different micro processes for OO design. The constructive micro process differs from the impressionistic micro process in that the former makes the analysis model executable before sequentializing the description and subsequently producing a second sequentialized model in the low-level design.

---

[3]It is perhaps humorous to observe that the title of [12] is *Object Oriented Design*. As mentioned before, "design" is to be interpreted here in the wide sense, as everything that precedes implementation.

The latter makes only a single executable model after implicitly sequentializing the analysis model. The two approaches share the same techniques for dealing with the static dimension. For example, relationships must be designed away because there is no support for them in the OO programming languages.

7.5 Further Reading

The constructivist approach was described first, as far as we know, in a contribution to an OOPSLA workshop by Tidwell [80], see also [23]:

> State models, which as a whole describe the behavior of the system, may be directly implemented using a technique called State Controlled Implementation (SCI). SCI provides for each object a template which defines a common implementation architecture as well as all control details. The information model and the state models can be described with regular data [and] thus lend themselves to automated generation of the architecture templates and program structure. The implementor is left with the task of coding each state's specific logic.[4] OOD and other design concepts can be applied to the state models of a system to determine domain boundaries, reusable components, processor allocation, and tasking considerations. Since the system's control has been removed into the template, a particular state's processing is generally straightforward.

The constructivist approach has been incorporated in a tool that is marketed by ObjectTime Inc. The method that is "reverse engineered" out of this tool is described in Selic et al. [71].

Most remarkable is that current OO books give scant attention to the process dimension of software development, especially of the process in the design phase. Given the widespread attention to ISO9000 certification, business reengineering, workflow studies, and the Carnegie-Mellon maturity levels which emphasize the importance of process, one would expect a much higher awareness of the process dimension.

---

[4]Tidwell uses the Shlaer-Mellor method [72, 73], which employs the *Moore* form of state machines, in which actions are associated with states. In contrast, we have used the *Mealy form*, in which actions are associated with transitions.

7.6   Exercises

1. Assume that we use the constructive design micro process. Our system requires the use of an algorithm for which there are different variants that trade simplicity versus efficiency. At what point during the design can we commit to these variants?

2. Now assume that the variants of the algorithm trade off space versus time. When must we commit in this trade-off?

3. The same as in Exercises 1 and 2, but assume now that the impressionistic micro process is followed.

Chapter 8

Design Metrics

This chapter revisits OO metrics. The design perspective demands more attention to be given to quality aspects of the design artifacts. Major solution aspects are "cast in concrete" during the design. Recognizing that an implementation artifact is likely to become a maintenance liability helps to launch early remedial action. Effort estimation remains of interest during the design. We begin by looking into this topic.

8.1   Effort Estimation Revisited

Effort estimation for design starts in a much better position than for analysis. Development effort for the total analysis is known (we assume), development effort of individual analysis artifacts are known (hopefully), and we have available an analysis model itself. (This information may pertain to a partial analysis and to a partial model in the case when an iterative macro process is used. If so, effort prediction applies to the design of the corresponding fragment of the target system.)

Estimation can be done at different levels of granularity. A coarse-grained approach consists of applying a multiplier to the measured total analysis effort. Alternatively, a system-wide product metric such as the number of classes and the number of relationships can be used in combination with a multiplier. Certainly, we can combine these two methods.

Effort estimation can be refined further by estimating the efforts to develop intermediate design deliverables. For example, a commitment to the constructivist micro process entails estimating the efforts of the executable model, the clustered model, the sequentialized model, and the optimized model. Obviously, we can omit the clustered model when the target system is not distributed. Effort estimations for these intermediate artifacts can be obtained as outlined above by using multipliers applied to the total analysis effort and/or applied to the analysis model product metrics. Tracking of progress is improved by this more detailed estimation procedure.

A commitment to the impressionistic approach, which has much less clear demarcations, entails estimating the effort to develop the sequentialized model and the optimized model (assuming a nondistributed system). Exploiting multipliers is again the obvious choice for estimating effort along this route.

Estimation at a finer level of granularity can be done as well. For each choice of a design micro process, one can estimate the work to be done in the design to elaborate class and relationship analysis artifacts. The design of classes is especially of interest. An effort estimate that relies on a product metric can be postulated to be a weighted sum of the number of transition diagrams. However, the weight for a transition diagram is a nonlinear function, say quadratic, of the number of states and linear in the number of transitions. A linear term for the number of attributes is realistic as well. Thus we obtain, for appropriate constants $\{c_i\}$,
estimated design time for a class =

$$c_1 * (\#\ attributes) +$$
$$\sum_{td\ a\ transition\ diagram} (c_2 * (\#\ states\ in\ td)^2 + c_3 * (\#\ transitions\ in\ td))$$

Further refinements can take into account the complexity of a transition: whether a guard depends on an event and/or a boolean expression, the number of actions, the number of generated events, and so on.

Estimating the design effort of other analysis artifacts goes along the same lines. The estimation of effort for a relationship may be a linear function of its arity. The estimation of effort for an enduring instance can be a linear function of the number of its attributes. The estimation of the design effort must be adjusted for:

1. The design mode: manual versus supported by tools

2. The inherent complexity of the domain

3. The familiarity with the domain

4. The availability of a domain design library

5. The availability of a low-level library for containers and the like

A tool has substantial impact, as is to be expected. It shapes the micro process by offering the ability to generate artifacts downstream automatically. The Rose tool from - Rational, for example -embodies, essentially, the impressionistic micro process. Analysis and design get blurred. C++ header files and code skeletons can be produced from diagrams that look very much like analysis diagrams. Relationships are conveniently restricted to binary and are coerced into attributes. Transition diagrams can be drawn but do not play a role in code generation. Hence, in the context of the other "more useful" notations that do lead to code generation, transition diagrams are typically ignored. The situation is drastically different with, for instance, the ObjectTime tool, which embodies the constructive micro process. Getting the transition diagrams right has high priority since they are extended into executable forms. Consequently, the estimation of design efforts depend strongly on the use of a tool, if any.

Next we have a closer look at quality metrics.

8.2 Quality Assessment

An operational definition for the quality of a software system is not obvious. Whether or not a system is working is not too relevant. It makes sense to talk about quality only *after* a system minimally satisfies its requirements. We will look some of these secondary features.

8.2.1 Size

Size is a well-known quality aspect that is usually adhered to implicitly. Other things being equal, an artifact that is half the size of another functionally equivalent artifact is clearly preferable. Nevertheless, there are exceptions to this rule. If A and B are equivalent design artifacts with $|A|$ less than $|B|$ but with the need to implement A while an implementation is available for B, then B is often preferable over A.

Size is typically a "subconscious" selector while design alternatives are contemplated: subconscious in the sense that design alternatives are usually not explicitly worked out and measured for making a rational and documented decision. Time pressures commonly prohibit working out alternatives in detail. Instead, group discussions are often used to legitimize far-reaching decisions on design alternatives.

8.2.2 Flexibility

Flexibility, also called *robustness*, of a software system can be defined as the ability to perform even outside an intended application domain, or at least it has the feature that its functionality degrades gradually outside its domain. As an example, consider numerical operations that are accurate and fast as long as values are within certain ranges, while the operations switch to approximate calculations when these ranges are surpassed or the operations switch to slower operations of arbitrary precision.

These are wonderful features that are easier to describe than to realize. Most desirable is flexibility that is unexpected. Physical systems can often be stretched beyond their normal range of operation, leading to heroic applications. Ordinary software systems are, however, very brittle.

Can the OO way help to make systems more flexible? It is not impossible. A system may use different algorithms that are encapsulated in different objects which are managed by a supervisor object. However, this is not exactly a case of unexpected flexibility. Rule-based systems appear to be genuinely flexible, possibly due to the fact that their application ranges are ill defined. Usage of OO for these types of systems is possible but not a necessity.

In any case, it is hard to conceive of a design metric that can be used as an assessor of this type of flexibility.

8.2.3   Modifiability

Maintainability is a key feature of a system. In essence it refers to the ease of modification of a system, and hence it stands for another kind of flexibility. Here we are interested in the ease of modifying the design and/or the code in order to correct errors and to accommodate changing requirements.

Modifiability of a system depends on numerous factors beyond design. Consistency of all descriptions with the code helps to do maintenance at the highest relevant abstraction level instead of having to reverse engineer code. Integrated tool support in combination with, for instance, a hyperlink-style integration of all development artifacts, from the requirements up to the executables, facilitates traversals. Automated support for versioning at all levels helps as well. Here, however, we look at features of the design that affect modifiability.

Modifications happen at three levels: (1) inside objects, (2) objects, and, (3) system-wide changes. We discuss each of these levels in turn.

8.2.4   Changes inside objects

A design's major deliverable consists of the realization of behavior: the transformation of transition diagrams into member functions. Modifiability of a member function depends primarily on its size and on its control complexity. Secondary factors are:

1. The number and complexity of arguments

2. The complexity of a return value, if any

3. The number of calls to other member functions, if any

In addition, we can distinguish whether a member function is local or is inherited. Hence we obtain for a member function *foo* a maintenance burden (MFMB) metric:

$$\mu_{MFMB}(foo) = c_1 * size(foo) + c_2 * VG(foo) + c_3 * \#arguments(foo) + ...$$

where c_i are certain constants; *size* is, for example, a function that counts tokens in the body of *foo*; and *VG* is the cyclomatic complexity of the control flow graph of *foo* (McCabe [52].

This metric can be improved. An extensive study by Coleman et al. [18] reported a set of metrics that were developed for C programs. These metrics can be applied to the system as a whole, to a file, or to a module. We conjecture that these metrics apply also to C++ member functions and hence to the descriptions of operations in the design phase.[1] We present only one of their metrics, which they formulated for application to a total system:

$$\mu_{ColemanMaintainability} =$$
$$171 - 3.42 * ln(aveE) - 0.23 * aveV(g') - 16.2 * ln(aveLOC) + 0.99 * aveCM$$

where we have the following interpretation for the variables: $aveE$ is the average Halstead Effort [31] per module, which is defined as:

$$(n1 * N2 * (N1 + N2) * log_2(n1 + n2))/(2 * n2)$$

where $n1$ is the number of unique operators, $n2$ is the number of unique operands, $N1$ is the number of operator occurrences, and $N2$ is the number of operand occurrences; $aveV(g')$ is the average extended cyclomatic complexity per module, where the extended cyclomatic complexity is defined as the number of decisions plus one; $aveLOC$ is the average number of lines of code per module; and $aveCM$ is the average number of lines of comments per module. This metric correlates 0.9 with the assessments of maintainers on a particular sample, see Coleman et al. [18] for details.

---

[1] Here we use the "trick" that our design language is a mixture of the graphical analysis notation for the structural aspects and the target language C++ for the dynamic dimension.

Obviously, we will *not* take averages when we apply this metric to a single member function.

Note that the meaning of μ_{MFMB} is different from $\mu_{ColemanMaintainability}$. Their signs are different. A high value of one corresponds with a low value of the other. Summation of μ_{MFMB} values is feasible, say for all member functions of a class, to obtain an estimated aggregate maintenance burden. In contrast, $\mu_{ColemanMaintainability}$ is geared to calculate averages, which, by the way, can be done as well with μ_{MFMB}.

To use the Coleman et al. result for measuring the maintenance burden of a member function (or its design equivalent), we use the derived metric μ_{CM}, defined as:

$$\mu_{CM} = -\mu_{ColemanMaintainability} + 171$$

Thus we have, after eliminating the "averages",

$$\mu_{CM} = 3.42 * ln(E) + 0.23 * V(g') + 16.2 * ln(LOC) - 0.99 * CM$$

8.2.5   Changing objects

There are two perspectives on objects: in isolation, i.e., independent of the context in which they operate, and in their roles as part of the target system. We look at each of these in turn.

Object in isolation

Maintenance of object (in fact we discuss here mainly the maintenance of classes) depends for most on their *size*. Other things being equal, larger classes are more difficult to grasp than smaller ones. We have two different kinds of sizes: the size made up by the local members only and the size made up by the local members and the inherited imported members. Hence a first measure of the maintenance burden of a class is the distance of the class to a root or to the most distant root when there is multiple inheritance. This gives us a sequence of metrics which are in turn more accurate and more laborious to calculate:

$\mu^1_{ClassMB}(class)$ = distance of *class* from the furthest root class

$\mu^2_{ClassMB}(class)$ = # direct and indirect super classes of *class*.
$\mu^3_{ClassMB}(class)$ =
$c_1 * \#$ *local member variables* +
$c_2 * \#$ *imported member variables* +

$c_3 * \#$ *local member functions* $+$
$c_4 * \#$ *imported member functions*

$\mu^4_{ClassMB}(class) =$
$c_1 * \#$ *local member variables* $+$
$c_2 * \#$ *imported member variables* $+$
$c_3 * \left(\sum_{local} \mu_{CM}(memberFunction_{local})\right) +$
$c_4 * \left(\sum_{imported} \mu_{CM}(memberFunction_{imported})\right)$

The reader is invited to invent further refinements.

These metrics do not assess whether a class has minimal size. A good design will give a class a single sharply demarcated responsibility. A class with multiple responsibilities should be split. Measuring a class for splitability is not possible in general. A crude attempt to measure splitability was described in part I, see the Lack Of Cohesion metric on page 121. The idea is to check whether the set of variables used in a member function intersects with similar sets of other member functions. If not, we have a strong indication that the class bundles more than one responsibility.

However, this test may fail to recognize tangled-up functionality that should be factored out. For example, consider an item that is passed around and undergoes a sequence of treatments. All the operations that correspond with the treatments could be bundled in one class, and the Lack Of Cohesion metric would not recognize that the operations could be split up because they all share the variable that refers to the item that undergoes the treatments.

Hence we prefer to use metrics that combine size and complexity in order to identify classes that are potential maintenance hazards.

Object in the system context

Another way to look at a design from the perspective of a single object is to investigate the communication connections that the corresponding class has with peer classes. This is traditionally known as coupling, see page 121. The different forms of coupling described there apply to design as well. We have the coupling induced by an object invoking a member function: the caller's fan-out (μ_{fanOut}) metric gets incremented, and the called object's fan-in (μ_{fanIn}) metric gets incremented also. In addition, we may count object types that flow-in (respectively, flow-out) as arguments of member functions. Clearly, we have that the sum of all fan-ins is equal to the sum of all fan-outs. The average fan-in/out can be calculated by dividing this sum by the number of classes. A high fan-in/out average, especially in combination with low average cohesion, suggests that certain objects have too much responsibility.

Of interest are objects where the difference between fan-in and fan-out is pronounced. If the fan-in is much larger than the fan-out, we have a highly reused server entity which is probably generic, and a candidate for a reuse library. In case the fan-in is much smaller than the fan-out, we have a managerial "nerve-center" entity that is probably application specific.

Another perspective on an object is whether it is enduring or transient and, if transient, whether it is generated due to lexical elaboration or due to explicit creation. An implementation environment lacking automatic garbage collection, such as C++, must penalize explicitly created, and deleted, objects heavily since their maintenance is notoriously problematic.

Consequently, we obtain as a maintenance burden for a class in a system context:

$$\mu_{systemContext}(class) = c_1 * \mu_{fanIn}(class) + c_2 * \mu_{fanOut}(class) + w(class)$$

where $w(class)$ is a term that is high for a class whose instances are explicitly generated and deleted.

8.2.6   Changing the system

The burden of maintaining a total system is again primarily a function of size. As a first approximation we can count the number of classes. There are many ways to replace simple counting by more elaborate sizing measures. For example, for each class we can combine its maintenance "size" based on its internal characteristics and based on its role in the system:

$$\mu^1_{system} = \sum_i (\alpha * \mu^4_{ClassMB}(class_i) + \beta * \mu_{systemContext}(class_i))$$

We can extend this global metric further by measuring the complexity of the graph that expresses the communication links between classes:

$$\mu^2_{system} = \mu^1_{system} + VG(system)$$

where $VG(system)$ measures, for example, the cyclomatic complexity of the class interaction graph.

8.3 Impact of a Quality Metric

We have defined design metrics that allow us to assess the maintenance costs of a system to be implemented. These metrics operate at different levels of granularity and permit us to zoom in on problematic areas. What should one do when a potential trouble spot is identified? Strangely enough, we do not recommend designing the trouble spot away when this would entail a discontinuity between the analysis model and the design. Instead, backtracking to the analysis model may be required to maintain consistency between the analysis and the design model. This may sound strange because the analysis model aims primarily at describing nondesign features of the system. However, to enhance maintainability it is very helpful to be able to move easily between all abstraction levels of a system and to know that everything is consistent.

8.4 Summary

In this chapter we describe several metrics for further effort estimation. Design efforts depend on which design micro process is followed, whether integrated development tools are used, whether the analysis model is complete, whether the intended system is distributed or not, whether frameworks are available for reuse, and so on. Effort metrics can be coarse grained and as simple as multipliers of the analysis efforts or can be fine grained and look at individual artifacts from the analysis model to be transformed.

At this point, it is perhaps not unwise to remember that there are sizable differences in productivity between developers. Hence actual effort estimations must take the experience level of developers into account.

Quality metrics are formulated indirectly as maintenance burden measures. These are formalized as size measures on artifact types with different scope. Maintenance burden metrics are defined for member functions, classes, and the total system.

Certainly, we cannot claim that all quality aspects are covered by the maintenance burden metrics. For example, it is not clear that splitting a large class into two or more classes will reduce a system's overall maintenance burden metric's value, although it may lead to reducing the average maintenance burden over all classes.

Use of polymorphism can affect the maintenance burden for subclasses and is *not* covered by our metrics. A penalty metric for polymorphism is hard to conceive since, without adhering to a style guide, a designer can associate arbitrary different functionality to equally named operations in different subclasses. As a consequence, the expression `x->foo()` can have as many different interpretations as there are subclasses to which x can be an instance.

Somewhat sneaky is that we have coupled effort metrics and quality metrics by reducing them both to size metrics.

8.5 Further Reading

The series of maintenance burden metrics defined in this chapter is based on extensive theoretical and empirical work done by Paul Oman and his team at the University of Idaho. They have cooperated with Hewlett-Packard since the early 1990s on developing maintainability metrics. Their metrics have been developed to assess non-OO code. Several of their papers are devoted to empirical validation. The list of papers consulted includes Oman et al. [56, 57, 58, 59, 60, 61, 62].

For a broad discussion of OO metrics, we refer again to Chapter 10 of Henderson-Sellers and Edwards [36]. This 65-page chapter gives an overview of pre-OO metrics and discusses potential modifications and extension to adapt the metrics to the realm of OO. The author acknowledges that many extensions are speculative and need further research. Such topics as: module metrics for semantic complexity, logic structure metrics, cognitive complexity model, cost-benefit metrics, and simulation of return on investment (regarding reuse) make for inspirational reading.

8.6 Exercises

1. Assume that an OO analysis tool recorded by artifact the cumulative effort to generate this artifact. Provide a detailed account of a fine-grained prediction technique for design efforts assuming a constructive micro process.

2. The same as Exercise 1 but assume an impressionistic micro process.

Chapter 9

Example: Home Heating System

This chapter is devoted to the design of a home heating system, elaborating on the analysis given in Chapter 5. The design has different variants that depend on the nature of the target system. Here are three systems in a spectrum:

1. A noncomputerized system with real rooms, a furnace, etc. in addition to some electromechanic switches

2. A partially computerized system with real rooms, a furnace, etc. in addition to a computerized controller

3. A computer-based simulator

We have taken the last choice because it gives us the best opportunity to illustrate OO design.

We have a choice as to micro processes: the constructive approach or the impressionistic approach. Each of these approaches is explored in turn. We will not develop full designs and highlight, only salient aspects.

9.1 Constructive Micro Process

We recollect that the constructive process produces in sequence: (1) an executable model, (2) a clustered model, (3) sequentialized clusters, and (4) optimized clusters. Most attention is given to development of the executable model.

9.1.1 Executable model

We follow in this section the sequence of steps formulated in Section 7.1 on page 262.

Replace acquaintance relationships

Figure 5.43 on page 204 shows the major acquaintance relationships that must be treated. (Notice that the diagram is incomplete. The clock can receive request for registration and deregistration of clients, and the furnace monitor makes use of these requests.) We investigate several of the links.

Two acquaintance relationships emanate from the clock toward objects from the class *Room* and toward an instance of the class *FurnaceMonitor*. Since we will typically have more than one room and only one furnace monitor, we expect to have to add to *Clock* a multivalued attribute for the rooms and a single-valued attribute for the furnace monitor. However, an investigation of *Clock* yields the insight that neither is required since there is already a multivalued attribute *clients* that is capable of handling rooms and a furnace monitor.[1]

The single acquaintance relationship that connects the valve controller class with the room class is also already accounted for. The multi-valued attribute *roomsThatNeedHeat* takes care of this relationship.

The class *Room* has an acquaintance relationship with the class *HeatFlowRegulator* to allow a room to register and unregister itself as illustrated in the dynamic diagram, see Figure 5.19 on page 168. Hence we must add an attribute to *Room* and - surprise - we did this already, see Figure 6.1 on page 231.

All other acquaintance relationships can be handled in similarly.

Incorporation by reference is typically the proper way and applies to the relationships depicted in Figure 5.43 on page 204. Bundling communication partners and shielding them may be achieved through attributes that have their value domains incorporated by value. One may contemplate this approach for the relationships of the class *Room* shown in Figure 5.5 on page 151. Indeed, no other entity needs to communicate directly with the implicit components of a room. Even the valve controller communicates via the room with a room's valve, see Figure 5.39 on page 195.

Eliminate regular relationships

The elimination of regular relationships can be bypassed. The analysis model does not have any. Otherwise, we would have applied the techniques outlined in Section 6.3.3 on page 231.

---

[1]A C++ implementation will require us to equip the class *Thing*, which is the value domain of *clients*, with a virtual member function *tic*, because *tic* events will be broadcast to all the clock's clients.

Replace multivalued attributes

The purpose of this activity is to replace multivalued attributes that use the $[N : M]$ notation and replace them with a single-valued attribute that uses a container construct. Again we can bypass this step because the analysis model already uses containers, see the heat flow regulator in Figure 5.11 on page 157 and the valve controller in Figure 5.37 on page 193.

Design attribute domains and their incorporation

Attributes must be investigated to check how value domains can be implemented. If a value domain is a class that is defined elsewhere or a container (or in general, a defined template) with a defined class (or defined classes as template parameters), we are done. Otherwise, we may have to introduce a new class, rely on a class available in a library, use a structure, or use a data type built in to the design language or the target implementation language.

In addition, we have to decide whether an attribute is to be incorporated by value or by reference. We consider some attributes.

The class *Switch/Indicator* class has an attribute *onOffStatus* with value domain {*On*, *Off*}, see page 154. Mapping *On* and *Off* to values like True and False or to, for example, the numbers one and zero are obvious choices. Incorporation by value is preferred over indirection by reference.

The *Clock* has the attribute *currentTime* with as value domain *DateTime*, see page 162. The application does not need to represent time for an extended period of time. The largest time period is a week for capturing the occupancy history information for a room and similarly for the living pattern. The actual number of data points depends on the chosen granularity. The finest-grained granularity of 1 second for a 1-week period requires less than 20 bits of data. Hence a 32-bit integer counter gives plenty of room to represent time.[2]

The class *Clock* also has an attribute with a set container as value domain. The "containee" is the class *Thing*, which is not defined elsewhere. Thus we must introduce this class. The class *Clock* does not prescribe requirements for the class *Thing* beyond the ability to accept a *tic* event. However, we have observed already that rooms and the furniture monitor will be inserted in the container to receive *tic* events. This can be realized by making the classes *Room* and *FurnaceMonitor* subclasses of *Thing*. This gives us the description in Figure 9.1.

---

[2]Trivia info: The number of seconds in 135 years can be represented by a 32-bit unsigned integer.

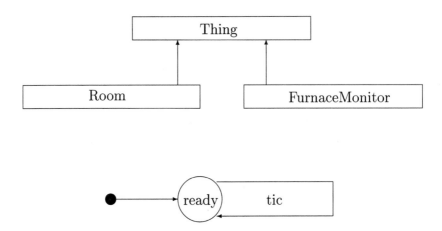

Figure 9.1: The clock refers in its *clients* attribute via the container *SET* to instances of the class *Thing* in order to send it *tic* events. The only thing we know about the class *Thing* is that it should support a transition that consumes *tic* events. In addition we know that rooms and the furnace monitor will be the actual instances. Hence we have made them subclasses of *Thing*.

A close look at the dynamics of a room, see Figure 5.18 on page 167, and the dynamics of the furnace monitor, see Figure 5.34 on page 188, shows that something is not 100% correct. The *tic* transition inside a *Thing* starts in the state *ready* and returns to the state *ready*. In contrast, the *tic* transition in a room starts in the state *wait for clock tic* and ends up in the state *decide whether to change heat request*. Similarly, we find a difference in the furnace monitor: *tic* starts in the *on* state and ends up in the *check* state. This violates the notion of inheritance that says that structure and behavior are inherited from superclasses. Thus we expect a *tic* transition in a room and in the furnace monitor to emanate from a *ready* state and to return to the same state. We can reconcile this problem by renaming the *tic* transitions in *Room* and *FurnaceMonitor* into *tic'* and adding to their dynamics the *ready-tic* transition diagram that we formulated for *Thing*. The *tic* transition inside *Room* would be elaborated as producing an internal *tic'* event and similarly for *FurnaceMonitor*. In a later phase we may observe that the *tic-tic'* forwarding is not strictly necessary. An optimization transformation may eliminate the *ready-tic* transition network and rename *tic'* back into *tic*.

The preceding paragraph may appear to belong to the hair-splitting category. Instead, it illustrates concisely the trade-off of adhering to strict rules, in this case about the meaning of inheritance, which furthers the ease of maintenance versus the desire to reduce the size of a design and implementation and the requirement of maximized efficiency. Hence this example illustrates the need for a tool that would do design optimizations analogously to modern compilers that do code optimizations.

The container *SET* is a parametrized class *SET(T)*, which we turn to next. At the time of this writing, we see the emergence of standard class libraries for C++ code that obviate the need to implement containers and many other constructs. We assume the availability of a corresponding design library.

We move on to the attributes of the class *Room*, see Figure 5.17 on page 165. Incorporation by value or by reference is covered by the heuristic: nonclass value domains are incorporated by value; class value domains are incorporated by reference. The two attributes *needsHeat?* and *registeredHeatRequest?* have Boolean values, and in conformance with the heuristic these values can be incorporated by value. The other attributes have classes as value domains. We can conform to the heuristic or not. Since all the object values are strictly private for a room, it is quite feasible to incorporate them all by value. Either way will work.

Most of the classes do not require further special attention. An exception is the attribute *occupancyRecord* in *OccupancyHistory*, see Figure 5.35 on page 5.35. The design for this attribute can be carried over to the design of the *livingPattern* attribute in *LivingPattern*. Since the analysis model has interpreted the requirements document as having to maintain the history and the living pattern for a week at a granularity of 1 second, a straightforward design uses a circular "array" with 60*60*24*7 bits. Putting 8 bits in a byte would require 75,600 bytes for an *occupancyRecord* and as much for a *livingPattern*. Decreasing the granularity to 1 minute and using or-logic each second reduces the storage requirement to 1260 bytes per room for an *occupancyRecord*. A data structure consisting of intervals during which occupancy does not change would be another approach to reducing storage space. We leave its design as an exercise.

Make operations on transitions executable

We recollect that executability presumes the availability of some kind of machinery that directly interprets transition networks, can generate arbitrary many instances of classes, can destroy instances, acts as a medium for the transmission of events and service requests, and can queue them where necessary. Thus we concentrate mostly on the action parts of the transitions.

We start with the simple transition network for the heat switch, which we show again in Figure 9.2.

The transition *turnOn* is activated by the event *turnOn()*, it has one action involv-

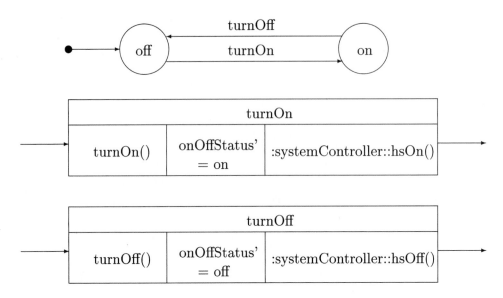

Figure 9.2: Transition network of the heat switch.

ing the attribute *onOffStatus*, and it generates an event for the *systemController*.[3]
The design of this transition is very straightforward. The only piece that is not executable is the action component, because the description *onOffStatus' = on* is an
equation and *not* an assignment statement. The equation stands for "*on* is the new
value of attribute *onOffStatus*" and it is obviously realized through the assignment
onOffStatus = on. Providing this replacement for the action specification of *turnOn*
yields an internal structure that may look as follows:

```
void HeatSwitch::turnOn {
startState:
     off;
queue?:
     nil;
inEvent:
     turnOn();
condition:
     true;
```

---

[3]Figure 5.4 on page 150 shows an acquaintance relationship between the heat switch and the
system controller. Its design has produced an additional attribute inside the heat switch that refers
to the system controller. Hence the heat switch can send an event to the system controller.

```
action:
    onOffStatus = on;
outEvent:
    systemController->hsOn();
goalState:
    on; };
```

Most of the items in this structure should be obvious. The item *queue?* describes whether incoming events can be queued. The value *nil* indicates that there is no queue; i.e., a turnOn event arriving at the heat switch while the switch is not in the *off* state will be discarded. The item *condition* is true since, beyond the arrival of a *turnOn* event, there is no additional restriction for firing the transition.

An example of a transition where an incoming event and a condition are specified can be found in Figure 5.12 on page 158. There are two transitions, *unRegisterRoomN* and *unRegisterRoomA*, that emanate from the state *aRNH*, which both need a firing event *uRR(room)*. Conditions check whether the last room is unregistered or not to disambiguate these transitions. Certainly, we can ask where the attribute *#room* is defined. We find an omission! Hence we have to add this attribute, and we need to maintain its value. The transition *registerRoomA* should increment *#room*, and the transition *unRegisterRoomA* should decrement it. The transitions *(un)registerRoomN* should set *#room* accordingly. For example, the action part of *registerRoomN* (respectively, *unRegisterRoomA*) is:

```
roomsThatNeedHeat->add(room); // roomsThatNeedHeat refers to a SET
#room = 1;
...
roomsThatNeedHeat->delete(room);
#room--;
```

The most complex transition in the system is the *tic* transition for a room. Fortunately, the need to clarify the requirements forced a precise reformulation of what was available in the requirements document, see page 166. That description translates easily into our design language. We obtain

```
currentOccupancy = occupancySensor->getOccupied?();
occupancyHistory->setOccupancy(dateTime, currentOccupancy);
previousOccupancy = occupancyHistory->getOccupancy(dateTime - 1week);
if (currentOccupancy == previousOccupancy)
then livingPattern->setPattern(dateTime, currentOccupancy);
```

```
// occupied? indicates whether the room is currently occupied or is
// expected to be occupied within 30 minutes
occupied? = currentOccupancy ||
              livingPattern->getPattern(dateTime, 30minutes);
td = desiredTempInputDevice->getDesiredTemperature();
if (occupied?) then tw = td else tw = td - 5;
temp = roomTemperatureSensor->getCurrentTemperature();
if temp <= tw - 2 then needsHeat = y else
if temp >= tw + 2 then needsHeat = n; // else
// needsHeat' = needsHeat; i.e. no change needed
```

This expansion assumes that the right thing happens in the expression

```
dateTime - 1week;
```

i.e., when time is represented as an integer, the minus operator can be a subtraction. Other encodings of time require an overloading of the minus operator.

One may wonder about the mechanism of transitions that emanate from super-states. Take, as an example, the transition *shutdown*, belonging to the *Furnace* network, see Figure 5.26 on page 177. A simplistic interpretation entails duplicating the *shutdown* transition for every substate in the unnamed superstate. Less wasteful solutions are conceivable, but since this is a matter for the interpreter or compiler of these diagrams, we can avoid this problem for now.

Some of the actions require attention because we are making a simulation model instead of constructing a real system. For example, the ignitor has a transition *ignite* with "do the ignition" as its action. We can replace this in the simulation by, for instance, an operation that writes a message on a log. Opening and closing of valves can receive similar treatments. A simulation using a graphical interface may depict the status of valves, temperature sensors, and so on.

A room temperature sensor requires some attention. Its value is deter-mined partially by a "force" that is external to a real system: the temper-ature outside. To represent this component, one may choose, for example, $temperature_{outside}(t) = \alpha * sin(t)$ as a function over time. The other component takes into account whether a room is being heated, which can be implemented by checking whether a room's valve is open. This yields a difference equation for certain constants p and q, as in

$$\Delta roomTemp(t) = p * (roomTemp(t) - temperature_{outside}(t)) + q * heated?(t)$$

Hence we obtain:

$$roomTemp(t+1) = roomTemp(t) + \Delta roomTemp(t)$$

Other components that reside on the system boundary can be made dependent on user input: for example, the fault reset switch, the optical combustion sensor, the fuel flow sensor, and so on.

All other transitions have action specifications that are easy to design.

Provide for event queues where necessary

The analysis model doesn't go into details as to how events are delivered and what happens when a server object is not in the proper state to honor a client's request. Often, these aspects are ignored because the implementation will be done in a sequential language anyway. However, these details need attention in our setting. The situation gets simplified considerably by assuming that the execution environment always provides for queuing to handle the situation when a recipient is in between states. There remains the problem of what to do when a recipient resides in a state that cannot handle an event or a service request. The analysis may have helped the situation by arranging for communication situations where the partners are always in sync. However, setting up these guarantees may be impossible at the system boundary with the external world: A device must be prepared to receive a turn off event while it is already turned off.

The user-interface objects have transition networks that have *on* and *off* states. These objects do not need to queue events that cannot be handled by the state in which the object resides.

The transition network of the heat-flow regulator, see Figure 5.12 on page 158, is a good example that avoids all problems. There are two types of events: *registerRoom* and *unRegisterRoom*. Both states in the network can handle both types of events, obviating the need for queues. Hence no queue is necessary.

The system controller has a transition network, see Figure 5.14 on page 161, that is an example in which the states are coordinated closely with their communication partners. There are four different types of events. The arrangements have been set up such that the system controller will always be in a state that can handle an arriving event. Again no queue is required, but the situation is not as safe as for the heat flow regulator. The system controller now depends on the arrangements with its communication partners.

The clock has another approach to obviate the need for a queue: It has only one state, the state *ready*, see page 162.

The room's transition network exploits yet another feature to avoid a queue, see page 167. The transitions *openValve* and *closeValve* can always be executed since a room always resides in the unnamed super state. The transitions *noChange*, *register*, and *unRegister* do not depend on events; they are driven by the values of local attributes. The *tic* transition remains. The room does not need a queue, provided that it can do all the processing required induced by a clock *tic* event before the next clock event arrives! In our simulator, we can arrange for this constraint by letting the clock wait until all activities induced by broadcasting a *tic* have died out.

The furnace sets up intricate arrangements with its communication partners that obviate the need for a queue, see page 177-178. The transition *turnOpenOilValve*, for example, is fired up as a result of the blower motor having reached the proper RPM value, while the preceding transition started up the blower motor and hence prepared it for the reception of the blower motor's notification event.[4]

Similar stories apply to the other objects. Hence there is no need for the simulation system to queue events explicitly.

Provide constructors and destructors

There is no mystery in this activity. For the simulation system to work, we need to create all its components. At least one constructor is required for each class. Destructors are not required. The home heating system does not need to create and destroy objects during execution. The simulator can simply terminate without cleanup on exit. A timer for the furnace can be preallocated and can be "recycled" after use.

Construct system initializer

A language such as C++ allows objects to be created in different ways:

1. Explicitly through **new**-constructs that are executed as part of transitions

2. Implicitly through **new**-constructs that are executed as part of lexical elaborations

3. Implicitly through lexical elaboration of declarations and leading to incorporation by value

---

[4]A prudent designer may extend the transition network with a time-out transition leading to an error exit.

Let's assume that our design language offers the same choices. The first type of creation is appropriate for the generation (and subsequent explicit deletion through **delete**) of transient objects, i.e., objects that have limited lifetimes. The latter types of creation are appropriate for enduring objects and hence can be used for system initialization. Using indirections through **new** or not is a matter of taste.

A recommended approach is to introduce a single object, called, say, *system*, a unique instance of the class *System* that takes care of the initialization. The attributes of *System* are the enduring subsystems, see Figure 5.43 on page 204, *room1*, *room2*, ..., *heatFlowRegulator*, *furnaceController*, etc. The ordering in which these objects are declared is significant. Each room needs to know the identity of the *heatFlowRegulator*. This suggests to declaring the *heatFlowRegulator* first and subsequently using its identity in the initializers for the rooms. However, taking a closer look at Figure 5.43 reveals that there is a "need-to-know" cycle: *furnaceController*, *furnace*, *furnaceMonitor*, *systemController*, *furnaceController*. This can be handled by declaring the elements of the cycle in reverse order: *furnaceController*, *systemController*, ... The head of the cycle, *furnaceController*, is partially initialized and after the missing attribute *furnace* has been declared, its identity is explicitly inserted in the *furnaceController*.

Lower-level subsystems, inside each room, inside the furnace, etc. can be treated similarly.

The initialization is completed by supplying *System* with a transition network having a transition named, say, *doIt*, that will initiate the simulation. Its effect is that the clock will receive a certain number of *ticToc* events. See Figure 9.3 for a possible setup. We omit the details for determining how many times the *ticToc* events are generated and how the *finished* and *not finished* guards are realized.

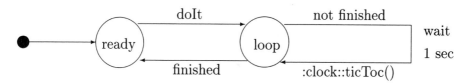

Figure 9.3: Transition network of the top-level *system* object. The *doIt* event starts the simulation. Let's assume that this event carries with it the length of the simulation, i.e., the number of *ticToc* events to be send to the clock.

There remains the question of who is responsible for introducing the *system* object and for sending it the startup event. We assume that our design execution environment can emulate the C++ **main** program.

This completes the construction of the executable model, except, of course, for filling in the details. The next major step is the construction of the clustered model.

9.1.2 Clustered model

The construction of the clustered model is very simple in our case. There is no need for distribution of the simulator. Hence the clustered model can consist of a single cluster. This obviates establishing CORBA-style machinery [55] to support cluster boundary-crossing object interaction.

9.1.3 Sequentialized clusters

This activity reduces to the sequentialization of a single cluster. A great majority of sequential processes consist of a "big" loop whose body starts with obtaining an event that is subsequently processed by an intricate maze that ultimately leads back to the beginning of the loop.

Main loop

In our case, this loop consists of invoking the *ticToc* operation on the unique clock instance. This operation leads to the generation of *tic* operations in the registered parties. Observe that where we used sending *events* before, here we use invocations of *operations* which correspond with C++ member function calls. In the previous model, the clock broadcasts events, allowing rooms, the furnace monitor, or a furnace timer to operate in parallel. Here a clock operation causes a "normal" nested chain of operations to be executed, ultimately returning to the clock that will serve a next client or that will enter a new iteration of the loop.

Flattening transition networks

The question remains as to how to realize this behavior. The object computational model of the earlier executable model is clearly different. In particular, we have to deal with an object having a transition diagram that can handle events only in certain states or, worse, that reacts to an event dependent on the state in which the object resides when the event arrives. The sequential model supports effectively only operations that emanate from a single state and that return to that state.

In Chapter 6 we described briefly techniques for flattening transition networks. Here, we elaborate the subclassing technique using an example. Consider the transition diagram of the heat switch, which we show again in Figure 9.4.

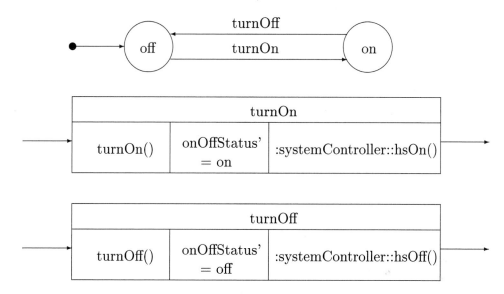

Figure 9.4: Transition network of the heat switch, in preparation for its sequentialized design.

The essence of this design "trick" is to use inheritance differently way than we have done before. Thus far, inheritance was employed to achieve the equivalence of concept classification. Instead, we will use subclassing to express the different behaviors that are available in the *off* and *on* states.

We need to make the following changes:

1. We add an attribute *state* that has as value domain *HeatSwitch*. Actual values will be unique instances of the classes *HeatSwitchOff* and *HeatSwitchOn*, see below.

2. We modify the transition network of the class *HeatSwitch* by using a single state, *ready*, and two transitions, *turnOn* and *turnOff*, which still depend on the invocation triggers *turnOn()* and *turnOff()*, respectively. However, their action part is forwarding *turnOn()* and *turnOff()*, respectively, to the object that is bound to the *state* attribute.

3. We add the class *HeatSwitchOff* as a subclass of *HeatSwitch*. It also has a single state, *ready*, and the two transitions, *turnOn* and *turnOff*, with the invocation triggers *turnOn()* and *turnOff()*. However, the transition *turnOff()* has *nothing* in its action part. It is a "no-op" because the heat switch is already in the off

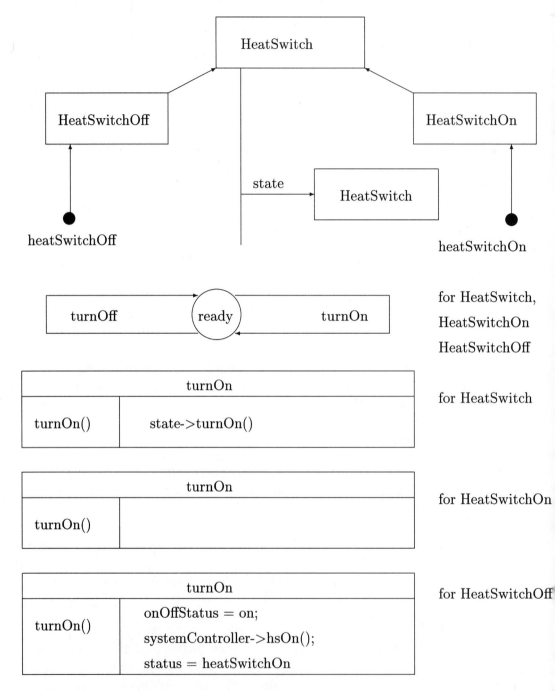

Figure 9.5: See the text for the subclassing used to represent the states of *HeatSwitch*.

state. In contrast, the action part of the transition *turnOn* has as action part

```
onOffStatus = on
systemController->hsOn() // an operation
state = heatSwitchOn // the unique instance of HeatSwitchOn
```

4. We add the class *HeatSwitchOn* as a subclass of *HeatSwitch*, etc.

Figure 9.5 shows the details of the subclassing and the transition networks. The coarse-grained view of the transition networks for the three classes is the same: the state *ready* with the two transitions. However, the details of the *turnOn* transition differs for the *HeatSwitch*, *HeatSwitchOn*, and *HeatSwitchOff* classes. Notice that the sequentialized transitions do *not* have an event section any longer. All communication is realized through operation invocations.

To be fair, we should acknowledge that this design trick has violated the inheritance rule, which states that transitions can only be modified through strengthening of postconditions (and weakening of preconditions). The situation can be saved by renaming the transitions and the events in the subclasses as *turnOn2* and *turnOff2*, respectively, and adjusting the action part in *turnOn* and *turnOff* in *HeatSwitch* accordingly. We will not change the notation in our diagram, but this correction will be visible by metrics, see below.

All the participating classes now have transitions that can always be invoked, but the meaning of the transition depends on the state in which the object resides. In essence, we have split off the bulk of behavior into separate stateless objects that are shared by all primary instances of *HeatSwitch* (which in our home heating example by itself has only a single instance). The same technique applies to all other classes that have transition networks with multiple states.

Using unique instances of subclasses to represent transition network states is a "nifty", elegant construct. However, one may object against its costs: the additional indirection involved in invoking an operation. The optimization section below gives an alternative.

Transitions fired through a condition

The wait states in the transition network of the furnace, see Figure 5.26 on page 177, still need some attention. The transition *startup* must arrange for the activation of a timer that will ultimately fire the transition *turnOnBlower*; similarly for the triggering of the *turnOffBlower* transition. We elaborate the design of this timer to illustrate what to do with a transition that is not triggered by an event but through a condition.

Analysis view of Timer

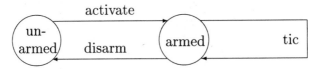

Design view of Timer

Unarmed subclass: Armed subclass:

Figure 9.6: Top: analysis view of a timer that can be used by the furnace to prevent starting up within 5 minutes since the last shutdown. The transition *disarm* is not driven by an event but is triggered by a local attribute having reached zero; the *tic* transition decreases this counter every second it is activated by the clock. Bottom: design view of the timer. See the text for the realization of the *disarm* transition.

Figure 9.6 shows the analysis and design views of a timer's behavior. The event or operation that leads to the *activate* transition transports the waiting time and the identity of the sender or client into the object. Its action consists of setting the wait time attribute and setting the attribute that represents the client to be resumed. In addition, the timer registers itself with the clock. The *tic* transition just decreases the wait-time attribute. The *disarm* transition in the analysis model is fired up by the condition that the wait-time attribute is not positive. The question is how to realize this transition in the timer's design. It gets absorbed by the *tic* operation:

```
waitTime--;
if (waitTime <= 0) {
    state = unarmed; // switch the timer to the unarmed state
    client->resume();
};
```

Superstates

The design of superstates also needs attention. Figure 9.7 illustrates how the unnamed superstate in the transition network of the blower motor is transformed. First, the transitions *setRPM* and *getRPM* are "pushed down" to the *off* and *on* states. Second, subclasses for the *off* and *on* states are introduced as discussed above. Hence all four operations are available for the class *BlowerMotor* and for its two subclasses. The operations in *BlowerMotor* forward to the operations in the subclasses. Although these transformations do the job, we can do better in this particular example. Since the two versions of the transition *setRPM* in the two subclasses are the same, we can lift them up into the *BlowerMotor* and remove them in the subclasses. The same optimization applies, of course, to the transition *getRPM*.

9.1.4 Optimized clusters

Sequentialized clusters yield an abundance of opportunities for optimization, especially when automatic design transformations have been employed. The treatment of a superset in the preceding section is an immediate illustration.

The use of subclassing to deal with transition networks having multiple states is quite heavy handed and introduces the overhead of indirections. A more efficient but less elegant approach avoids state subclassing. Instead, one uses operations which start off with a case statement that branches on the value of the *state* attribute and invokes in each branch the proper version of the operation.

Optimizations usually exploit ad hoc features of a design. The system controller and the furnace controller can certainly be optimized, see, for example, Figure 5.14 on page 161. The key feature they have in common is that the four states in their transition networks can be represented by two independent Boolean-valued attributes. Hence we can simplify the system controller by the following modifications:

1. Introduce the attributes *heatSwitch* and *faultResetSwitch* and initialize them both with *false*.

2. Replace the transition network having four states and eight transitions by the single state *ready* and the following operations:

3. Define the operation *frOn()* as

```
heatSwitch = true;
if (faultResetSwitch) furnaceController->enable();
```

Analysis view

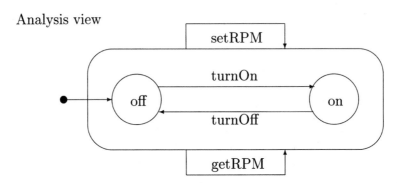

Design step 1

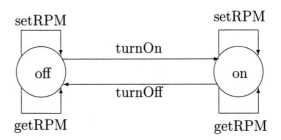

Design step 2: operations for Blower Motor and for its two subclasses

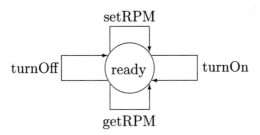

Figure 9.7: Treatment for a superset regarding the transitions *setPRM* and *getPRM*. See the text for details.

4. Define the operation *frOff()* as

```
heatSwitch = false;
if (faultResetSwitch) furnaceController->disable();
```

5. Define the operation *hsOn()* as

```
faultResetSwitch = true;
if (heatSwitch) furnaceController->enable();
```

6. Define the operation *hsOff()* as

```
faultResetSwitch = false;
if (heatSwitch) furnaceController->disable();
```

Of course, this change affects only the internals of the system controller. The clients and the server of the system controller are undisturbed. Whether this optimization of the system controller is appropriate is another matter. The price we pay is that the optimized design differs from the analysis description. In fact, the gain, in this case, is negligible. The home heating system will not perform better by this optimization. In general, one can argue that this system is not compute bound and hence does not require optimization. Thus we may want to do the reverse: replace fast procedures by less efficient procedures that reduce memory requirements. Consequently, we will not hunt for further design optimizations.

9.2 Metrics for the Constructive Micro Process

This section is devoted to the application of several metrics defined in Chapter 8. We look first in detail at one class, again the heat switch, after it has been transformed into the optimized phase. Subsequently, we apply these metrics to all the other classes.

9.2.1 Heat Switch Metrics

The heat switch ends up with a main class and with two subclasses that represent the *on* and *off* states. We recollect that we defined several metrics that measure the maintenance burden of a class in isolation ($\mu^1_{ClassMB}$, $\mu^2_{ClassMB}$, $\mu^3_{ClassMB}$, $\mu^4_{ClassMB}$)

and a single metric that measures the maintenance burden given the place of the class in the target system ($\mu_{systemContext}$). Below we repeat each definition before applying it.

$\mu^1_{ClassMB}(class)$ = distance of *class* from the furthest root class
    We recollect that the *HeatSwitch* is a subclass of the class *Switch/Indicator*. Hence:
$\mu^1_{ClassMB}(HeatSwitch) = 1$
$\mu^1_{ClassMB}(HeatSwitchOff) = 2$
$\mu^1_{ClassMB}(HeatSwitch) = 2$

$\mu^2_{ClassMB}(class)$ = # direct and indirect super classes of *class*.
    There is no multiple inheritance, so we get the same values as for $\mu^1_{ClassMB}$:
$\mu^2_{ClassMB}(HeatSwitch) = 1$
$\mu^2_{ClassMB}(HeatSwitchOff) = 2$
$\mu^2_{ClassMB}(HeatSwitch) = 2$

$\mu^3_{ClassMB}(class) =$
$c_1 * \#$ *local member variables* $+$
$c_2 * \#$ *imported member variables* $+$
$c_3 * \#$ *local member functions* $+$
$c_4 * \#$ *imported member functions*.
    Remember that we have introduced a *status* attribute in *HeatSwitch*. The only other attribute *onOffStatus* is defined in *Switch/Indicator*. Notice that the subclasses have the imported member functions *turnOn* and *turnOff* (which are not used!) in addition to the local member functions *turnOn2* and *turnOff2*. Hence we obtain
$\mu^3_{ClassMB}(HeatSwitch) = c_1 * 1 + c_2 * 1 + c_3 * 2 + c_4 * 0$
$\mu^3_{ClassMB}(HeatSwitchOff) = c_1 * 0 + c_2 * 2 + c_3 * 2 + c_4 * 2$
$\mu^3_{ClassMB}(HeatSwitchOn) = c_1 * 0 + c_2 * 2 + c_3 * 2 + c_4 * 2$
Local entities are easier to deal with than imported entities. Member functions are more complex than member variables. For the sake of these calculations, let's give c_i the values
$c_1 = 1, c_2 = 2, c_3 = 3, c_4 = 4$
This gives
$\mu^3_{ClassMB}(HeatSwitch) = 9$
$\mu^3_{ClassMB}(HeatSwitchOff) = 18$
$\mu^3_{ClassMB}(HeatSwitchOn) = 18$

$\mu^4_{ClassMB}(class) =$

$c_1 * \#$ local member variables $+$
$c_2 * \#$ imported member variables $+$
$c_3 * (\sum_{local} \mu_{CM}(member Function_{local})) +$
$c_4 * (\sum_{imported} \mu_{CM}(member Function_{imported}))$.

We repeat as well the definition of the Coleman et al. maintainability metric:
$\mu_{CM}(member Function) =$
$3.42 * ln(E) + 0.23 * V(g') + 16.2 * ln(LOC) - 0.99 * CM$.
E is the Halstead Effort [31], per module, which is defined as
$(n1 * N2 * (N1 + N2) * log_2(n1 + n2))/(2 * n2)$
where $n1$ is the number of unique operators, $n2$ is the number of unique operands, $N1$ is the number of operator occurrences, and $N2$ is the number of operand occurrences; $V(g')$ is the extended cyclomatic complexity per module, where the extended cyclomatic complexity is defined as the number of decisions plus one; LOC is the number of lines of code per module; and CM is the number of lines of comments per module.

We will work our way through by calculating $\mu^4_{ClassMB}(HeatSwitch)$. Applying the formula, we obtain
$\mu^4_{ClassMB}(HeatSwitch) =$
$c_1 * 1 + //\ c_1 * \#$ local member variables
$c_2 * 1 + //\ c_2 * \#$ imported member variables
$c_3 * (\mu_{CM}(turnOn) + \mu_{CM}(turnOff)) + //\ c_3 * (\sum_{local} \mu_{CM}(member Function_{local}))$
$c_4 * 0\ //\ c_4 * (\sum_{imported} \mu_{CM}(member Function_{imported}))$
Subsequently, we expand $\mu_{CM}(turnOn)$:
$3.42 * ln(E) + 0.23 * V(g') + 16.2 * ln(LOC) - 0.99 * CM$
Recollect that the action part of $turnOn$ in $HeatSwitch$ is only $state$->$turnOn()$. Thus we have as operators, $->turnOn()$ and as operand, $state$. Hence we have
$n1$ is the number of unique operators $= 1$
$n2$ is the number of unique operands $= 1$
$N1$ is the number of operator occurrences $= 1$
$N2$ is the number of operand occurrences $= 1$
This gives
$E = (n1 * N2 * (N1 + N2) * log_2(n1 + n2))/(2 * n2)$
$= (1 * 1 * (1 + 1) * log_2(1 + 1))/(2 * 1) = log_2(2) = 1$
The number of decisions is zero; hence $V(g') = 1$.
The number of lines of code is one; hence $LOC = 1$.
The number of lines of comments is zero; hence $CM = 0$.
This gives:

$\mu_{CM}(turnOn) = 3.42 * ln(1) + 0.23 * 1 + 16.2 * ln(1) - 0.99 * 0 = 0.23$

Obviously, we also have $\mu_{CM}(turnOff) = 0.23$. This gives us
$\mu^4_{ClassMB}(HeatSwitch) =$
$c_1 * 1+ \; // \; c_1 * \# \; local \; member \; variables$
$c_2 * 1+ \; // \; c_2 * \# \; imported \; member \; variables$
$c_3 * 0.46+ \; // \; c_3 * (\mu_{CM}(turnOn) + \mu_{CM}(turnOff))$
$c_4 * 0 \; // \; c_4 * (\sum_{imported} \mu_{CM}(memberFunction_{imported}))$
Using also the weights $c_1 = 1, c_2 = 2, c_3 = 3, and c_4 = 4$ yields
$\mu^4_{ClassMB}(HeatSwitch) = 4.38$

Next we attack $\mu^4_{ClassMB}(HeatSwitchOn)$. We obtain
$\mu^4_{ClassMB}(HeatSwitchOn) =$
$c_1 * 0+ \; // \; c_1 * \# \; local \; member \; variables$
$c_2 * 2+ \; // \; c_2 * \# \; imported \; member \; variables$
$c_3 * (\mu_{CM}(turnOn2) + \mu_{CM}(turnOff2))$
$// \; c_3 * (\sum_{local} \mu_{CM}(memberFunction_{local}))$
$c_4 * (\mu_{CM}(turnOn) + \mu_{CM}(turnOff))$
$// \; c_4 * (\sum_{imported} \mu_{CM}(memberFunction_{imported}))$

The term multiplied by $c_4 = 0.46$ since these are the transitions belonging to *HeatSwitch*. The calculations of $\mu_{CM}(turnOn2)$ and $\mu_{CM}(turnOff2)$ remains. The action part of the transition *turnOn2* is empty; thus $\mu_{CM}(turnOn2) = 0$. It turns out that $\mu_{CM}(turnOff2) = 28.4$. Using the same weights, we get
$\mu^4_{ClassMB}(HeatSwitchOn) = c_1 * 0 + c_2 * 2 + c_3 * 28.4 + c_4 * 0.46 = 91.0$
Due to symmetry, we also have $\mu^4_{ClassMB}(HeatSwitchOff) = 91.0$.

The calculated measures are summarized in Table 9.1. The fact that the absolute values for each class in the table are drastically different is not of concern. We can multiply each metric with an arbitrary positive parameter. Of interest, however, are the ratios between the header class *HeatSwitch* and its subclasses. These ratios are 2 in the top three rows and over 20 in the case of $\mu^4_{ClassMB}$. The ratio of 2 is certainly too low. A subclass has twice as many transitions, one of which has three action statements, whereas, the parent transitions have only a single statement. In addition, we have to deal with the obtuseness of inheritance. On the other hand, a ratio of 20 seems to be too high. At this point, however, we do not have enough data to adjust the c_i coefficients in the different metrics.

As discussed above, an alternative design of the class *HeatSwitch* does not use instances of subclasses but instead, uses a conditional expression inside the *turnOn* and *turnOff* transitions. For example, the action part of *turnOn* consists of

Metric	HeatSwitch	HeatSwitchOff	HeatSwitchOn	Sum
$\mu^1_{ClassMB}$	1.00	2.0	2.0	5.00
$\mu^2_{ClassMB}$	1.00	2.0	2.0	5.00
$\mu^3_{ClassMB}$	9.00	18.0	18.0	45.00
$\mu^4_{ClassMB}$	4.38	91.0	91.0	186.38

Table 9.1: Summarizes the values obtained by applying four different metrics to measure the maintenance burden on the class *HeatSwitch* and on the two subclasses *HeatSwitchOff* and *HeatSwitchOn*. The two subclasses have been added during the design. The last column adds up the values in each row and will be used below.

```
if ( onOffStatus == Off )
then { onOffStatus = On;
       systemController->hsOn(); }
// else ignore the turnOn() event
```

We recalculate the metrics for this design.
The metric $\mu^1_{ClassMB}$ measures the distance to the furthest root and thus
$\mu^1_{ClassMB}(HeatSwitch) = 1$

The metric $\mu^2_{ClassMB}$ counts the number of direct and indirect super classes:
$\mu^2_{ClassMB}(HeatSwitch) = 1$

The metric $\mu^3_{ClassMB}$ takes more aspects into account:
$\mu^3_{ClassMB}(class) =$
$c_1 * \#$ *local member variables*
$c_2 * \#$ *imported member variables*
$c_3 * \#$ *local member functions*
$c_4 * \#$ *imported member functions*
Notice that we don't have the attribute *state* any longer. Thus we obtain
$\mu^3_{ClassMB}(HeatSwitch) = c_1 * 0 + c_2 * 1 + c_3 * 2 + c_4 * 0 = 8$

We repeat also last metric:
$\mu^4_{ClassMB}(class) =$
$c_1 * \#$ *local member variables* $+$
$c_2 * \#$ *imported member variables* $+$
$c_3 * (\sum_{local} \mu_{CM}(memberFunction_{local})) +$
$c_4 * (\sum_{imported} \mu_{CM}(memberFunction_{imported})).$

The only term of interest is $\mu_{CM}(turnOn)$ (and the same value for *turnOff*). The elaboration of $3.42*ln(E)+0.23*V(g')+16.2*ln(LOC)-0.99*CM$ for $\mu_{CM}(turnOn)$ yields the value 31.04. Consequently, we obtain

$\mu^4_{ClassMB}(HeatSwitch) =$

$c_1 * 0 + //c_1 * \#$ *local member variables* +

$c_2 * 1 + //c_2 * \#$ *imported member variables* +

$c_3 * (31.04 + 31.04) + //c_3 * (\sum_{local} \mu_{CM}(memberFunction_{local})) +$

$c_4 * 0 //c_4 * (\sum_{imported} \mu_{CM}(memberFunction_{imported})) = 188.24$

In Table 9.2 we compare the two different designs against the four different maintenance burden metrics. Of interest are the ratios $design_1/design_2$ for the four different metrics. They are, respectively, 5, 5, 5.6, and 1.0. Design 2 is much easier to maintain according to the first three metrics, while the fourth metric considers them virtually equally easy (or hard). The first design avoids conditional expressions. The second design avoids the introduction of subclasses. We tend to agree with the fourth metric. However, empirical studies are needed to investigate which type of design is easier in the long run.

A surprising argument in favor for the first three metrics is that the first design is amenable to automation. The second design exploits the insight that the existing attribute *onOffStatus* could be utilized in the conditional expressions.

Metric	Design 1	Design 2
$\mu^1_{ClassMB}$	5.00	1.00
$\mu^2_{ClassMB}$	5.00	1.00
$\mu^3_{ClassMB}$	45.00	8.00
$\mu^4_{ClassMB}$	186.38	188.24

Table 9.2: Comparison of the maintenance burden metric values applied to the design of the *HeatSwitch*. The first design uses the two subclasses *HeatSwitchOff* and *HeatSwitchOn*; the second design uses conditional expressions to deal with the two *off* and *on* states in the analysis model. See the text for a discussion of the essentially two different ratios of the four different pairs of metric values.

9.2.2   HHS design statistics

Of interest is whether our analysis artifact metrics correlate with our design artifact metrics. To restrict the number of computations, we have calculated the values of the metric $\mu^4_{ClassMB}$ applied to the designs of the home heating system where we used

Class	μ_{vocab}	Ψ_A	$\mu^4_{ClassMB}$	μ_{fanOut}	μ_{fanIn}	Ψ_D
HS	5	10	188	1	0	288
FRS/I	5	10	188	1	1	388
FSI	5	10	188	0	1	288
HFR	5	14	339	2	1	639
SC	8	19	433	1	2	733
Clock	5	14	132	3	2	632
Room	14	32	245	7	2	1145
OS	4	8	11	0	1	111
RTS	4	8	11	0	1	111
DTID	4	8	11	0	1	111
WV	4	9	11	0	1	111
FC	8	19	433	1	2	733
Furnace	14	44	1054	8	2	2054
BM	6	16	217	0	1	317
OilValve	4	11	222	0	1	322
Ignitor	2	6	34	0	1	134
WTS	4	8	11	0	1	111
FM	10	23	353	4	2	953
FFS	4	8	11	0	1	111
OCS	4	8	11	0	1	111
OH	4	9	42	0	1	142
LP	4	9	42	0	1	142
VC	NA	24	307	1	2	607

Table 9.3: Metric values for the home heating system classes. The first column has data from μ_{vocab} which can be captured early in the analysis. The second column has data from Ψ_A, the synthetic metric introduced in Chapter 5, which can be obtained late in the analysis phase. (The data for these two metrics were presented in Chapter 5.) The next three columns have the values obtained from the design metrics $\mu^4_{ClassMB}$, μ_{fanOut}, and μ_{fanIn}, respectively. The last column has the synthetic design metric Ψ_D, which is defined as: $\mu^4_{ClassMB} + 100 * \mu_{fanOut} + 100 * \mu_{fanIn}$. These have been applied to the design, which does *not* use subclasses when multiple states are involved. The next table shows the correlations between these metric values.

the approach that does *not* use subclasses for dealing with multiple states. Table 9.3 shows the results. The data in the first two columns come from the analysis phase and have been shown in Table 5.2 on page 198. The metric $\mu^4_{ClassMB}$ does not take into account the role that a class plays in the target system. The metrics μ_{fanOut} and μ_{fanIn} address that dimension. The values for these metrics are also shown in Table 9.3. A combination of these design metrics is defined as

$$\Psi_D = \mu^4_{ClassMB} + 100 * \mu_{fanOut} + 100 * \mu_{fanIn}$$

The values of this synthetic metric are represented in the table as well.

Metric 1	Metric 2	β_0	β_1	Correlation
μ_{vocab}	Ψ_A	-2.3267	2.7888	0.96491
μ_{vocab}	$\mu^4_{ClassMB}$	-151.6525	59.2390	0.78259
Ψ_A	$\mu^4_{ClassMB}$	-123.9374	22.4604	0.87682
μ_{vocab}	Ψ_D	-349.8717	136.8833	0.91706
Ψ_A	Ψ_D	-242.3386	48.5253	0.96311

Table 9.4: The values for β_0 and β_1 are the best fits for the available data in the equation $\mu_{Metric2} = \beta_0 + \beta_1 * \mu_{Metric1}$.

The correlations between these metrics are shown in Table 9.4. The correlation between μ_{vocab} (early in the analysis) and Ψ_A (late in the analysis) was shown on page 199. The correlation between the analysis vocabulary metric and the design metric $\mu^4_{ClassMB}$, 0.78, is quite respectable. As is to be hoped, the correlation between the analysis class metric Ψ_A and the design class metric $\mu^4_{ClassMB}$, 0.88, is even better. Taking into account the fan-out and fan-in metrics improves the correlations even more and raises them to 0.92 and 0.96, respectively. Assuming that these product metrics correlate themselves with effort metrics, we obtain more credence that measuring efforts early in the life cycle can be used to come up with a reliable estimate for the total development effort.

At this point we are able to calculate the maintenance burden for the total system according to formulas given in Section 8.2.6 on page 278:

$$\mu^1_{system} = \sum_i (\alpha * \mu^4_{ClassMB}(class_i) + \beta * \mu_{systemContext}(class_i))$$

$$\mu^2_{system} = \mu^1_{system} + VG(system)$$

The actual values are at this point not relevant. These values become of interest when actual maintenance efforts for deployed systems are available. Then one can correlate these calculated system maintenance burdens against actual expenditures. Keeping track of the actual maintenance efforts per class (e.g., by measuring the mutation ratio of classes) is also useful and can be correlated with the calculated values for $\mu_{systemContext}(class_i)$.

9.3 Impressionistic Micro Process

The impressionistic micro process was described in Section 7.2 on page 265. Bypassing the construction of an executable model that has one thread of control per object is the main difference with the constructive process. Most activities in the constructive process apply to the impressionistic process and yield the same results. Subsequently, we can apply the same product metrics. Consequently, we avoid redoing our home heating example.

9.4 Summary

This chapter illustrates how to apply the constructive design micro process to the home heating example. Many of the design steps apply to the impressionistic micro process as well. By choosing to implement a simulator for the home heating system one has to introduce classes that represent the "outside world". The heat switch class was used to illustrate in more detail how to flatten a multistate transition network by using subclasses.

Metrics developed in Chapter 8 were illustrated using the heat switch. A synthetic metric Ψ_D has been defined that uses $\mu_{ClassMB}^4$, μ_{fanOut}, and μ_{fanIn}. Values calculated on all classes of the home heating system for Ψ_D correlate well with Ψ_A with a value of 0.96. This result suggests that measurements taken during the analysis can be used as predictors for design efforts. Whether these values will actually correlate with maintenance efforts of the corresponding implementation artifacts is to be researched.

9.5 Further Reading

As we mentioned in Chapter 5, only Booch [12] discusses details of the home heating system.

9.6   Exercises

1. Define and design a class that can be the value domain of the *livingPattern* attribute in *livingPattern* and that uses internally a representation of a circular list of intervals of periods during which the pattern does not change. Make sure that this class can also be used as a value domain for *occupancyRecord* in *OccupancyHistory*.

2. Select a few classes of the home heating system, work out their designs, and calculate their Ψ_D values.

Part III

Implementation

Chapter 10

Implementation Concepts

10.1 Purpose

The purpose of this chapter is to prepare the translation or transformation of the design model into C++. Does it make sense for us to discuss C++ or any other OO programming language? Let's look at what this would entail.

Traditionally, one distinguishes:
- Syntax: the form and structure of the language
- Semantics: the meaning of its terms
- Pragmatics: use of the language

Texts on C++ or a similar language usually assume that the reader is already familiar with computer languages. Hence they avoid detailed descriptions of the syntax. Most attention is given to a systematic treatment of the meaning of key language concepts. Small examples are provided to explain the meanings beyond a definition. Well-known texts that follow this route are Lippman [48] and Stroustrup [77]. These examples are the beginnings of the pragmatics of the language. They illustrate how to obtain small goals.

Pragmatics is, however, a huge area and one can argue whether one can effectively teach pragmatics when interpreted in a wide sense. A complete program is a detailed solution. It resembles a proof of a theorem, and it resembles a coherent text that is produced in response to a particular need. However. we are not yet able to teach effectively how to generate proofs. Neither are we able to teach how to write good text.[1] These skills rely on many other cognitive abilities that go beyond understanding

---

[1]Consider the *New York Times Book Review*, August 21, 1994 of William H. Gass's, *On Experimental Writing: Some Clues for the Clueless:* "Pick a sentence at random from a randomly selected

the syntax and meanings of the key concepts of languages.

The pragmatics of using a programming language as the thinking medium for system development is hopeless anyway. That is why analysis and design have been introduced as "detours". Programming languages force attention to detail that is irrelevant for "thinking about what can be done".[2] A language such as C++ offers a wealth of options to do trivial things. For example, incrementing a counter can be expressed in at least three different ways. The rich expressive power of programming languages helps to cater for the needs of the machine - squeezing machine cycles out of a implementation - but the price to pay is that they stand in the way of *our* global problem solving.

Using a programming language as an interhuman communication vehicle also yields disasters. It is the cause of the high costs of maintenance when systems are described primarily through their code, Grady [29].

In the view of Brito e Abreu [1], implementation activities are quite constricted,

> Object-Orientation is well suited for what is called "seamless development", which basically stands for using the same formalism and corresponding notation throughout the life cycle, by means of stepwise refinement. The traditional barriers between analysis an design and particularly between design and coding, characterized by formalism shifts with corresponding translation rules, are bound to diminish. Therefore, analysis and design play an even more important role than ever. *Coding, for example, can be considered just as a "fill-in-the-blanks" activity.*[3]

Does that mean that nothing is left for the pragmatics of (OO) programming languages? No, until there are optimizing "compilers" or sufficiently efficient interpreters for design languages, we must still *realize*, i.e., translate, a design into a machine-friendly formalism. As a "detail", performance and resource restriction requirements must be met. However, we emphasize that the implementation phase has little room to maneuver. When, say, a performance requirement is not met by the

---

book, and then another from another volume, also chosen by chance; then write a paragraph that will be a reasonable bridge between them"; or "do dialogue in dialect: a Welshman and a Scott arguing about an onion". Even if these suggestions for getting a grip on writing are a joke, is there still anybody around who wants to teach the full pragmatics of language?

[2]The expression quoted comes from Stroustrup [77]. The quote is somewhat perverse because Stroustrup suggests that a programming language "... provides a set of concepts for the programmer to use when thinking about what can be done". He may, in fact, have an opposite opinion about what can be done with programming languages.

[3]Emphasis added.

code, the solution is *not* to change the code in the first place. Instead, the design must be changed (or requirements may have to be adjusted first). Subsequently, design modifications are propagated into the code.

Implementation activities depend on how far the design went into detail. A non-detailed design may ignore memory reclamation or gory details of exception handling or may make assumptions about the infrastructure that turn out to have nontrivial consequences. What is the implementer to do in these circumstances? Our preferred answer is to go back to the design phase.

In summary, in this chapter we concentrate on the pragmatics of transforming the design into code. Implementation activities that require genuine thinking are ignored because we adhere to the "implementation = coding" philosophy. To present the translation actions, we follow the core concepts introduced in the analysis phase. However, relations are ignored because they have been designed away. Before getting into the translation rules, we make some general observations on OO programming languages and on C++ in particular.

10.2 What OOP Languages Have in Common

OO programming languages have many basic features in common. Encapsulated objects are expected. Classes as template descriptions are usually available as well, although research continues on class-free languages; see Smith [75]. Object interaction as a variant of function invocation is obviously shared as well. Since OO programming languages conform to the restriction of a normal process, all objects in a process share a single thread of control. Again research is in progress to allow for lightweight threads; see Arjomandi et al. [5]. They also share the fact that there is no support for the encapsulation of subsystems. Exploiting clusterings in multiple files is the only poor man's way to emulate subsystems; see Section 10.12.

10.3 Where OOP Languages Differ

Some differences between OOP languages are captured in Table 10.1.

10.4 Obvious Features of C++

C++ has inherited the obtuseness of C. Stroustrup [77] explains the use of references with

	C++	CLOS	Eiffel	Objective-C	Smalltalk	Java
Multiple inheritance	Yes	Yes	Yes	No	No	Yes
Meta class	No	Yes	No	No	Yes	Yes
Typing	Yes	No	Yes	Yes	No	Yes
Templates	Yes	No	No	No	No	No

Table 10.1: Some differences among major OO programming languages.

```
int ii = 0;
int& rr = ii;
rr++;            // ii is incremented to 1
```

Why is *ii* incremented instead of *rr*?

C++ is, like C, a system's building language. Control of squeezing the last byte out of an implementation or the last nanosecond out of a CPU has not been surrendered.

Readability of C++ is as poor as that of C. For example, the key word "static" requires even more interpretation in C++ than in C. The language appears to be optimized for minimum typing by developers, but since maintenance is a much larger part of a system's life cycle cost, this choice is a liability.

C++ is as popular as C.[4] Thus, although we are no fans of C++, we agree that for now it is the prevailing OO language. Hence its use in this book.

10.5   Unexpected Features of C++

The availability of arrays with run-time defined boundaries is a pleasant surprise. For example, one can have
```
int nn = 5; // array size
int *i = new int[nn]; // define i[0] up to i[4]
i[4] = -3; // set the last one
```

---

[4]The popularity of C and C++ is amazing. On the other hand, supremacy of the questionable is not uncommon: C has prevailed over Algol68, Pascal, and Ada; DOS prevailed over Unix; Unix prevailed over VMS; and Windows surpassed X11. Ranting and raving more: VHS video prevailed over Beta; the inferior granularity of U.S. television was chosen over European TV. Sociologists to the rescue for explanations.

The inability to turn on array-bound checking remains a continuing embarrassment. Booleans were recently added to the language after no little amount of deliberations. Given that they were already available in Algol60, one wonders.

A pleasant surprise is that input and output operations of C have been overhauled. The new stream primitives `cin` and `cout` are easier to work with than C's `scanf` and `printf`.

10.6 Perspective

C++ is a "huge" language. We do not attempt to cover it. Only those features are touched upon that emerge as obvious targets for design constructs. Hence there is plenty of room for an C++ expert to exploit additional insights about the semantics of a design to go beyond the mappings that we present. Having acknowledged this, we want to remind readers as well that using exceptional features may save a few nanoseconds, but probably at the cost of maintainability and portability. Hence we recommend using only a minimal subset of C++ and using it in "robotic" fashion. Current C++ code generation tools are a good example.

10.7 Class Statics

In this section we describe the transformation of attributes. These transformations are straightforward and have been incorporated in all OO CASE tools that generate code. The next two subsections treat the cases where the value domain is or is not a class. We assume that attributes are single valued; i.e., multiple-valued attributes have been designed away using containers or the like. Figure 10.1 shows the two different cases.

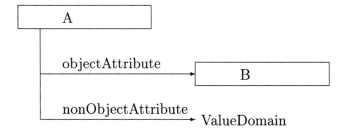

Figure 10.1: Ground cases for an object-valued attribute and a non-object-valued attribute to be translated in C++.

Attributes, called data members in C++, can be implemented in different ways. The dimensions are:

– *External exposure:* public, protected, private

– *Physical:* by value, by reference

An attribute can always be accessed by local operations. Protected is the recommended exposure choice for attributes. Protected means that an attribute cannot be accessed from outside the class but is accessible by derived classes (and by so-called "friend classes"). Declaring an attribute public gives full access from outside, but this is against the object encapsulation philosophy. A private attribute is not accessible by derived classes (although friend classes can access them). The proper role of a private attribute is only to support a local computation; i.e., a private attribute can not play a role in the conceptualization of a class.

Let O be an object. Along the physical dimension one can choose whether the entity referred to by an attribute is being incorporated inside O (this is the "by value" designation) or whether the attribute entity is outside O and is attached through a pointer (this is the "by reference" designation). The former yields a strong notion of encapsulation. On the other hand, encapsulation is relative. A referenced attribute entity can still have excellent privacy: When an object O creates a referenced entity E, it is up to O whether or not it will reveal the identity of E to third parties. The encapsulation of a "by value" entity can be illusory as well, as shown in[5]

```
class indecentExposer {
private:
    any privateMember;
    any *pprivateMember = &privateMember;
public:
    any *expose(){ return pprivateMember; };
};
```

Moral: Encapsulation is in the mind of the beholder and can be broken by the foolhardy.

10.7.1   Object-valued attributes

The choices along both dimensions mentioned above are available for object-valued attributes. In case an attribute has been introduced during analysis, we recommend implementing it as "protected". This will guarantee that subclasses have this

---

[5]We are sympathetic to readers who have difficulty appreciating this example.

attribute as well. If the attribute has been introduced during design, an implementation in the "private" section is likely to be sufficient. When a subclass needs access to the attribute, the subclass can be made into a friend of the attribute or of the class to which the attribute belongs. Regarding physical incorporation, we recommend "by reference", see below for some arguments. Hence we obtain for the two cases of *objectAttribute*:

```
class A {
...
protected:
   B *objectAttribute1; // introduced in analysis
private:
   B *objectAttribute2; // introduced in design
:...
};
```

As a result, *objectAttribute* is a pointer to an instance of class B (provided, of course, that there has been proper initialization or assignment).

One can certainly deviate from the incorporation by reference treatment and do an incorporation by value, as in

```
class A {
protected:
   B objectAttribute;
};
```

However, automatic code generation can get into trouble when attributes are always translated into by value incorporations, as we will see.

Two classes *A* and *B* can have each other as value domains of attributes. For example, the class *Employee* can have an attribute *worksIn* with as value domain *Department*, and the class *Department* can have the attribute *headOfDepartment* with as value domain *Employee*. It is possible to use for both attributes incorporation by reference, as in

```
class Employee {
protected:
   Department *worksIn;
};
class Department {
protected:
```

```
    Employee *headOfDepartment;
};
```

It is *not* possible to use incorporation by value for both attributes. This can be argued as follows. Let $size(X)$ be the size, say in bytes, of an object of class X. Assume that A is incorporated by value in B and the other way around as well. We get $size(A) < size(B) < size(A)$, which is a contradiction. An alternative argument considers the compilation sequence of A and B. The compilation of A requires that the compilation of B has already been done to determine the size of an instance of A. The same holds for the compilation of B. Again we have a contradiction. Hence at least one of the mutual attributes must be an incorporation by reference. This supports the recommendation that objects always be incorporated through references.

Yet another argument are recursive classes that refer to themselves directly or indirectly in attributes. Obviously, these can be implemented only through "by reference" attribute domains.

10.7.2   Non-object-valued attributes

Non-object-valued attributes have value domains such as *bool, char, int, double, float*, and user-defined *struct*s. As for object-valued attributes, the choices for the type of external exposure and for the type of physical incorporation are available.

The exposure choice remains the same. A "conceptual" attribute introduced during the analysis should be made available to subclasses; hence they are to be implemented as protected. Design attributes introduced to help a local computation should be made into private members.

The proper way for non-object-valued attributes is incorporation by value. The sizes of these entities are known and there is no good reason to refer to them through a pointer. An exception would be an entity that is to be shared with other objects. However, this would lead to an aliased structure, which has a notorious bad reputation.[6] Side effects through aliased structures are hard to control. Consequently, incorporation by value is the proper way. Hence we translate our example into

```
class A {
protected:
    ValueDomain nonObjectAttribute1; // introduced in analysis
private:
```

---

[6]Aliasing is impossibly hard for proof obligation generators that adhere to the compositionality principle.

```
    ValueDomain nonObjectAttribute2; // introduced in design
};
```

Enumeration

Value domains defined by enumeration translate directly into C++. Consider an attribute *color* with the values *red, orange, yellow, green, blue, violet* as shown in Figure 10.2. The translation of this attribute can be done as in:

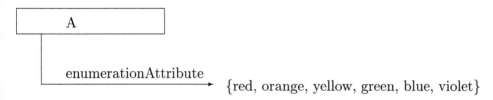

Figure 10.2: Attribute with an enumeration value domain.

```
class A {
protected:
    enum {red, orange, yellow, green, blue, violet};
};
```

Note that an **enum** is an abbreviation for a sequence of **const**s. Hence an equivalent implementation of our example is

```
class A {
protected:
const red = 0;
const orange = 1;
const yellow = 2;
const green = 3;
const blue = 4;
const violet = 5;
};
```

10.7.3   Constraints

The design has taken care of all constraints formulated during design.

10.7.4 Class globals

Objects partition a process-wide state space. This phenomenon, known as *encapsulation* and is a hallmark of the OO approach. However, sometimes it is useful to maintain global information that pertains to all instances of a class. How many instances does a class have? What has been the maximum number of instances? What is the average lifetime for an instance? Suppose that each instance of a class has a unique sequence number. Where do we store the counter that gets incremented when a new instance is produced?

Analysis and design notations do not have special notations for this kind of meta information. Hence to maintain these data for, say, a class A one would have to introduce a class *classAData* with the proper attributes. This class will have a single instance, say *theClassAData*, and the constructors and destructors of A should refer to operations in this unique instance, *theClassAData*.

C++ has a special notation for class-specific meta data. It supports the notion of class attributes, which are called *static* data members. The examples given above are introduced, as in

```
class A {
static int numberOfInstances;
static int maxNumberOfInstances;
static List<A> listOfAInstances; // List is a parametrized class
static float averageLifeTime;
static int instanceIdentifierCounter;
};
```

These static variables are manipulated by static functions. For example, we can have

```
class A {
...
static void incrementNumberOfInstances(){numberOfInstances++;};
static int maxNumberOfInstancesF(){return maxNumberOfInstances;};
...
};
```

10.8 Class Dynamics

The low-level design has produced a description of algorithms, storage structures, and their access mechanisms. The level of detail of these descriptions may differ.

Memory management may have been ignored by the design, assuming that garbage collection will take care of it. Alternatively, the design may have taken care of storage reclamation.

As an other example, the design may have exploited multiple inheritance while the target programming language has only single inheritance. Backtracking into the design, and/or into analysis, is here the recommended line of action.

Things get more laborious when the implementation language is not OO. Object encapsulation will be achieved through a programming discipline that simulates the conventions of, say, C++. Inheritance is more cumbersome. Cut-and-paste and modify is a cheap way to obtain the effects of inheritance (and avoid the costs of dynamic lookup while losing polymorphism). However, this cheapness may turn expensive during maintenance when all copies have to be remodified.

10.8.1 Abstract class

A class is a description of potential instances. Due to generalization where commonalities are factored out, one may introduce abstract classes for which instances are never to be introduced. Only their (indirect) nonabstract subclasses, which are extended with commitments on dynamic features, will have instances.

An operation that has different refinements in subclasses and that needs to be activated in a polymorphic setting - i.e., where operation selection occurs at run time - needs to have a "virtual" presence in the superclass.

A class is called abstract in C++ when it has at least one undefined operation; i.e., a *virtual function*. As an example, an undefined function *setZip*, a placeholder to be defined in a subclass, is defined as in

```
class StreetAddress {
protected:
   String street;
   Integer number;
public:
   virtual void setZip(Integer) = 0; // setZip has a zero body
};
```

Virtual functions are discussed in greater detail in Section 10.10.

10.8.2   Self reference

Member functions can refer directly to local members. For example, assume that a class S has the member
```
int ex
```
Then a member function can have as body
```
{ return ex; };
```
An alternative (unnecessary) way would explicitly mention the object in which the member *ex* resides. This can be done through
```
{ return this->ex; };
```
because in every member function of the class S there is the implicit definition
```
S *const this;
```
and the value of *this* is the object for which the function is invoked.

This self-knowledge can be exploited when an object needs to export its identity to another party. Registration and deregistration of objects in servers are main examples of usages of *this*. A room in the home heating system can register itself with the heat flow regular through
```
theHeatFlowRegulator->registerRoom(this);
```
Similarly, the furnace monitor can deregister itself from the clock through
```
theClock->removeClient(this);[7]
```

10.9   Object Management

Multiple mechanisms play a role in object creation and destruction. Entering and leaving a scope can lead to object creation and subsequent destruction. For example, if we have a class *Person*, we will obtain a new instance named *John* of *Person* through encountering
```
Person John;
```
Objects can be created and deleted explicitly through the **new** and **delete** operations, as in

```
Person *p;
...
p = new Person;
...
```

---

[7]The addition of the "this"-concept is a remarkable addition to the computer-science arsenal. The naming process could have been better. The me-generation missed a chance for immortality: "me" would have been half as much typing.

```
delete p;
```

Passing an object by value into the argument of a function is yet another way that an object gets created. In this case, the object is copied faithfully byte per byte. Values inside the object get copied over while entities referred to by pointers are not copied - only their pointers are copied. A function can return an object as a value. Copying the returned object into the recipient object will occur in a similar fashion. A special copy constructor deals with these cases. Both of these types of object creations are not recommended. It is better to pass object pointers around in function arguments and in function returns. Hence we ignore copy constructors.

Constructors play a role when a scope is entered and when the function **new** is used. C++ allows the specification of multiple constructors for a class. Constructors all have the same name: the name of the class for which they generate instances that is *Person* in our running example. The constructors differ through their signatures. A default constructor for the class *Person* would be

```
Person::Person()
{ name = "";
  ssn = "";
};
```

This constructor assumes that the class *Person* has the memberss *name* and *ssn*. This constructor is not doing much. It ensures only that nonrandom values are assigned to the attribute values of the new instance. This minimal constructor will be invoked when we enter a scope with

```
Person anonymous = Person();
Person somebody(); // abbreviated form
Person *psomebody = new Person();
```

A more interesting constructor allows us to specify initialization values: for example

```
Person::Person(char *n, char *s)
{ name = n;
  ssn = s;
};
```

Having this constructor available allows us to declare

```
Person aPerson = Person("John Doe", "123-45-6789");
Person someoneElse("Goofey", "000-00-0001"); // abbreviated form
Person *psomebody = new Person("Dilbert", "000-00-0002");
```

Yet another constructor that provides for a default of the *ssn* attribute is

```
Person::Person(char *n)
{ name = n;
  ssn = "777-77-7777";
};
```

The `delete` operation is a potential troublemaker. Deleting the same object twice is a good recipe for trouble. Accessing a deleted object yields a disaster as well. Hence the best strategy is not to delete any object at all.

Enduring objects are okay. These are anchor points of the application that will be around during the lifetime of the process and need not be recycled.

Garbage collection can help out where the time-out due to a garbage collection is inconsequential or where this time has an acceptable upper bound. Garbage collection in Emacs is a good example. Garbage collection is called *conservative* when it removes true garbage while not necessarily capturing everything. Rumor has it that memory leaks are negligible in conservative garbage collection.

If garbage collection is unacceptable, one has to do careful object lifetime studies. Defining a delete operation on the spot when a new operation is introduced helps to establish a lifetime scope. A special case is the creation of a "thread" object that will take care of its own destruction:

```
Thread *mission;
...
mission = new Thread(...);
mission->start(...); // set mission into motion
mission = 0;
...
```

How does `mission` eliminate itself? Through an operation like
`delete this;`

Observe that `mission` is rebound immediately to the nil-pointer after the (deleted!) thread object has returned. This coding sequence ensures that no object still has a handle on the deleted object - provided that the `mission` object did not give its identity away to a third party.

Pointers are troublesome in general. OO is not improving the situation. Consider the following situation:

```
WhateverClass *p, *q;
p = new WhateverClass(...); // create a fresh initialized instance
q = p; // copy the pointer to the instance
```

```
q->foo(..); // foo changes what q is pointing to;
            // hence the meaning of p changes also
```

This situation looks simple but is quite nasty. *We* see immediately in this example that p is also affected by the **foo** operation. Things get harder when the q->foo operation is far removed from the q-p pointer copying. It turns out that theoretical semantics has a hard time with the q->foo operation, due to the "immediate" side effect on p. If this is a surprise, consider the following:
– The creation of a new object entails the attachment to p of all properties associated with being an **WhateverClass** and all properties added by initialization arguments.
– The copying of the p-pointer will give q all the p properties to q.
– Both of these operations affect only the players mentioned in the operation.
– In contrast, the operation q->foo affects the properties of an entity not mentioned at all in the operation.

The moral of this example: Stay away from aliasing; it is more troublesome than the infamous *gotos*.

10.10   Inheritance

Inheritance is dealt with more or less as expected. One can declare a class A to have a superclass B as in

```
class A : public B {
...
};
```

The prefix **public** of B guarantees that the right things happen: Public members of B remain public and protected members of B remain protected as well.[8] A superclass can have instead of **public**, the **private** or **protected** qualifier. None of these other qualifiers fit the dictum that a subclass shares the structure and behavior of its superclass. Hence we ignore them.[9]

C++ assumes quite some discipline. A subclass can redefine a member function in a superclass as if the member in the superclass does not exist. Needless to say, a redefinition of a member function that violates the purpose and behavior of the function in the superclass may be advantageous for a quick fix, but such a practice

---

[8]It is to be observed that the access qualifiers public, protected, and private apply not only to attributes but also to functions.

[9]Having these three different ways of inheritance in C++ suggests that a committee ran amok.

spells disaster for maintenance. As a guideline: A subclass member should only *add* to the semantics of the equivalent member function in a parent.

The desire to extend the reach of typing in C++ as far as possible is the cause of the use of virtual functions as mentioned before. The consequence for inheritance is explained with an example. We revisit the class `StreetAddress` with the virtual function `setZip`:

```
class StreetAddress {
protected:
   String street;
   Integer number;
public:
   virtual void setZip(Integer) = 0; // setZip has a zero body
};
```

Now we can introduce two subclasses of *StreetAddress* that have two different Zip attributes - a short five-digit version and a long nine-digit version - and two different *setZip* functions:

```
class ShortStreetAddress : public StreetAddress {
protected:
   ShortZip zip;
public:
   void setZip(Integer i){ zip = stringifyShort(i);};
};
```

```
class LongStreetAddress : public StreetAddress {
protected:
   LongZip zip;
public:
   void setZip(Integer i){ zip = stringifyLong(i);};
};
```

The pragmatics of these virtual functions is problematic. They are defined with zero semantics. So why introduce them in the first place? Consider the following situation:

```
ShortStreetAddress aShortStreetAddress;
StreetAddress *sa = & aShortStreetAddress;
sa->setZip(95124);
```

The variable *sa* refers to an instance of *ShortStreetAddress*. Hence *we* know that the function *setZip* is well defined because the class *ShortStreetAddress* has a definition with the right signature. However, the compiler sees only the object *sa*, which is of the type *StreetAddress*. Thus one can argue that the declaration of the virtual function in *StreetAddress* helps out the compiler. In addition, one may advance the thesis that the class *StreetAddress* is enriched by the function *setZip*, although it has no meaning beyond its signature.

Would it make sense to extend analysis languages with an equivalent construct? Such an extension would help the transformation of a design into C++. Our example does not support such an extension. We can already create a disjoint transition network with a single state and a single transition labeled *setZip* without further details. Such a network does not need a special notation. Obviously, we encounter here a case of polymorphism.

Would it make sense to adjoin such a special notation for the design? This would help the design-implementation transition. Again we have doubts. Interpreted languages can do run-time checking as they see fit. Interpretation of `sa->setZip(95124)` will lead to the question of whether `aShortStreetAddress` entertains a `setZip` operation - which is the case indeed. Thus it is again the fact that C++ needs a compiler (and the philosophy that run-time checks are to be avoided to boost performance), which is the rationale behind virtual functions. Hence the virtual function construct is truly a C++ specific notion and is *not* to be exported into design.

10.10.1 Constructors in a subclass

A constructor in a subclass can refer to a constructor in a superclass. The following example formulates constructors for the class `StreetAddress` and for the subclass `ShortStreetAddress`. The latter refers to the former:

```
StreetAddress::StreetAddress(String streetName, Integer streetNumber)
   : street(streetName) // this is one way to initialize
   { number = streetNumber; }; // this is another way

ShortStreetAddress::ShortStreetAddress
   (String streetName, Integer streetNumber, ShortZip zipX)
   : StreetAddress(streetName, streetNumber),
               // invoke superclass constructor
   zip(zipX)    // specific for ShortStreetAddress
   {};          // empty body, since nothing else to do
```

Note the two different ways that attributes (members) can be initialized. For example, for `ShortStreetAddress` we could have done the initialization of `zip` inside the body of constructor through `zip = zipX`.

10.10.2   Multiple inheritance

We have advocated avoiding clashes of attributes when multiple inheritance is being used in analysis. Hence we can usually avoid these issues in C++. However, the diamond situation discussed on page 63 deserves attention. We repeat the relevant figure, as Figure 10.3.

The translation in C++ of the "channel" diamond is the easy, normal case:

```
class Channel {
protected:
    Number channelId;
...
};
class AudioChannel : public Channel {
...
channelId = 1;
};
class ImageChannel : public Channel {
...
channelId = 2;
};
class Video : public AudioChannel, public ImageChannel {
...
    // the next two lines demonstrate how to disambiguate the access to
    // the two different channelId's
filter(AudioChannel::channelId, ...);
clip(ImageChannel::channelId, ...);
```

The crux of the matter is the need to disambiguate the two different attribute *channelId*'s, as illustrated above.

We now turn to the case where attributes get merged. The merging of attributes in the class *ClientEmployee* is done by a surprising maneuver: The subclasses *Employee* and *Client* are made into virtual subclasses of *Person*:

```
class Person {
```

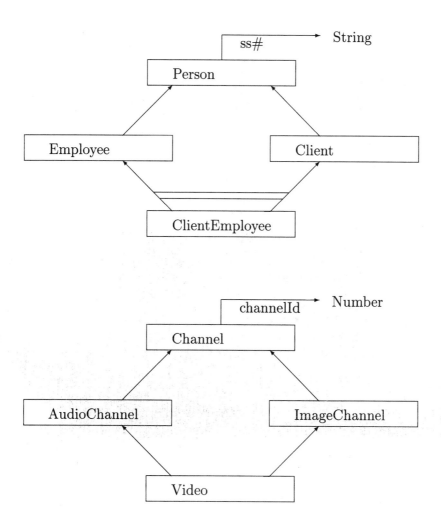

Figure 10.3: As discussed in Chapter 2, the two attributes inherited from *Person* along the two different inheritance chains are merged in *ClientEmployee*; in contrast, *Video* will need two copies of the attribute *channelId*. See the text for an explanation of how these two different cases are dealt with in C++.

```
protected:
    String ssn = "000-00-0000";
...
};
class Employee : public virtual Person {/* ... */};

class Client : public virtual Person  {/* ... */};

class ClientEmployee : public Employee, public Client {
...
    // the next line demonstrates that disambiguation is not required
ssn = "000-00-1111";
};
```

10.11   Templates

Parametrized analysis classes map directly on the template construct in C++. For example, consider making a list of objects where these objects are instances of the class T. An element of the list is say an instance of the class *Pair*. One component of a pair is an object in the class T and the other component is the tail of the list. This can be implemented as

```
template <class T> class Pair {
private:
    T *first;
    Pair<T> *next;
public:
    Pair(T *e, Pair *p) : first(e), next(p) {};
    T *elem() { return first; };
    Pair<T> *tail() { return next; };
    void rplacd(Pair<T> *p) { next = p; };
};
```

An actual list of integers can be introduced as
```
Pair<int> *list;
```
The implementation of the parametrized container class *SET* in the home heating system uses the class *Pair*.

10.12   Subsystems

A system in execution consists primarily of cooperating objects. Controlling the complexity of interactions between the ocean of objects is done through clusterings in subsystems, as discussed in analysis. A subsystem is defined, or prescribed, as a collection of objects that have a relative high interaction in comparison with other objects (in other subsystems).

C++ has no notion that corresponds with subsystems. Instead, C++ has an orthogonal notion of *translation unit* which can be interpreted first as just the content of a file. A translation unit is a sequence of declarations of types, functions, variables, constants, classes, and instances. An optional prefix of a translation unit consists of declarations of externals and/or of references to files to be supplied first to a translation unit. Things get more convoluted because one cannot have forward references in C++ (as an unpleasant inheritance of C). The standard solution is to put declarations in separate "header" files. If a translation unit file does not compile due to unknown entities, another header file is to be added to the prefix.

One can ask the question of whether a subsystem structure can drive the delineation of translation units. As a first approximation we can introduce a translation unit for each subsystem. Prefixes for such a translation unit are:

- Descriptors of all types in the file itself - this prevents problems ensuing from forward references, recursion, etc.

- Descriptors of all types in other subsystems that are referenced.

- Descriptors of all utility types. This consists of structs, if any, and of standard container classes and the like.

For large systems, one may want to elaborate this scheme by having more translation units per subsystem. One can use a layering structure. If layer 0 corresponds with a top subsystem, the translation unit at layer N needs as prefix, at least, all the descriptors of its subsystems at layer N+1.

Distributed objects systems are somewhat different. Object communication that crosses process boundaries must be supported by an infrastructure that mediates between:

- Different address spaces

- Different implementations, because different OO programming languages may be used

- Different dynamics, because some OO programming languages permit to generate new classes or redefine them at run time

- Differences, like byte orders, that are caused by differences in underlying hardware

This infrastructure can be considered to be a subsystem in its own right. In the next section we touch on CORBA [55] as an example of such an infrastructure.

10.13   CORBA

Corba facilitates a client, an object, to invoke an operation in a remote object. Whether or not a client should suspend until a reply is obtained can be specified. Invocation descriptions have minimally signature descriptions and can be extended with exception handlers. Contextual items can be mentioned as well. Object handlers can be translated in a format that can be stored and that can be shipped around between different address spaces.

The infrastructure, called *Object Request Broker* (ORB), requires at each site a run-time component and/or a support server, likely to be supplemented by library additions. The accommodation of languages such as Smalltalk and CLOS that allow the introduction of new classes at run time can be handled by the ORB as well. Invocations out of static languages, such as C++, are handled through stubs defined in an Interface Definition Language (IDL). An Interface Repository with equivalent capabilities is available at run time for dynamic languages.

10.14   User Interfaces

User interfaces are relatively large components of applications. Their specification is usually done through some sketches, exploiting the maxim "a picture is worth 1000 words". Recent developments obviate the need to hack them out. A package such as Tcl/TK, for instance, has a powerful script language that facilitates the generation of windows for the X environment, Ousterhout [63]. An interpreter for this script language facilitates rapid development and bypasses the edit-compile-execute cycle. Ousterhout [63] even mentions XF, an interactive interface for manipulating window objects on the screen that can generate Tcl/TK scripts. The Tcl/TK package is in the public domain.

Galaxy is a commercial package. Its documentation claims that it permits the development of applications that can be moved to "Unix, Windows, Windows NT, Macintosh, OS/2, and OpenVMS without changing a single line of code". They claim as well to make available "a rich set of platform-independent abstractions - such as file management, networking, memory management and distributed services", see [27].

10.15 Persistency

Commercial OO databases are available. They struggle in an uphill battle against relational technology because the SQL interoperability standard, grounded in relational calculus, is unavailable. Multiple efforts are under way to converge on a standard, see Loomis et al. [49].

An alternative consists of mapping objects into a relational database. A class corresponds with a table. At least one commercial tool, from Persistence, generates C++ classes and import and output mechanisms from a relational database schema.

10.16 Generic Implementation Framework

A populist definition of a framework is: a large system that doesn't do anything. In a more serious vein; it is skeleton code that has to be filled in. A framework need not aim to represent a total system. It can be a skeleton for a subsystem. Examples of subframeworks are: ISIS, which handles interprocess communication for distributed systems, see [9]; packages such as X-windows and its specializations such as Motif for user interfaces; and (relational) (object-oriented) databases for the support of persistent entities. See Figure 10.4 for a pictorial representation of a generic single process "master" framework with subframeworks.

This master framework can be represented in C++ as

```
// put UI stuff here
class UInput {
/* TheUInput forwards from the UI to the application */
};
class UOutput {
/* TheUOutput forwards from the application to the UI */
};
class ComInput {
/* TheComInput forwards from the Communication Package
```

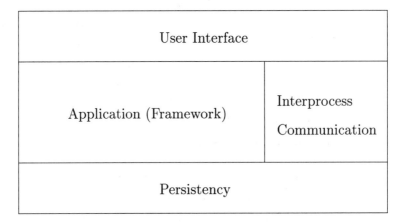

Figure 10.4: Generic single-process "master" framework. The application can be filled in with an application-specific framework.

```
    to the application */
};
class ComOutput {
/* TheComOutput forwards from the application to the
   Communication Package */
};
class Persistent {
/* ThePersistent handles all interactions with a repository */
};
// More classes, etc. here
main{
UInput : TheUInput;
UOutput : TheUOutput;
ComInput : TheComInput;
ComOutput : TheComOutput;
Persistent : ThePersistent;
bool: notReady = true;
// More initializations here
while (notReady) {
event = getNextEvent();
  /* This can be hairy to implement, since events can
     come in from the UI and from an external process */
```

```
if (UIevent(event)) {
   TheUInput.dispatch(event); }
else if (ComEvent(event)) {
   TheComInput.dispatch(event); }
else
   error("Input event from unknown source.");
}; // end of while (notReady)
exit(0);
}
```

The key players here are the two instances *TheUInput* and *TheComInput*. They will receive all input events, whether coming from the user interface or from an external process.

As mentioned in a comment, the statement *event = getNextEvent()* hides a sizable amount of complexity. Operating systems have low-level facilities for listening at multiple ports without having to poll. A user interface package, such as X, helps to shield the programmer from low-level event processing at the hefty price that listening at ports other than the user interface requires no obvious "gymnastics". A communication package such as Isis also takes control of event processing and provides hooks to squeeze in events that originate from a user interface. Obviously, one needs a generic high-level primitive such as *getNextEvent*.

A possible style for an implementation lets the two players *TheUInput* and *TheComInput* generate thread objects which receive control after they have been constructed. Such a thread object would have a narrowly defined mission. After completing its objectives, it would self-destruct and allow another event to be processed.

10.17 Summary

In this chapter we describe implementation activities from a transformational, "implementation is coding", perspective. Since we committed to C++ in this book, we look at a fragment of the C++ pragmatics: how to realize in code the low-level design (and possibly auxiliary aspects). Data members realize the different variants of attributes: incorporation by value versus incorporation by reference, value domains that are classes versus value domains that are nonobjects. Member functions are just translations from the design operations that result from flattening transition networks. C++ has three versions of inheritance. Public inheritance guarantees that members in a superclass carry over with their visibility properties in a subclass. Multiple inheritance is discussed, in particular the variations where a common class is inherited along multiple routes.

10.18   Further Reading

Lippman [48] is a classic introduction to C++. An alternative is Winder's *Developing C++ Software* [86]. Stroustrup [77] gives newer extensions. More recent is Stroustrup [78]. An advanced treatment of C++ with intriguing idioms is Coplien [19]. Many other texts are available.

10.19   Exercises

1. The template for the class *Pair* contains the member function `rplacd` to change one component of a pair. Modify the class so that the other component can be changed as well.

2. Select several classes from the home heating system, implement them in C++, and compare your solution against solutions given in Chapter 13 and in Appendix B.

Chapter 11

Implementation Process

An implementation micro process prescribes (or recommends, to be more programmer friendly) a family of partially ordered steps for transforming a design into a compilable set of translation units. Assuming that we have obtained a detailed design, which possibly can even be executed given the proper CASE tool, we still have great latitude to formulate these ordered steps. To obtain some constraints, we investigate first some minimal requirements for an implementation process. Another look at Figure 1.1 on page 7 is recommended.

11.1 Requirements for an Implementation Process

Genericity

A development micro process should be generic; that is, the process should not depend on features of the design, the domain of the application, the application itself, corporate conventions, the size of the design, and so on. Certainly, we agree that these other features are important as well, but they should only play a role in the *instantiation* of the generic implementation process that yields an implementation plan.

This requirement is quite strong if we expect that every implementation plan can be obtained solely by instantiation, i.e., by choosing proper values for parameters. In actuality, the generic process acts more like a guideline for the creation of an implementation plan.

Instantiable

As discussed above, we cannot expect an implementation process to be formulated in great detail and in sufficient parametrized form that only instantiation is required to produce a plan. Hence the instantiability requirement here eliminates process descriptions that are very unspecific, such as "do the implementation" or "implement what cannot be obtained through reuse". In other words, an implementation process should outline numerous, partially ordered activities in which each generic activity can be replaced by a sequence of actions that prescribe an implementation step that is specific for a particular project.

Induces Assignable Chunks

The assignable chunk requirement applies to the size of chunks. The instantiation of a process component should yield a chunk that is not too small – implement the `else` part of this conditional statement – and not too big – implement a communication package that supports tunable fault tolerance. Certainly, one wants also to obtain chunks for which successful completion is easy to assess. A process activity prescribing "a natural, elementary, maintainable realization of a design component" is an example that does *not* lead to easy objective assessment of a successful completion.

Accommodates Incrementality

An implementation process should allow for an incremental approach. This requirement applies equally to the other micro processes in the overall life cycle. Each micro process should be compatible with whatever (paradigm independent) macro process is chosen: waterfall, spiral, fountain, cleanroom, etc. This requirement does not put a real constraint on an implementation process. Incrementality is obtained in selecting which fragment and/or aspect of a system to concentrate on. This choice is usually done outside and significantly before an implementation plan for a fragment is to be constructed.

Accommodates Process Metrics

The requirement that an implementation plan, an instance of a generic implementation process, will accommodate the use of process metrics is quite a weak constraint. One should be able to measure durations of assigned activities that lead from one milestone to another, possibly measuring the consumption of auxiliary resources as well. As long as the generic process itself has an implicit notion of milestone, we should be safe.

Accommodates Incremental Testing

Testing can be scheduled, in principle, at any time after an implementation artifact is constructed. In practice, it is attractive to interleave implementation activities and testing activities. This helps to obtain fast feedback and prevents rot to propagate. Again, this is a weak constraint and can be considered to be subsumed by the "Induces Assignable Chunks" requirement.

However, we should recognize that the amount of scaffolding required to achieve incremental testing can depend on the process adopted. In particular, a bottom-up process will facilitate a smooth transition from unit testing up to system testing. Artifacts developed and tested earlier can become parts of the scaffold to test an artifact in a next layer.

Accommodates Reuse

The "mechanics" of development *with* reuse (in contrast to development *for* reuse) are surprisingly multifaceted. Reuse of low-level generic components can be accommodated fairly easily. Wherever a plan prescribes the development of an artifact, one can replace this activity by looking for an artifact that satisfies the requirement or that can be modified easily. In case a reusable artifact cannot be found, a new one is to be developed after all.

In contrast, a design may have been made with the deliberate aim of reusing a high-level component. The implementation of such a component becomes more driven by the circumstances. For example, the code for this high-level component may be available together with the code for all its constituents. If so, one jumps right into testing, and perhaps one can even reuse tests that are associated with the code. Another example would be where "slight" adjustments have to be made. The activities are then driven by the identification of the deltas and their replacements. Yet another example requires the development of all the constituents of the high-level components. A bottom-up approach will work provided that the artifacts which end up interacting directly with the reused high-level component can be hooked up seamlessly.

Accommodates a Team

Obviously, a generic process should lead to a plan that, in general, allows more than one person to enact plan steps. This entails that the generic process leaves ample room for nondeterminism.

In summary, we have the following requirements for an implementation micro process:

1. Generic

2. Instantiable into implementation plans

3. Induced plans have assignable chunks that are not too small and not too large

4. Accommodates incrementality; in fact, it should be compatible with any chosen macro process

5. Accommodates process metrics to be applied during plan enactment

6. Accommodates incremental testing and in particular prescribes bottom up implementation plans

7. Accommodates reuse in an implementation plan

8. Accommodates plan enactment by teams

11.2   Implementation Micro Process

The implementation process is represented graphically in Figure 11.1. The boxes represent input and output to the process. The ovals represent intermediate implementation artifacts. The necessity of the Design input box is unquestionable. The other input box, Framework/ Libraries, is optional and depends on whether reuse of frameworks and/or code is to be included.

The process depicted can be interpreted to apply to a novel development and applies to a first iteration of an iterative life cycle. However, this process can also be applied to the modification of an existing system or to subsequent iterations. This can be achieved by adding the existing (partial) system to the Frameworks/ Libraries box.

The process description has an object-oriented character through the emphasis on the artifacts that are produced and consumed in the process. Descriptive labels have been added to the diagram to indicate what kind of activity is involved in producing an artifact from its sources. For example, an *Enduring Instance* is obtained through instantiation from its corresponding *Class*; an *Adjusted Imported Component* is obtained through specialization of an *Imported Component*; the *Implementation* is obtained through integration of all the source components.

Figure 11.1 should be self-explanatory, with the possible exception of the artifacts in *Fire-walls and Glue Components*. Importing a component has the advantage that one does not have to develop it. On the other hand, the system becomes vulnerable to changes that can be made to the component after it has been adopted. Encapsulating an imported component through a fire-wall/glue component reduces ripple affects when a new version of the imported component has to be accommodated.

Figure 11.2 shows a classic decomposition of a system with fire-walls/glue components that shield the core system against modifications in the peripheral subsystem. In fact, this architecture allows complete replacement of a peripheral with minimal impact on other components of the system. A glue component acts here as a twoway forwarding agency.

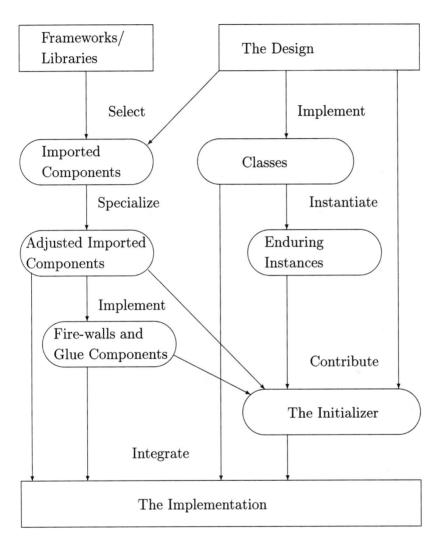

Figure 11.1: Global view of the generic implementation micro process. The boxes represent the input and output, respectively. The ovals represent intermediate artifacts. Additional labels indicate what kind of activity plays a role in the generation of an artifact from its source artifacts.

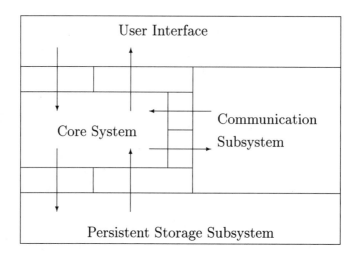

Figure 11.2: Generic system components that are shielded from each other through fire-walls/glue components. The arrows indicate how information flows through one half of a fire-wall. This setup facilitates the replacement of a peripheral subsystem and shields the core system against modifications in a peripheral subsystem.

The generic process allows for nondeterminism. One has freedom to work on imported components, on classes, or on both categories. Nothing is specified regarding which imported component to work on first or on the order in which design classes are implemented. A plausible strategy is to work on each subsystem at the time or to work in parallel as a team on multiple subsystems. This process is also uncommitted as to whether an implementation is to proceed in a top-down or bottom-up fashion.

11.2.1   Class implementation

The process of the implementation of a class can unsurprisingly be expanded into the following steps:

1. Decide which class components will be private, protected, or public.

2. Define all attribute members; follow the design regarding whether a member is incorporated by value or through an indirection.

3. Define all member functions.

4. Define all constructors.

5. Define a destructor.

Although not part of the implementation process, it is recommended that the class be tested by itself and in its context of usage before system-wide testing is done.

11.2.2 Instance implementation

Initializing the system requires the creation of its enduring instances. "Need-to-know" dependencies will prescribe an ordering of their creations. Circular dependencies must be resolved by partial initializations and completing the initializations when all enduring instances are created.

11.3 Satisfaction of the Process Requirements

This section is devoted to the evaluation of the implementation micro process against the requirements formulated earlier. This provides an opportunity to elaborate the process further.

Genericity

Our process is indeed generic in that it does not depend on special features of a design, on the domain of the application, on the application itself, on corporate conventions, and so on. The process is quite high level. It is certainly not possible to use only instantiation to obtain an implementation plan. For example, the process allows great freedom in selecting the order in which classes are implemented. Similarly for the sequence in which components are imported, if any.

Induces Assignable Chunks

This requirement prescribes that tasks in an implementation plan be of the proper size and that completion of a task can be assessed easily. The generic process given does not guarantee that this requirement will be satisfied. On the other hand, the process also does not preclude this requirement. It is certainly possible to derive plans that reveal a micro management mindset. The opposite is possible as well. Hence satisfying this requirement relies on a tasteful instantiation.

Accommodates Incrementality

As argued before, the accommodation of incrementality is easy to satisfy. Nothing in our micro process precludes using an incremental macro process.

Accommodates Process Metrics

Our process has many milestones. When a class is implemented, a milestone is reached. The instantiation of each enduring instance is a little milestone. Obtaining a specialized imported component is yet another milestone. Plans derived from the micro process will inherit all these milestones, and hence process metrics can be supported easily.

Accommodates Incremental Testing

As mentioned above this requirement is quite weak and is easy to satisfy. Nondeterminism in the generic process permits us to use a bottom-up strategy (or any other). Thus it is feasible to interleave testing with development.

Accommodates Reuse

This requirement is certainly satisfied: the micro process has a separate input stream for frameworks and libraries. Attention is also given to the adjustment of imported artifacts. In addition, shields are provided to protect imported subsystems from each other as necessary.

Accommodates a Team

Again, due to the abundance of nondeterminism, nothing precludes deriving plans that call for enactment by a team.

11.4   Summary

In this chapter we describe a micro process for OO implementations. The main sequence of activities consists of realizing the classes, constructing the enduring instances, and creating a system initalizer. Bringing the system down in an orderly fashion is part of the system initializer. No commitment is made about the order in which classes are implemented. A bottom-up strategy facilitates the implementation of classes and the construction of scaffolds for testing. A secondary sequence of activities deals with the optional incorporation of frameworks and components of libraries. An integration step brings everything together. This micro process is compatible with any macro process chosen.

11.5   Further Reading

We are not aware of publications that deal with implementation micro processes.

11.6   Exercises

1. Suppose that a bottom-up strategy is chosen to implement the home heating system to facilitate interleaving of testing. Devise a partial ordering that de-

scribes whether a class is to be implemented before another class. Are there circular dependencies?

2. Suppose that classes C_1 and C_2 which belong to the same layer in a bottom-up strategy, are ready to be implemented. What criteria would you use, if any, to prescribe the order in which C_1 and C_2 are to be implemented?

Chapter 12

Implementation Metrics

We recall that metrics are used for distinctly different purposes. Process metrics are used for tracking expended costs and for estimating remaining effort. Product metrics aim primarily at capturing quality aspects in order to obtain artefacts (or modules) that will be easy to maintain. Alternatively, size product metrics provide another route to estimate development effort for dependent, downstream artefacts. Third, dynamic metrics are used to measure run-time resource consumptions. The latter play a key role during testing: verifying that performance goals are met and checking that a system will not run out of resources (memory, swap, file descriptors, disk space, ports, locks, etc.) Since dynamic metrics do not contribute to implementation activities, they are not discussed further. At the same time, we should acknowledge that interleaving testing with implementation activities provides fast feedback that can force reimplementations (or worse) when resource consumption is unacceptable.

Hence we limit ourselves to process and product metrics. Applying product metrics to assess quality is still in its infancy, the reason being that although one can measure artefacts believing that somehow a quality aspect is addressed, no one can yet interpret the numbers and say which ranges are good, which ones are acceptable, and which ones are bad. At this point, these numbers allow us only to recognize outliers: artefacts that are exceptional: for instance, a class that has an unusual number of subclasses, a "spider" class that is involved in many communications with other classes, a class that has an exceptional number of (inherited) attributes or member functions, and so on.[1]

---

[1] Abreu [2] describes the following technique to define "good" ranges for quality metrics: – a set of well-established libraries is identified; – a metric is applied to all relevant elements in all libraries; – a good value range is defined as the range that contains 50% of the values falling between the 25th and 75th percentiles; – if a library deviates substantially from the norm, it may be deleted from the defining set.

The question of which product aspects to measure does not have an easy answer. As a warm-up we list two sets of metrics for which tools have been developed. The first set is incorporated in an experimental tool used in-house by IBM. The second set of metrics is part of a commercial tool. Below many more metrics are listed that are for the most part extracted from the literature and from recent contributions to metric workshops held at OOPSLA conferences.

The following quote describes metrics that are incorporated in the CPPSTATS tool, which is used inside IBM [83]:

Method details . The lines of code (LOC) in a method. From this can be calculated the LOC per class, average LOC per method, and number of methods in a class. Also recorded are the method's access scope, i.e., public, protected, or private, the return type, and the parameters.

Class instance variables . The variable's name, type. and access scope are recorded.

Class LOC . This is LOC not associated with any method, and the class definition.

File LOC . If no class-related information is found, the LOC in the file should be recorded.

Superclass . The subclass/superclass relationship is recorded.

Method complexity . The McCabe complexity measure for a method is recorded.

Another set of metrics can be found in an OO tool from McCabe Associates. Their description clusters them as follows:

Encapsulation
    – Lack of Cohesion in Methods
    – Percent of Public and Protected
    – Access to Public Data

Polymorphism
    – Percent of Non-overloaded Calls
    – Weighted Methods per Class
    – Response for a Class

Inheritance
- Number of Roots
- Fan-in
- Number of Children
- Depth

Quality
- Maximum Cyclomatic Complexity of Methods in a Class
- Maximum Essential Complexity of Methods in a Class
- Number of Classes Dependent on Descendants

The metrics in the quality category are, in fact, also product size metrics. Interpreting their values into quality judgments is the user's responsibility.

After this warm-up, we describe in the next two sections metrics for effort estimation product and metrics that may be used for quality assessment.

12.1 Effort Metrics

Measuring expended effort can be done very coarsely simply by recording how many person-months have already been consumed as part of an implementation. Less coarsely, one can record the amount of effort spend per artifact type; i.e., for the development of classes, the creation of enduring instances, the construction of adjusted imported components, etc. More fine grained, one can record the amount of effort spend per artifact for each artifact type. One can go further and record the amount of effort devoted to a member type in a class, and so on.

For each metric that records the past, we have corresponding metrics that "measure the future", that is metrics that estimate the required effort for the development of a (component of) an implementation artifact or of all the artifacts belonging to an artifact type. These estimation metrics take their input from product and/or effort metrics that were applied to design artifacts or to artifacts residing in reuse libraries. For example, we can have for an individual implementation class ic that is to be obtained from a design class dc the effort estimation function

$$efes(ic) = \mu_1 * efm(dc) + \mu_2 * pr(dc) + \nu$$

Where $efes(ic)$ is the estimate for the effort of the implementation class ic based on the design class dc; $efm(dc)$ is the actual effort used to develop the design class dc; $pr(dc)$ is a (synthetic) product metric that takes multiple aspects of the design class dc into account; and μ_1, μ_2, and ν are constants whose values are determined empirically.

Clearly, this formula assumes that design efforts have been recorded at least with the granularity of individual classes. If that is not the case, we can still use an estimation based on a product metric, using a modified formula with different empirical coefficients μ_{pr} and ν_{pr}:

$$efes(ic) = \mu_{pr} * pr(dc) + \nu_{pr}$$

Since we have no illusion that reuse is free, we need similar formulas to estimate the effort to incorporate imported components. We expect that the contribution of the constant term will dominate contributions of the design development costs and the size of the imported component.

The estimated costs of specialization of imported components can be a function of their sizes. The effort to develop firewalls is a function of the number of communications that have to be forwarded. As a first approximation, the sizes of adjacent communication partners can be used. Along the lines detailed in Section 4.1, induction can be used to estimate the remaining effort at any point during an implementation.

In current practice, where maintaining (automatically) detailed records is not a routine affair, we may have to fall back on a much coarser estimation of the implementation as a whole. As a rule of thumb, we can use the heuristic that an implementation takes roughly as much effort as the design. At the same time, we recommend strongly, to measure effort at a fine granularity in order to improve effort estimations.

We finish this section on effort with a somewhat unexpected process metric that is noted by Lorenz [50]: the rate by which methods and classes are thrown away. According to Lorenz, "... classes and methods thrown away should occur at a steady rate throughout most of the development process".

This metric is not a pure implementation metric. Lorenz indicates that "this item is a bit of a cross between design and project metrics." We can go a step further by observing that domain-specific classes are introduced predominantly during the analysis. Hence we modify the metric as the rate in which classes and transitions are thrown away during analysis and we have another metric that measures the rate by which generic classes, operations, and member functions are thrown away during design. This modification emphasizes that all the hard thinking – conceptualization and problem solving – is to be done *outside* implementation activities. It may take awhile though before this vision is acknowledged with a yawn.

Noteworthy is Lorenz's statement "I know of at least one O-O company that uses this metric as an indication of projects going awry." If classes are not thrown away, "you are probably doing an incremental development instead of performing true iterations on areas of the system. You are probably not pulling out problem domain abstractions along the way either." We do not ascribe completely to the former, but we do agree with the latter.

12.2 Product Metrics

Implementation product metrics are not of much help for effort estimation. Instead they may be useful for quality assessments provided that one has established guidelines to interpret numeric ranges. Most of these metrics have already been encountered. We list them here to concentrate them in one place. They are grouped according to their application scope: member functions, classes, inheritance, and the implementation as a whole, i.e., the system. In the next subsections we provide a short description of each metric, together with a reference, if any. Notice that some metrics in later subsections use metrics in earlier subsections.

12.2.1 Member function metrics

Size of a member function This can be measured in many different ways:

1. The number of lines of code

2. The number of statements

3. The number of semicolons in the body of the member function

4. The number of (input and output) parameters

5. The number of member variables used

6. The Halstead length metric, see [31]

We give a brief definition of the Halstead metric following Henderson-Sellers [36]. Any symbol or keyword to represent data is classified as an *operand*. A keyword used to specify an action is classified as an *operator*. Hence arithmetic symbols, assignment symbols, Boolean operators, function names, and control keywords are operators. Let N_1 be the total number of operators and N_2 be the total number of operands. The Halstead length metric $= N_1 + N_2$.

Complexity of a member function We can use the cyclomatic complexity, see McCabe [52]. We give a brief definition of this metric following Shooman [74]. A member function (or any other algorithm or "normal" program) can be associated with a directed graph G that represent the flow of control. Nodes in this graph correspond with the entry point, exit, and control choice points such as if-then, if-then-else, while, for and loop statements and (implicit) labels. Arcs in the graph represent the executable statements that lead from one node to another; i.e., an arc represents one or more statements that lead from one node to another. By adding one phantom arc from the (single) exit node to the entry point we obtain a strongly connected graph with one component (each node is reachable from each other node). For such a graph the cyclomatic number $V(G)$ is equal to $m - n + 1$, where m is the number of arcs in the graph G and n is the number of nodes in the graph G.

Fan-in of a member function This metric counts the number of places outside the class to which the member function belongs where the member function is invoked. Hence such a place contributes to the fan-out (see below) of the class to which that place belongs. Maximizing fan-in – to reuse functionality – is clearly incompatible with minimizing fan-out – to boost the reusability of a class by minimizing its dependence on other classes.

Fan-out of a member function This counts the number of references out of the member function to external objects.[2] This notion is also referred to as *coupling*. For example, Chidamber and Kemerer [16] write: "... an object is coupled to another object if one of them acts on the other, i.e., methods of one use methods or instance variables of another". Accessing directly an instance variable (= attribute) in another object violates encapsulation and is to be avoided.

12.2.2   Class metrics

Class attributes There are different ways to count attributes. If the class is not obtained through inheritance and is not a friend, we have
number of all attributes = private + protected + public attributes

When we have inheritance and/or friendships
number of all attributes =
inherited + friendship attributes + locally defined attributes

Another way of looking at attributes is whether or not they are object valued
number of all attributes = object-valued + non-object-valued attributes

---

[2]Note that we have changed slightly the fan-out notions as given originally by Henry and Kafura [38] and mentioned by Henderson-Sellers et al. [36]. They also considered for the fan-out count the number of data structures updated and the number of global data. These additions are clearly pre-OO and hence we have streamlined them away.

Yet another way to categorize attributes considers whether an attribute entity is incorporated by value or is being referred to

number of all attributes = value + reference attributes

These distinctions allow us to define such secondary (quality?) metrics as

attribute closure = (private attributes) / (number of all attributes)

attribute external dependence = (inherited + friendship attributes) / (number of all attributes)

attribute OO-ness = (object valued attributes) / (number of all attributes)

attribute incorporation = (value attributes) / (number of all attributes)

The use of public attributes violates encapsulation and is against OO philosophy. Thus we can have as a warning metric

non-OO attribute alert = 2 ** (number of public attributes)

Number of static attributes of a class A static attribute of a class is shared by all instances of a class. Static attributes are subject to the same access control regimes as those of regular attributes. Thus we can have equations similar to those for the regular attributes. However, since static attributes are far less prevalent than regular attributes, we do not bother to elaborate them. Possibly of interest is the ratio

(number of static attributes) / (number of regular attributes)

Number of member functions of a class Again we can distinguish on the basis of access control and whether or not a return value, if any, is an object. Locally defined member functions versus unmodified and modified inherited member functions can also be distinguished.

Weighted methods for a class Chidamber and Kemerer [16] introduced a secondary metric for a class that consists of summing over all member functions their "weight". They are uncommitted as to what constitutes the weight of a member function. It can be a size metric, a complexity metric, or a combination of them. A deteriorated weight is the number 1, in which case we are simply back at the number of member functions per class.

Fan-in of a class This metric sums up all the fan-ins of the member functions of a class. A high fan-in for a class suggests that the system is vulnerable to changes in its interface.

Fan-out per class Summing up the fan-outs for all member functions gives the fan-out for a class. Chidamber and Kemerer [16], refer to this as the coupling of a class.

Response for a class This metric is defined by Chidamber and Kemerer [16] as the size of the set consisting of the member functions in the class and the member functions that can be directly invoked by them. This metric is fairly close to the sum of the number of member functions and the fan-out. A difference comes in when an external member function *foo* is invoked twice. The fan-out count will go up by 2, while the response for a class count goes up only by 1.

Lack of cohesion in methods This metric was also defined in Chidamber and Kemerer [16]. Its purpose is to measure the cohesion of the member functions; i.e., whether or not the class can potentially be split up. The name *lack of cohesion* makes this metric somewhat confusing, in our opinion. The definition in [16] is also somewhat opaque. Although they give a formal definition, it is incomplete. We give an alternative characterization.

Pairs of member functions can be checked whether or not they share instance variables. A pair is "good" when the two member functions share at least one variable. A pair is "bad" when they do not share a variable. Consider now the set of good pairs and the set of bad pairs. We take it that a pair having the same member function twice (which would obviously make the pair good) is ignored and is *not* a member of the set of good pairs. We assume as well that two pairs that differ only in the ordering of the member functions are *not* considered to be different. Now measure the size of the good and bad sets and denote them by G and B, respectively. Finally the metric is defined as $B - G$ when $B > G$, and otherwise the value is 0. Thus the lack of cohesion value is large when there are many bad pairs compared with good pairs.

Chidamber and Kemerer [16] give the following example: M1 is a member function that uses the variables a, b, c, d, e. Similarly, M2 uses a, b, e and M3 uses x, y, z. The good set has only the pair (M1, M2). The bad set has the pairs (M1, M3) and (M2, M3). Hence the lack of cohesion metric is 2 minus 1 = 1. The cohesion in this example is not good. We can clearly shrink the class by splitting off the M3 member function with its variables x, y, z.

At the same time one should not jump to the conclusion that a class having a positive lack of cohesion metric value entails that it can be split. The next example has a lack of cohesion metric value 3 but none of its member functions can be split off. The admittedly artificial class has six member functions, M1 - M6, which use the pool of variables a, b, c, d, e, f as follows: M1 has a, b; M2 has b, c; M3 has c, d; M4 has d, e; M5 has e, f; M6 has f, a; The set of good pairs is (M1, M2), (M2, M3), (M3, M4), (M4, M5), (M5, M6), (M6, M1) and has a size of 6. The set of bad pairs is (M1, M3), (M1, M4), (M1, M5), (M2, M4), (M2, M5), (M2, M6), (M3, M5), (M3, M6), (M4, M6) and has a size of 9. Hence the lack of cohesion metric is 9 minus 6 = 3. At the same time, none of the member functions can be split off.

Using the pattern of this example, we can create classes with arbitrary large values for the lack-of-cohesion metric while none of its member functions can be split off. This observation leads to the next metric.

Number of member function clusters for a class A member function cluster is constructed by the transitive closure of the "good" relationship defined above for pairs of member functions. In other words, for every pair of member functions in a cluster (provided that the cluster has more than one member function), we can find a chain of intermediate member functions that connect the two so that all adjacent member functions in the chain have at least one instance variable in common. A cluster is maximal in that no other member function can be added to it. The example given by Chidamber and Kemerer [16], see above, has two clusters: {M1, M2} and {M3}. The other example given above has only one cluster: {M1, M2, M3, M4, M5, M6}.

Number of comment lines This metric can be refined into the number of comment lines per attribute, per member function class, and per class.

12.2.3 Inheritance metrics

Inheritance depth of a class This is the distance to a root class. The distance is zero when the class is a root class itself. If multiple inheritance is involved, it is the maximum length from the class to a root.

Number of ancestors of a class This is the depth when there is no multiple inheritance.

Number of direct subclasses of a class This metric indicates the magnitude of ripples in direct descendant classes when a class is modified.

Number of direct and in-direct subclasses of a class As the preceding metric, this metric measures the vulnerability of the system when a class is changed. Here the potential ripples in all descendant classes are measured.

12.2.4   Implementation system metrics

Number of global enduring instances

These instances are created at initialization time and stay around during execution. Some of them may represent ensemble or subsystem entities.

Min, max, median, and average number of attributes per class

Lorenz [50] advises that the average number should be less than 6.

Min, max, median, and average number of member functions per class

Lorenz suggests that the average should be less than 20.

Min, max, median, and average size of member functions

Lorenz suggests that the average should be less than 15 statements for C++.

Min, max, median, and average complexity of member functions

Obviously, it is attractive to keep this number low.

Min, max, median and average inheritance depth of the classes

These metrics indicate the amount of internal reuse. Lorenz suggests that the maximum should be less than 6.

Min, max, median and average fan-in of the classes

This allows us to identify high fan-in classes. The correctness of these classes has a high priority.

Min, max, median, and average fan-out of the classes

This allows us to identify high fan-out classes that are probably nonreusable and to check whether that is acceptable; i.e., whether they represent system-specific features.

Number of classes

This metric is the OO equivalent of "lines of code" from the pre-OO era and gives a coarse indication of a system's size. Refinements of this metric are:
– Number of reused as-is classes
– Number of reused but modified classes
– Number of newly developed classes
Two class reuse metrics can be defined as:
pure reuse rate = (reused as-is) / (number of classes)
leveraged reuse rate = (reused as-is + modified classes) / (number of classes)

Number of root classes

This metric is another coarse measure of the system size. A secondary metric,
1 - (number of root classes) / (total number of classes)
gives another perspective on how much inheritance and hence conceptual reuse
is built into the system.

Average number of comment lines

Lorenz recommends that the averages for classes, attributes, and member functions should be greater than 1.

12.2.5 More product metrics?

The number of the product metrics listed above is overwhelming, and certainly one can
define more of them. For example, classes can be split up into abstract and concrete
classes; a class can designate friends; and so on. All these things can be counted.
Are all these numbers relevant? Many of these metrics will correlate and hence it
will be possible to prune this product metrics collection. Whether these metrics are
relevant at all remains to be seen. The way to find out will be to build metric tools,
apply them to many projects, identify patterns, and compare the patterns against
maintenance data.

Note that many of the values of these product metrics should not be a surprise -
they should already be known after the design!

12.2.6 Fewer product metrics?

Facing the torrent of OO metrics, one can argue that there is still a place for the
"old" metrics. This is exactly what is done by Welker [82] in a contribution titled
"Traditional Software Metrics - Hold On!" In particular, he argues that lines of code
and cyclomatic complexity are useful. He illustrates his point by comparing reimplementations into Ada of systems done originally in Fortran and C. When comparing
non-OO versus OO systems, it is certainly not feasible to use OO metrics.

While the Ada that was used is only object-based, since it does not support inheritance, the reimplementations score by and large better on LOC, Halstead complexity,
cyclomatic complexity, and the so Oman Maintainability Index, see Table 12.1.
The number of modules is remarkably larger in the Ada systems than in the pre-Ada
systems.

Keeping things simple is also suggested in a study by Li and Henry [47]. They
compare using two different sets of metrics for predicting the maintenance efforts of

System	Language	LOC	Halstead	V(G)	Subroutines	OMI
IMOM 1.0	C	75357	1.66E8	13.17	298	32.58
	Ada	61300	5.70E7	3.21	1562	74.84
IMOM 2.0	C	109182	2.51E8	14.22	422	31.77
	Ada	76641	6.53E7	3.36	1976	75.35
COMJAM	Fortran	55279	6.56E7	10.27	218	35.35
	Ada	61230	5.55E7	3.19	1540	72.84
PD	Fortran	41645	5.18E7	7.24	295	47.52
	Ada	62867	5.79E7	3.23	1568	74.45
RECCE	Fortran	108885	1.93E8	15.73	335	27.50
	Ada	54451	5.11E7	3.26	1374	74.61

Table 12.1: Comparison of reimplementation into Ada from C and Fortran. Most remarkably are the decreases in the LOC, Halstead complexity, cyclomatic complexity $\dot{V}(G)$ and the increases in the number of subroutines and the Oman Maintainability Index OMI.

various applications. One set had eight metrics:

1. Inheritance level

2. Number of direct subclasses

3. Number of local methods and methods called

4. Number of disjoint sets of methods

5. Sum of the cyclomatic complexity for all methods

6. Number of requests

7. Number of abstract data types defined

8. Number of methods

The other set had only two metrics:

1. Number of semicolons in a class

2. Number of methods and attributes

Both of these sets were effective in predicting maintenance efforts. According to this study, there was *no* significant advantage in using one over the other.

12.3   Our Metrics

Most of the metrics discussed in this chapter can be lifted up to the design phase or even to the analysis phase. Or, turning the argument the other way around, we can reuse the metrics that we developed in the design phase. We admit that this tactic does not allow to exploit us the fine points of C++ (or another chosen implementation language), but given the state of the art, we don't believe that anything is lost. Hence, we refer to Chapter 8, where we defined:

1. $\mu^4_{ClassMB}(class_i)$, to measure the predicted maintenance burden for a class in isolation

2. $\mu_{systemContext}(class_i)$, to measure the predicted maintenance burden for a class due to its role in the context of a system

3. μ^1_{system} and μ^2_{system}, which summarize the predicted maintenance burden for a total system

In addition, we have available the old standby, LOC, the number of lines of code per member function. Since we have already used $\mu^4_{ClassMB}$ as part of Ψ_D in the design, we will switch to LOC in the implementation; see Chapter 13.

12.4   OO Metric Abuse

Metrics can be good. They help to track progress, they help in effort and cost estimations, and they help to improve quality by facilitating adherence to guidelines. They also raise the level of awareness if only by the constructions of these guidelines. However, metrics can be misused as well, as the following contribution to a metric workshop at the OOPSLA 1993 conference testifies (Hamilton [32]).

> Where Things Went Wrong
>
> This was our first major Object Oriented development effort. We had a little experience with a small prototype project, using Coad/Yourdon OO Analysis and Design and C++. We were just learning the language and avoided inheritance, both in the design and in the implementation. We had some experience with C before the prototype, but not with C++.
>
> As we entered the major project, we generated our manpower and schedule estimates using past experience in Fortran but on a similar application. Our development metrics in the past had been fairly basic;

number of subroutines and lines of code, number designed, number coded, number unit tested, number integrated. Our customers in the past had not looked over our shoulders a lot, as long as we seemed to be making reasonable progress.

For the new OO project we had a more concerned customer, who was fully aware of our lack of experience with the methods and the language. The new customer was much more interested in the finer detail of our progress and in our ability to accurately estimate the effort and schedule. Management and technical alike were being asked to prove themselves in a new environment, and to provide evidence that everything was under control.

Not realizing the extent of potential class proliferation within the detail design and coding tasks, we selected number of classes as the basic metric for reporting system size and development progress. A class is here defined as a C++ class or a main routine. Our problem domain analysis produced about 75 classes. As we added from the solution domain classes in the design, the total went to about 500 classes. This became the basis for our total effort and schedule estimates as we entered detailed design and implementation.

Our monthly meetings with the customer to summarize progress now began to focus on the total number of classes expected and the number designed, coded, unit tested, and integrated. The stability of this number was being used to judge the ability of management to estimate the size of the project. As that number started to rise above 500, the customer started to question our ability to plan and manage effectively.

At about this point, the impact of inheritance began to become more clear. I personally was reviewing nearly all of the detail design and code that was being generated. And I began to find places where good design practice would suggest that classes be divided into a number of subclasses, as a substitute for numerous case statements or to provide for the easy reuse of classes as base classes. As I found such situations, I recommended local redesign and the creation of multiple subclasses. This plus the evolution of groups of class attributes into their own classes, caused the number of classes metric to start to climb, and caused a minor panic among our managers.

From the customer's point of view, changing the metric was not appropriate. From our manager's point of view, getting berated by the customer for letting a project get out of control was not acceptable. So the edict went out – no new classes. From that point, very few new classes were created. As situations arose where new classes were called for, another mechanism had to be used; case statements instead of subclasses, overly complex classes instead of multiple simple classes, and so on. We had gotten ourselves into a situation where the metrics were driving the design.

A result of our particular selection of metrics, and the meaning that we and our customer attached to those metrics, was that many of our classes were too large and complex, and the generated tasks using these classes were much larger than necessary. A very significant lesson was learned: it is crucial to select appropriate metrics to be collected and to assign realistic meanings to those metrics, if a project is to be managed, and perceived to be managed, in a credible manner.

There are more lessons. Embarking on a project of this magnitude without a sufficient understanding of inheritance is certainly to be avoided. Questionable is the blowup of classes from 75 to 500 in the transition from analysis to detailed design. Possibly, they rushed out of a preliminary analysis into the design. The expansion of classes during the implementation phase was caused by the new appreciation for inheritance. Backtracking into the design would have been more appropriate.

This example gives indirect support for using a weighted class metric instead of a straight class count. Due to exponential effects, it is likely that splitting up a complex class in multiple classes will bring a weighted class metric down.

12.5　Summary

The major content in this chapter is an enumeration of 29 different product metrics (many of which have several variants). They are grouped according to the size of the unit to which they apply: member function (4), class (10), inheritance (4), and system (11). Many of these metrics can be promoted to design artifacts if not to analysis artifacts. In a sense, at this point we have too many metrics given the lack of experience we have with them. LOC, the number of lines of code, one of the size metrics on member functions, is used in Chapter 13. In the section on metric abuse we describe a case where OO metrics were severely misused.

12.6   Further Reading

Some of the metrics rules of thumb quoted in this chapter come from Lorenz [50], an early book that devotes an appendix to metrics and measurements. A more theoretical discussion of OO metrics can be found in an extensive chapter in Henderson-Sellers and Edwards [36], which has been expanded into a book (Henderson-Sellers [37]).

12.7   Exercises

1. Apply the Weyuker metric features, see page 111, on as many product metrics defined in this chapter as you care to.

2. Define additional C++-specific product metrics and provide arguments for why they are necessary.

Chapter 13

Example: Home Heating System

In this chapter we illustrate the transformation of the design of the Home Heating System into C++. The micro process formulated in Section 11.2 and depicted on page 341 will be followed. Subsequently we discuss the application of metrics.

13.1   Implementing the Design

It is time to acknowledge that the design of the home heating system is quite incomplete. We decided earlier that we would make a simulation model of a home heating system. However, we omitted to specify the details of what is to be simulated. How many rooms are there in the model? What is the periodic function that describes the outside temperature as a function of time, which is to be used (in addition to the information of the desired temperature, the actual temperature and whether or not the room gets heated) to calculate the temperature deltas for a room at every tick of the clock? What are the initial settings? What are the driver functions that describe the occupancies for the rooms as a function of time? What is the (graphical?) output of the model? Does the simulation allow dynamic intervention, or is it a batch style of computation? And before we forget, what is the purpose of the simulation? We are lucky that we don't have to answer all these questions because our aim here is only to illustrate how to transform in principle a complete design into a working target system.

Still we felt the need to make a working simulation program in order to test the correctness of the code presented. The core classes are described in this chapter. Auxiliary classes that model an environment and the hardware and code of the `main()` program as well as some other files are given in Appendix B. The code of many classes has been extended with print statements that contribute to a trace of the execution.

The micro process advises us to check whether we should use an existing framework. In case our simulation program needs a graphical interface (GUI), we definitely should hunt around for a generator that runs on the target platform. Right away we should verify for such a generator whether the system can be structured according to the following schema (or a similar schema if multiple runs are to be supported):

```
...                                     // initialize


while ( notFinished )
    { if ( GUIeventAvailable )          // check user input, if any
         switch ( ... ) { ... }         // do whatever the user wants
      else { clock->ticToc();           // do one round of simulation
           display->adjust(); };        // adjust the display
    };


exit(0);                                // terminate
```

This schema decouples the impact of the user's actions – setting the desired temperatures for a room, inducing a furnace fault, changing a room's occupancy, and so on. Displaying the system's state is also decoupled. The idea is that modifications for the display are accumulated in the display object. Thus those core objects whose attribute values need to be displayed must be extended so that they push their modifications into the display object.

Our simulation program does not use a GUI; still we have used a display object. However, we have not been consistent, due to being impatient. In many places, we have simply inserted raw "cout << ..." statements.

13.2   Classes

The next step is to implement the classes, which begs the question of where to start. As argued before, a bottom-up approach helps to build up scaffolds for testing. A scaffold at level N uses the classes developed at level $N - 1$. It is also useful at this point to check libraries to avoid the development of classes that are readily available. One can't compete against excellent commercial libraries with generic classes that sell for less than $200.[1] Container classes are most likely available in these libraries.

---

[1]We refer here to the STL library developed by Alex Stepanov, for which there are at least two commercializations. Of courseD, despite this advice, we wrote our own parametrized SET class.

Classes that can benefit are:
- *HeatFlowRegulator*, which needs a *SET* for its *roomsThatNeedHeat* attribute
- *Clock*, which needs a *SET* for its *clients* attribute
- *ValveControl*, which needs a *SET* for its *roomsThatNeedHeat* attribute

The first class in this list needs minimal set functionality: Elements are to be added and deleted in addition to determining the magnitude of the set. The other two require, in addition, the ability to "broadcast" an operation to all the members of the set. This could be done "manually" by a cursor mechanism that accesses each member of the set in turn, but it is more convenient when a set supports a generic *apply* or a *for_each* operation, where one can specify a particular operation that can be applied to all members of the set. Thus we have to search for a parametrized class that looks like

```
template<class T, function F> class SET {
public:
    void insert(T);
    void delete(T);
    int size();
    bool empty();
    bool has(T);
    void apply(F);
};
```

If such a class cannot be found, one should try harder; one should resist trying to build systems from scratch. Otherwise, we will never develop an engineering discipline.[2] Hence we proceed by constructing the classes that are specific for our system.

To facilitate testing, we follow a bottom-up strategy. We look first at classes that do not depend on anything else; then we look at the next layer, which depends only on the classes already developed; etc. We have to watch for cycles, of course. In the meantime we extend classes in an ad hoc fashion to cater for the needs of a simulation.

13.2.1 Furnace Status Indicator

The *FurnaceStatusIndicator* class is straightforward. The header file is

---

[2]As mentioned earlier, we kludged our own SET class. Due to problems with C++, we had to write two different apply functions, called *forEachElement* and *forEachElement1*. The first permits us to formulate a zero-argument member function to be applied to all elements of the set. The second makes it possible to formulate a one-argument function that expects an integer argument.

```
#ifndef FurnaceStatusIndicator_H
#define FurnaceStatusIndicator_H

#include "HHStypes.h"

class FurnaceStatusIndicator {
private:
    bool status;
    DisplayOut* theDisplayOut;
public:
    FurnaceStatusIndicator(DisplayOut*);
    void turnOn();
    void turnOff();
};
#endif
```

It is not strictly the case that the class *FurnaceStatusIndicator* is independent. We have added a dependency on the class *DisplayOut*. In case a simulation needs to depict the status of the furnace status indicator, there is now a way to reach the user interface. We have here an application of the model-view-controller pattern. The class *FurnaceStatusIndicator* is the model, the class *DisplayOut* corresponds with the view, and a class *DisplayIn*, not used here, would be the controller. The classes *DisplayOut* and *DisplayIn* shield the core classes from the user interface. To capture these dependencies we have thrown in the include file "HHStypes.h". This file will contain at least class DisplayOut.

Subsequently, we can construct the source file,

```
#include "FurnaceStatusIndicator.h"
#include "DisplayOut.h"

FurnaceStatusIndicator::FurnaceStatusIndicator(DisplayOut* displayOut)
      : theDisplayOut(displayOut), status(false) {}
void FurnaceStatusIndicator::turnOn() {
    if (!status) {
        status = true;
        theDisplayOut->displayStatus(status); }; }
void FurnaceStatusIndicator::turnOff() {
    if (status) {
        status = false;
```

```
theDisplayOut->displayFurnaceStatus(status); }; }
```

Inclusion of the file `DisplayOut.h` is done to avoid trouble with the invocation of display operations by `turnOn()` and `turnOff()`. Observe that we invoke these operations only provided that the furnace status indicator is in the proper state. For example, turning the indicator on for the second time in a row is a no-op. The constructor initializes the `status` member in the off state, which is represented by `false`.

13.2.2 Clock Client

The clock has different kinds of clients that expect *tic* events: rooms, the furnace monitor, timers, and others, see below. We can introduce an abstract superclass *ClockClient* that subsumes them. This will help the implementation of the clock: In particular, this will allow for the introduction of the value domain of the clock's *client* attribute. The header file is

```
#ifndef ClockClient_H
#define ClockClient_H

class ClockClient {
protected:
    char* name;
public:
    ClockClient(char*);
    virtual void tic(int tim) = 0;
    char* getName();
};
#endif
```

Notice that we cannot make instances of this class. Only subclasses that provide an implementation for the `tic` operation can be instantiated. The clock will pass on the time in the *tic*-event, which a client can use or not. To facilitate tracing, we have added a `name` attribute. This attribute is "protected" because we want to make it available to the subclasses of *ClockClient*. The code is simply

```
#include "ClockClient.h"

ClockClient::ClockClient(char* nm) : name(nm) {}
char* ClockClient::getName() { return name; }
```

13.2.3   Occupancy Sensor

The occupancy sensor class is also very simple and is an example that can be generated almost automatically. The header file is

```
#ifndef OccupancySensor_H
#define OccupancySensor_H

#include "HHStypes.h"

class OccupancySensor {
private:
   bool occupied;
   DisplayOut* theDisplayOut;
   Room* myRoom;
public:
   OccupancySensor();
   void setDisplayOut(DisplayOut*, Room*);
   void setOccupied(bool);
   bool getOccupied();
};
#endif
```

Notice that we prepare again for the display of the **occupied** value. The source file becomes

```
#include "OccupancySensor.h"
#include "DisplayOut.h"

OccupancySensor::OccupancySensor()
      : occupied(false) {};
void OccupancySensor::setDisplayOut(DisplayOut* dO, Room* rm) {
      theDisplayOut = dO;
      myRoom = rm; };
void OccupancySensor::setOccupied(bool value) {
      occupied = value;
      theDisplayOut->displayOccupancySensor(myRoom, occupied); }
bool OccupancySensor::getOccupied() {
      return occupied; }
```

Setting the attribute `occupied` has the potential side effect that its new value will be displayed. Since there can be more than one occupancy sensor in the system, we have added to the display request the identity of the room to which the sensor belongs.

This implementation is faithful to the analysis and design model. However, we have a little problem. We have assumed that real sensors in the rooms will generate `setOccupied` events. In our simulation model, we have to introduce an auxiliary class that represents these devices. Hence we obtain the header file

```
#ifndef OccupancySensorDevice_H
#define OccupancySensorDevice_H

#include "HHStypes.h"
#include "ClockClient.h"

class OccupancySensorDevice : public ClockClient {
private:
   Room* myRoom;
   OccupancySensor* myOccupancySensor;
   bool foo(int); // provides occupancy at a particular time
public:
   OccupancySensorDevice(char*, Room*, OccupancySensor*);
   void tic(int);
};
#endif
```

We have made this class a subclass of *ClockClient*. In the initialization of the system, we will create for each room an occupancy sensor, and for each one we will create an occupancy sensor device. The room will be initialized with the sensor to pull the information out. The device must be initialized with the sensor to push values in. Each device instance must become a member of the clock client attribute to receive *tic* events so that it can update the sensor before a room queries the sensor. The actual data is provided by a function `foo`, which is indexed by the time. A possible source file could be

```
#include "OccupancySensorDevice.h"
#include "OccupancySensor.h"

OccupancySensorDevice::OccupancySensorDevice
```

```
     (char* nm, Room* rm, OccupancySensor* myOccSen)
      : ClockClient(nm), myRoom(rm), myOccupancySensor(myOccSen) {}
void OccupancySensorDevice::tic(int value) {
   myOccupancySensor->setOccupied(foo(value)); }
bool OccupancySensorDevice::foo(int value) { return true; }
```

This source file makes every room occupied at all times. More sophisticated occupancy patterns can be defined as required. The `foo` function has access to the time and it also knows the identity of the associated room. Tracing in the `tic` function can be added in a quick-and-dirty fashion by something like

```
cout << "Occupancy Sensor Device: " << name
     << " Occupancy of room: " << myRoom->getName()
     << " at time: " << value
     << " is: " << foo(value) << "\n";
```

Alternatively, we would have to construct this output string and pipe it to a member function of a *DisplayOut* object.

Observe that the constructor invokes the constructor of `ClockClient` in order to initialize the **name** member.

13.2.4   Other sensors and simple classes

The home heating system has the following additional sensor types: room temperature, water temperature, fuel flow sensor, and optical combustion sensor. It should be clear that we can implement these in the same fashion as for the occupancy sensor. In addition, for all of them we need to introduce an additional class to represent the devices in the simulation.

The class that represents the desired temperature input device requires similar treatment. Again we need an additional class, this time to simulate the input from a room occupant.

We have two kinds of valves: for water and for oil. They have no effect on the simulation. They can be implemented like the furnace status indicator, provided that we want to display their open-closed status. Otherwise, we omit their display.

An even simpler class is the ignitor, with only a single operation *ignite* that does nothing in a simulation. Success or failure of an ignition is monitored by the optical combustion sensor and the fuel flow sensor that we discussed earlier.

The implementation of all these classes is given in Appendix B.

13.2.5 Blower Motor

The implementation of the blower motor is quite simple but requires for a simulation an auxiliary class that takes care of increasing the *rpm* of the motor when the motor is turned on (see the comments in the code for details). The header file is

```
#ifndef BlowerMotor_H
#define BlowerMotor_H

#include "HHStypes.h"

class BlowerMotor {
private:
    bool turnedOn;
    int theRPM;
public:
    BlowerMotor(bool, int);
    bool isOn(); // for the simulation
    void turnOn();
    void turnOff();
    void setRPM(int);
    int getRPM();
};
#endif
```

The code is of more interest:

```
#include "BlowerMotor.h"

BlowerMotor::BlowerMotor(bool onOff, int rpm)
        : turnedOn(onOff), theRPM(rpm) {}
bool BlowerMotor::isOn() {
    return turnedOn; }
void BlowerMotor::turnOn() {
    if (!turnedOn) {
        turnedOn = true; }; }
void BlowerMotor::turnOff() {
    if (turnedOn) {
        turnedOn = false;
```

```
         theRPM = 0; }; }    // for the simulation
void BlowerMotor::setRPM(int rpm) {
    theRPM = rpm; }
int BlowerMotor::getRPM() {
    return theRPM; }
```

Conforming to the analysis dynamic model, we have that the *TurnOn* and *TurnOff* operations are state sensitive, while the get and set operations are effective unconditionally.

We assume that there is a blower motor device object that checks at every clock tick whether the blower motor is on, and if so, increases the motor speed to a certain maximum RPM value. The header file of such a class is

```
#ifndef BlowerMotorDevice_H
#define BlowerMotorDevice_H

#include "HHStypes.h"
#include "ClockClient.h"

class BlowerMotorDevice : public ClockClient {
private:
   BlowerMotor* theBlowerMotor;
public:
   BlowerMotorDevice(char*, BlowerMotor*);
   void tic(int tim);
};
#endif
```

A possible realization of the ramp up of the **theRPM** attribute is

```
#include "BlowerMotorDevice.h"
#include "BlowerMotor.h"

BlowerMotorDevice::BlowerMotorDevice(char* nm, BlowerMotor* bm)
    : ClockClient(nm), theBlowerMotor(bm) {}
void BlowerMotorDevice::tic(int tim) {
   if (theBlowerMotor->isOn()) {
      int currentRPM = theBlowerMotor->getRPM();
      cout << "BlowerMotorDevice::tic currentRPM " << currentRPM
```

```
        << "\n";
  if (currentRPM < blowerMotorOKspeed )
     theBlowerMotor->setRPM(3 + currentRPM); }; }
```

A *tic* event will increase the motor speed by three, provided that the motor is on and the speed is still under **blowerMotorOKspeed** (which is defined in the global file **HHStypes.h**; see Appendix B).

13.2.6 Heat Switch

The heat switch is a second-level class: It needs to know about the system controller. The heat switch is also special, in that it is part of the user interface: At all times an inhabitant can set the switch in another position. Hence a simulation with a graphical user interface probably needs to provide an on/off button that the simulation user can "click on" which causes the proper transition in the heat switch to fire. The header file is

```
#ifndef HeatSwitch_H
#define HeatSwitch_H

#include "HHStypes.h"

class HeatSwitch {
private:
   bool status;
   DisplayOut* theDisplayOut;
   SystemController* theSystemController;
public:
   HeatSwitch(SystemController*, DisplayOut*);
   void turnOn();
   void turnOff();
};
#endif
```

The display fire-wall is added to accommodate a visual representation of the heat status. A system controller attribute is added to provide a handle on this unique object in the home heating system. The corresponding code is

```
#include "HeatSwitch.h"
```

```
#include "DisplayOut.h"
#include "SystemController.h"

HeatSwitch::HeatSwitch(SystemController* sc, DisplayOut* displayOut)
    : theSystemController(sc), theDisplayOut(displayOut),
      status(false) {};
void HeatSwitch::turnOn() {
    if (!status) {
        status = true;
        theDisplayOut->displayHeatSwitchStatus(status);
        theSystemController->hsOn(); }; }
void HeatSwitch::turnOff() {
    if (status) {
        status = false;
        theDisplayOut->displayHeatSwitchStatus(status);
        theSystemController->hsOff(); }; }
```

Notice that we have taken the liberty to change the internal representation of the status attribute. Instead of the values *on* and *off*, we use the Boolean values *true* and *false*. In addition, we have changed the name of the attribute from *onOffStatus* to *status*. These changes have no impact on other objects. On the other hand, in actual practice it is recommended that the analysis and design descriptions be changed to maintain notational consistency.

13.2.7   Fault Reset Switch/Indicator

The fault reset switch indicator is virtually identical to the heat switch. Only the member function invocations of the system controller have to be modified: *hsOn()* and *hsOff()* are replace by *frOn()* and *frOff()*, respectively; see Appendix B for details.

13.2.8   System Controller

To appreciate the implementation of the system controller, it pays to backtrack to its design. The analysis model has four states in the transition diagram, see Figure 5.14 on page 161. Due to the special format of the diagram, we can recognize that these four states decompose as the combinations of two binary, state variables that represent whether the heat switch is *on* or *off*, and whether the fault reset switch is *on* or *off*, respectively. Hence we introduce two attributes, *heatSwitchStatus* and *faultResetSwitchStatus*. After these additions the design is easy. Certainly, we also need to introduce a handle on the furnace controller. Thus we obtain as the header file

```
#ifndef SystemController_H
#define SystemController_H

#include "HHStypes.h"

class SystemController {
private:
    bool heatSwitchStatus;
    bool faultResetSwitchStatus;
    FurnaceController* theFurnaceController;
public:
    SystemController(FurnaceController*);
    void hsOff();
    void hsOn();
    void frOn();
    void frOff();
};
#endif
```

All that remains is the code that provides the details of the member functions:

```
#include "SystemController.h"
#include "FurnaceController.h"

SystemController::SystemController(FurnaceController* fc)
        : theFurnaceController(fc),
          heatSwitchStatus(false),
          faultResetSwitchStatus(false) {}
void SystemController::hsOff() {
    if (heatSwitchStatus) {
        heatSwitchStatus = false;
        if (faultResetSwitchStatus) {
            cout << "SystemController::hsOff \n";
            theFurnaceController->disable(); }; }; }
void SystemController::hsOn() {
```

```
    if (!heatSwitchStatus) {
        heatSwitchStatus = true;
        if (faultResetSwitchStatus) {
            cout << "SystemController::hsOn \n";
            theFurnaceController->enable(); }; }; }
void SystemController::frOff() {
    if (faultResetSwitchStatus) {
        faultResetSwitchStatus = false;
        if (heatSwitchStatus) {
            cout << "SystemController::frOff \n";
            theFurnaceController->disable(); }; }; }
void SystemController::frOn() {
    if (!faultResetSwitchStatus) {
        faultResetSwitchStatus = true;
        if (heatSwitchStatus) {
            cout << "SystemController::frOn \n";
            theFurnaceController->enable(); }; }; }
```

As usual, we track whether we are in the proper state before honoring an event. If so, we set the corresponding state attribute and we proceed by checking whether the other state attribute warrants propagating an event to the furnace controller. The similarity with the semantics of an *and*-gate should be obvious. We have sprinkled output statements in the code to facilitate tracing of events.

13.2.9   Heat-Flow Regulator

The heat-flow regulator is our next target. As observed earlier, the analysis uses in the dynamic model an attribute that counts the number of rooms that need heat, while the static model omits this attribute. The heat-flow regulator needs to communicate with both the valve controller and furnace controller. Hence the design will have introduced attributes for them also. Thus we obtain the header file

```
#ifndef HeatFlowRegulator_H
#define HeatFlowRegulator_H

#include "HHStypes.h"
#include "SET.h"

class HeatFlowRegulator {
```

```
private:
   int roomCnt;
   SET<Room>* roomsThatNeedHeat;
   ValveController* theValveController;
   FurnaceController* theFurnaceController;
public:
   HeatFlowRegulator(ValveController*, FurnaceController*);
   void registerRoom(Room* room);
   void unRegisterRoom(Room* room);
};
#endif
```

We rely here on the parametrized *SET* class that is instantiated by the *Room* class to keep track of all rooms that have decided that they need heat. The code follows:

```
#include "HeatFlowRegulator.h"
#include "ValveController.h"
#include "FurnaceController.h"
#include "Room.h" // To support the trace operations

HeatFlowRegulator::HeatFlowRegulator
        (ValveController* vc, FurnaceController* fc)
    : theValveController(vc), theFurnaceController(fc), roomCnt(0) {
          roomsThatNeedHeat = new SET<Room>(); }
void HeatFlowRegulator::registerRoom(Room* room) {
   cout << "HeatFlowRegulator register room "
        << room->getName() << "\n";
   roomCnt++;
   roomsThatNeedHeat->add(room);
   theValveController->addRoom(room);
   if (1 == roomCnt) theFurnaceController->startup(); }
void HeatFlowRegulator::unRegisterRoom(Room* room) {
   cout << "HeatFlowRegulator Unregister room "
        << room->getName() << "\n";
   roomCnt--;
   roomsThatNeedHeat->delet(room);
   theValveController->removeRoom(room);
   if (0 == roomCnt) theFurnaceController->shutdown(); }
```

Notice that the constructor sets the room count to zero and initializes the multivalued attribute that tracks the rooms that need heat with the empty set. The references to the valve controller and furnace controller are initialized also.

We have in the analysis two transitions that deal with registering a room and similarly, with deregistering a room. Each time we combine them into a single member function. Whether or not to send a message to the furnace controller is decided after the common activities are completed. This "smart" simplification is best done in the design phase, where there is less clutter. Conceivably, a design optimizer could propose those meaning-preserving transformations. Whether such a change could be propagated further up in the analysis model would depend on whether "understandability" of the analysis description would be hampered. Decreasing the clarity of the analysis in favor of increasing the continuity of the descriptions between the different development phases is a difficult trade-off. Smarter compilers exploiting meaning-preserving transformations, guided by heuristics, will alleviate these trade-offs.

13.2.10   Clock

The clock class is the "king of the hill": It drives the events that make all other objects work. Still it depends also on the class *ClockClient* (which was called *Thing* in the analysis model) for the characterization of its *clients* attribute. All classes whose instances can appear in the clock's client container should be a subclass of *ClockClient* and should define a *tic* operation. The header file is

```
#ifndef Clock_H
#define Clock_H

#include "HHStypes.h"
#include "SET.h"
#include "ClockClient.h"

class Clock {
private:
    int currentTime;
    SET<ClockClient>* clients;
public:
    Clock();
    void ticToc();
```

```
    void addClient(ClockClient* cc);
    void removeClient(ClockClient* cc);
    int getTime();
};
#endif
```

The operation `ticToc` is driven by an external entity, a "real" clock in an actual realization of the Home Heating System. In the simulation, the driver will be a for-loop. The code is as follows:

```
#include "Clock.h"

Clock::Clock ()
      : currentTime(0) {
          clients = new SET<ClockClient>(); }
void Clock::ticToc() {
      currentTime++;
      cout << "Clock time ************** " << currentTime << "\n";
      clients->forEachElement1(&ClockClient::tic, currentTime); }
void Clock::addClient(ClockClient* cc) {
      cout << "Clock::addClient "
          << cc->getName() << "\n";
      clients->add(cc); }
void Clock::removeClient(ClockClient* cc) {
      cout << "Clock::removeClient "
          << cc->getName() << "\n";
      clients->delet(cc); }
int Clock::getTime() {
      return currentTime; }
```

The constructor initializes the time, maintained in *currentTime*, to zero and initializes *clients* to the empty set by calling up the constructor for *SET*. Notice that the clock sends out the time when its sends out a *tic* event as part of the broadcast to all members of the set.

Somewhat tricky is the implementation of the *ticToc* operation. The clock needs to broadcast to all the entities that have registered an interest in *tic* events. All these entities are "inside" the set. Due to the way that typing is handled in C++, it is not sufficient to have a single *apply* function in *SET*. We need to "pipe through" different kinds of operations to the elements inside the set. Here we need to have applied

"`...->tic(currentTime)`" to the set elements. The valve controller, see below, must request application of "`...->openValve()`". The key difference being that the former member function has an argument and the latter does not. Consequently, the clock code requires the *SET* to support the *forEachElement1* operation in addition to a different apply operation for the valve controller class.[3]

Much more tricky is the consequence of the iterative realization of the `tic` broadcast by the `forEachElement` operation. This is, in fact, a design topic, but we will address it here. Since the analysis model assumes asynchronous communication where the exact timing of the arrival of events is not critical, it appears that the iterative implementation is fine. We have to look closer. The clock broadcasts in the analysis model to all recipients, waits "an eternity", and then repeats the cycle. While waiting, it takes in requests for new clients to join and for existing clients to leave the set of *tic*-recipients. In the iterative implementation, these leave and join operations happen *during* the broadcast. Disaster looms when a set iterator interferes with the set insertion and deletion operations. This delicate issue is resolved in our implementation by making an internal copy of the set when an insertion or deletion happens during a set iteration. For details, see the implementation of the *SET* class in Appendix B. This is a "dirty" trick and was possible only because we wrote our own *SET* class. An alternative design and implementation require the `ticToc` operation to obtain a copy of its set of clients. Hence we would get inside the `ticToc` operation

```
SET<ClockClient> clientsCopy = clients;
clientsCopy.forEachElement1(&ClockClient::tic, currentTime);
```

However, this will work only if the *SET* class supports a copy constructor.

13.2.11   Valve Controller

The valve controller has a complex-looking transition network in the analysis model; see Figure 5.40 on page 196. The situation gets simplified by the observation that the *furnaceOn* and *furnaceOff* operations can be designed and implemented separately: They do not depend on the states *ready*, *add*, and *del*. Subsequently, one can recognize that the transitions *openValve* and *noOp* exclude each other, and since they are not triggered by events, they can be combined with the *addRoom* operation. Similarly, the transitions *closeValve* and *noOp* can be combined with *deleteRoom*. This yields the unsurprising header file

---

[3]The typing in C++ is not powerful enough to avoid this duplication. Proposals for enhancements (see John Rose, John.Rose@eng.sun.com) are floating around but seem not to have sufficient support.

```
#ifndef ValveController_H
#define ValveController_H

#include "HHStypes.h"
#include "SET.h"

class ValveController {
private:
    bool furnaceIsOn;
    SET<Room>* roomsThatNeedHeat;
public:
    ValveController();
    void furnaceOn();
    void furnaceOff();
    void addRoom(Room* room);
    void removeRoom(Room* room);
};
#endif
```

Expansion of the member functions gives

```
#include "ValveController.h"
#include "Room.h"

ValveController::ValveController ()
    : furnaceIsOn(false) {
      roomsThatNeedHeat = new SET<Room>(); }
void ValveController::furnaceOn() {
   if (!furnaceIsOn) {
      cout << "ValveController::furnaceOn \n";
      furnaceIsOn = true;
      roomsThatNeedHeat->forEachElement(&Room::openValve); }; }
void ValveController::furnaceOff() {
   if (furnaceIsOn) {
      cout << "ValveController::furnaceOff \n";
      furnaceIsOn = false;
      roomsThatNeedHeat->forEachElement(&Room::closeValve); }; }
void ValveController::addRoom(Room* room) {
      cout << "ValveController add room "
```

```
                << room->getName() << "\n";
           roomsThatNeedHeat->add(room);
           if (furnaceIsOn) room->openValve(); }
   void ValveController::removeRoom(Room* room) {
       cout << "ValveController delete room "
               << room->getName() << "\n";
           roomsThatNeedHeat->delet(room);
           if (furnaceIsOn) room->closeValve(); }
```

The *noOp* transition from the analysis description has disappeared because the conditional statements in *addRoom* and *deleteRoom* do not have an **else** branch. Notice also that we rely on a different "apply" operation in the *SET* class to broadcast the *openValve* and *closeValve* events than the one we used in the *Clock* class. This operation **forEachElement** is also aware of possible interference with set insertions and deletions, although *we* know that the **roomsThatNeedHeat** member will not be modified during the iterative broadcast.[4]

13.2.12   Furnace Controller

The furnace controller analysis model follows the same "pattern" as the system controller. The header files and the code files are similar as well. Hence we refer to Appendix B for the details.

13.2.13   Room

The room class belongs to the largest classes in the system as measured by the number of attributes. We have added the attribute **DisplayOut*** to support the display of sensor values in a simulation. Noticeable in the Room's header file is the list of include-files. This is required since the corresponding attributes are incorporated by value - hence these header files are used to determine the amount of storage in a room object that must be reserved for these attributes.

```
#ifndef Room_H
#define Room_H

#include "HHStypes.h"
```

---

[4]We hope that the reader gets a positive appreciation for executable high-level design models that obviate the need for dealing with these pesky design puzzles.

```
#include "OccupancyHistory.h"
#include "LivingPattern.h"
#include "RoomTemperatureSensor.h"
#include "RoomTemperatureSensorDevice.h"
#include "OccupancySensor.h"
#include "OccupancySensorDevice.h"
#include "DesiredTempInputDevice.h"
#include "DesiredTempInputDeviceDev.h"
#include "WaterValve.h"
#include "ClockClient.h"
#include "DisplayOut.h"

class Room : public ClockClient {
private:
   bool needsHeat;
   bool registeredHeatRequest;
   bool heating;
   OccupancyHistory myOccupancyHistory;
   LivingPattern myLivingPattern;
   RoomTemperatureSensor myRoomTemperatureSensor;
   RoomTemperatureSensorDevice myRoomTemperatureSensorDevice;
   OccupancySensor myOccupancySensor;
   OccupancySensorDevice myOccupancySensorDevice;
   DesiredTempInputDevice myDesiredTempInputDevice;
   DesiredTempInputDeviceDev myDesiredTempInputDeviceDev;
   WaterValve myWaterValve;
   HeatFlowRegulator* theHeatFlowRegulator;
   DisplayOut* theDisplayOut;
   Clock* theClock;
public:
   Room(char*, HeatFlowRegulator*, DisplayOut*, Clock*);
   void tic(int);
   void openValve();
   void closeValve();
   bool isHeating(); // for the simulation
   void printName(); // for testing
};
#endif
```

The dynamic model in the analysis has three transitions whose guards depend only on the values of *needsHeat* and *registeredHeatRequest* and *not* on a triggering event. As we saw earlier, these transitions are absorbed in operations that are triggered by events, in this case by *tic*.

The code part for the *tic* operation is relatively large. But observe that the code follows closely the specification given on page 166. It is perhaps necessary to emphasize that the specification there was *not* intended to become the code - it aimed to clarify the requirements - but it is certainly pleasant that this description carries over by and large. The if-then-else construct at the end of the `tic`-body realizes the absorbed transitions.

```
#include "Room.h"
#include "HeatFlowRegulator.h"
#include "Clock.h"

Room::Room(char* nm, HeatFlowRegulator *hfr, DisplayOut* dO,
        Clock* cl) :
      ClockClient(nm),
      theClock(cl),
      needsHeat(false),
      registeredHeatRequest(false),
      heating(false),
      myRoomTemperatureSensorDevice("RTSD",
                              this, &myRoomTemperatureSensor),
      myOccupancySensorDevice("OSD", this, &myOccupancySensor),
      myDesiredTempInputDeviceDev("DTID", this,
                              &myDesiredTempInputDevice),
      theHeatFlowRegulator(hfr),
      theDisplayOut(dO)
      { myRoomTemperatureSensor.setDisplayOut(dO, this);
        myOccupancySensor.setDisplayOut(dO, this);
        theClock->addClient(&myRoomTemperatureSensorDevice);
        theClock->addClient(&myOccupancySensorDevice);
        theClock->addClient(&myDesiredTempInputDeviceDev); }
void Room::tic(int dateTime) {
      cout << "Room " << name << " heating " << heating;
      bool currentOccupancy = myOccupancySensor.getOccupied();
      myOccupancyHistory.setOccupancy(dateTime, currentOccupancy);
```

```
    bool previousOccupancy =
            myOccupancyHistory.getOccupancy(dateTime - week);
    if (currentOccupancy == previousOccupancy)
        myLivingPattern.setPattern(dateTime, currentOccupancy);
    const int minute30 = 30*60; // # seconds in 30 minutes
    // occupied indicates whether the room is currently occupied or
    // is expected to be occupied within 30 minutes
    bool occupied = (currentOccupancy) ? currentOccupancy :
            myLivingPattern.occupancyExpected(dateTime, minute30) ;
    int td = myDesiredTempInputDevice.getDesiredTemperature();
    int tw = (occupied) ? td : (td - 5);
    int temp = myRoomTemperatureSensor.getCurrentTemperature();
    if (temp <= tw - 2) needsHeat = true; else
    if (temp >= tw + 2) needsHeat = false; // else no change
    cout << " td " << td
         << " temp " << temp
         << " needsHeat " << needsHeat << "\n";
    if (needsHeat && !registeredHeatRequest) {
        registeredHeatRequest = true;
        theHeatFlowRegulator->registerRoom(this); }
    else
    if (!needsHeat && registeredHeatRequest) {
        registeredHeatRequest = false;
        theHeatFlowRegulator->unRegisterRoom(this); }; }
void Room::openValve() {
    cout << "Room::openValve " << name << "\n";
    heating = true;
    myWaterValve.open(); }
void Room::closeValve() {
    cout << "Room::closeValve " << name << "\n";
    heating = false;
    myWaterValve.close(); }
bool Room::isHeating() { return heating; }
void Room::printName() {
    cout << "Room::printName " << name << "\n"; }
```

Observe that the constructor of *Room* passes the `DisplayOut*` reference (and the identity of the room) to the two sensors in the room. The open and close valve functions are just forwarding operations. The code makes use of two numeric constants, `week` and `minute30`. They represent the number of seconds in a week and in 30 minutes, respectively. The `week` constant is defined through a global `#define#` instruction in the file `HHStypes.h`; see appendix B.

13.2.14   Occupancy History

The class occupancy history class is "traditionally" (together with living pattern class) problematic.[5] Assuming that the reader has made the side trip to the footnote, we assume that the design has adopted a brute-force solution and we are happy to follow this lead in the implementation: Occupancy is recorded for a full week with a granularity per second in a "dumb" manner. Thus we do not maintain intervals during which the occupancy doesn't change, but dutifully store the state of occupancy for every tick of the clock. We have the comfort of object-oriented-ness so that we can change this policy at any time without fearing ripple effects. This said, we present the header file

```
#ifndef OccupancyHistory_H
#define OccupancyHistory_H

#include "HHStypes.h"

class OccupancyHistory {
private:
   bool occupancyRecord[week];
public:
   OccupancyHistory();
   void setOccupancy(int, bool);
   bool getOccupancy(int);
};
#endif
```

We must admit that this brute-force approach has a price tag. Since a Boolean is represented by one byte, an instance of this class takes over 600 kB. The code is

---

[5]Students who follow an analysis class and are confronted with these classes usually cannot avoid digging into their design and implementation. Often, they feel the need to reduce the time granularity to 5 minutes, or even 30 minutes, with which the history, and living pattern, is to be maintained. The arguments range from: "the room will be preheated 30 minutes before expected occupation" to "it is not realistic to keep track of occupancies below X minutes". Maintaining a time granularity of 1 second is deemed extravagant.

```
#include "OccupancyHistory.h"

OccupancyHistory::OccupancyHistory() {
        for (int i = 0; i<week; ++i) occupancyRecord[i] = false; }
void OccupancyHistory::setOccupancy(int dateTime, bool occupancy) {
    if (dateTime < 0) setOccupancy(dateTime + week, occupancy); else
    if (week <= dateTime) setOccupancy(dateTime % week, occupancy);
    else occupancyRecord[dateTime] = occupancy; }
bool OccupancyHistory::getOccupancy(int dateTime) {
    if (dateTime < 0) getOccupancy(dateTime + week); else
    if (week <= dateTime) getOccupancy(dateTime % week); else
    return occupancyRecord[dateTime]; }
```

The key idea is to treat the array that keeps track of the occupancies as a circular data structure. Other subtleties are left to the curiosity of the reader. It is certainly possible to avoid the duplication of code in the set and get functions by defining a global normalizeTime function, as in

```
int normalizeTime(int dateTime) {
    if (dateTime < 0) return (dateTime + week); else
    if (week <= dateTime) return (dateTime % week); else
    return dateTime; }
```

This also allows us to simplify the next class.

13.2.15 Living Pattern

The living pattern class is nearly identical to the occupancy history class. The header file is

```
#ifndef LivingPattern_H
#define LivingPattern_H

#include "HHStypes.h"

class LivingPattern {
private:
   bool livingPatternR[week];
public:
```

```
    LivingPattern();
    void setPattern(int, bool);
    bool occupancyExpected(int, int);
};
#endif
```

The difference is that the operation *occupancyExpected* takes two arguments because we need to know whether occupancy can be expected in a certain interval. Yes, an alternative design would use only one argument to indicate the beginning of the interval of interest and would build the length of the interval into the class. The design chosen leaves the determination of the interval length in the hands of the client. This time we use the `normalizeTime` function:

```
#include "LivingPattern.h"

LivingPattern::LivingPattern() {
        for (int i = 0; i<week; ++i) livingPatternR[i] = false; }
void LivingPattern::setPattern(int dateTime, bool occupancy) {
        livingPatternR[normalizeTime(dateTime)] = occupancy; }
bool LivingPattern::occupancyExpected(int dateTimeI, int length) {
        int dateTime = normalizeTime(dateTimeI);
        // return true iff there is an i such that:
        //    dateTime <= i < dateTime + length and
        //    livingPatternR[i] = true
        // j = i % week
        // to deal with the circularity of livingPatternR[week]
        int end = dateTime + length;
        for (int i = dateTime; i < end; i++)
            { int j = ( i < week) ? i : i - week;
                if (livingPatternR[j]) return true; };
        return false; }
```

This class (and the occupancy history class) demonstrates nicely that we can change the data representation inside the class without having a ripple effect on the outside system. In fact, we can change the representation in the living pattern class and *not* change the representation in the occupancy history class, or the other way around.

13.2.16   Furnace

The furnace class is the other sizable class in the home heating system. As in case for the *Room* class, there are several **include** files to deal with members that are incorporated by value. A **furnaceStatus** member tracks the state in the dynamic model. This is required due to the greater complexity of the dynamic model. An enumeration clause defines the set of legal states. A tiny **max** function is defined, as a private member function in the header file, to avoid dependence on an external library. The number of public member functions is less than one might expect from the dynamic model. The reason is that several of them have become internal transitions, driven by a **resume** operation.

```
#include "WaterTemperatureSensorDevice.h"

class Furnace {
private:
    enum states {
        furnaceOff, waitToFireUp, waitForBlowerMotor,
        oilValveOpened, waitForHotWater, furnaceOn,
        oilValveClosed };
    states furnaceStatus;
    int lastShutDownTime;
    int waitPeriod;
    Clock* theClock;
    BlowerMotor theBlowerMotor;
    BlowerMotorDevice theBlowerMotorDevice;
    OilValve theOilValve;
    Ignitor theIgnitor;
    FurnaceMonitor* theFurnaceMonitor;
    ValveController* theValveController;
    FurnaceStatusIndicator* theFurnaceStatusIndicator;
    Timer<Furnace>* myTimer;
    WaterTemperatureSensor theWaterTemperatureSensor;
    WaterTemperatureSensorDevice theWaterTemperatureSensorDevice;
    int max(int x, int y) { return ( (x < y) ? y : x ); };
    void turnOnBlower();
    void ignite();
    void turnOffBlower();
    void checkRPMBlowerMotor();
```

```
   void turnOpenOilValve();
   void checkWaterTemperature();
   void openWaterValves();
public:
   Furnace(Clock*, FurnaceMonitor*, ValveController* vc,
           FurnaceStatusIndicator* fsi);
   void startup();
   void resume();
   void shutdown();
};
#endif
```

The internal transitions have become private member functions. They are driven by a timer. Recollect that the furnace cannot start within 5 minutes of it being shut down; it has to wait until the blower motor has gained enough speed; and it has to wait until the water temperature in the boiler is okay. For each of these situations a timer is activated that will cause the furnace to resume at the appropriate time. Sometimes the furnace can proceed right away; sometimes the furnace must reactivate the timer again. The **resume** operation in the furnace decides which transition to activate based on the current state of the furnace. The reader is invited to scrutinize the code:

```
#include "Furnace.h"
#include "Clock.h"
#include "FurnaceMonitor.h"
#include "ValveController.h"
#include "FurnaceStatusIndicator.h"

Furnace::Furnace(Clock* clock, FurnaceMonitor* fm,
           ValveController* vc,
           FurnaceStatusIndicator* fsi) :
     theClock(clock), theFurnaceMonitor(fm), theValveController(vc),
     theFurnaceStatusIndicator(fsi),
     theBlowerMotor(false, 0),
     theBlowerMotorDevice("BMD", &theBlowerMotor),
     theWaterTemperatureSensorDevice("WTSD",
                                       &theWaterTemperatureSensor)
     {
       lastShutDownTime = -1000;
       furnaceStatus = furnaceOff;
```

```
        myTimer = new Timer<Furnace>("Timer", this, theClock);
        theClock->addClient(&theBlowerMotorDevice);
        theClock->addClient(&theWaterTemperatureSensorDevice); }
void Furnace::startup() {
   if (furnaceStatus == furnaceOff) {
      cout << "Furnace::startup \n";
      const int minute5 = 5*60; // # seconds in 5 minutes
      furnaceStatus = waitToFireUp;
      int waitPeriod =
            max(0, minute5 -
                  (theClock->getTime() - lastShutDownTime));
      if (0 < waitPeriod)
         myTimer->alarm(waitPeriod); else
      turnOnBlower(); }; }
void Furnace::resume() { switch ( furnaceStatus ) {
   case waitToFireUp:
        turnOnBlower();
        break;
   case waitForBlowerMotor:
        checkRPMBlowerMotor();
        break;
   case waitForHotWater:
        checkWaterTemperature();
        break;
   case oilValveClosed:
        turnOffBlower();
        break; }; }
void Furnace::turnOnBlower() {
      if (furnaceStatus == waitToFireUp) {
         cout << "Furnace::turnOnBlower \n";
         furnaceStatus = waitForBlowerMotor;
         theBlowerMotor.turnOn();
         myTimer->alarm(1); }; }
void Furnace::checkRPMBlowerMotor() {
      if (blowerMotorOKspeed <= theBlowerMotor.getRPM()) {
         cout << "Furnace::checkRPMBlowerMotor \n";
         turnOpenOilValve(); } else
      myTimer->alarm(1); }
```

```
void Furnace::turnOpenOilValve() {
    if (furnaceStatus == waitForBlowerMotor) {
        cout << "Furnace::turnOpenOilValve \n";
        furnaceStatus = oilValveOpened;
        theOilValve.open();
        ignite(); }; }
void Furnace::ignite() {
    if (furnaceStatus == oilValveOpened) {
        cout << "Furnace::ignite \n";
        furnaceStatus = waitForHotWater;
        theIgnitor.ignite();
        theFurnaceMonitor->enable();
        myTimer->alarm(1); }; }
void Furnace::checkWaterTemperature() {
    if (waterTempOK <=
        theWaterTemperatureSensor.getCurrentTemperature() )
        openWaterValves(); else
    myTimer->alarm(1); }
void Furnace::openWaterValves() {
    if (furnaceStatus == waitForHotWater) {
        cout << "Furnace::openWaterValves \n";
        furnaceStatus = furnaceOn;
        theValveController->furnaceOn();
        theFurnaceStatusIndicator->turnOn(); }; }
void Furnace::shutdown() {
    if (furnaceStatus == waitToFireUp ||
        furnaceStatus == waitForBlowerMotor ||
        furnaceStatus == oilValveOpened ||
        furnaceStatus == waitForHotWater ||
        furnaceStatus == furnaceOn) {
        cout << "Furnace::shutdown \n";
        furnaceStatus = oilValveClosed;
        myTimer->unarm();
        theOilValve.close();
        theFurnaceMonitor->disable();
        myTimer->alarm(5); }; }
void Furnace::turnOffBlower() {
    if (furnaceStatus == oilValveClosed) {
```

```
cout << "Furnace::turnOffBlower \n";
furnaceStatus = furnaceOff;
theBlowerMotor.turnOff();
theFurnaceStatusIndicator->turnOff();
theValveController->furnaceOff(); }; }
```

The furnace imports several references through its constructor. In addition, the constructor initializes the internal components. Noticeable is the private timer that is created. All this structure is new, because the analysis model of the furnace was quite incomplete and we did not elaborate these details in the design phase. An interpreter for the design would have forced us to address earlier the details that were filled in during the implementation.

The **shutdown** operation activates the timer to let the blower continue for 5 seconds before turning it off. Notice that the timer is unarmed before activating it. Whether the timer is actually unarmed, (i.e., removed from the set of clock clients) depends on the state in which the shutdown took place. Hence the timer's **unarm** operation will be effective only when the timer is a client of the clock. For details, see below.

13.2.17 Timer

The class *Timer* has only a single instance that is used by the furnace, which is by itself a single instance of the class *Furnace*. Since a timer is a general concept, it has been implemented as a parametrized class where the type of the object that needs a timer service is variable. All the information is captured by the header file:

```
#ifndef Timer_H
#define Timer_H

#include "HHStypes.h"
#include "ClockClient.h"
#include "Clock.h"

template <class T> class Timer : public ClockClient {
private:
    int remainingTime;
    bool armed;
    T* theSB;
    Clock* theClock;
public:
```

```
    Timer(char* nm, T* aSB, Clock* clock)
      : ClockClient(nm), theSB(aSB), theClock(clock), armed(false) {};
    void alarm(int tim) {
        armed = true;
        remainingTime = tim;
        theClock->addClient(this); };
    void tic(int tim) {
        if (armed) {
            remainingTime--;
            if (remainingTime-- <= 0) {
                armed = false;
                theClock->removeClient(this);
                theSB->resume(); }; }; };
    void unarm() {
        armed = false;
        theClock->removeClient(this); };
};
#endif
```

In case the reader wonders about *SB*, see the footnote.[6]

The normal operation for a timer is to become activated by the **alarm** operation and to unarm itself when the timer expires in a **tic** operation. However, the timer may have been prematurely unarmed by the **unarm** operation. Hence we have the test inside the **tic** operation.

13.2.18   Furnace Monitor

The *Furnace* class is the last main class that we describe in this chapter. It is a subclass of *ClockClient* because when the furnace is fired up, it has to check continuously that the fuel is flowing and that the combustion is okay. During normal operation it is the furnace that removes the monitor from the clock's clients. In case the monitor finds an anomaly, it shuts down the furnace and removes itself from the clock. This explains why the furnace monitor has a handle on the clock. The header file is

```
#ifndef FurnaceMonitor_H
#define FurnaceMonitor_H
```

---

[6] "SB" stands for "sleeping beauty".

```
#include "HHStypes.h"
#include "ClockClient.h"

class FurnaceMonitor : public ClockClient {
private:
    bool off;
    bool oilFlow;
    bool combustion;
    FuelFlowSensor* theFuelFlowSensor;
    OpticalCombustionSensor* theOpticalCombustionSensor;
    FaultResetSwitch* theFaultResetSwitch;
    Clock* theClock;
public:
    FurnaceMonitor(char*, Clock*, FuelFlowSensor*,
                   OpticalCombustionSensor*);
    // to resolve a circular reference in the HH System ....
    void setFaultResetSwitch(FaultResetSwitch*);
    void enable();
    void disable();
    void tic(int);
};
#endif
```

The analysis model revealed a cycle in the class-relationship diagram. This was a sign for potential trouble when these classes were instantiated so that the instantiated objects were actually forming a circular chain of references. In fact, we have run into this situation: We have the following circular chain: furnace monitor → fault reset switch → system controller → furnace controller → furnace → furnace monitor. As a result, one of the members in this cycle cannot use its constructor to initialize the reference it needs. Instead, it has to wait until the entity to which it is referring is actually declared.[7] This explains why we have the operation setFaultResetSwitch inside the furnace monitor.[8] The resulting code is

```
#include "FurnaceMonitor.h"
#include "FaultResetSwitch.h"
```

---

[7]This is the awful consequence of the one-pass compilation policy that "tyrannizes" C and that burdens C++ as well. Are we ever growing beyond the aha-delight of one-pass translation?

[8]Awgrr!

```cpp
#include "Clock.h"
#include "FuelFlowSensor.h"
#include "OpticalCombustionSensor.h"

FurnaceMonitor::FurnaceMonitor(char* nm, Clock* clock,
    FuelFlowSensor* ffs, OpticalCombustionSensor* ocs) :
    ClockClient(nm),
    theClock(clock), theFuelFlowSensor(ffs),
    theOpticalCombustionSensor(ocs) {
        off = true;
        oilFlow = false;
        combustion = false; }
void FurnaceMonitor::setFaultResetSwitch(FaultResetSwitch* frs) {
    theFaultResetSwitch = frs; }
void FurnaceMonitor::enable() {
    cout << "FurnaceMonitor::enable \n";
    off = false;
    theClock->addClient(this); }
void FurnaceMonitor::disable() {
    cout << "FurnaceMonitor::disable \n";
    off = true;
    theClock->removeClient(this);}
void FurnaceMonitor::tic(int value) {
    if (!off) {
        cout << "FurnaceMonitor::tic " << value <<"\n";
        oilFlow = theFuelFlowSensor->getFuelFlow();
        combustion = theOpticalCombustionSensor->getCombustion();
        if (!oilFlow || !combustion) {
            theClock->removeClient(this);
            theFaultResetSwitch->turnOff(); } ; }; }
```

Again, as we saw with the timer, the furnace monitor will be removed normally from the clock's clients, inside the disable operation, or by the furnace monitor itself when it observes trouble inside tic. No trouble occurs when the monitor is already removed from the clock's clients. Everything else is straightforward.

13.3   Stepping Back

The reader is invited to check Appendix B for additional classes and Appendix C for some sample output of the simulation program. This is a good time to compare the analysis model description and the final code.

Quite uninteresting is the need to have the file `HHStypes.h`. It is required due to the inability in C++ (and in C) to have forward references. Remarkable is the community of programmers' willingness to live with the inconveniences of this harness. It makes the writing of the `main` file a headache. The introduction of a class, called, say, `System`, would still face the anomaly of the circular object references that we encountered in the preceding section. This is a serious impediment for the automatic generation of C++ code.

Several classes have to be introduced as a result of embedding the Home Heating System into a simulation. We introduced drivers for the sensors: one for the blower motor to simulate its coming up to speed and one for the desired temperature input device. Another extension would be required to simulate an external modification of the heat switch.

The class *ClockClient* had to be introduced to deal with the heterogeneity of the set of the clock's clients, and polymorphism was exploited to give each time a different interpretation of the `tic` operation in the different subclasses. The class *Timer* was introduced to deal with the fuzzy characterization of the furnace's behavior. Finally, we had to introduce the *SET* class because we did not have ready access to a container library.

The most salient phenomenon in the behavioral realm is the disappearance of transitions that are not driven by external events, as we saw most clearly in the *Room* class: the transitions *register*, *unRegister*, and *noChange* were all absorbed by the room's `tic` operation. The emergence of internal transitions in the *Furnace* class is an anomaly caused by a design that emerged during the implementation phase. At this point a single timer resumes the furnace and an "ugly" switch statement decides which internal transition to fire up. Specialized timers would obviate the need for the resume operation and its switch statement. Another approach would partially eliminate the timers, and give more responsibility to the blower motor and water temperature sensor, or the like, to resume a specific transition of the furnace. See the exercise at the end of the chapter.

Dealing with insertions and deletions in the clock's set of clients while iterating over that set is the trickiest aspect of the implementation. Unsurprisingly, the problem is caused by aliasing - multiple access paths to the same memory location - one of the most hideous sources of errors (for the theory behind this problem see de Champeaux and de Bruin [20]). We feel that this problem, and its solution, is the most formidable argument in favor of adopting software development techniques that obviate the need to descend in the "programming hell". The approach outlined in the part of design is thus far the most promising candidate, in our opinion.

Adherence to the implementation micro process was quite straightforward. There was no reuse and we did not import a framework. Hence we simply plunged into the implementation of classes in a bottom-up fashion. The separation in header files and code files was certainly helpful, but even better was the detailed analysis and design (the latter is not spelled out in this book).

13.4   Metrics for the Implementation

No data are available for the effort it took to implement these classes and the supporting files. We look forward to the opportunity to work with student groups to obtain sets of empirical data.

We can apply to the code the same set of product metrics that we introduced in Chapter 9. Instead, we will simply count the number of lines and correlate them with the metrics obtained in the analysis and design phases. Table 13.1 shows the raw data. We show only entries from the implementation phase for which there are corresponding entries in the earlier phases.

The total number of lines listed in Table 13.1 for the header files, code files, and the total LOC are 509, 544, and 1053, respectively. In contrast, when we include the files required for the simulation, the auxiliary files, and the main program, the numbers are 850, 734 and 1584 respectively. The amount of code required for a "real" Home Heating System is likely in between 1053 and 1584, and given that we deal with a "toy" application, is not of genuine concern.

The next step entails calculating the correlations of the implementation metric against the analysis and design metrics. Table 13.2 has the results.

Obviously, the correlations found for the Home Heating System are quite encouraging. If we believe that product metrics correlate with effort metrics, then based on these results, we have available a quite reliable estimator for OO system development efforts.

Class	μ_{vocab}	Ψ_A	Ψ_D	.h file	.cc file	LOC
HS	5	10	288	20	18	38
FRS/I	5	10	388	20	19	39
FSI	5	10	288	19	13	32
HFR	5	14	639	19	27	46
SC	8	19	733	22	33	55
Clock	5	14	632	20	19	39
Room	14	32	1145	46	64	110
OS	4	8	111	20	14	34
RTS	4	8	111	22	15	37
DTID	4	8	111	23	10	33
WV	4	9	111	18	12	30
FC	8	19	733	22	31	53
Furnace	14	44	2054	49	104	153
BM	6	16	317	22	17	39
OilValve	4	11	322	18	11	29
Ignitor	2	6	134	14	7	21
WTS	4	8	111	18	10	28
FM	10	23	953	26	34	60
FFS	4	8	111	18	12	30
OCS	4	8	111	18	11	29
OH	4	9	142	18	12	30
LP	4	9	142	18	21	39
VC	NA	24	607	19	30	49

Table 13.1: More metric values for the home heating system classes. The data in the first three columns were presented earlier. The first column consists of data from μ_{vocab} which can be captured early in the analysis. The second column consists of data from Ψ_A, the synthetic analysis metric introduced in Chapter 5. The third column is the synthetic metric Ψ_D, defined in Chapter 9. The next three columns are the number of lines in the header files, the number of lines in the code files, and the last column is the sum of the two previous columns, respectively. The next table shows the correlations between these metric values.

Metric 1	Metric 2	β_0	β_1	Correlation
μ_{vocab}	LOC	-5.3757	8.8367	0.93281
Ψ_A	LOC	2.7704	3.0253	0.94849
Ψ_D	LOC	19.0813	5.9659	0.94238

Table 13.2: The values for β_0 and β_1 are the best fits for the available data in the equation: $\mu_{Metric2} = \beta_0 + \beta_1 * \mu_{Metric1}$.

13.5 Summary

In this chapter we have illustrated how to transform a low-level design into C++. Some realizations require care since the design was not worked out in detail. The inability to have forward references in C++ code requires to break reference cycles in objects that get initialized. This is an impediment for automatic code generation.

Product metric values obtained by measuring lines of code for all classes correlate favorably with $Sigma_A$ and $Sigma_D$, the product metrics from the analysis and design, respectively.

13.6 Exercises

1. We have argued that the implementation and design of the `ticToc` operation in the *Clock* may have to do its own copying of the *clients* attribute, to avoid interference with set iteration. These deliberations clearly should take place during the transition from a thread-per-object design to a single-thread-per-process design. Would it be possible to automatize the proper design decision? Argue both ways.

2. The implementation of the *Furnace* was done against a fuzzy and incomplete analysis model. Redo its analysis, design, and implementation. Would the introduction of a boiler class be helpful?

Part IV

Last Words

Chapter 14

One Step Beyond

14.1 Programming Problem

Motto: The best way to solve a problem is to run away from it as fast as possible.
(Anonymous)

We agree with the motto in the case of programming. This has been the subliminal message of most of this book, while we, of course, respect all the hard work done (and ongoing!) by object-oriented programming language designers, without which we would not be where we are today. At the same time, we still cannot seriously suggest throwing away programming as part of software development and rely instead on powerful analysis and design machinery. There are many reasons for this state of affairs. We can ignore the obvious political reasons of momentum: There is much vested interest in the programming industry. Instead, we should acknowledge that using only (OO) analysis and design does not produce a complete system. We see at least the following deficiencies:

- There are too few tools that support OO software development with only analysis and design, although these are rapidly evolving.

- A system typically requires a graphical user interface (GUI). Other machinery is required to develop that subsystem. "Gluing" the core logic with the GUI requires the skill, mind set, and tedium of programming. Annoying are the "tyrannical" demands by the GUI that impose a strict software framework on the overall software architecture.

- Having to make objects persistent creates another major headache that requires careful manipulation and the tedious development of another "glue" layer.

- A distributed system introduces yet another set of complexities, especially because the necessary infrastructure (CORBA, [55]) is less stable than desired. Noteworthy as well is the fact that a persistence component as well as a facilitator for interprocess communication may impose their own architectural frameworks. These force a developer to descend into quite murky areas to reconcile their demands.

- A new system may have to cooperate with an existing system, which typically causes the development of subtle wrapping and/or bridging components.

Initiatives such as OpenDoc and OLE2 are under way to demarcate once and for all encompassing software architectures that obviate the need to develop these pesky glue components time and again. However, at this point we are not convinced that these initiatives, or similar ones, have a solid foundation and will be accepted widely.

Hence, Part III of this book, which illustrates how to transform the analysis and the design models into a programming language, is unfortunately quite necessary. At the same time, we believe that much more automatic code generation can be done than is offered by extant OO CASE tools.

14.2   Effort Estimation Again

At the time of this writing we read in the *Communications of the ACM* [64]:

> ... it is surprisingly difficult to measure object systems. Reliable measurement units for predicting progress, assessing productivity, and evaluating cost are not currently available for OO designs and applications.

Although this book does not provide a complete answer, it is a step in the right direction. We recall our programme as sketched in Figure 1.2 on page 10. The postulated correlations in this figure would lead to derived correlations in Figure 1.3 on page 11, which is the rationale of downstream effort prediction based on upstream effort measurements. At this point we have support for some of the "horizontal" correlation arrows connecting product artifacts - see Figure 14.1 for a summary of the correlation coefficients reported in previous chapters - and we have support for "horizontal" correlation arrows connecting efforts inside the analysis phase - see again Figure 5.9 on page 218. At this point we have no empirical support for the "vertical" correlation arrows between product metrics on artifacts and the efforts to develop these artifacts. This is certainly an area for further study. It goes without saying that controlled studies in this realm are quite costly and are as yet beyond our means.

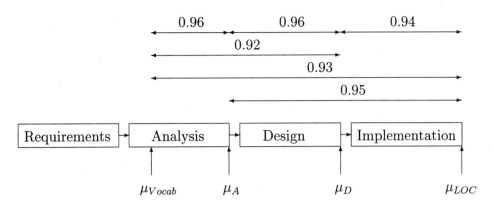

Figure 14.1: Summary of the correlations we measured between product metrics applied to the vocabulary entries in the analysis model and the corresponding classes in analysis, design, and implementation for the Home Heating System.

Although we are pleased with the excellent correlation coefficients found for the product metrics, see again Figure 14.1, we are quite aware that the sample size is small. Repeat studies on a larger scale are required to confirm these findings.

Figure 14.1 reminds us that formal effort estimation based on product metrics has to wait until an initial fragment of the analysis has been completed. Estimates earlier in the life cycle are, of course, desired in practice. As an example, consider the situation where the development costs of a commercial product are critical and it is to be decided whether to proceed with the generation of an extensive requirements document based on a costly market study. It would be attractive to decide early whether a product is feasible at all given a reasonably accurate estimation of the development costs. Unfortunately, we have little to offer on this problem. Experience with similar projects is an obvious asset for producing a ballpark estimate. When several experts are available, they can engage in rounds of estimations, possibly looking separately at analysis, design, and implementation in order to obtain consensus. Object oriented-ness has little to offer here unless fine-grained estimation is done exploiting the micro processes that we presented in previous chapters.

14.3   Quality Metrics

By now it should be clear that we aimed our product metrics at effort estimation and that we ignored their application to assess the quality of artifacts. The main reason is that OO quality metrics are still in their infancy. There are two problems:

1. What should be measured? The complexity of a class inheritance graph? The complexity of class interaction graph? The complexity of state charts? The complexity of member functions?

2. What are good and bad value ranges? Is it good or bad that a class inherits 15 attributes, 55 states, and 280 transitions?

Some recent advances in this area are described in Appendix A. This area is ripe for aggressive research.

14.4   Testing Metrics

Quality assurance is creeping up in the life cycle. Traditionally, one distinguished between unit testing, integration testing, system testing for first-time deployment, and regression testing for the validation of newer versions. Better defined intermediate (executable) deliverables as the result of detailed micro processes permit to do quality assessments earlier. All the tricks of the trade of measuring error densities as a function of time, mutation rate of artifacts, and so on can be pushed up in the life cycle. This important topic is to be dealt with in another work.

14.5   Maintenance Metrics

Maintenance metrics is another area where fantasies can run wild by exploiting OO-ness. To mention a few metrics:

- Number of new classes after first release

- Number of complaint reports for a class

- Number of versions for a class after first release

- Number of errors for a member function

- Number of new member functions after first release

- Number of discarded member functions after first release

- Number of discarded classes after first release

All of these measures can be transformed into functions over time, (pseudo) derivatives can be defined, (moving) averages can be calculated, and so on. Again, we leave this for another work.

14.6 Effort Prediction Curve Balls

A fundamental assumption in this book has been stability. Although every project is unique and is to be handled by a unique team (one cannot step in the same river twice), we have assumed that the unique features are small in comparison with the common features of previous projects. This is the basis for prescribing a standard process and using analogy reasoning for effort estimation. Our fundamental assumption can be violated in many ways:

1. A project is for a new product in a new product stream and there is no overlap with previous products.

2. A "manual" development process is replaced by a process supported by a CASE tool.

3. The members of a team may have earlier development experiences, but have never used OO before.

4. A reuse library is obtained.

Obviously, in these situations, we have to fall back onto a data-gathering mode to provide baseline data to be used for future projects. In the meantime, we have to rely on gut-level guesses.

14.7 In Closing

Software development remains a laborious activity. Although one doesn't get dirty hands, too often one has to drag things around repetitively, hammer things in place, struggle with stupid tools that have zero understanding of what one is trying to achieve; in short, it is too much of a hassle. We have no illusions: the metric business does not make things simpler right away. Collecting metric data by hand as we did for the examples in this book cannot be expected from overloaded developers.

Hence we look forward to CASE tool builders taking up the challenges.

Appendix A

Category Quality Metric

This appendix is the print version of a report that became available on the Internet in 1994. The author, Robert Martin, kindly granted permission to make it available for this book.[1]

A.1 Abstract

This paper describes a set of metrics that can be used to measure the quality of an object-oriented design in terms of the interdependence between the subsystems of that design. Designs that are highly interdependent tend to be rigid, unreusable, and hard to maintain. Yet interdependence is necessary if the subsystems of the design are to collaborate. Thus, some forms of dependency must be desirable, and other forms must be undesirable. This paper proposes a design pattern in which all the dependencies are of the desirable form. Finally, this paper describes a set of metrics that measure the conformance of a design to the desirable pattern.

A.2 Introduction

What is it about OO that makes designs more robust, more maintainable, and more reusable? This is a poignant question since there have been many recent examples where applications designed with so-called OO methods have turned out not to fulfill those claims. Are these qualities of robustness, maintainability, and reusability in-

---

[1]The title of the report is "OO Design Quality Metrics: An Analysis of Dependencies". Robert Martin, Object Mentor, can be reached at rmartin@oma.com.

trinsic to OOD? If so, why don't all applications designed with OOD have them? If not, what other characteristics does a object-oriented design require in order to have these desirable qualities?

This paper presents the case that simply using objects to model an application is insufficient to gain robust, maintainable, and reusable designs, that there are other attributes of a design that are required, and that these attributes are based on a pattern of interdependencies between the subsystems of the design that support communications within the design, isolate reusable elements from nonreusable elements, and block the propagation of change due to maintenance.

Moreover, this paper presents a set of metrics that can easily be applied to a design and that measure the conformance of that design to the desired pattern of dependencies. These metrics are *design quality* metrics. They provide information to designers regarding the ability of their design to survive change or to be reused.

Interested readers are referred to Martin [51] for a more in-depth look at these metrics and the design principles that they measure.

A.3   Dependency

What is it that makes a design rigid, fragile, and difficult to reuse? It is the interdependence of the subsystems within that design. A design is rigid if it cannot easily be changed. Such rigidity is due to the fact that a single change to heavily interdependent software begins a cascade of changes in dependent modules. When the extent of that cascade of change cannot be predicted by the designers or maintainers, the impact of the change cannot be estimated. This makes the cost of the change impossible to estimate. Faced with such unpredictability, managers become reluctant to authorize changes. Thus the design becomes rigid.

Fragility is the tendency of a program to break in many places when a single change is made. Often, the new problems are in areas that have no conceptual relationship with the area that was changed. Such fragility greatly decreases the credibility of the design and maintenance organization. Users and managers are unable to predict the quality of their product. Simple changes to one part of the application lead to failures in other parts that appear to be completely unrelated. Fixing those problems leads to even more problems, and the maintenance process begins to resemble a dog chasing its tail.

A design is difficult to reuse when the desirable parts of the design are highly dependent on other details which are not desired. Designers faced with the task of investigating the design to see if it can be reused in a different application may be impressed with how well the design would do in the new application. However, if the design is highly interdependent, the designers will also be daunted by the amount of work necessary to separate the desirable portion of the design from the other portions of the design that are undesirable. In most cases, such designs are not reused because the cost of the separation is deemed to be higher than the cost of redevelopment of the design.

A.4 Example: The Copy Program

A simple example may help to make this point. Consider a simple program that is to copy characters typed on a keyboard to a printer. Assume, furthermore, that the implementation platform does not have an operating system that supports device independence. Then we might conceive of a structure for this program that looks as shown in Figure A.1.

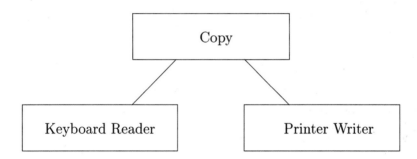

Figure A.1: Structure of the Copy program, with its two submodules.

There are three modules. The Copy module calls the other two. One can easily imagine a loop within the Copy module. The body of that loop calls the Read Keyboard module to fetch a character from the keyboard; it then sends that character to the Write Printer module, which prints the character.

The two low-level modules are nicely reusable. They can be used in many other programs to gain access to the keyboard and the printer. This is the same kind of reusability that we gain from subroutine libraries.

However, the Copy module is not reusable in any context that does not involve a keyboard or a printer. This is a shame since the intelligence of the system is maintained in this module. It is the Copy module that encapsulates a very interesting policy that we would like to reuse.

For example, consider a new program that copies keyboard characters to a disk file. Certainly, we would like to reuse the Copy module since it encapsulates the high-level policy that we need; i.e., it knows how to copy characters from a source to a sink. Unfortunately, the Copy module is dependent on the Write Printer module and so cannot be reused in the new context.

We could certainly modify the Copy module to give it the new desired functionality. We could add an *if* statement to its policy and have it select between the Write Printer module and the Write Disk module depending on some kind of flag. However, this adds new interdependencies to the system. As time goes on and more and more devices must participate in the copy program, the Copy module will be littered with *if/else* statements and will be dependent on many lower-level modules. It will eventually become rigid and fragile.

A.5 Inverting Dependencies with OOD

One way to characterize the problem above is to notice that the module that contains the high-level policy; i.e., the Copy module is dependent on its details. If we could find a way to make this module independent of the details that it controls, we could reuse it freely. We could produce other programs that used this module to copy characters from any input device to any output device. OOD gives us a mechanisms for performing this dependency inversion.

Consider the simple class diagram in Figure A.2.

Here we have a Copy class that contains an abstract Reader class and an abstract Writer class. One can easily imagine a loop within the Copy class which gets characters from its Reader and sends them to its Writer. Yet this Copy class does not depend at all on the Keyboard Reader nor the Printer Writer. Thus the dependencies have been inverted. Now the Copy class depends upon abstractions, and the detailed Readers and Writers depend on the same abstractions.

Now we can reuse the Copy class, independent of the Keyboard Reader and the Printer Writer. We can invent new kinds of Reader and Writer derivatives which we can supply to the Copy class. Moreover, no matter how many kinds of Readers and Writers are created, Copy will depend on none of them. There will be no interdependencies to make the program fragile or rigid.

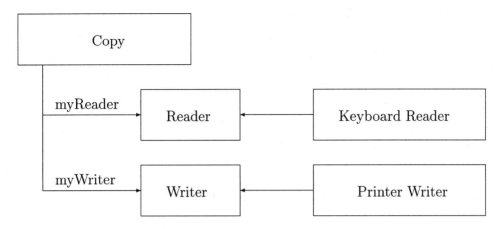

Figure A.2: The class Copy has attributes with as value domains two abstracted classes, Reader and Writer. These value domains have as subclasses Keyboard Reader and Printer Writer.

A.6 Good Dependencies

What makes the OO version of the copy program robust, maintainable, and reusable? It is its lack of interdependencies. Yet it does have some dependencies, and those dependencies do not interfere with those desirable qualities. Why not? Because the targets of those dependencies are extremely stable; i.e., they are unlikely to change.

Consider the nature of the Reader and Writer classes. In C++ they could be represented as follows:
```
class Writer {public: virtual void Write(char) = 0;};
class Reader {public: virtual char Read() = 0;};
```
These two classes are very unlikely to change. What forces exist that would cause them to change? Certainly, we could imagine some if we stretched our thinking a bit. But in the normal course of events, these classes are extremely stable.

Thus there are very few forces that could cause Copy to be changed. Copy is an example of the open/closed principle at work. Copy is open to be extended since we can create new versions of Readers and Writers for it to drive. Yet Copy is closed for modification since we do not have to modify it to achieve those extensions.

Thus we can say that a Good Dependency is a dependency on something that is very stable. The more stable the target of the dependency, the more Good the dependency is. By the same token a Bad Dependency is a dependency on something that is unstable. The more unstable the target of the dependency is, the more Bad the dependency is.

A.7   Stability

How does one achieve stability? Why, for example, are Reader and Writer so stable? Consider again the forces that could make them change. They depend on nothing at all, so a change from a dependee cannot ripple up to them and cause them to change. I call this characteristic *independence*. Independent classes are classes that do not depend on anything else.

Another reason that Reader and Writer are stable is that they are depended on by many other classes: Copy, Keyboard Reader, and Keyboard Writer among them. In fact, the more varieties of Reader and Writer exist, the more dependents these classes have. The more dependents they have, the harder it is to make changes to them. If we were to change Reader or Writer, we would have to change all the other classes that depended on them. Thus there is a great deal of force preventing us from changing these classes and enhancing their stability.

I call classes that are heavily depended on, *responsible*. Responsible classes tend to be stable because any change has a large impact.

The most stable classes of all are classes that are both independent and responsible. Such classes have no reason to change and lots of reasons not to change.

A.8   Class Categories: The Granule of Reuse and Release

Seldom can a class be reused in isolation. Copy provides a good example. It must be reused with the abstract Reader and Writer classes. It is generally true that a class has a set of collaborating classes from which it cannot easily be separated. To reuse such classes, one must reuse the entire group. Such a group of classes is highly cohesive, and Booch calls them a *class category*.

A class category (hereinafter referred to simply as a *category*) is a group of highly cohesive classes that obey the following three rules:

1. The classes within a category are closed together against any force of change. This means that if one class must change, all of the classes within the category are likely to change. If any of the classes are open to a certain kind of change, they are all open to that kind of change.

2. The classes within a category are reused together. They are strongly interdependent and cannot be separated from each other. Thus if any attempt is made

to reuse one class within the category, all the other classes must be reused with it.

3. The classes within a category share a common function or achieve a common goal.

These three rules are listed in order of importance. Rule 3 can be sacrificed for rule 2, which can, in turn, be sacrificed for rule 1.

If categories are to be reused, they must also be released and given release numbers. If this were not the case, reusers would not be able to rely on the stability of the reused categories since the authors might change it at any time. Thus the authors must provide releases of their categories and identify them with release numbers so that reusers can be assured that they can have access to versions of the category that will not be changed.

The dependencies between categories are the ones we want to manage. Since categories are both the granule of release and reuse, it stands to reason that the dependencies that we wish to manage are the dependencies between categories rather than the dependencies within categories. After all, within a category, classes are expected to be highly interdependent. Since all the classes within a category are reused at the same time, and since all classes in a category are closed against the same kinds of changes, the interdependence between them cannot do much harm.

Thus we can move our discussion of dependency up a level and discuss the independence, responsibility and stability of categories instead of classes. The categories with the highest stability are categories that are both independent and highly responsible, and dependencies upon stable categories are good dependencies.

A.9   Dependency Metrics

The responsibility, independence, and stability of a category can be measured by counting the dependencies that interact with that category. Three metrics have been identified:

Ca *Afferent Couplings*: The number of classes outside this category that depend upon classes within this category.

Ce *Efferent Couplings*: The number of classes outside this category that are depended on by classes inside this category.

I *Instability*: $(Ce/(Ca + Ce))$. This metric has the range [0,1]. I = 0 indicates a maximally stable category; I = 1 indicates a maximally instable category.

Not all categories should be stable.

If all the categories in a system were maximally stable, the system would be unchangeable. In fact, we want portions of the design to be flexible enough to withstand a significant amount of change. How can a category that is maximally stable (I = 0) be flexible enough to withstand change? The answer is to be found in the open/closed principle. This principle tells us that it is possible and desirable to create classes that are flexible enough to be extended without requiring modification. What kind of classes conform to this principle? Abstract classes.

Consider the Copy program again. The Reader and Writer classes are abstract classes. They are highly stable since they depend on nothing and are depended on by Copy and all its derivatives. Yet Reader and Writer can be extended, without modification, to deal with many different kinds of I/O devices.

Thus, if a category is to be stable, it should also consist of abstract classes so that it can be extended. Stable categories that are extensible are flexible and do not constrain the design.

If stable categories should be highly abstract, one might infer that instable categories should be highly concrete. In fact, this stands to reason. An abstract category must have dependents since there must be classes, outside the abstract category, that inherit from it and implement the missing pure interfaces. However, we do not want to encourage dependencies upon instable categories. Thus, instable categories should not be abstract; they should be concrete.

We can define a metric that measures the abstractness of a category as follows:

A *Abstractness*: (# abstract classes in category / total # of classes in category).
This metric range is [0,1]; 0 means concrete and 1 means completely abstract.

A.10   The Main Sequence

We are now in a position to define the relationship between stability (I) and abstractness (A). We can create a graph with A on the vertical axis and I on the horizontal axis. If we plot the two good kinds of categories on this graph, we will find the categories that are maximally stable and abstract at the upper left at (0,1). The categories that are maximally instable and concrete are at the lower right at (1,0).

But not all categories can fall into one of these two positions. Categories have degrees of abstraction and stability. For example, it is very common that one abstract class derives from another abstract class. The derivative is an abstraction that has a dependency. Thus, although it is maximally abstract, it will not be maximally stable. Its dependency will decrease its stability.

Consider a category with A = 0 and I = 0. This is a highly stable and concrete category. Such a category is not desirable because it is rigid, it cannot be extended because it is not abstract, and it is very difficult to change because of its stability.

Consider a category with A = 1 and I = 1. This category is also undesirable (perhaps impossible) because it is maximally abstract and yet has no dependents. It, too, is rigid because the abstractions are impossible to extend.

But what about a category with A = 0.5 and I = 0.5? This category is partially extensible because it is partially abstract. Moreover, it is partially stable, so that the extensions are not subject to maximal instability. Such a category seems balanced. Its stability is in balance with its abstractness.

Consider again the Abstract-Instability graph in Figure A.3. We can draw a line from (0,1) to (1,0). This line represents categories whose abstractness is balanced with stability. Because of its similarity to a graph used in astronomy, I call this line the "Main Sequence".

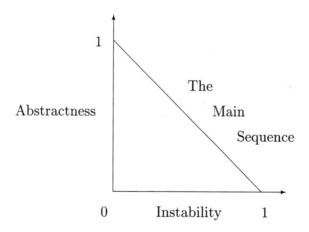

Figure A.3: Main Sequence. See the text for a discussion.

A category that sits on the main sequence is not too abstract for its stability, nor is it too instable for its abstractness. It has the right number of concrete and abstract classes in proportion to its efferent and afferent dependencies. Clearly, the most desirable positions for a category to hold are at one of the two endpoints of the main sequence. However, in my experience only about half the categories in a project can have such ideal characteristics. Those other categories have the best characteristics if they are on or close to the main sequence.

A.11   Distance from the Main Sequence

This leads us to our last metric. If it is desirable for categories to be on or close to the main sequence, we can create a metric which measures how far away a category is from this ideal.

D *Distance*: $|(A + I - 1)/\sqrt{2}|$. The perpendicular distance of a category from the main sequence. This metric ranges from $[0,0.707]$. (One can normalize this metric to range between $[0,1]$ by using the simpler form $|(A + I - 1)|$. I call this metric D').

Given this metric, a design can be analyzed for its overall conformance to the main sequence. The D metric for each category can be calculated. Any category that has a D value that is not near zero can be reexamined and restructured. In fact, this kind of analysis have been a great aid to the author in helping to define categories that are more reusable and less sensitive to change.

Statistical analysis of a design is also possible. One can calculate the mean and variance of all the D metrics within a design. One would expect a conformant design to have a mean and variance that were close to zero. The variance can be used to establish control limits which can identify categories that are exceptional in comparison to all the others.

A.12   Conclusion and Caveat

The metrics described herein measure the conformance of a design to a pattern of dependency and abstraction which the author feels is a good pattern. Experience has shown that certain dependencies are good and others are bad. This pattern reflects that experience. However, a metric is not a god; it is merely a measurement against an arbitrary standard. It is certainly possible that the standard chosen in this paper is appropriate only for certain applications and is not appropriate for others. It may also be that there are far better metrics that can be used to measure the quality of a design.

Thus, I would deeply regret it if anybody suddenly decided that all their designs must unconditionally be conformant to The Martin Metrics. I hope that designers will experiment with them, find out what is good and what is bad about them, and then communicate their findings to the rest of us.

Appendix B

Additional Code

B.1 Global Initialization File

B.1.1 Header file

```
#ifndef HHStypes_h
#define HHStypes_h

// basic standard libraries used

#include <time.h>
#include <stdlib.h>
#include <string.h>
#include <iostream.h>

class BlowerMotor;
class BlowerMotorDevice;
class Clock;
class ClockClient;
class DesiredTempInputDevice;
class DesiredTempInputDeviceDev;
class DisplayOut;
class FaultResetSwitch;
class FuelFlowSensor;
class FuelFlowSensorDevice;
class Furnace;
```

```
class FurnaceController;
class FurnaceMonitor;
class FurnaceStatusIndicator;
class HeatFlowRegulator;
class HeatSwitch;
class Ignitor;
class LivingPattern;
class OccupancyHistory;
class OccupancySensor;
class OccupancySensorDevice;
class OilValve;
class OpticalCombustionSensor;
class OpticalCombustionSensorDevice;
class Room;
class RoomTemperatureSensor;
class RoomTemperatureSensorDevice;
class SystemController;
class Timer;
class ValveController;
class WaterTemperatureSensor;
class WaterTemperatureSensorDevice;
class WaterValve;

#define hday 250
#define day hday * 2
#define week day * 7
#define blowerMotorOKspeed 20
#define waterTempOK 200
#define beta 40.0
#define alpha beta/hday
#define beta2 120.0

#endif
```

B.2 Desired Temperature Input Device

B.2.1 Header file

```
#ifndef DesiredTempInputDevice_H
#define DesiredTempInputDevice_H

#include "HHStypes.h"

class DesiredTempInputDevice {
private:
   int desiredTemperature;
public:
   DesiredTempInputDevice();
   void setDesiredTemperature(int);
   int getDesiredTemperature();
};
#endif
```

B.2.2 Code file

```
#include "DesiredTempInputDevice.h"

DesiredTempInputDevice::DesiredTempInputDevice()
     : desiredTemperature(50) {}
void DesiredTempInputDevice::setDesiredTemperature(int temp) {
     desiredTemperature = temp; }
int DesiredTempInputDevice::getDesiredTemperature() {
     return desiredTemperature; }
```

B.3 Desired Temperature Input Device Device

B.3.1 Header file

```
#ifndef DesiredTempInputDeviceDev_H
#define DesiredTempInputDeviceDev_H

#include "HHStypes.h"
```

```
#include "ClockClient.h"
#include "DesiredTempInputDevice.h"

class DesiredTempInputDeviceDev : public ClockClient {
private:
   Room* myRoom;
   DesiredTempInputDevice* myDesiredTempInputDevice;
   int foo(int); // provides desired temp at a particular time
public:
   DesiredTempInputDeviceDev(char*, Room*, DesiredTempInputDevice*);
   void tic(int);
};
#endif
```

B.3.2   Code file

```
#include "DesiredTempInputDeviceDev.h"
#include "Room.h"

DesiredTempInputDeviceDev::DesiredTempInputDeviceDev
      (char* nm, Room* rm, DesiredTempInputDevice* myDTID)
    : ClockClient(nm), myRoom(rm),
      myDesiredTempInputDevice(myDTID) {}
void DesiredTempInputDeviceDev::tic(int value) {
  myDesiredTempInputDevice->setDesiredTemperature(foo(value)); }
int DesiredTempInputDeviceDev::foo(int value) {
   char* st = myRoom->getName();
   if (st[0] == 'A') return 60; else
   if (st[0] == 'B') return 70; else
     { cout << "DesiredTempInputDeviceDev error \n";
       return -1; }; }
```

B.4   Display Out

B.4.1   Header file

```
#ifndef DisplayOut_H
```

```
#define DisplayOut_H

#include "HHStypes.h"

class DisplayOut {
public:
   DisplayOut();
   void displayFurnaceStatus(bool);
   void displayOccupancySensor(Room*, bool);
   void displayHeatSwitchStatus(bool);
   void displayRoomTemperatureSensor(Room*, float);
};
#endif
```

B.4.2   Code file

```
#include "DisplayOut.h"
#include "Room.h"

DisplayOut::DisplayOut() {}

void DisplayOut::displayFurnaceStatus(bool status) {
    cout << "DisplayOut::displayFurnaceStatus " << status <<"\n" ; }
void DisplayOut::displayOccupancySensor(Room* rm, bool value) {
//    cout << "DisplayOut::displayOccupancySensor Room " <<
//         rm->getName() << " " << value <<"\n" ;
}
void DisplayOut::displayHeatSwitchStatus(bool status) {
    cout << "DisplayOut::displayHeatSwitchStatus " <<
            status <<"\n"; }
void DisplayOut::displayRoomTemperatureSensor(Room* rm, float value) {
    cout << "DisplayOut::displayRoomTemperatureSensor Room "
        << rm->getName() << " " << value <<"\n"; }
```

B.5   Fault Reset Switch

B.5.1   Header file

```
#ifndef FaultResetSwitch_H
#define FaultResetSwitch_H

#include "HHStypes.h"

class FaultResetSwitch {
private:
   bool status;
   DisplayOut* theDisplayOut;
   SystemController* theSystemController;
public:
   FaultResetSwitch(SystemController*, DisplayOut*);
   void turnOn();
   void turnOff();
};
#endif
```

B.5.2   Code file

```
#include "FaultResetSwitch.h"
#include "DisplayOut.h"
#include "SystemController.h"

FaultResetSwitch::FaultResetSwitch(SystemController* sc,
                                   DisplayOut* displayOut)
     : theSystemController(sc), theDisplayOut(displayOut),
       status(false) {}
void FaultResetSwitch::turnOn() {
     if (!status) {
        status = true;
        theDisplayOut->displayHeatSwitchStatus(status);
        theSystemController->frOn(); }; }
void FaultResetSwitch::turnOff() {
     if (status) {
```

```
        status = false;
        theDisplayOut->displayHeatSwitchStatus(status);
        theSystemController->frOff(); }; }
```

B.6   Fuel Flow Sensor

B.6.1   Header file

```
#ifndef FuelFlowSensor_H
#define FuelFlowSensor_H

#include "HHStypes.h"

class FuelFlowSensor {
private:
    bool fuelFlow;
public:
    FuelFlowSensor();
    void setFuelFlow(bool);
    bool getFuelFlow();
};
#endif
```

B.6.2   Code file

```
#include "FuelFlowSensor.h"

FuelFlowSensor::FuelFlowSensor()
        : fuelFlow(false) {}
void FuelFlowSensor::setFuelFlow(bool value) {
    fuelFlow = value; }
bool FuelFlowSensor::getFuelFlow() {
    return fuelFlow; }
```

B.7   Fuel Flow Sensor Device

B.7.1   Header file

```
#ifndef FuelFlowSensorDevice_H
#define FuelFlowSensorDevice_H

#include "HHStypes.h"
#include "ClockClient.h"

class FuelFlowSensorDevice : public ClockClient {
private:
   FuelFlowSensor* myFuelFlowSensor;
   bool foo(int); // provides flow at a particular time
public:
   FuelFlowSensorDevice(char*, FuelFlowSensor*);
   void tic(int);
};
#endif
```

B.7.2   Code file

```
#include "FuelFlowSensorDevice.h"
#include "FuelFlowSensor.h"

FuelFlowSensorDevice::FuelFlowSensorDevice
        (char* nm, FuelFlowSensor* ffs)
     : ClockClient(nm), myFuelFlowSensor(ffs) {}
bool FuelFlowSensorDevice::foo(int) { return true; }
void FuelFlowSensorDevice::tic(int value) {
  myFuelFlowSensor->setFuelFlow(foo(value)); }
```

B.8   Furnace Controller

B.8.1   Header file

```
#ifndef FurnaceController_H
#define FurnaceController_H
```

```
#include "HHStypes.h"

class FurnaceController {
private:
   bool systemControlStatus;
   bool needsHeatStatus;
   Furnace* theFurnace;
public:
   FurnaceController(Furnace*);
   void disable();
   void enable();
   void shutdown();
   void startup();
};
#endif
```

B.8.2   Code file

```
#include "FurnaceController.h"
#include "Furnace.h"

FurnaceController::FurnaceController(Furnace* furnace)
      : theFurnace(furnace),
        systemControlStatus(false),
        needsHeatStatus(false) {}
void FurnaceController::disable() {
    if (systemControlStatus) {
       systemControlStatus = false;
       if (needsHeatStatus) {
          cout << "FurnaceController Disable \n";
          theFurnace->shutdown(); }; }; }
void FurnaceController::enable() {
    if (!systemControlStatus) {
       systemControlStatus = true;
       if (needsHeatStatus) {
          cout << "FurnaceController Enable \n";
          theFurnace->startup(); }; }; }
```

```
void FurnaceController::shutdown() {
    if (needsHeatStatus) {
        needsHeatStatus = false;
        if (systemControlStatus) {
            cout << "FurnaceController Shutdown \n";
            theFurnace->shutdown(); }; }; }
void FurnaceController::startup() {
    if (!needsHeatStatus) {
        needsHeatStatus = true;
        if (systemControlStatus) {
            cout << "FurnaceController Startup \n";
            theFurnace->startup(); }; }; }
```

B.9   Ignitor

B.9.1   Header file

```
#ifndef Ignitor_H
#define Ignitor_H

#include "HHStypes.h"

class Ignitor {
public:
    void ignite();
};
#endif
```

B.9.2   Code file

```
#include "Ignitor.h"

void Ignitor::ignite() {}
```

B.10 OilValve

B.10.1 Header file

```
#ifndef OilValve_H
#define OilValve_H

#include "HHStypes.h"

class OilValve {
private:
   bool status;
public:
   OilValve();
   void open();
   void close();
};
#endif
```

B.10.2 Code file

```
#include "OilValve.h"

OilValve::OilValve() : status(false) {}
void OilValve::open() {
    if (!status) status = true; }
void OilValve::close() {
    if (status) status = false; }
```

B.11 Optical Combustion Sensor

B.11.1 Header file

```
#ifndef OpticalCombustionSensor_H
#define OpticalCombustionSensor_H

#include "HHStypes.h"
```

```
class OpticalCombustionSensor {
private:
   bool combustion;
public:
   OpticalCombustionSensor();
   void setCombustion(bool);
   bool getCombustion();
};
#endif
```

B.11.2   Code file

```
#include "OpticalCombustionSensor.h"

OpticalCombustionSensor::OpticalCombustionSensor()
     : combustion(false) {}
void OpticalCombustionSensor::setCombustion(bool value) {
     combustion = value; }
bool OpticalCombustionSensor::getCombustion() {
     return combustion; }
```

B.12   Optical Combustion Sensor Device

B.12.1   Header file

```
#ifndef OpticalCombustionSensorDevice_H
#define OpticalCombustionSensorDevice_H

#include "HHStypes.h"
#include "ClockClient.h"
#include "OpticalCombustionSensor.h"

class OpticalCombustionSensorDevice : public ClockClient {
private:
   OpticalCombustionSensor* myOpticalCombustionSensor;
   bool foo(int); // provides combustion at a particular time
public:
```

```
    OpticalCombustionSensorDevice(char*, OpticalCombustionSensor*);
    void tic(int);
};
#endif
```

B.12.2 Code file

```
#include "OpticalCombustionSensorDevice.h"
#include "OpticalCombustionSensor.h"

OpticalCombustionSensorDevice::OpticalCombustionSensorDevice
        (char* nm, OpticalCombustionSensor* ocs) :
            ClockClient(nm), myOpticalCombustionSensor(ocs) {}
void OpticalCombustionSensorDevice::tic(int value) {
    myOpticalCombustionSensor->setCombustion(foo(value)); }
bool OpticalCombustionSensorDevice::foo(int value) { return true; }
```

B.13 Room Temperature Sensor

B.13.1 Header file

```
#ifndef RoomTemperatureSensor_H
#define RoomTemperatureSensor_H

#include "HHStypes.h"

class RoomTemperatureSensor {
private:
    float currentTemperature;
    DisplayOut* theDisplayOut;
    Room* myRoom;
public:
    RoomTemperatureSensor();
    void setDisplayOut(DisplayOut*, Room*);
    void setCurrentTemperature(float);
    int getCurrentTemperature();
    float getTemp();
```

```
};
#endif
```

B.13.2   Code file

```
#include "RoomTemperatureSensor.h"
#include "DisplayOut.h"

RoomTemperatureSensor::RoomTemperatureSensor()
      : currentTemperature(50.0) {}
void RoomTemperatureSensor::setDisplayOut(DisplayOut* dO, Room* rm) {
    theDisplayOut = dO;
    myRoom = rm; };
void RoomTemperatureSensor::setCurrentTemperature(float value) {
    currentTemperature = value;
    theDisplayOut->displayRoomTemperatureSensor(myRoom, value); }
int RoomTemperatureSensor::getCurrentTemperature() {
    return (int) currentTemperature; }
float RoomTemperatureSensor::getTemp() { return currentTemperature; }
```

B.14   Room Temperature Sensor Device

B.14.1   Header file

```
#ifndef RoomTemperatureSensorDevice_H
#define RoomTemperatureSensorDevice_H

#include "HHStypes.h"
#include "ClockClient.h"

class RoomTemperatureSensorDevice : public ClockClient {
private:
    Room* myRoom;
    RoomTemperatureSensor* myRoomTemperatureSensor;
    float foo(int); // provides temperature at a particular time
public:
    RoomTemperatureSensorDevice(char*, Room*, RoomTemperatureSensor*);
```

```
    void tic(int);
};
#endif
```

B.14.2 Code file

```
#include "RoomTemperatureSensorDevice.h"
#include "RoomTemperatureSensor.h"
#include "Room.h"

RoomTemperatureSensorDevice::RoomTemperatureSensorDevice
      (char* nm, Room* rm, RoomTemperatureSensor* myRTS)
    : ClockClient(nm), myRoom(rm), myRoomTemperatureSensor(myRTS) {}
float RoomTemperatureSensorDevice::foo(int value ) {
      float oldTemp = myRoomTemperatureSensor->getTemp();
      bool heating = myRoom->isHeating();
      int index = value % day;
      float outside = ((index <= hday) ?
                        alpha * index + beta :
                        -alpha * index + beta2 );
      float newTemp = oldTemp +
            (outside - oldTemp) * 0.01 +
            ( heating ? 0.5 : 0.0);
      return newTemp; }
void RoomTemperatureSensorDevice::tic(int value) {
  myRoomTemperatureSensor->setCurrentTemperature(foo(value)); }
```

B.15   SET

B.15.1   Header file

```
#ifndef SET_H
#define SET_H

#include "HHStypes.h"

template <class T> class Pair {
```

```
private:
    T* first;
    Pair<T>* next;
public:
    Pair(T* e, Pair* p) : first(e), next(p) {};
    T* elem() { return first; };
    Pair<T>* tail() { return next; };
    void rplacd(Pair<T>* p) { next = p; };
};

template <class T> class SET {
private:
    Pair<T>* list;
    int siz;
    T* el;
    int x;
    void (T::*foox)();
    void (T::*foox1)(int);
    bool iterating;
    bool copied;
    Pair<T>* listCopy;
    Pair<T>* lx;
    Pair<T>* copyList(Pair<T>* in) {
        if (0 == in) return 0;  else
        return new Pair<T>(in->elem(), copyList(in->tail())); };
    void delList(Pair<T>* in) {
        if (0 != in) {
            delList(in->tail());
            delete in; }; };
public:
    SET() : siz(0), list(0), iterating(false), copied(false),
            listCopy(0) {};
    bool empty() { return (siz == 0) ; };
    int size() { return siz ; };
    bool in1(Pair<T>* lis) {
        if (0 == lis)
            return false ; else
        if (el == lis->elem())
```

```
                 return true; else
                 return in1(lis->tail()); };
   bool in(T* elemx) {
        el = elemx;
        if (copied) lx = listCopy; else
        if (iterating) {
           copied = true;
           listCopy = copyList(list);
           lx = listCopy; } else
        lx = list;
        return in1(lx); };
   void add(T* elx) {
        if (!in(elx)) {
           siz++;
           if (copied) {
              Pair<T>* p1 = new Pair<T>(elx, listCopy);
              listCopy = p1; } else {
              Pair<T>* p2 = new Pair<T>(elx, list);
              list = p2; }; }; };
   void delet1(Pair<T>* lis) {
        Pair<T>* p1 = lis->tail();
        if (el == p1->elem()) {
           lis->rplacd(p1->tail());
           delete p1; } else
        delet1(p1); };
   void delet(T* elemx) {
        if (in(elemx)) {
           siz--;
           if (copied) {
              if (elemx == listCopy->elem()) {
                 Pair<T>* p1 = listCopy;
                 listCopy = listCopy->tail(); delete p1; } else
                 { el = elemx; delet1(listCopy); }; } else
           if (elemx == list->elem()) {
              Pair<T>* p2 = list;
              list = list->tail();
              delete p2; } else
           { el = elemx; delet1(list); }; }; };
```

```
    void fEE(Pair<T>* lis) {
        if (!(0 == lis)) {
            el = lis->elem();
            (el->*foox)();
            fEE(lis->tail()); }; };
    void forEachElement(void (T::*foo)()) {
        foox = foo;
        iterating = true;
        fEE(list);
        iterating = false;
        if (copied) {
            copied = false;
            delList(list);
            list = listCopy; }; };
    void fEE1(Pair<T>* lis) {
        if (!(0 == lis)) {
            el = lis->elem();
            (el->*foox1)(x);
            fEE1(lis->tail()); }; };
    void forEachElement1(void (T::*fooy)(int), int y) {
        cout << "forEachElement1 -- size: " << siz << "\n";
        x = y;
        foox1 = fooy;
        iterating = true;
        fEE1(list);
        iterating = false;
        if (copied) {
            copied = false;
            delList(list);
            list = listCopy; }; };
  };
#endif
```

B.16 Water Temperature Sensor

B.16.1 Header file

```
#ifndef WaterTemperatureSensor_H
#define WaterTemperatureSensor_H

#include "HHStypes.h"

class WaterTemperatureSensor {
private:
   int currentTemperature;
public:
   WaterTemperatureSensor();
   void setCurrentTemperature(int);
   int getCurrentTemperature();
};
#endif
```

B.16.2 Code file

```
#include "WaterTemperatureSensor.h"

WaterTemperatureSensor::WaterTemperatureSensor()
      : currentTemperature(50) {}
void WaterTemperatureSensor::setCurrentTemperature(int value) {
      currentTemperature = value; }
int WaterTemperatureSensor::getCurrentTemperature() {
      return currentTemperature; }
```

B.17 Water Temperature Sensor Device

B.17.1 Header file

```
#ifndef WaterTemperatureSensorDevice_H
#define WaterTemperatureSensorDevice_H

#include "HHStypes.h"
```

```
#include "ClockClient.h"

class WaterTemperatureSensorDevice : public ClockClient {
private:
   WaterTemperatureSensor* myWaterTemperatureSensor;
   int foo(int); // provides temperature at a particular time
public:
   WaterTemperatureSensorDevice(char*, WaterTemperatureSensor*);
   void tic(int);
};
#endif
```

B.17.2   Code file

```
#include "WaterTemperatureSensorDevice.h"
#include "WaterTemperatureSensor.h"

WaterTemperatureSensorDevice::WaterTemperatureSensorDevice
         (char* nm, WaterTemperatureSensor* myWTS)
    : ClockClient(nm), myWaterTemperatureSensor(myWTS) {}
void WaterTemperatureSensorDevice::tic(int value) {
  myWaterTemperatureSensor->setCurrentTemperature(foo(value)); }
int WaterTemperatureSensorDevice::foo(int value) { return 300; }
```

B.18   Water Valve

B.18.1   Header file

```
#ifndef WaterValve_H
#define WaterValve_H

#include "HHStypes.h"

class WaterValve {
private:
   bool status;
public:
```

```
    WaterValve();
    void open();
    void close();
};
#endif
```

B.18.2   Code file

```
#include "WaterValve.h"

WaterValve::WaterValve()
     : status(false) {}
void WaterValve::open() {
     if (!status) status = true; }
void WaterValve::close() {
     if (status) status = false; }
```

B.19   Main Program

```
#include "HHStypes.h"

#include "BlowerMotor.h"
#include "Clock.h"
#include "DisplayOut.h"
#include "FaultResetSwitch.h"
#include "FuelFlowSensor.h"
#include "FuelFlowSensorDevice.h"
#include "Furnace.h"
#include "FurnaceController.h"
#include "FurnaceMonitor.h"
#include "FurnaceStatusIndicator.h"
#include "HeatFlowRegulator.h"
#include "HeatSwitch.h"
#include "LivingPattern.h"
#include "OpticalCombustionSensor.h"
#include "OpticalCombustionSensorDevice.h"
#include "Room.h"
```

```
#include "SET.h"
#include "Timer.h"
#include "OccupancyHistory.h"
#include "OccupancySensor.h"
#include "OccupancySensorDevice.h"
#include "SystemController.h"
#include "ValveController.h"
#include "WaterValve.h"

main() {
  Clock theClock;
  DisplayOut* theDisplayOut = new DisplayOut;
  FurnaceStatusIndicator theFurnaceStatusIndicator(theDisplayOut);
  ValveController theValveController;
  FuelFlowSensor theFuelFlowSensor;
  FuelFlowSensorDevice theFuelFlowSensorDevice("FFSD",
                                                &theFuelFlowSensor);
  theClock.addClient(&theFuelFlowSensorDevice);

  OpticalCombustionSensor theOpticalCombustionSensor;
  OpticalCombustionSensorDevice
      theOpticalCombustionSensorDevice("OCSD",
                                        &theOpticalCombustionSensor);
  theClock.addClient(&theOpticalCombustionSensorDevice);

  FurnaceMonitor theFurnaceMonitor
      ("FM", &theClock, &theFuelFlowSensor,
       &theOpticalCombustionSensor);
  Furnace theFurnace(&theClock, &theFurnaceMonitor,
                     &theValveController,
                     &theFurnaceStatusIndicator);
  FurnaceController theFurnaceController(&theFurnace);
  SystemController theSystemController(&theFurnaceController);
  HeatSwitch theHeatSwitch(&theSystemController, theDisplayOut);
  FaultResetSwitch theFaultResetSwitch(&theSystemController,
                                        theDisplayOut);

  theFurnaceMonitor.setFaultResetSwitch(&theFaultResetSwitch);
```

```
    HeatFlowRegulator theHeatFlowRegulator(&theValveController,
                                           &theFurnaceController);

    Room aRoom("A", &theHeatFlowRegulator, theDisplayOut, &theClock);
    theClock.addClient(&aRoom);
    Room bRoom("B", &theHeatFlowRegulator, theDisplayOut, &theClock);
    theClock.addClient(&bRoom);

    cout << "\n HHS Welcomes you!\n";
    int inx;
    for (inx = 0; inx <= 1; inx++) theClock.ticToc();
    theHeatSwitch.turnOn();
    theFaultResetSwitch.turnOn();
    for (inx = 2; inx <= 320; inx++) theClock.ticToc();
}
```

Appendix C

Fragments of Example Output

C.1   Initialization and the First Two Cycles

```
Clock::addClient FFSD
Clock::addClient OCSD
Clock::addClient BMD
Clock::addClient WTSD
Clock::addClient RTSD
Clock::addClient OSD
Clock::addClient DTID
Clock::addClient A
Clock::addClient RTSD
Clock::addClient OSD
Clock::addClient DTID
Clock::addClient B

HHS Welcomes you!
Clock time ******************** 1
forEachElement1 -- size: 12
Room B heating 0 td 50 temp 50 needsHeat 0
DisplayOut::displayRoomTemperatureSensor Room B 49.9032
Room A heating 0 td 50 temp 50 needsHeat 0
DisplayOut::displayRoomTemperatureSensor Room A 49.9032
Clock time ******************** 2
forEachElement1 -- size: 12
```

```
Room B heating 0 td 70 temp 49 needsHeat 1
HeatFlowRegulator register room B
ValveController add room B
DisplayOut::displayRoomTemperatureSensor Room B 49.8106
Room A heating 0 td 60 temp 49 needsHeat 1
HeatFlowRegulator register room A
ValveController add room A
DisplayOut::displayRoomTemperatureSensor Room A 49.8106
DisplayOut::displayHeatSwitchStatus 1
DisplayOut::displayHeatSwitchStatus 1
SystemController::frOn
FurnaceController Enable
Furnace::startup
Furnace::turnOnBlower
Clock::addClient Timer
```

C.2   Cycle 10 and 11

```
Clock time ******************** 10
forEachElement1 -- size: 13
Clock::removeClient Timer
Furnace::checkRPMBlowerMotor
Furnace::turnOpenOilValve
Furnace::ignite
FurnaceMonitor::enable
Clock::addClient FM
Clock::addClient Timer
Room B heating 0 td 70 temp 49 needsHeat 1
DisplayOut::displayRoomTemperatureSensor Room B 49.2146
Room A heating 0 td 60 temp 49 needsHeat 1
DisplayOut::displayRoomTemperatureSensor Room A 49.2146
BlowerMotorDevice::tic currentRPM 21
Clock time ******************** 11
forEachElement1 -- size: 14
Clock::removeClient Timer
Furnace::openWaterValves
ValveController::furnaceOn
```

```
Room::openValve A
Room::openValve B
DisplayOut::displayFurnaceStatus 1
FurnaceMonitor::tic 11
Room B heating 1 td 70 temp 49 needsHeat 1
DisplayOut::displayRoomTemperatureSensor Room B 49.6577
Room A heating 1 td 60 temp 49 needsHeat 1
DisplayOut::displayRoomTemperatureSensor Room A 49.6577
BlowerMotorDevice::tic currentRPM 21
```

C.3 Cycle 41

```
Clock time ******************** 41
forEachElement1 -- size: 13
FurnaceMonitor::tic 41
Room B heating 1 td 70 temp 62 needsHeat 1
DisplayOut::displayRoomTemperatureSensor Room B 62.4288
Room A heating 1 td 60 temp 62 needsHeat 0
HeatFlowRegulator Unregister room A
ValveController delete room A
Room::closeValve A
DisplayOut::displayRoomTemperatureSensor Room A 61.9288
BlowerMotorDevice::tic currentRPM 21
```

C.4 Cycle 66

```
Clock time ******************** 66
forEachElement1 -- size: 13
FurnaceMonitor::tic 66
Room B heating 1 td 70 temp 72 needsHeat 0
HeatFlowRegulator Unregister room B
ValveController delete room B
Room::closeValve B
FurnaceController Shutdown
Furnace::shutdown
Clock::removeClient Timer
```

```
FurnaceMonitor::disable
Clock::removeClient FM
Clock::addClient Timer
DisplayOut::displayRoomTemperatureSensor Room B 71.9309
Room A heating 0 td 60 temp 60 needsHeat 0
DisplayOut::displayRoomTemperatureSensor Room A 60.933
BlowerMotorDevice::tic currentRPM 21
```

Glossary

Action A terminating operation that causes a local change in state or that invokes a service request in an external object.

Analysis The elaboration of a system's requirements in terms of a precise, usually graphical, paradigm specific formalism.

Architecture In a (software) system, the structure that connects the top-level subsystems.

In a logical architecture, the subsystems represent functional components and the structure typically reflects interaction dependencies.

In a physical software architecture, the components - called clusters in the design - correspond with distinct processes, possibly residing on different processors. See also page 77.

Attribute A function on the set of instances of a class to a value domain, which can be a set of instances of a class or a set of nonclass elements. An attribute has a unique attribute name, sometimes called a role name.

CASE Computer-Aided Software Engineering.

Class A concept that describes the minimal set of properties - structural and behavioral - that are shared by intended items in a collection (the object instances of that class).[1]

Class interaction diagram A directed labeled graph where the nodes are classes, and a directed labeled vertex between, say, $C1$ and $C2$ represents "each instance of $C1$ knows an instance in $C2$ and is prepared to invoke an operation in $C2$

---

[1] A class is certainly *not* "a set of objects that share a common structure and a common behavior" as defined by Booch [12, 13]; although it is certainly the case that the collection of instances of a class is a set of varying size over time.

whose name is represented by the label". An operation can be a service request or a one-way invocation.

Clean-room macro process A special case of the spiral macro development process. Each iteration, containing analysis, design, implementation, test, and documentation, lasts less than a month. This applies when the functionality of a target system decomposes into nested subsets. See page 6 for details.

Cluster A component in the physical architecture of the design that will be realized as a process in the implementation.

Cohesion The degree to which the tasks performed by a unit (e.g., a class) are functionally related. See page 354 for an attempt to operationalize this concept.

Concurrent processing Two processes are concurrent when the second one starts before the first one terminates, while only one executes at the time. See also Parallel processing.

Coupling A measure of interdependence between units, which can be classes, modules in a program, etc. Coupling can be defined in terms of the fan-in and fan-out of a unit, see also page 121.

Cyclomatic complexity A metric based on a measure in the theory of graphs: it calculates the number of potential paths through an algorithm; see McCabe [52]. Following Jalote [42], we simplify the definition to the number of decisions plus one.

Design The construction of a "blueprint" solution that conforms to the analysis description of a target system. Performance requirements, among others, may not be demonstrably satisfied by the design output.

Design pattern Systematically names, motivates, and explains a general design that addresses a recurring design problem in OO systems. It describes the problem, the solution, when to apply the solution, and its consequences. It also gives implementation hints and examples. The solution is a general arrangement of objects and classes that solves the problem. The solution is customized and implemented to solve the problem in a particular context. (This definition is taken from [28].)

Ensemble An object representing a subsystem that has the following features:

1. An ensemble has other objects and/or subensembles as its functional components.

2. A constituent is a part of at least one and at most one ensemble (thus the constituent-ensemble relationship is *not* transitive).

3. An ensemble mediates all interaction between constituents and entities outside the ensemble.

4. Constituents may interact among each other.

5. An ensemble is responsible for the construction and deletion of constituents.

Event A one-way communication between the issuing object and the audience of the event.

Fan-in/out Fan-in is the number of calls to a given unit.
Fan-out is the number of calls from a given unit.

Fountain macro process A macro development process where at any time during the development a new insight can lead to a return to the analysis phase or even to the requirements phase. See Henderson-Sellers and Edwards [35].

Function points A synthetic metric that can be applied at the requirements stage to estimate the size of a system. It is mainly applied to management information systems (MISs). The original formula with its weights is:
function points =
number of inputs * 4 +
number of outputs * 5 +
number of enquiries * 4 +
number of master files * 10 +
number of interfaces * 7
For more details, see page 15 and Albrecht and Gaffney [3].

Guard On a transition, a condition to be satisfied and/or an event that has to occur (or that has occurred when events can be queued). The guard must be satisfied for the transition to fire.

GUI Graphical User Interface.

Halstead effort Defined as Halstead [31]:

$$(n1 * N2 * (N1 + N2) * log_2(n1 + n2))/(2 * n2)$$

where $n1$ is the number of unique operators, $n2$ is the number of unique operands, $N1$ is the number of operator occurrences, and $N2$ is the number of operand occurrences.

IFPUG International Function Point User Groups.

Implementation The realization of a design in a programming language (or languages) so that all requirements are satisfied.

Inheritance The class Q inherits from the class P if and only if:

1. Every attribute A of P is an attribute of Q.
2. Every constraint C of P is a constraint of Q.
3. Every state S of P is a state of Q.
4. Every transition T of P is a transition of Q, while it is allowed in Q to weaken a guard in a transition and/or the strengthen an effect.
5. When P appears in a relationship, Q can appear in the same role as well.
6. Q formulates an additional restriction.

See also Multiple inheritance.

Instance An object seen within the context of its associated, unique, class.

Interaction diagram An alternative way to depict scenario diagrams. An instance of a class is represented by a vertical line with a characterization of the instance at the top. A numbered link in the scenario diagram is represented by an arrowed horizontal line that starts and ends at the vertical lines of the originator and the target of the interaction, respectively. The number of the link corresponds with the vertical ordering of the horizontal lines (with the first one at the top) and hence corresponds with the ordering in the originating script.

LOC Lines Of Code.

Maintenance Removing imperfections of an implementation and/or design, or the modification of a system to accommodate changed requirements.

Maintenance burden For a unit, a size metric. This metric is defined for the following units:

- Member function (or its design equivalent):
  $\mu_{CM} = 3.42 * ln(E) + 0.23 * V(g') + 16.2 * ln(LOC) - 0.99 * CM$ See
  Section 8.2.4 on page 274 for details.

- Class(design or implementation) in isolation:
  $\mu^4_{ClassMB}(class) =$
  $c_1 * \#\ local\ member\ variables +$
  $c_2 * \#\ imported\ member\ variables +$
  $c_3 * \left(\sum_{local} \mu_{CM}(member Function_{local})\right) +$
  $c_4 * \left(\sum_{imported} \mu_{CM}(member Function_{imported})\right)$

- Class as part of a system:
  $\mu_{systemContext}(class) = c_1 * \mu_{fanIn}(class) + c_2 * \mu_{fanOut}(class) + w(class)$
  where $w(class)$ is a term that is high for a class whose instances are explicitly generated and deleted.

- System (without class interaction complexity):
  $\mu^1_{system} = \sum_i(\alpha * \mu^4_{ClassMB}(class_i) + \beta * \mu_{systemContext}(class_i))$

- System (with class interaction complexity):
  $\mu^2_{system} = \mu^1_{system} + VG(system)$
  where $VG(system)$ measures, for example, the cyclomatic complexity of the class interaction graph.

Method, software development

- Well-defined core concepts for which there exist agreed upon notations; to be used in describing domain artifacts and models of the intended system from different perspectives.

- A process that outlines the steps for utilizing core concepts, which defines intermediate deliverables, and that characterizes dependencies between these deliverables.

- A criterion for measuring progress which can indicate that a development (sub)activity has been completed.

Methodology Study of methods. The secondary meaning is *method*. We see no reason, beyond pomposity, to use *methodology* in the secondary meaning.[2]

---

[2]Similarly, we are not thrilled with the current abundant usage of *technology*; *techniques* is often a better term.

Metric A function with, as range, a domain of interest and, as value domain, the nonnegative numbers. A classification according to the domains in our field:

1. Effort metrics measure the human, machine, etc. resources spent during a particular time period on a specific set of development tasks.

2. Static product metrics measure the volume and complexity of artifacts produced in the life cycle.

3. Dynamic product metrics measure the volume of fixed and transient objects of an executing target system and the complexity of the communication graph of the objects.

A teleological classification:

1. Measurement of actual development costs for a particular time period, possibly qualified per type of development activity

2. Measurement of development fragments in order to predict/estimate future subsequent development costs

3. Measurement of quality aspects in order to predict/estimate subsequent development costs to achieve acceptable product quality

4. Measurement of development aspects to enhance a general awareness of "where we are and where we are going"

Multiple inheritance Occurs when a class is engaged in more than one inheritance relationships; i.e., has more than one superclass.

Object A conceptual entity that:

1. Is identifiable

2. Has features which span a local state space

3. Has operators that can change the status of the system locally, while these operations may induce invocations of operations in peer objects

An analysis object has the additional requirement that it refers to a thing that is identifiable by the users of the target system - either a tangible thing or a mental construct.

OOA Object-oriented analysis, an analysis method that uses objects as a key concept and which usually prepares for an object-oriented design.

OOD Object-oriented design, a design method that uses objects as a key construct and which usually prepares for an object-oriented implementation.

OOP Object-oriented program(ming).

Parallel processing A period when two processes execute at the same time. See also Concurrent processing.

Polymorphism An operation is polymorphic when its semantics depend on the context of its invocation. For example, the operation *foo* can have different effects in different peer subclasses that inherit from a common superclass. Polymorphism existed pre-OO. A print command that can handle integers, reals, booleans, and strings is an example of a polymorphic operation. The + operation as used by mathematicians for addition of natural numbers, integers, reals, complex numbers, quaternions, vectors, matrices, elements of Abelian groups, and so on is a noncomputer language example.

Process "A series of actions or operations conducive to an end", Webster's [81].

- A macro development process is a generic process that prescribes the scheduling of requirements gathering, analysis, design, implementation, and test activities.
- A micro development process is a paradigm-specific generic process that prescribes analysis, design, implementation, and testing activities.
- A micro process should be compatible with any macro process.
- The combination of a macro process and micro processes must be instantiated into a development plan.

Relationship Mathematically, a subset in the space generated by the Cartesian product of some domains, where a domain can be the extension of a class or of "plain" data domain such as numbers, strings, etc.
An instance of a relationship is an element of the subset and can be represented by a tuple of entities that reside in the constituting domains.

Relationship, acquaintance A binary relationship between objects that is used for object communication so that a sender object knows the identity of a recipient object.

Requirements gathering The demarcation of what a target system is supposed to do.

Scenario An extension of a use case by filling in "obvious" actions that decompose "large" operations, where the intermediate actions involve intermediate objects and/or subsystems.

Although scenarios are extensions of use cases, they cannot refine into details that entail design commitments.

Scenario diagram A "rewritten" version of a scenario in terms of the formally developed analysis classes. The nodes in a scenario diagram are (prototypical) instances of classes. A numbered, directed link between these instances stands for an operation invocation that corresponds with a transition in the end-of link instance. The number on the link is the sequence number of the operation event and should correspond with a line number in the scenario.

SEI Software Engineering Institute, associated with Carnegie-Mellon University.

Spiral macro process A macro process with multiple iterations of analysis, design, and implementation. A risk analysis precedes each cycle and determines the set of issues to be addressed in an iteration. See Boehm [11].

State A mode of being. A passive state represents a state in which nothing changes except the passage of time. A state is active when it has an interruptible executing process.

Subclass A class Q is a subclass of the class P if Q inherits from P.

Substitutability The substitutability dictum proclaims that a subclass instance can be substituted in the position where a superclass instance is expected *and* that the substituted instance behaves consistently with the behavior of any superclass instance in that position.

Subsystem A constituting component of a system.

Superclass A class P is a superclass if there is a class Q that inherits from P.

Transition An object leaving a state, performing (optionally) an action or multiple actions, optionally creating events targeted for other objects and entering a successor state, which can be the same state as the originating state.

Transition network A notation for expressing behavior of objects consisting of states and guarded transitions between these states. A transition is said to "fire" when control resides in the transition's start state and: – a transition-specific event arrives and a guard condition of the transition, if any, evaluates to true; or

– the transition does not depend on an event and its guard condition evaluates to true.

Use case A user-system interaction sequence where intermediate states can be included as necessary. A user need not be a human being but can be another system.

Waterfall macro process A macro development process where the analysis phase is, by and large, completed before design activities start and where the design phase is completed before implementation activities start. A pure form never existed; the inventor, Royce [68], equipped the waterfall with "salmon ladders".

Whirlpool macro process A macro development process where backtracking occurs with even less provocation than in the fountain macro process. This applies to explorative situations where no progress can be made by the production of a requirements document.

Bibliography

[1] Abreu, F. Brito e, "Object-Oriented Software Design Metrics", contribution to the metrics workshop at Oopsla 1994, distributed by B. Henderson-Sellers, email: brian@socs.uts.edu.au; email Abreu: fba@inesc.pt.

[2] Abreu, F. Brito e, R. Esteves, and M. Goulao, "The Design of Eiffel Programs: Quantative Evaluation Using the MOOD Metrics", Report INESC, Lisbon, Portugal, 1995.

[3] Albrecht, A.J., and J.E. Gaffney, Jr, "Software Function, Source Lines of Code, and Development Effort Prediction: A Software Science Validation", *IEEE Trans. Software Eng.*, vol. SE-9, no. 6, pp. 639-64, November 1983.

[4] Allen, E., and D. de Champeaux, "Extending the Statechart Formalism: Event Scheduling and Disposition", *Proceedings of Oopsla 1995*, Austin, TX, pp. 1-16, 1995.

[5] Arjomandi, E., et al., "Concurrency Support for C++", *C++ Report*, pp. 44-50, 1994.

[6] Beck, K. and W. Cunningham, "A Laboratory for Teaching Object-Oriented Thinking", *Oopsla 1989 Conference Proceedings*, *SIGPLAN Notices*, vol. 24 no. 10, 1989.

[7] Berard, E.V., *Essays on Object-Oriented Software Engineering* Prentice Hall, Upper Saddle River, NJ, 1993.

[8] Best, L., "What Is Architectural Software Development?" available on the WWW http://c2.com/ppr/ams.html.

[9] Birman, K. and K. Marzullo, "ISIS and the META Project", *Sun Technol.*, pp. 90-104, Summer 1989.

[10] Boehm, B.W., *Software Engineering Economics*, Prentice Hall, Upper Saddle River, NJ, 1981.

[11] Boehm, B.W., "A Spiral Model of Software Development and Enhancement", *IEEE Comput.*, vol. 21, no. 5, pp. 61-72, 1988.

[12] Booch, G., *Object Oriented Design with Applications*, Benjamin-Cummings, Redwood City, CA, 1990.

[13] Booch, G., *Object Oriented Analysis and Design with Applications*, Benjamin-Cummings, Redwood City, CA, 1993.

[14] Bunt, H.C., "The Formal Semantics of Mass Terms", Ph.D. thesis, University of Amsterdam, 1981.

[15] Chidamber, S.R., and C.K. Kemerer, "Towards a Metrics Suite for Object Oriented Design", *Proceedings of Oopsla 1991*, Phoenix, AZ, pp. 197-211, 1991.

[16] Chidamber, S.R. and C.K. Kemerer, "A Metrics Suite for Object-Oriented Design", MIT Center for Information Systems Research Working Paper 249, 1993.

[17] Coad, P., and E. Yourdon, *Object-Oriented Design*, Yourdon Press, Prentice Hall, Upper Saddle River, NJ, 1991.

[18] Coleman, D., B. Lowther, and P. Oman, "The Application of Software Maintainability Models on Industrial Software Systems", Report 93-03 TR, Software Engineering Test Lab, University of Idaho, Moscow, ID, 1993.

[19] Coplien, J., *Advanced C++: Programming Styles and Idioms*, Addison-Wesley, Reading, MA, 1991.

[20] de Champeaux, D., and J. de Bruin, "Symbolic Evaluation of LISP Functions with Side Effects for Verification", in *Advance Papers of the 7th International Joint Conference on Artificial Intelligence*, Vancouver, British Columbia, pp. 519-527, August 1981 ; and in *Algorithmic Languages*, ed. J.W. de Bakker and J.C. van Vliet, North-Holland, New York, pp. 271-291, 1982.

[21] de Champeaux, D., "Verification of Some Parallel Algorithms", *Proceedings of the 7th Annual Pacific Northwest Software Quality Conference*, Portland, OR, pp. 149-169, 1989.

[22] de Champeaux, D., A. Anderson, M. Dalla Gasperina, E. Feldhousen, F. Fulton, M. Glei, C. Groh, D. Houston, D. Lerman, C. Monroe, R. Raj, and D. Shultheis, "Case Study of Object-Oriented Software Development", Report HPL-91-170, 1991; and in *Oopsla 1992 Conference Proceedings.*

[23] de Champeaux, D., "Toward an Object-Oriented Software Development Process", Report HPL-92-149, 1992.

[24] de Champeaux, D., D. Lea, and P. Faure, *Object-Oriented System Development*, Addison-Wesley, Reading, MA, 1993.

[25] Embley, D.W., B. Kurtz, and S.N. Woodfield, *Object-Oriented Systems Analysis*, Yourdon Press, Prentice Hall, Upper Saddle River, NJ, 1992.

[26] Firesmith, D.G., *Object-Oriented Requirements Analysis and Logical Design*, Wiley, New York, 1993.

[27] Galaxy is a product of Visix Software, Inc., 11440 Commerce Park Drive, Reston, VA, 22091.

[28] Gamma, E., R. Helm, R. Johnson, and J. Vlissides, *Design Patterns: Elements of Reusable OO Software*, Addison-Wesley, Reading, MA, 1995.

[29] Grady, B., "An Investment Model for Software Process Improvement", a note of Hewlett-Packard Corporate Engineering, 1992.

[30] Grady, B., *Practical Software Metrics for Project Management and Process Improvement*, Prentice Hall, Upper Saddle River, NJ, 1992.

[31] Halstead, M.H., *Elements of Software Science*, Elsevier Scientific Publishing Company, Amsterdam, 1977.

[32] Hamilton, J., "Where Things Went Wrong", contribution to the Process and Metric Workshop at Oopsla 1993.

[33] Harel, D., "Statecharts: A Visual Formalism for Complex Systems", in *Sci. Comput. Program.* vol. 8, pp. 231-274, 1987.

[34] Harel, D., "On Visual Formalisms", in *Commun.ACM*, vol. 31, no. 5, pp. 514-530, 1988.

[35] Henderson-Sellers, B., and J.M. Edwards, "The Object-Oriented Systems Life Cycle", in *Commun.ACM*, vol. 33, no. 9, pp. 142-159, 1988.

[36] Henderson-Sellers, B., and J.M. Edwards, *BOOKTWO of Object-Oriented Knowledge: The Working Object*, Prentice Hall, Upper Saddle River, NJ, 1994.

[37] Henderson-Sellers, B., *Object-Oriented Metrics, Metrics of Complexity*, Prentice Hall, Upper Saddle River, NJ, 1996.

[38] Henry, S., and D. Kafura, "Software Structure Metrics Based on Information Flow", *IEEE Trans. Software Eng.*, vol. SE-7, no. 5, pp. 510-518, 1981.

[39] Humphrey, W.S., *Managing the Software Process*, Addison-Wesley, Reading, MA, 1990.

[40] Jacobson, I., "Object-Oriented Development in an Industrial Environment", *Proceedings of Oopsla 1987*, Orlando, FL, pp. 183-191, 1987.

[41] Jacobson, I., M. Christerson, P. Jonsson, and G. Overgaard, *Object-Oriented Software Engineering*, Addison-Wesley, Reading, MA, 1992.

[42] Jalote, P., *An Integrated Approach to Software Engineering*, Springe- Verlag, New York, 1991.

[43] Kemerer, C.F., "An Empirical Validation of Software Cost Estimation Models", *Commun.ACM*, vol. 30, no. 5, pp. 416-429, 1987.

[44] Kemerer, C.F., "Reliability of Function Points Measurement: A Field Experiment", *Commun.ACM*, vol. 36, no. 2, pp. 85-97, 1993.

[45] Kerth, N., Personal communication reported in [12].

[46] Klausner, S., personal Communication, 1992-1993.

[47] Li, W., and S. Henry, "Object-Oriented Metrics That Predict Maintainability", *J. Syst. Software*, pp. 111-122, 1993.

[48] Lippman, S.B., *C++ Primer*, Addison-Wesley, Reading, MA, 1989.

[49] Loomis, M., R. Cattell, F. Manola, R. Soley, and J. Sutherland, "Panel Objects and Database Standards", *Proceedings of Oopsla 1995*; also in *ACM Sigplan Notices*, vol. 30, no. 10, pp. 331-332, 1995.

[50] Lorenz, M., *Object-Oriented Software Development*, Prentice Hall, Upper Saddle River, NJ, 1993.

[51] Martin, R.C., *Designing Object Oriented C++ Applications Using the Booch Method*, Prentice Hall, Upper Saddle River, NJ, 1995.

[52] McCabe, T.J., "A Complexity Measure", *IEEE Trans. Software Eng.*, vol. SE-2, no. 4, pp. 308-320, 1976.

[53] Menga, G., "G++, A Framework for Object-Oriented Design and Prototyping of Manufacturing Systems", Dipartimento di Automatica e Informatica, Politecnico di Torino, Torino, Italy, 1993.

[54] Mills, E.E., "Software Metrics, SEI Curriculum Module SEI-CM-12-1.1", Carnegie Mellon University, Pittsburgh, PA, 1988.

[55] *Object Management Architecture Guide*, 2nd ed., R.M. Soley, ed., The Object Management Group, 1992.

[56] Oman, P., J. Hagemeister, and D. Ash, "A Definition and Taxonomy for Software Maintainability", Report 91-08 TR, Software Engineering Test Lab, University of Idaho, Moscow, ID, email: oman@cs.uidaho. edu, 1991.

[57] Oman, P., and J. Hagemeister, "Metrics for Assessing a Software System's Maintainability", Report 92-01 TR, *Proceedings of the 1992 IEEE Conference on Software Maintenance*, Orlando, FL, pp. 337-344, 1992.

[58] Oman, P., and J. Hagemeister, "Construction and Validation of Polynomials for Predicting Software Maintainability", Report 92-06 TR, Software Engineering Test Lab, University of Idaho, Moscow, ID, 1992.

[59] Oman, P., J. Hagemeister, F. Zhuo, and B. Lowther, "Constructing and Testing Software Maintainability Assessment Models", Report 92-08 TR, Software Engineering Test Lab, University of Idaho, Moscow, ID, 1992.

[60] Oman, P., B. Lowther and D. Coleman, "The Application of Software Maintainability Models on Industrial Software Systems", Report 93-03 TR, Software Engineering Test Lab, University of Idaho, Moscow, ID, 1993.

[61] Oman, P., D. Ash, B. Lowther, and L. Yao "The Application of Software Maintainability Models on Industrial Software Systems", Report 94-03 TR, Software Engineering Test Lab, University of Idaho, Moscow, ID, 1994.

[62] Oman, P., and T. Pearse, "Maintainability Measurements on Industrial Source Code Maintenance Activities", Report 95-01 TR, Software Engineering Test Lab, University of Idaho, Moscow, ID, 1994.

[63] Ousterhout, J.K., *Tcl and the Tk Toolkit*, Addison-Wesley, Reading, MA, 1994.

[64] Pancake, C.M., "The Promise and the Cost of Object Technology: A Five Year Forecast", *Commun.ACM*, vol. 38, no. 10, pp. 33-49, 1995.

[65] Putnam, L.H., "A General Empirical Solution to the Macro Software Sizing and Estimating Problem", *IEEE Trans. Software Eng.*, vol. SE-4, no. 4, 1978.

[66] Reenskaug, T., P. Wold, and O.A. Lehne, *Working With Objects* Manning, Greenwich, CT, 1996.

[67] Reinold, K., "OO Metrics", contribution to the Oopsla 1993 Workshop on Process and Metrics for Object-Oriented Software Development. (A copy can be obtained, hopefully, from "K.Reinold@bull.com".)

[68] Royce, W.W., "Managing the Development of Large Software Systems", *Proceedings of IEEE WESCON*, 1970.

[69] Rubin, H.A., "Macro-Estimation of Software Development Parameters: The ESTIMACS System", *Proceedings of Softfair: A Conference on Software Development Tools, Techniques, and Alternatives*, IEEE, New York, pp. 109-118, 1983.

[70] Rumbaugh, J., M. Blaha, W. Premerlani, F. Eddy, W. Lorensen, *Object-Oriented Modeling and Design*, Prentice Hall, Upper Saddle River, NJ, 1991.

[71] Selic, B., G. Gullekson, P.T. Ward, *Real-Time Object-Oriented Modeling*, Wiley, New York, 1994.

[72] Shlaer, S., and S.J. Mellor, *Object-Oriented Systems Analysis*, Yourdon Press, Prentice Hall, Upper Saddle River, NJ, 1988.

[73] Shlaer, S., and S.J. Mellor, *Object Life Cycles: Modeling the World in States*, Englewood Cliffs, New Jersey: Yourdon Press, Prentice Hall, Upper Saddle River, NJ, 1991.

[74] Shooman, M.L., *Software Engineering*, McGraw-Hill, New York, 1983.

[75] Smith, R.B., "Prototype-Based Languages: Object Lessons from Class-Free Programming", *Proceedings of Oopsla 1994*, also in *ACM Sigplan Notices*, vol. 29, no. 10, pp. 102-112, 1994.

[76] Sprouls, J., *IFPUG Function Point Counting Practitioners Manual Release 3.0*, International Function Point Users Group, Westerville, OH, 1990.

[77] Stroustrup, B., *The C++ Programming Language*, Addison-Wesley, Reading, MA, 1991 (2nd ed., 1993).

[78] Stroustrup, B., *The Design and Evolution of C++*, Addison-Wesley, Reading, MA, 1994.

[79] Thebaut, S.M., and V.Y. Shen, "An Analytic Resource Model for Large-Scale Software Development", *Inform. Process. Management*, vol. 10, no. 1-2, pp. 293-315, 1984.

[80] Tidwell, B.K., "Object-Oriented Analysis State Controlled Implementation", *Proceedings of the Workshop on Object-Oriented (Domain) Analysis, Oopsla 1991*, 1991.

[81] *Webster's Ninth New Collegiate Dictionary*, Merriam-Webster, Springfield, MA, 1988.

[82] Welker, K.D., "Traditional Software Metrics - Hold On!" contribution to the Metrics Workshop at Oopsla 1994, distributed by B. Henderson-Sellers, email: brian@socs.uts.edu.au.

[83] West, M., communication on the discussion group at oometrics@andrews.edu on November 15, 1994.

[84] Weyuker, E., "Evaluating Software Complexity Measures", *IEEE Trans. Software Eng.*, vol. 14, no. 9, pp. 1357-1365, 1988.

[85] White, S., "Panel Problem: Software Controller for an Oil Hot Water Heating SYSTEM", *Proceedings of COMPSAC*, Computer Society Press of the IEEE, New York, pp. 276-277, 1986.

[86] Winder, R., *Developing C++ Software*, Wiley, Chichester, West Sussex, England, 1991.

[87] Wirfs-Brock, R., B. Wilkerson, and L. Wiener, *Designing Object-Oriented Software*, Prentice Hall, Upper Saddle River, NJ, 1990.

[88] Wolverton, R.W., "The Cost of Developing Large-Scale Software", *IEEE Trans. Comput.* vol. C-23, no. 6, pp. 615-636, 1974; reprinted in L.H. Putnam, *Tutorial, Software Cost Estimating and Life-Cycle Control: Getting the Software Numbers*, IEEE, New York, pp. 282-303, 1980.

Index